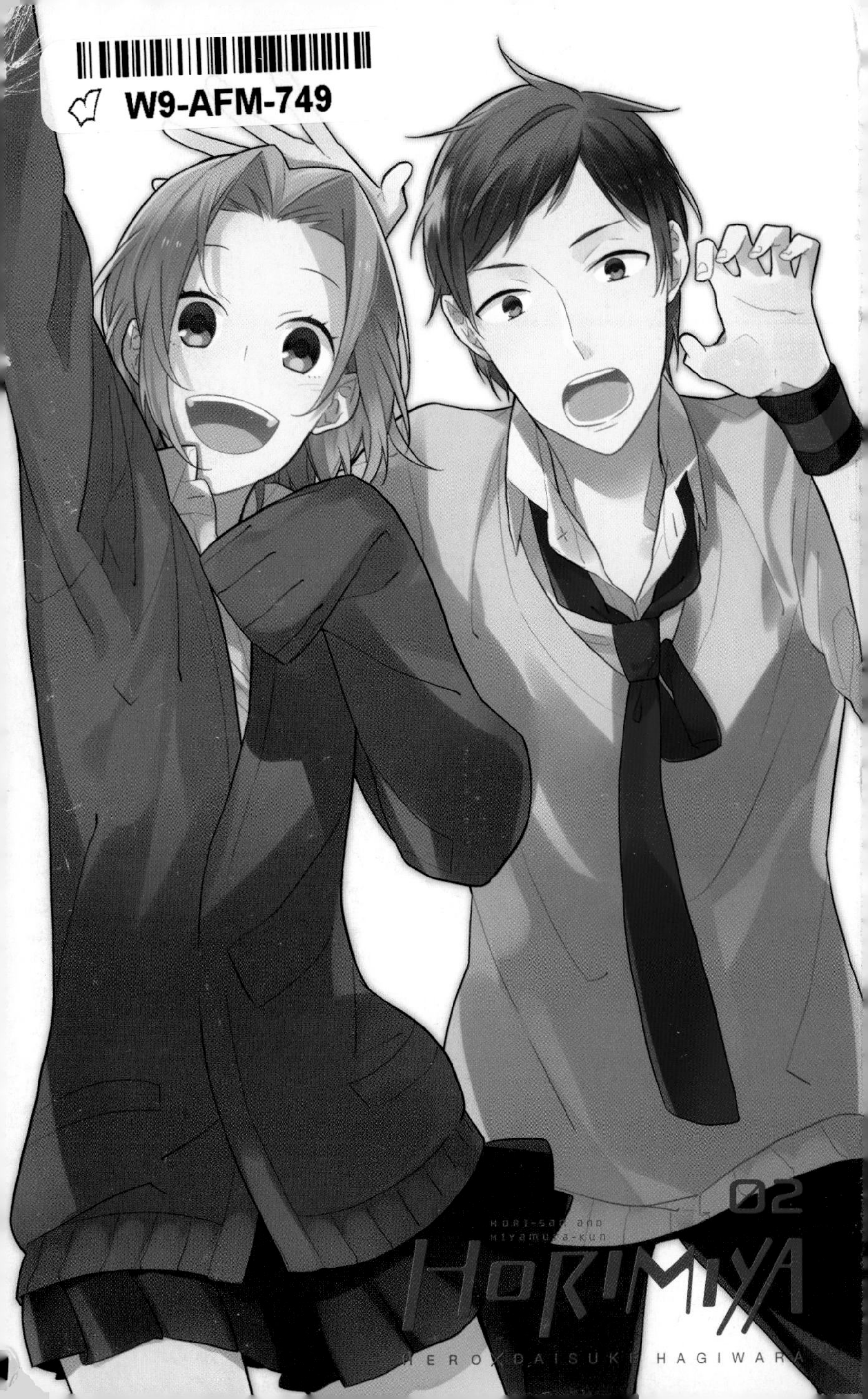
02
HORI-san and
MIYAMURA-KUN
HORIMIYA
HERO × DAISUKE HAGIWARA

HORI-san and
MIYAMURA-kun

HORIMIYA

02

C ONTENTS ✳

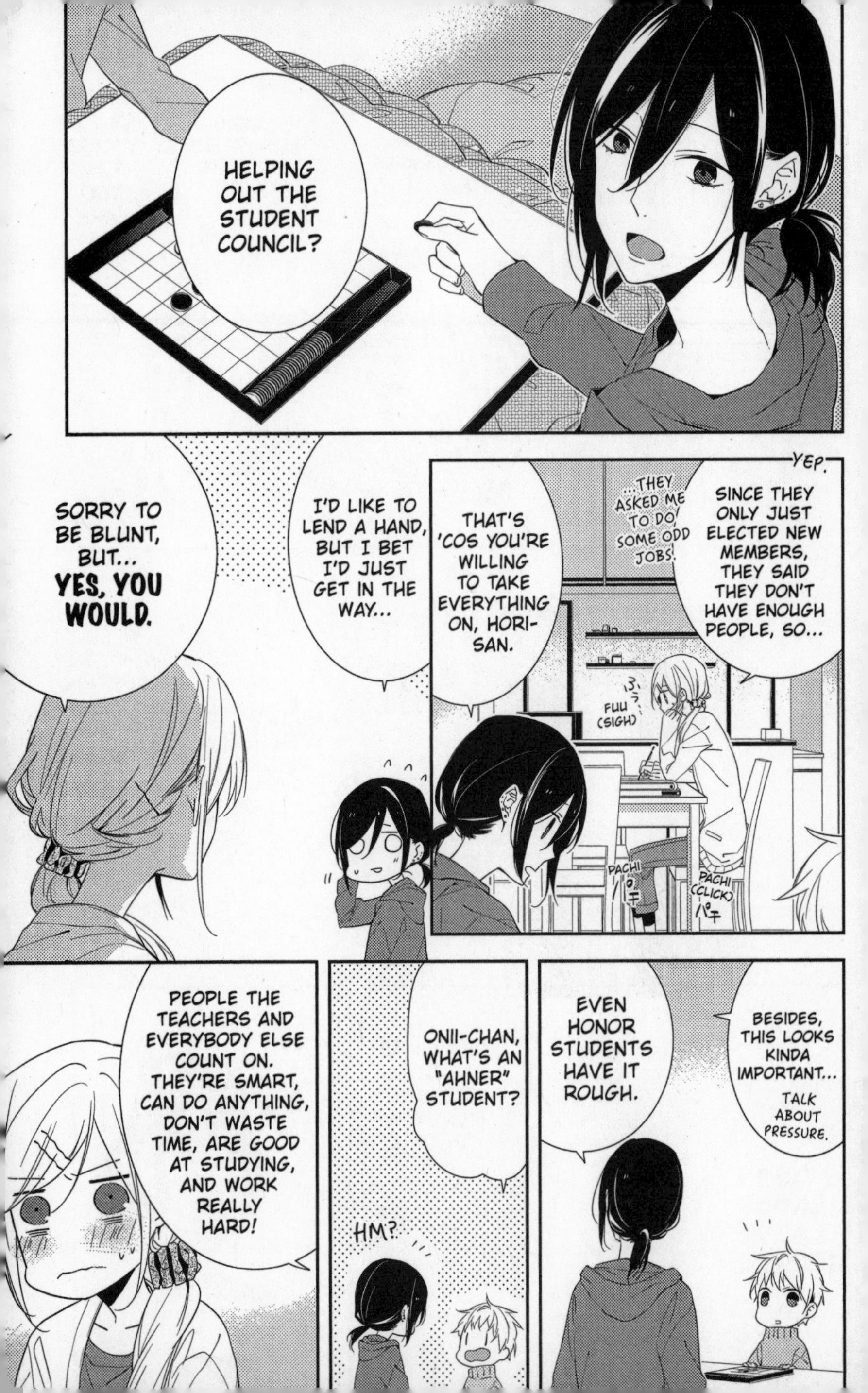
HELPING OUT THE STUDENT COUNCIL?
YEP.
SINCE THEY ONLY JUST ELECTED NEW MEMBERS, THEY SAID THEY DON'T HAVE ENOUGH PEOPLE, SO...
...THEY ASKED ME TO DO SOME ODD JOBS!
THAT'S 'COS YOU'RE WILLING TO TAKE EVERYTHING ON, HORI-SAN.
FUU (SIGH)
PACHI
PACHI (CLICK)
I'D LIKE TO LEND A HAND, BUT I BET I'D JUST GET IN THE WAY...
SORRY TO BE BLUNT, BUT... **YES, YOU WOULD.**
BESIDES, THIS LOOKS KINDA IMPORTANT...
TALK ABOUT PRESSURE.
EVEN HONOR STUDENTS HAVE IT ROUGH.
ONII-CHAN, WHAT'S AN "AHNER" STUDENT?
HM?
PEOPLE THE TEACHERS AND EVERYBODY ELSE COUNT ON. THEY'RE SMART, CAN DO ANYTHING, DON'T WASTE TIME, ARE GOOD AT STUDYING, AND WORK REALLY HARD!

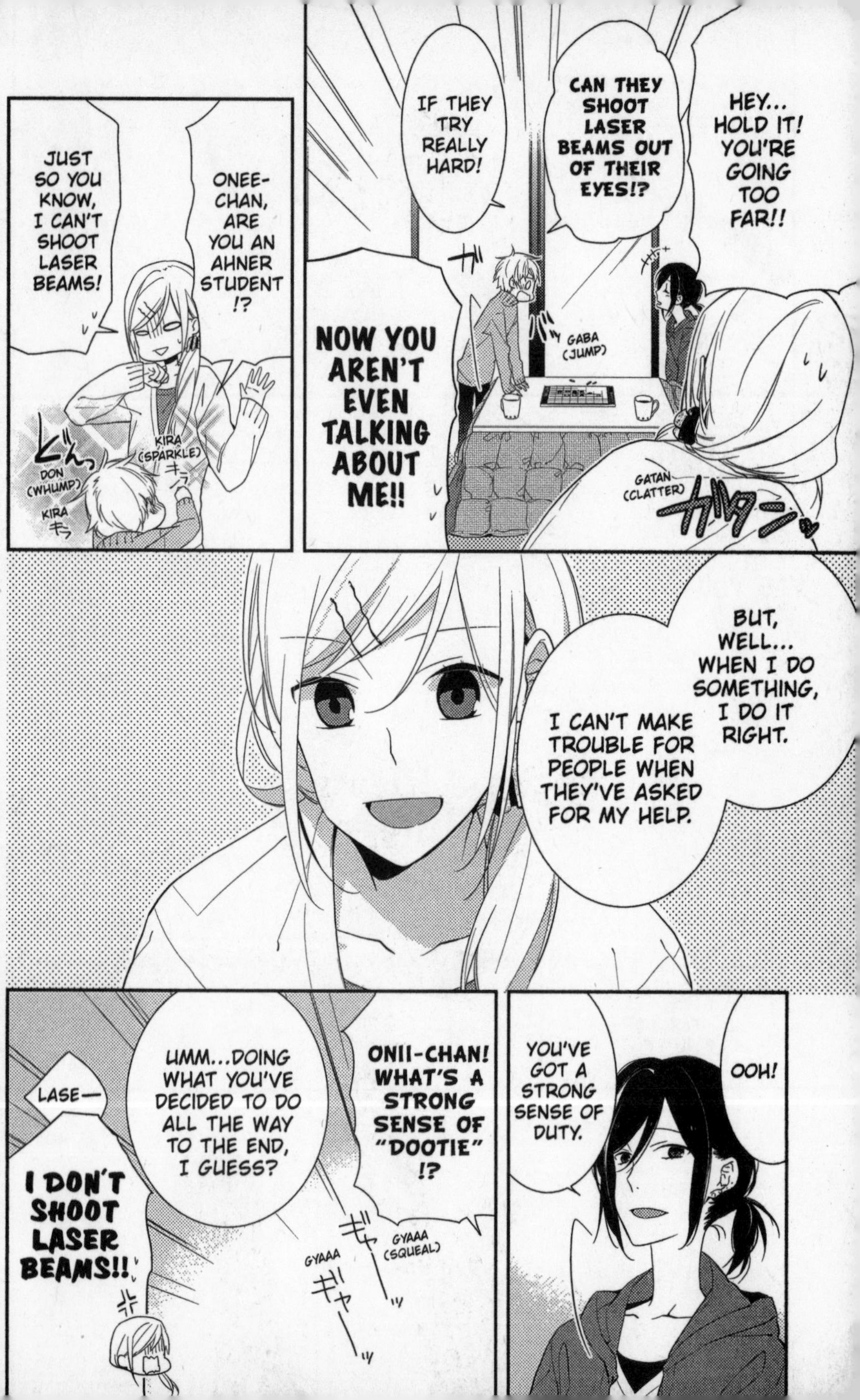
HEY... HOLD IT! YOU'RE GOING TOO FAR!!
CAN THEY SHOOT LASER BEAMS OUT OF THEIR EYES!?
IF THEY TRY REALLY HARD!
GABA (JUMP)
NOW YOU AREN'T EVEN TALKING ABOUT ME!!
GATAN (CLATTER)
ONEE-CHAN, ARE YOU AN AHNER STUDENT !?
JUST SO YOU KNOW, I CAN'T SHOOT LASER BEAMS!
KIRA (SPARKLE)
DON (WHUMP)
KIRA
BUT, WELL... WHEN I DO SOMETHING, I DO IT RIGHT.
I CAN'T MAKE TROUBLE FOR PEOPLE WHEN THEY'VE ASKED FOR MY HELP.
OOH!
YOU'VE GOT A STRONG SENSE OF DUTY.
ONII-CHAN! WHAT'S A STRONG SENSE OF "DOOTIE" !?
GYAAA (SQUEAL)
GYAAA
UMM...DOING WHAT YOU'VE DECIDED TO DO ALL THE WAY TO THE END, I GUESS?
LASE—
I DON'T SHOOT LASER BEAMS!!

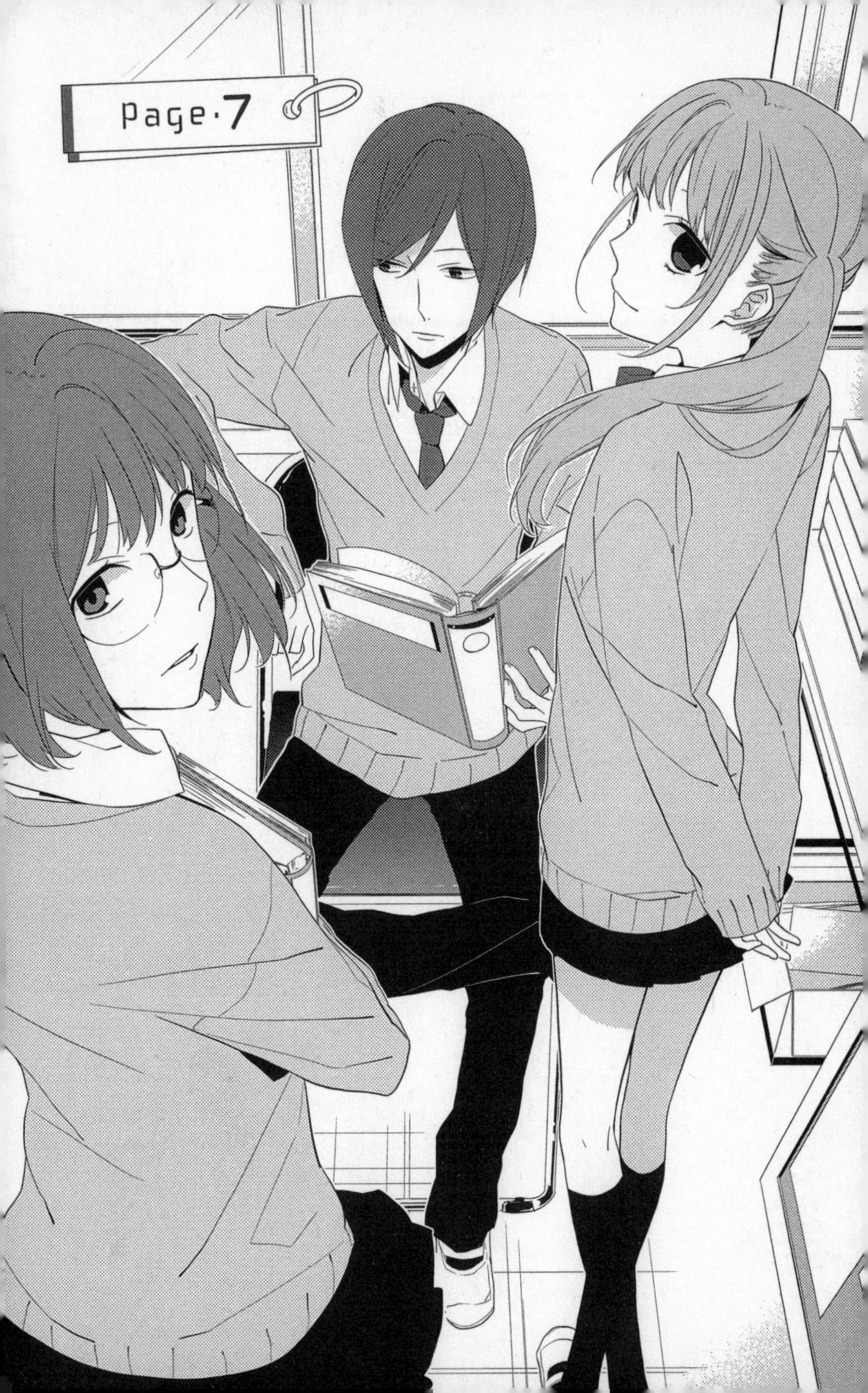
Page・7

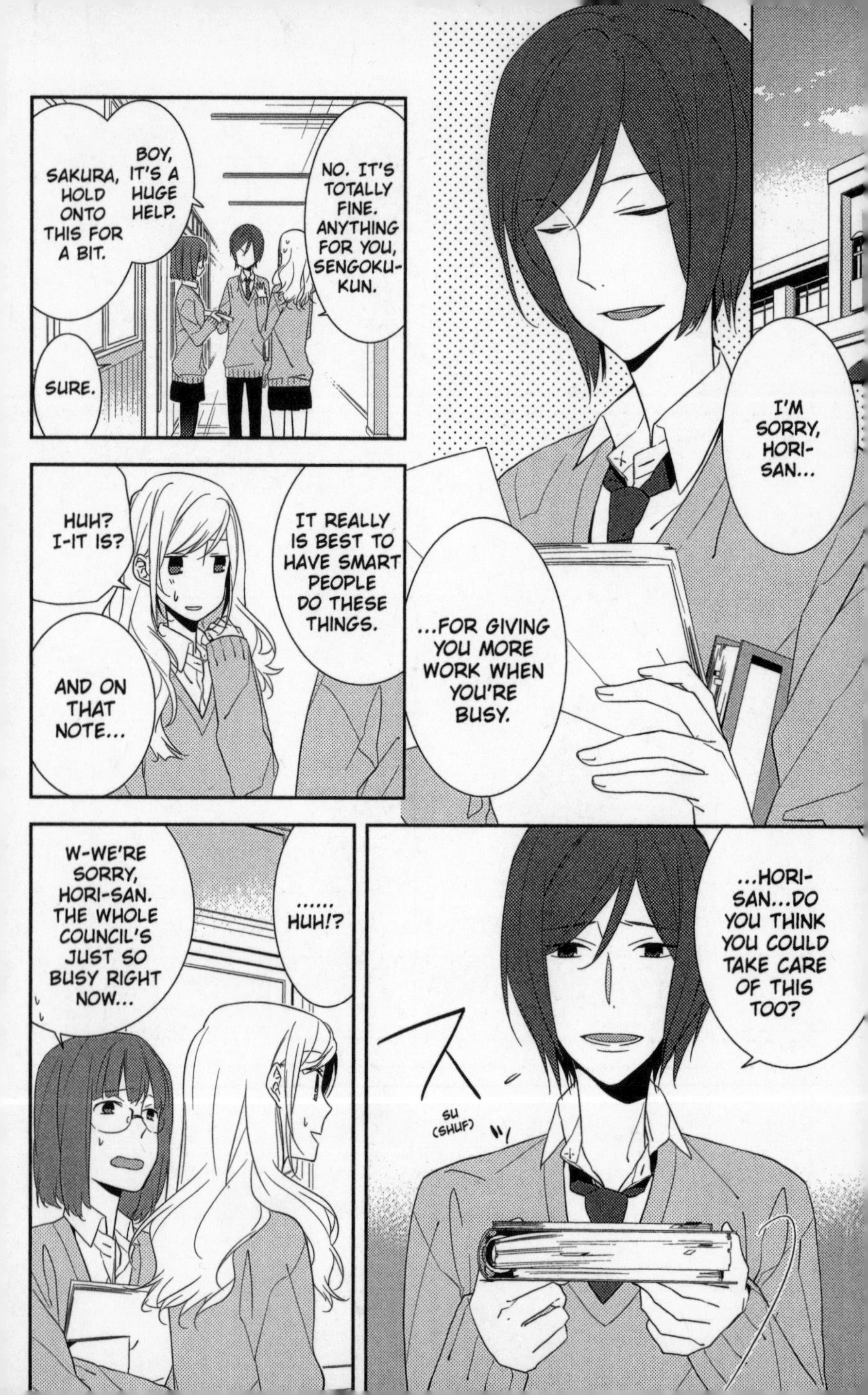
I'M SORRY, HORI-SAN...
...FOR GIVING YOU MORE WORK WHEN YOU'RE BUSY.
NO. IT'S TOTALLY FINE. ANYTHING FOR YOU, SENGOKU-KUN.
BOY, IT'S A HUGE HELP.
SAKURA, HOLD ONTO THIS FOR A BIT.
SURE.
IT REALLY IS BEST TO HAVE SMART PEOPLE DO THESE THINGS.
HUH? I-IT IS?
AND ON THAT NOTE...
...HORI-SAN...DO YOU THINK YOU COULD TAKE CARE OF THIS TOO?
SU (SHUF)
......HUH!?
W-WE'RE SORRY, HORI-SAN. THE WHOLE COUNCIL'S JUST SO BUSY RIGHT NOW...

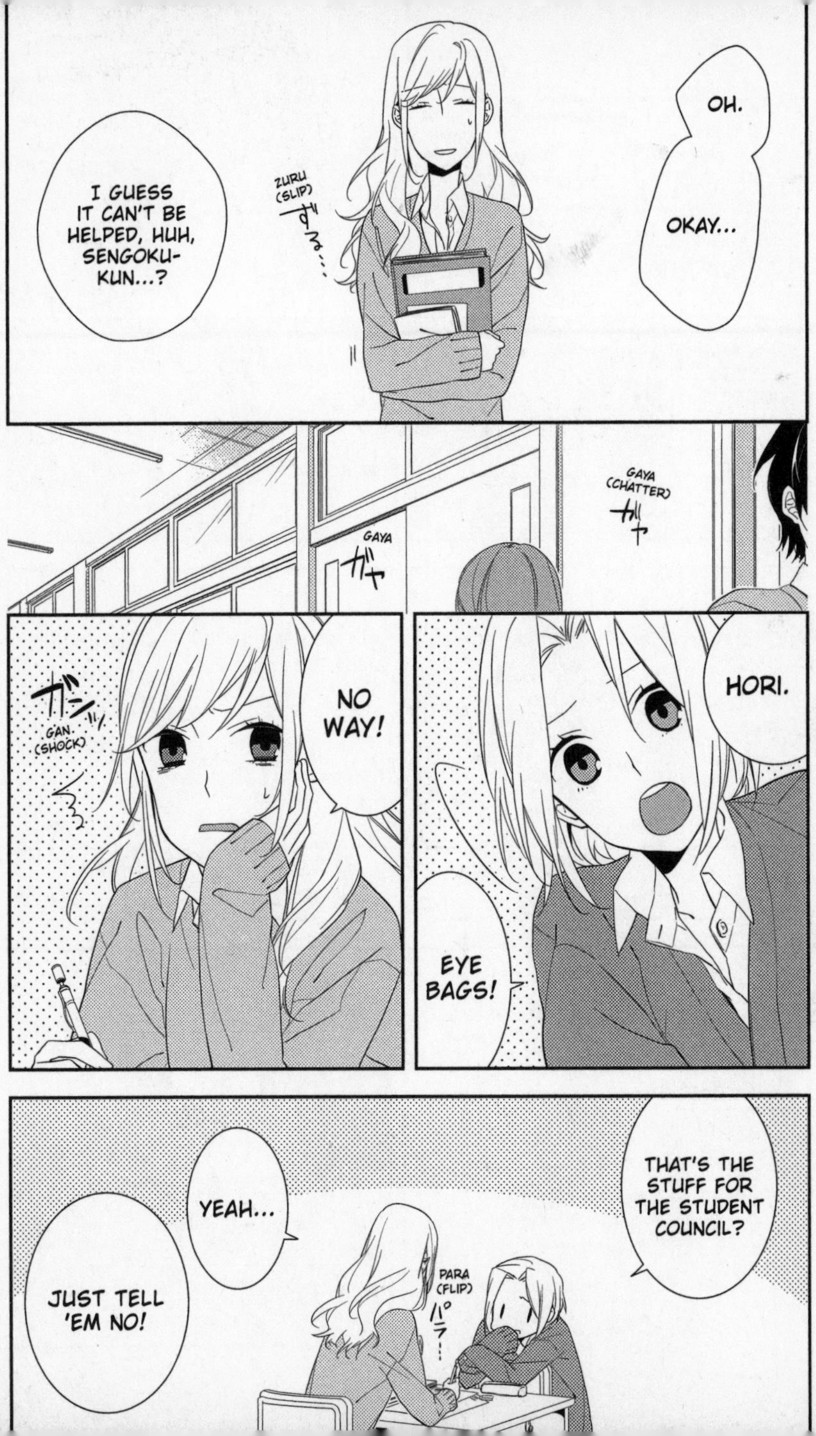
OH.
OKAY...
ZURU (SLIP)
I GUESS IT CAN'T BE HELPED, HUH, SENGOKU-KUN...?
GAYA (CHATTER)
GAYA
HORI.
EYE BAGS!
NO WAY!
GAN (SHOCK)
THAT'S THE STUFF FOR THE STUDENT COUNCIL?
PARA (FLIP)
YEAH...
JUST TELL 'EM NO!

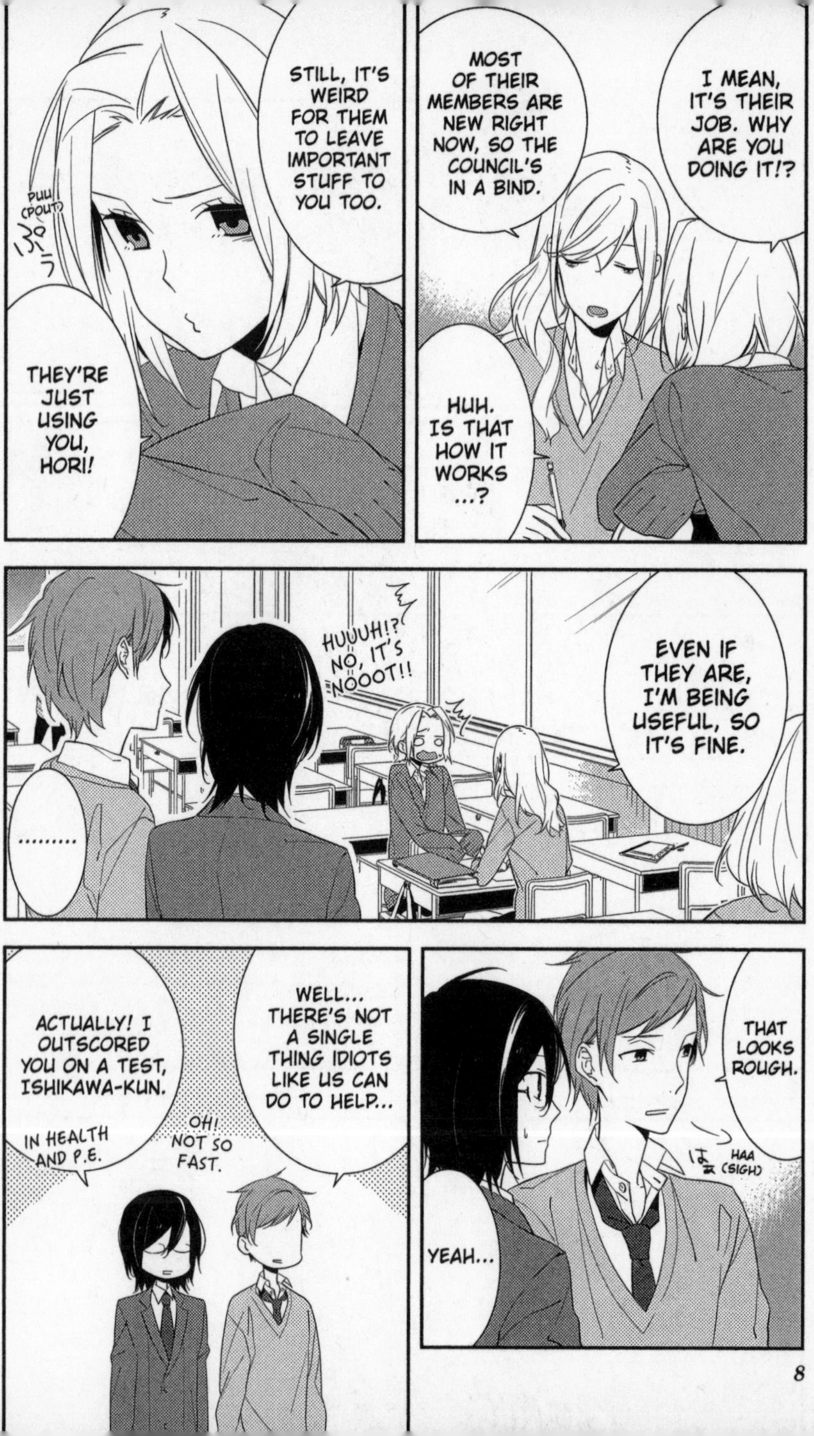
I MEAN, IT'S THEIR JOB. WHY ARE YOU DOING IT!?
MOST OF THEIR MEMBERS ARE NEW RIGHT NOW, SO THE COUNCIL'S IN A BIND.
HUH. IS THAT HOW IT WORKS ...?
STILL, IT'S WEIRD FOR THEM TO LEAVE IMPORTANT STUFF TO YOU TOO.
PUU (POUT)
THEY'RE JUST USING YOU, HORI!
EVEN IF THEY ARE, I'M BEING USEFUL, SO IT'S FINE.
HUUUH!? NO, IT'S NOOOT!!
....
THAT LOOKS ROUGH.
HAA (SIGH)
YEAH...
WELL... THERE'S NOT A SINGLE THING IDIOTS LIKE US CAN DO TO HELP...
ACTUALLY! I OUTSCORED YOU ON A TEST, ISHIKAWA-KUN.
OH! NOT SO FAST.
IN HEALTH AND P.E.

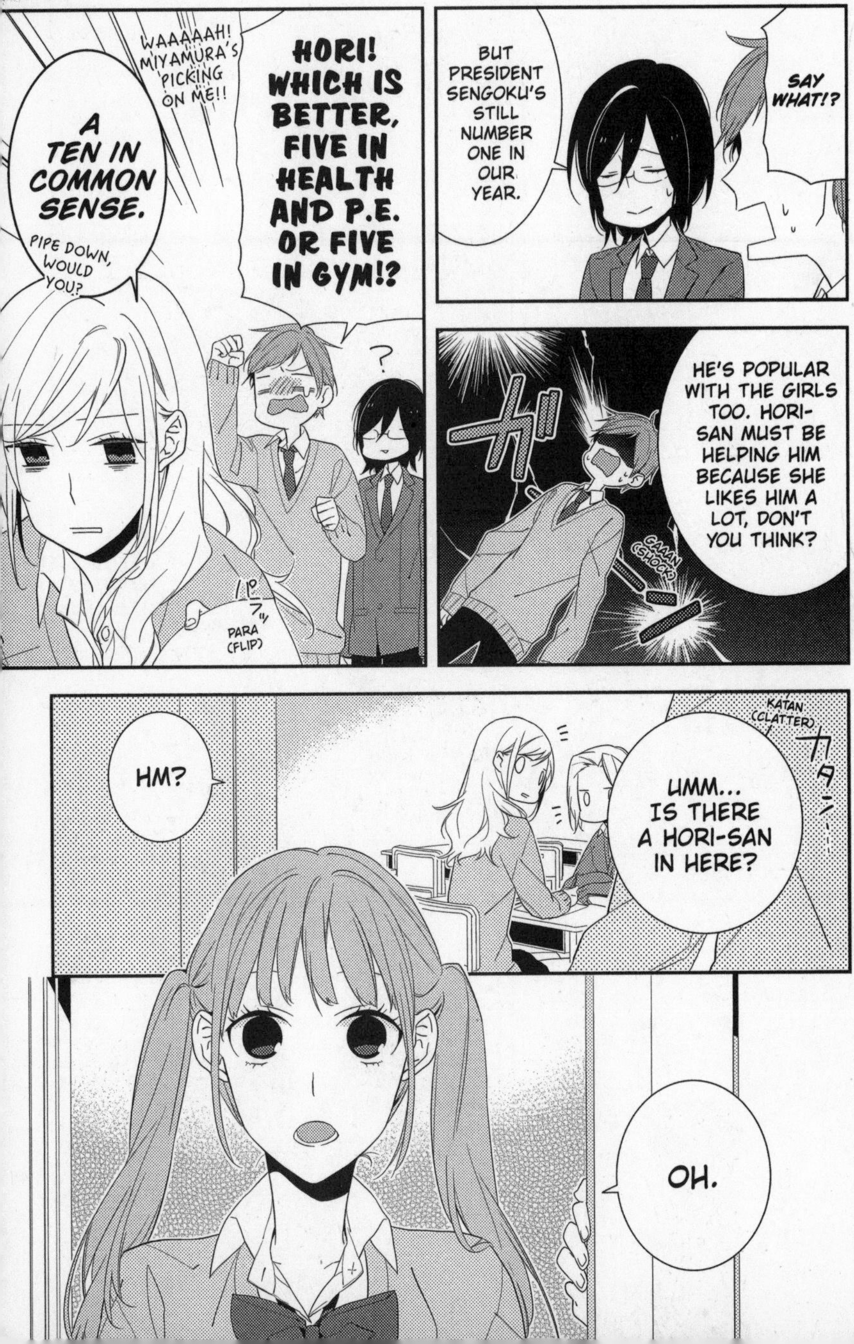

BUT PRESIDENT SENGOKU'S STILL NUMBER ONE IN OUR YEAR.
SAY WHAT!?
HE'S POPULAR WITH THE GIRLS TOO. HORI-SAN MUST BE HELPING HIM BECAUSE SHE LIKES HIM A LOT, DON'T YOU THINK?
GAAAN (SHOCK)
HORI! WHICH IS BETTER, FIVE IN HEALTH AND P.E. OR FIVE IN GYM!?
WAAAAAH! MIYAMURA'S PICKING ON ME!!
A TEN IN COMMON SENSE.
PIPE DOWN, WOULD YOU?
?
PARA (FLIP)
KATAN (CLATTER)
UMM... IS THERE A HORI-SAN IN HERE?
HM?
OH.

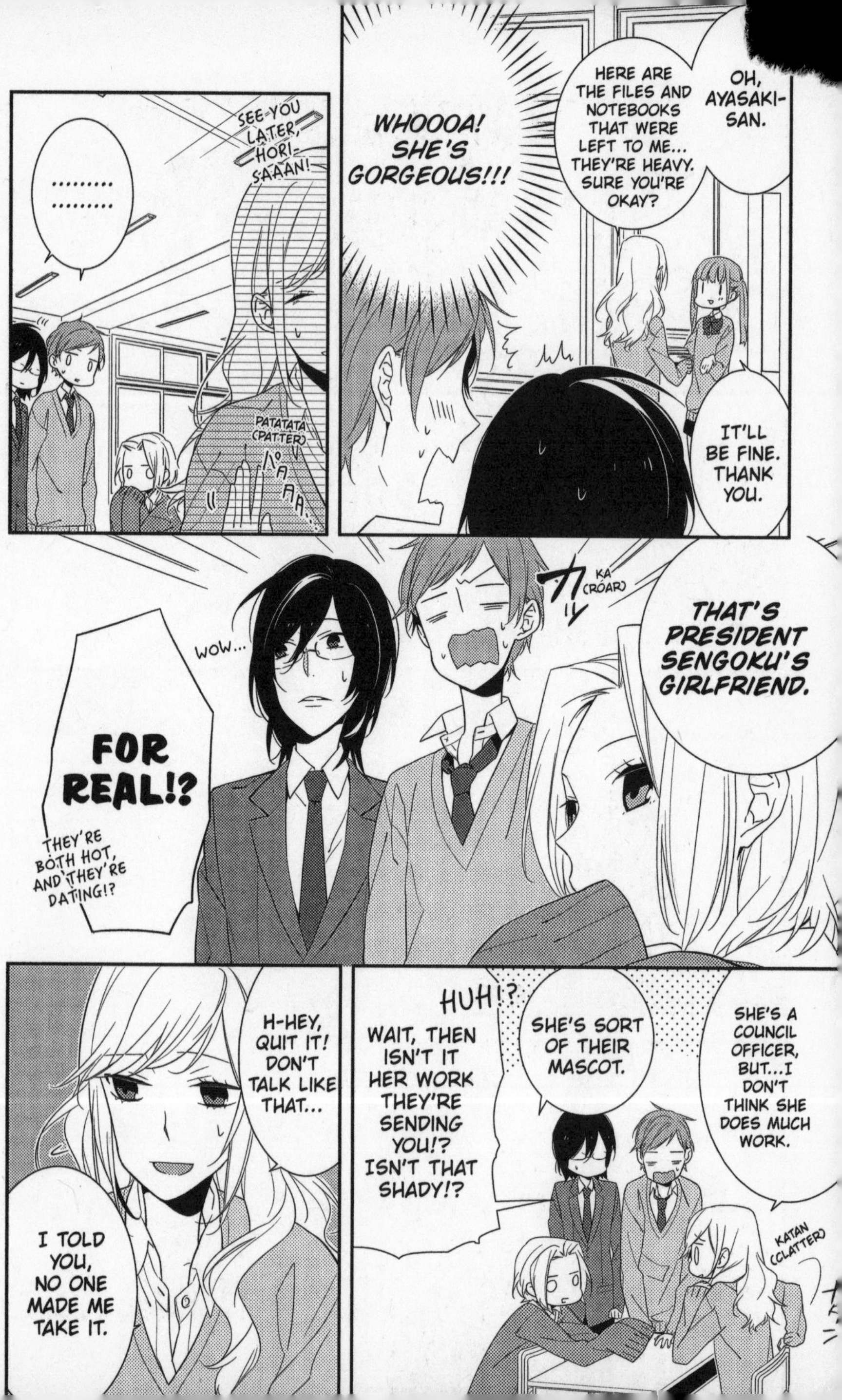
OH, AYASAKI-SAN.
HERE ARE THE FILES AND NOTEBOOKS THAT WERE LEFT TO ME... THEY'RE HEAVY. SURE YOU'RE OKAY?
WHOOOA! SHE'S GORGEOUS!!!
IT'LL BE FINE. THANK YOU.
SEE YOU LATER, HORI-SAAAN!
....
....
PATATATA (PATTER)
THAT'S PRESIDENT SENGOKU'S GIRLFRIEND.
KA (ROAR)
WOW...
FOR REAL!?
THEY'RE BOTH HOT, AND THEY'RE DATING!?
SHE'S A COUNCIL OFFICER, BUT...I DON'T THINK SHE DOES MUCH WORK.
SHE'S SORT OF THEIR MASCOT.
HUH!?
WAIT, THEN ISN'T IT HER WORK THEY'RE SENDING YOU!? ISN'T THAT SHADY!?
KATAN (CLATTER)
H-HEY, QUIT IT! DON'T TALK LIKE THAT...
I TOLD YOU, NO ONE MADE ME TAKE IT.

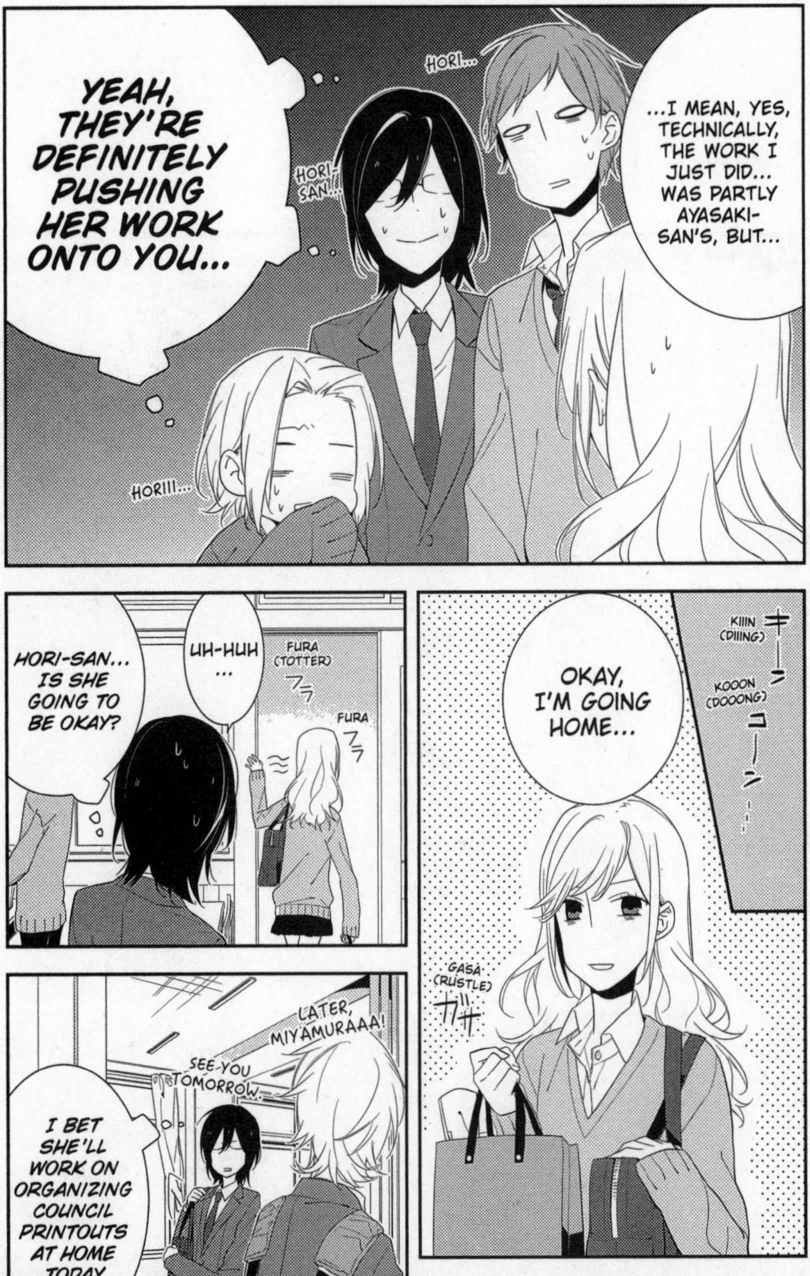
...I MEAN, YES, TECHNICALLY, THE WORK I JUST DID... WAS PARTLY AYASAKI-SAN'S, BUT...
HORI...
HORI-SAN...
YEAH, THEY'RE DEFINITELY PUSHING HER WORK ONTO YOU...
HORIII...
KIIIN (DIIING)
KOOON (DOOONG)
OKAY, I'M GOING HOME...
GASA (RUSTLE)
UH-HUH...
FURA (TOTTER)
FURA
HORI-SAN... IS SHE GOING TO BE OKAY?
LATER, MIYAMURAAA!
SEE-YOU TOMORROW.
I BET SHE'LL WORK ON ORGANIZING COUNCIL PRINTOUTS AT HOME TODAY TOO.

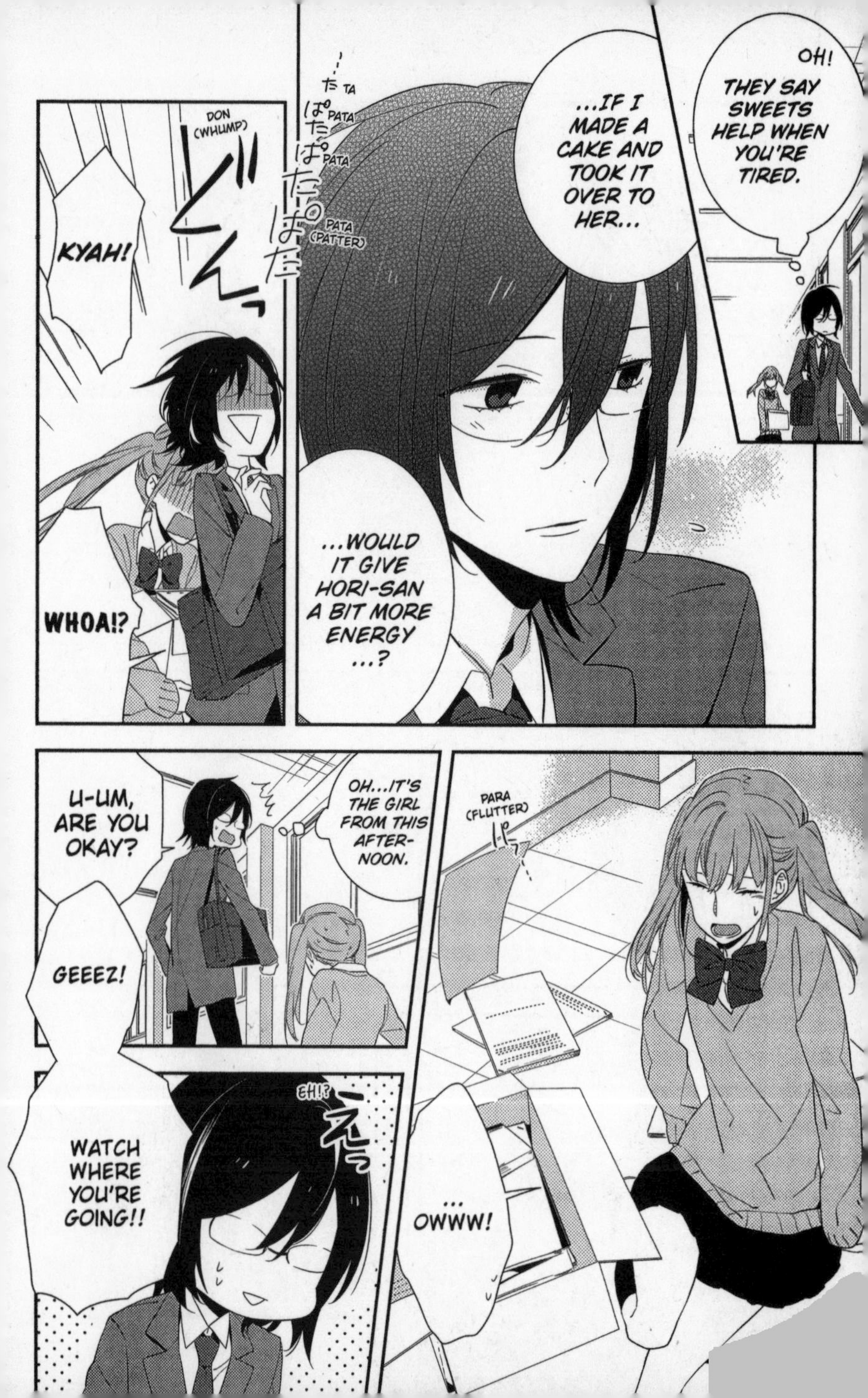
OH!
THEY SAY SWEETS HELP WHEN YOU'RE TIRED.
...IF I MADE A CAKE AND TOOK IT OVER TO HER...
...WOULD IT GIVE HORI-SAN A BIT MORE ENERGY ...?
TA
PATA
PATA
PATA (PATTER)
DON (WHUMP)
KYAH!
WHOA!?
PARA (FLUTTER)
... OWWW!
OH...IT'S THE GIRL FROM THIS AFTER-NOON.
U-UM, ARE YOU OKAY?
EH!?
GEEEZ!
WATCH WHERE YOU'RE GOING!!

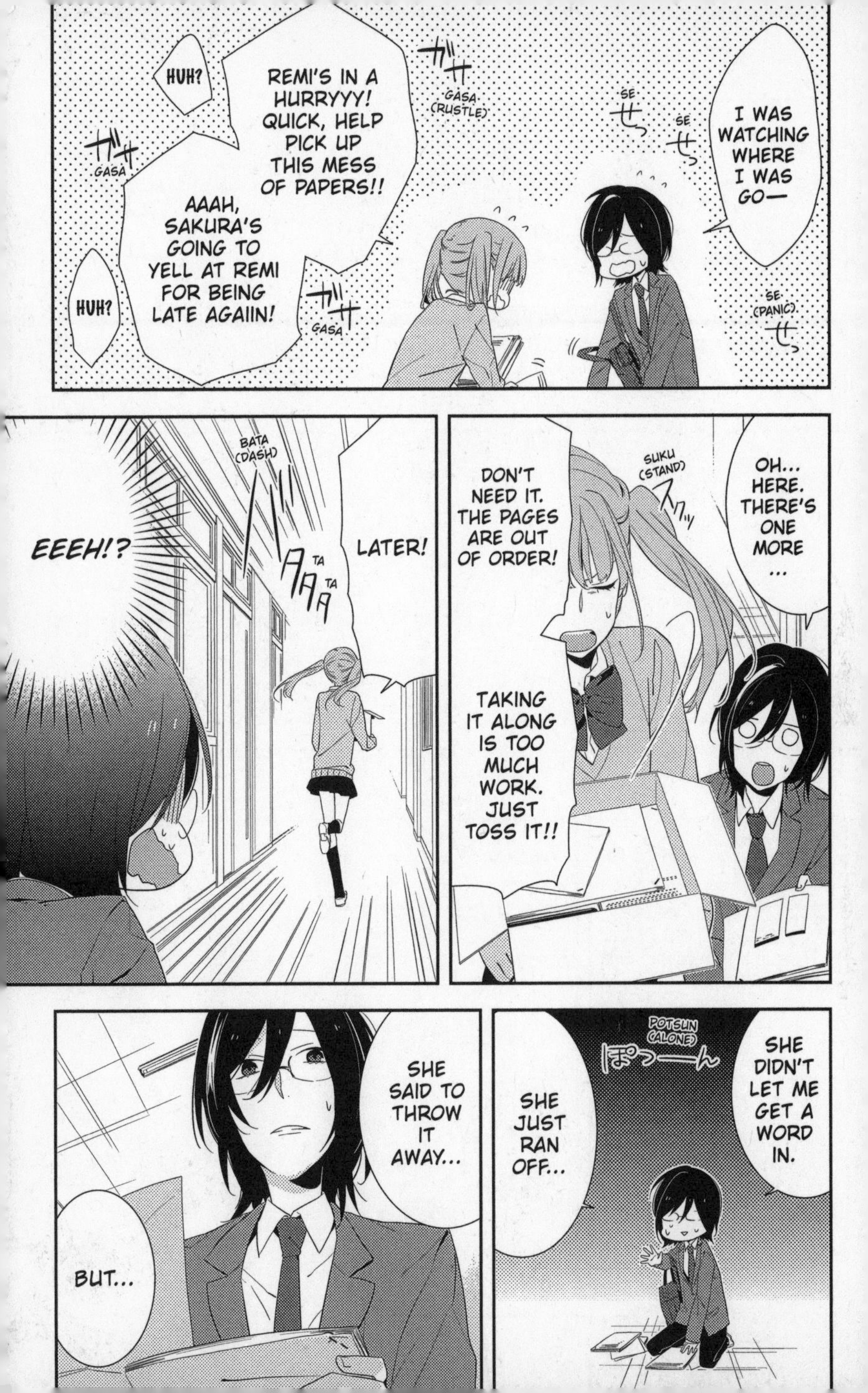
I WAS WATCHING WHERE I WAS GO—
SE
SE
SE (PANIC)
GASA (RUSTLE)
REMI'S IN A HURRYYY! QUICK, HELP PICK UP THIS MESS OF PAPERS!!
HUH?
GASA
AAAH, SAKURA'S GOING TO YELL AT REMI FOR BEING LATE AGAIIN!
GASA
HUH?
OH... HERE. THERE'S ONE MORE...
SUKU (STAND)
DON'T NEED IT. THE PAGES ARE OUT OF ORDER!
TAKING IT ALONG IS TOO MUCH WORK. JUST TOSS IT!!
LATER!
BATA (DASH)
TA
TA
EEEH!?
SHE DIDN'T LET ME GET A WORD IN.
POTSUN (ALONE)
SHE JUST RAN OFF...
SHE SAID TO THROW IT AWAY...
BUT...

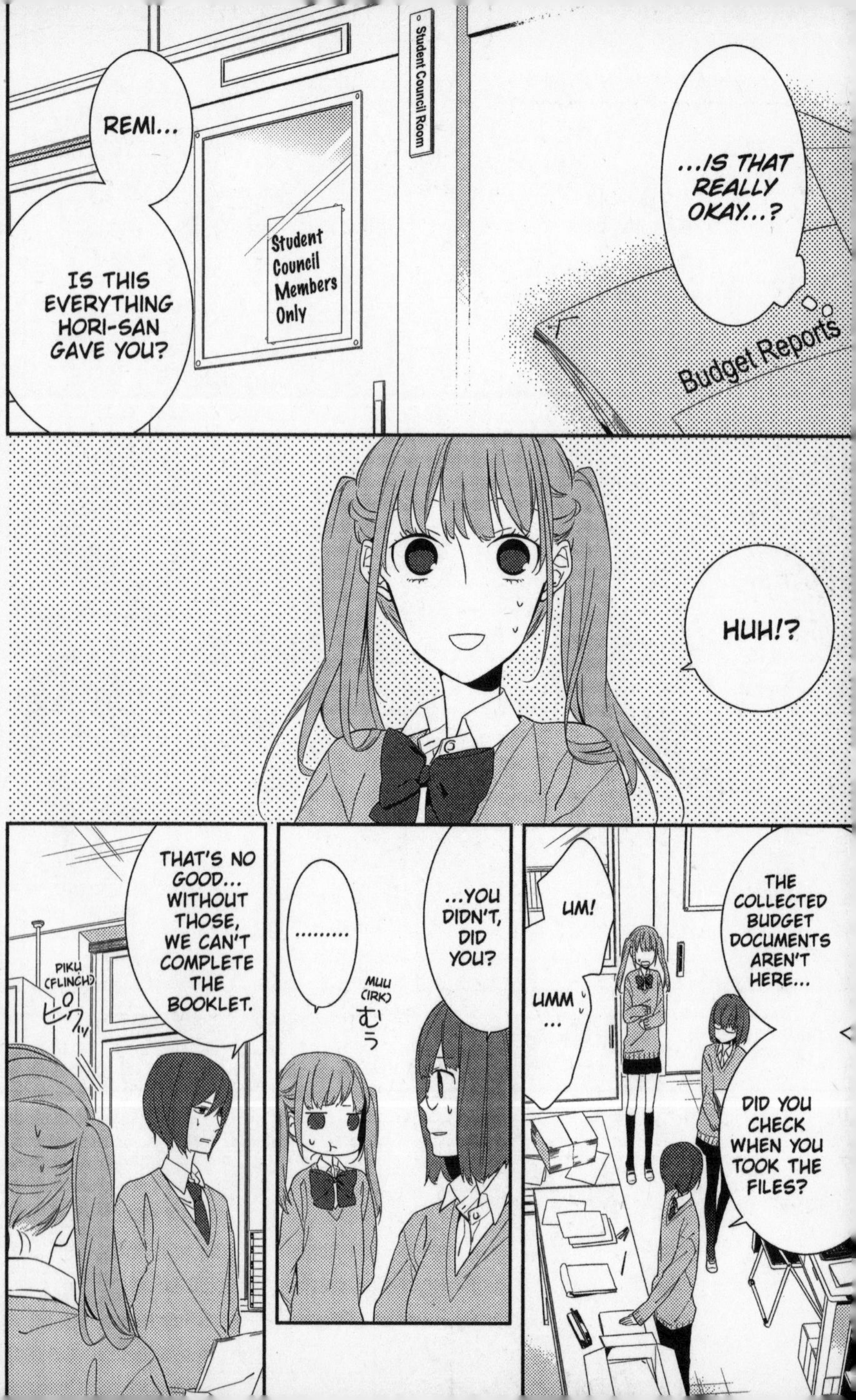
...IS THAT REALLY OKAY...?
Budget Reports
Student Council Room
REMI...
Student Council Members Only
IS THIS EVERYTHING HORI-SAN GAVE YOU?
HUH!?
THE COLLECTED BUDGET DOCUMENTS AREN'T HERE...
UM!
UMM...
DID YOU CHECK WHEN YOU TOOK THE FILES?
...YOU DIDN'T, DID YOU?
....
MUU (IRK)
むぅ
THAT'S NO GOOD... WITHOUT THOSE, WE CAN'T COMPLETE THE BOOKLET.
PIKU (FLINCH)
ピクッ

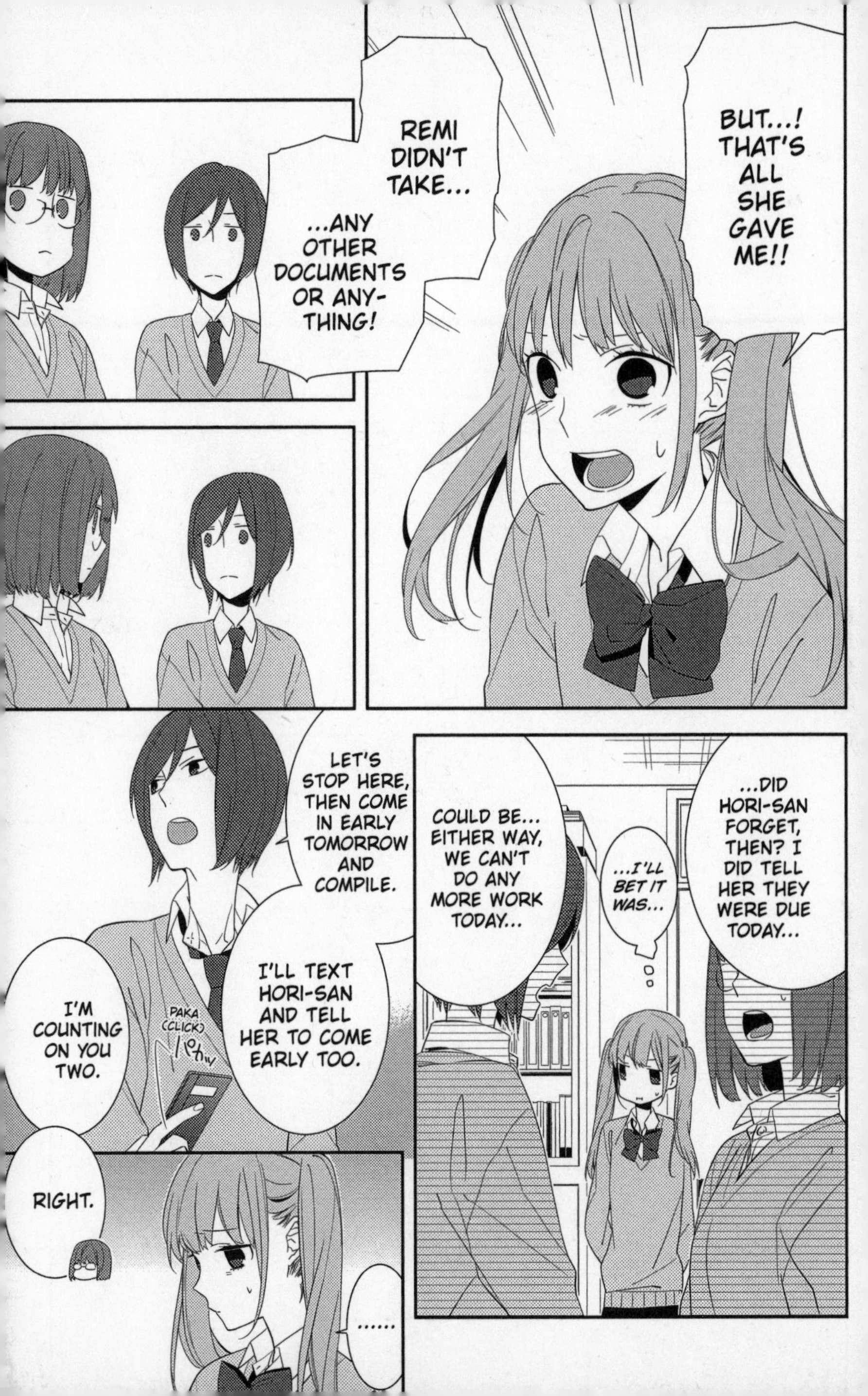
BUT...! THAT'S ALL SHE GAVE ME!!
REMI DIDN'T TAKE...
...ANY OTHER DOCUMENTS OR ANY-THING!
...DID HORI-SAN FORGET, THEN? I DID TELL HER THEY WERE DUE TODAY...
...I'LL BET IT WAS...
COULD BE... EITHER WAY, WE CAN'T DO ANY MORE WORK TODAY...
LET'S STOP HERE, THEN COME IN EARLY TOMORROW AND COMPILE.
I'LL TEXT HORI-SAN AND TELL HER TO COME EARLY TOO.
PAKA (CLICK)
パカッ
I'M COUNTING ON YOU TWO.
......
RIGHT.

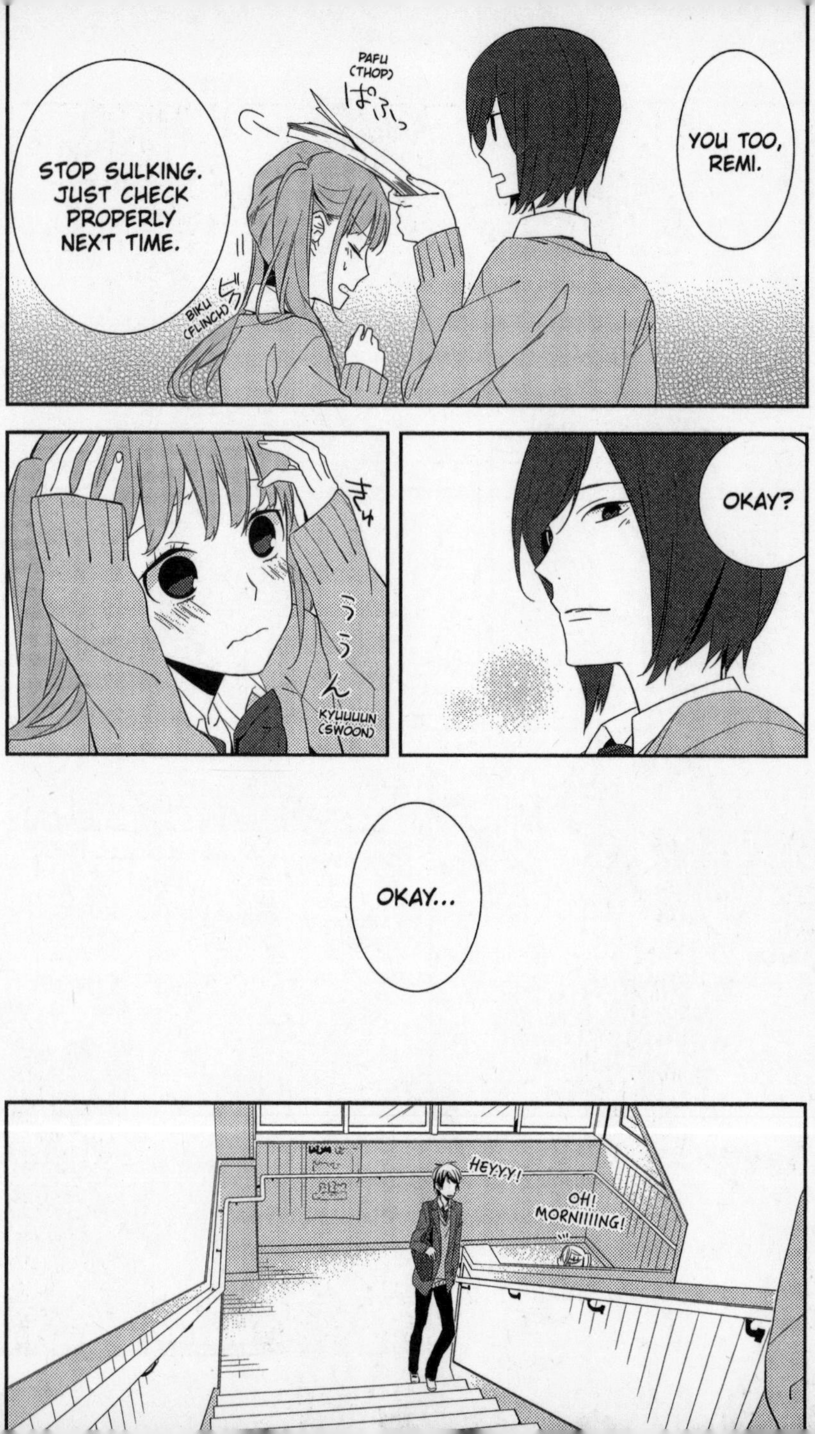
YOU TOO, REMI.
PAFU (THOP) ぱふっ
STOP SULKING. JUST CHECK PROPERLY NEXT TIME.
BIKU (FLINCH) ビク
OKAY?
きゅ
ううん
KYUUUUN (SWOON)
OKAY...
HEY-Y-Y!
OH! MORNIIIING!

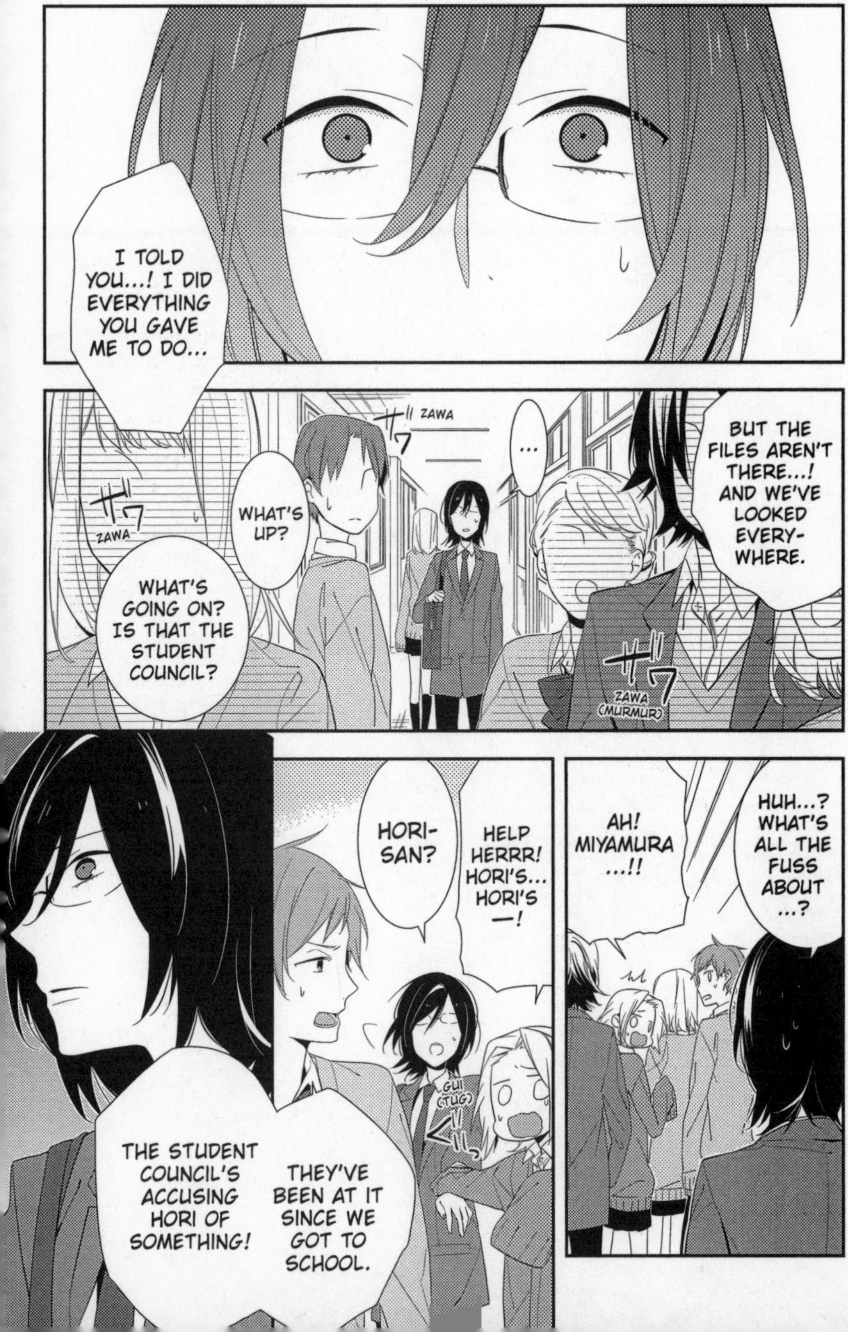
I TOLD YOU...! I DID EVERYTHING YOU GAVE ME TO DO...
BUT THE FILES AREN'T THERE...! AND WE'VE LOOKED EVERY-WHERE.
...
ZAWA
WHAT'S UP?
ZAWA (MURMUR)
ZAWA
WHAT'S GOING ON? IS THAT THE STUDENT COUNCIL?
HUH...? WHAT'S ALL THE FUSS ABOUT...?
AH! MIYAMURA...!!
HELP HERRR! HORI'S... HORI'S—!
HORI-SAN?
GUI (TUG)
THE STUDENT COUNCIL'S ACCUSING HORI OF SOMETHING!
THEY'VE BEEN AT IT SINCE WE GOT TO SCHOOL.

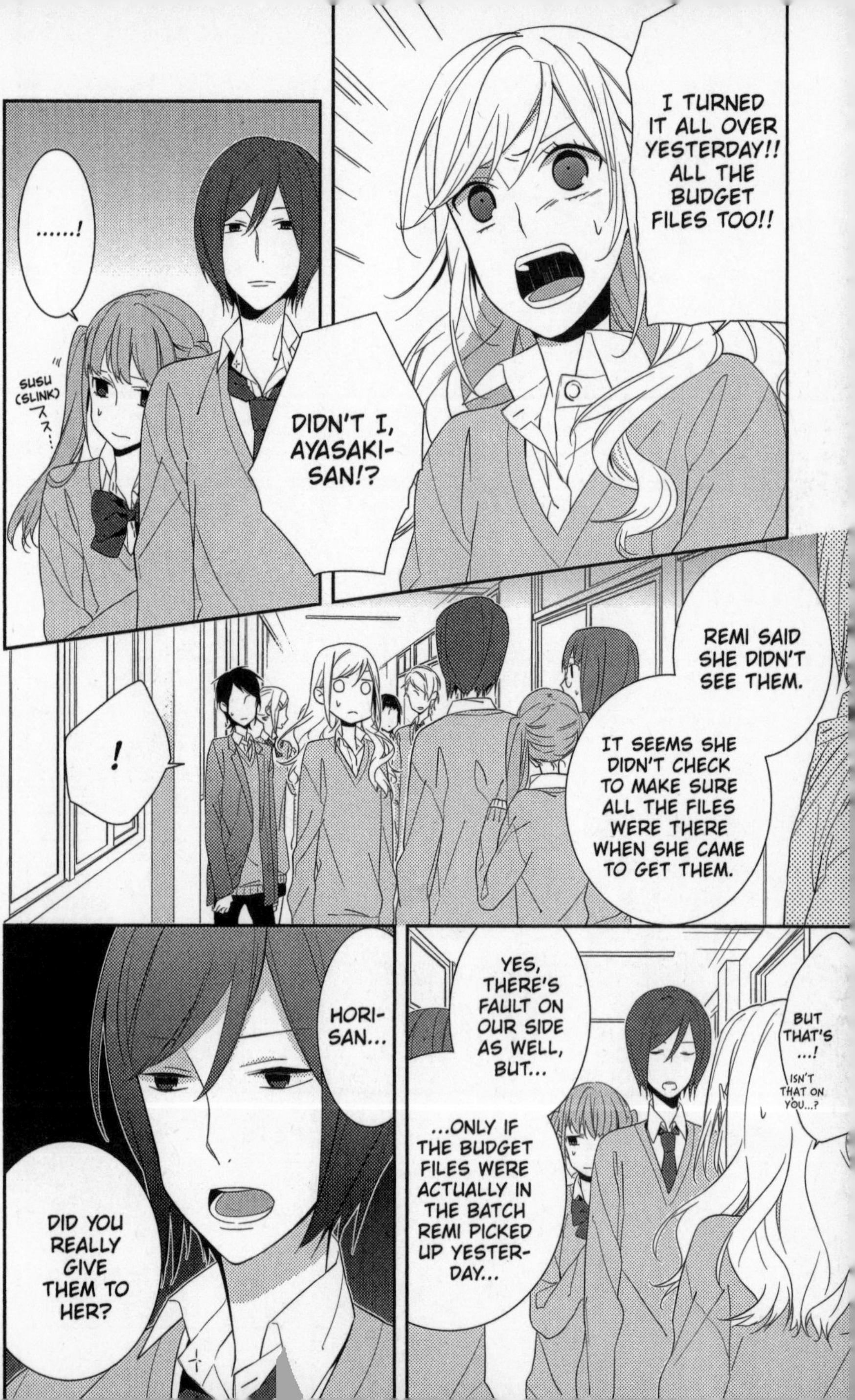
I TURNED IT ALL OVER YESTERDAY!! ALL THE BUDGET FILES TOO!!
DIDN'T I, AYASAKI-SAN!?
......!
SUSU (SLINK)
スス…
REMI SAID SHE DIDN'T SEE THEM.
IT SEEMS SHE DIDN'T CHECK TO MAKE SURE ALL THE FILES WERE THERE WHEN SHE CAME TO GET THEM.
!
YES, THERE'S FAULT ON OUR SIDE AS WELL, BUT...
BUT THAT'S ...!
ISN'T THAT ON YOU...?
...ONLY IF THE BUDGET FILES WERE ACTUALLY IN THE BATCH REMI PICKED UP YESTER-DAY...
HORI-SAN...
DID YOU REALLY GIVE THEM TO HER?

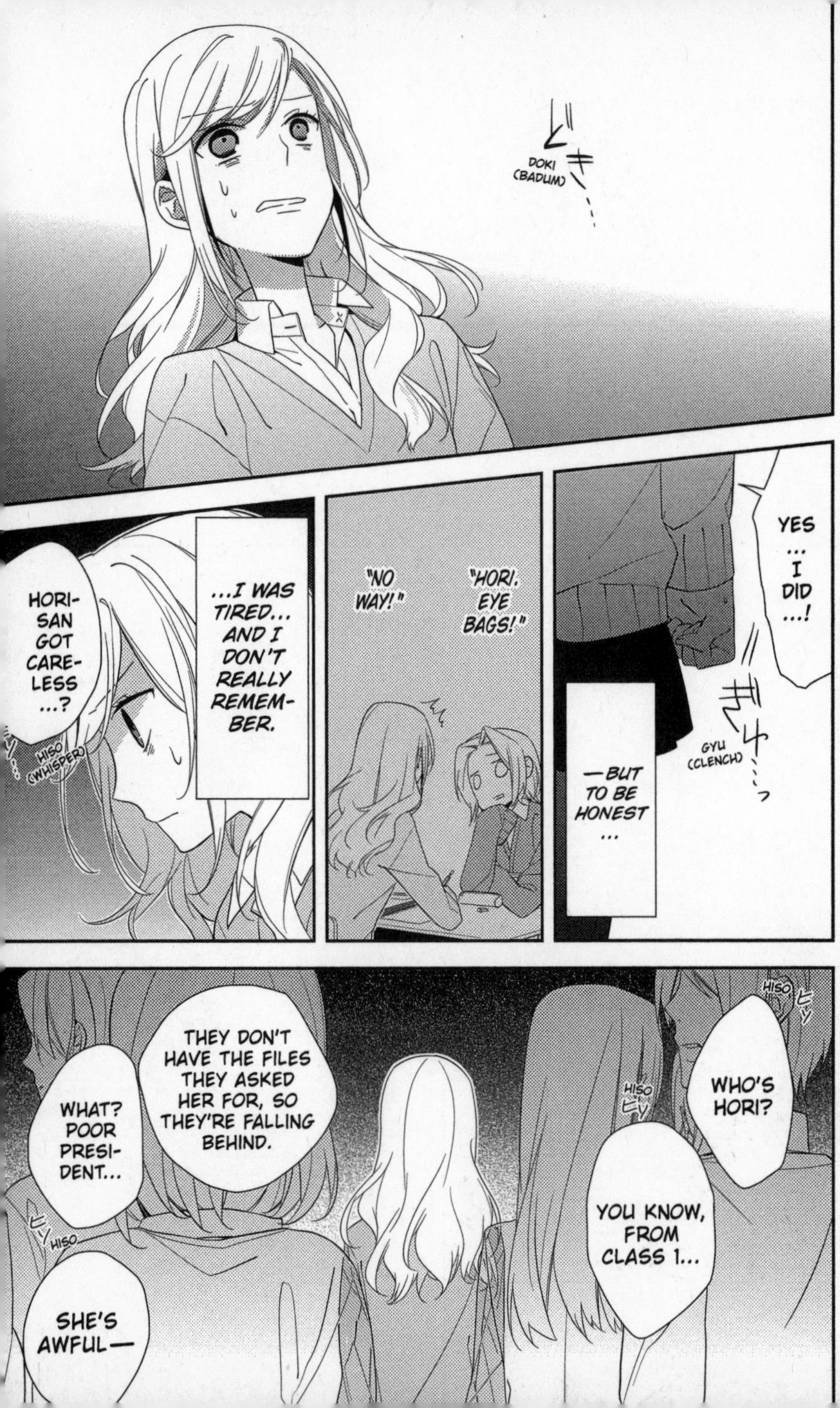
ドキ
DOKI (BADUM)
YES... I DID...!
ギュ
GYU (CLENCH)
—BUT TO BE HONEST...
"HORI. EYE BAGS!"
"NO WAY!"
...I WAS TIRED... AND I DON'T REALLY REMEMBER.
HORI-SAN GOT CARELESS...?
HISO (WHISPER)
HISO
WHO'S HORI?
HISO
YOU KNOW, FROM CLASS 1...
THEY DON'T HAVE THE FILES THEY ASKED HER FOR, SO THEY'RE FALLING BEHIND.
WHAT? POOR PRESIDENT...
HISO
SHE'S AWFUL—

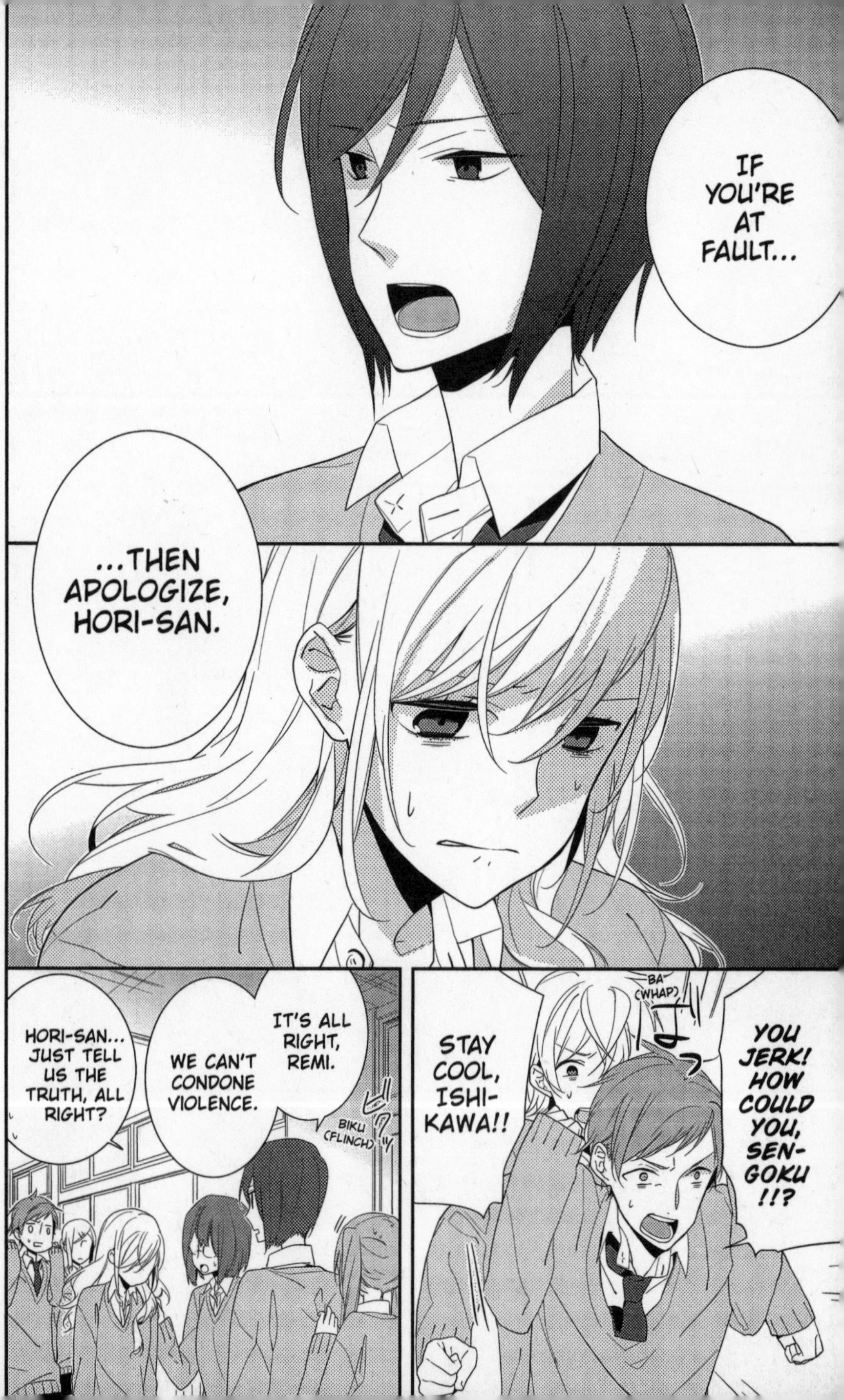
IF YOU'RE AT FAULT...
...THEN APOLOGIZE, HORI-SAN.
YOU JERK! HOW COULD YOU, SEN-GOKU!!?
BA (WHAP)
STAY COOL, ISHI-KAWA!!
IT'S ALL RIGHT, REMI.
BIKU (FLINCH)
WE CAN'T CONDONE VIOLENCE.
HORI-SAN... JUST TELL US THE TRUTH, ALL RIGHT?

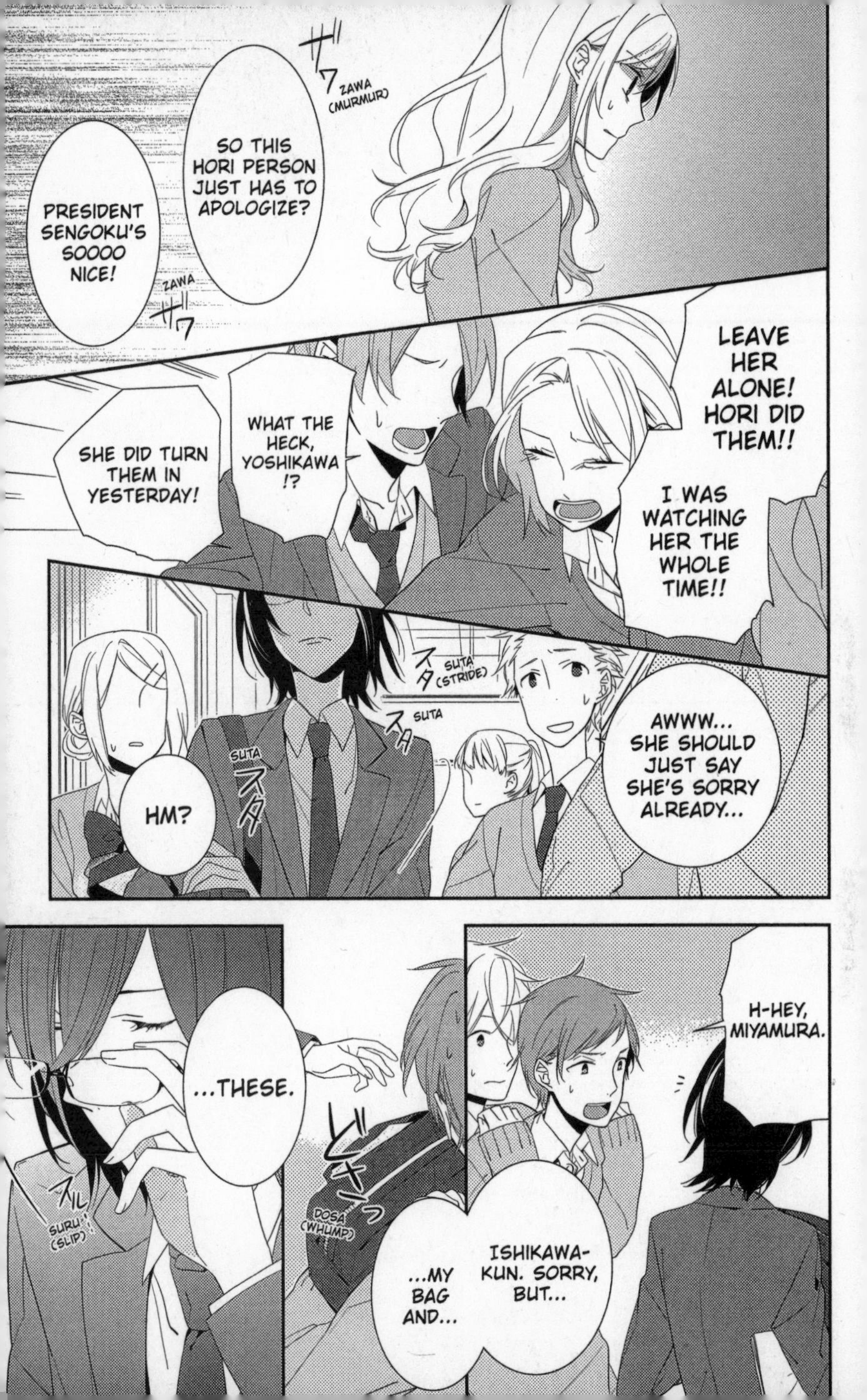
ZAWA (MURMUR)
SO THIS HORI PERSON JUST HAS TO APOLOGIZE?
PRESIDENT SENGOKU'S SOOOO NICE!
ZAWA
LEAVE HER ALONE! HORI DID THEM!!
I WAS WATCHING HER THE WHOLE TIME!!
WHAT THE HECK, YOSHIKAWA!?
SHE DID TURN THEM IN YESTERDAY!
AWWW... SHE SHOULD JUST SAY SHE'S SORRY ALREADY...
SUTA (STRIDE)
SUTA
SUTA
HM?
H-HEY, MIYAMURA.
ISHIKAWA-KUN. SORRY, BUT...
...MY BAG AND...
DOSA (WHUMP)
...THESE.
SURU (SLIP)

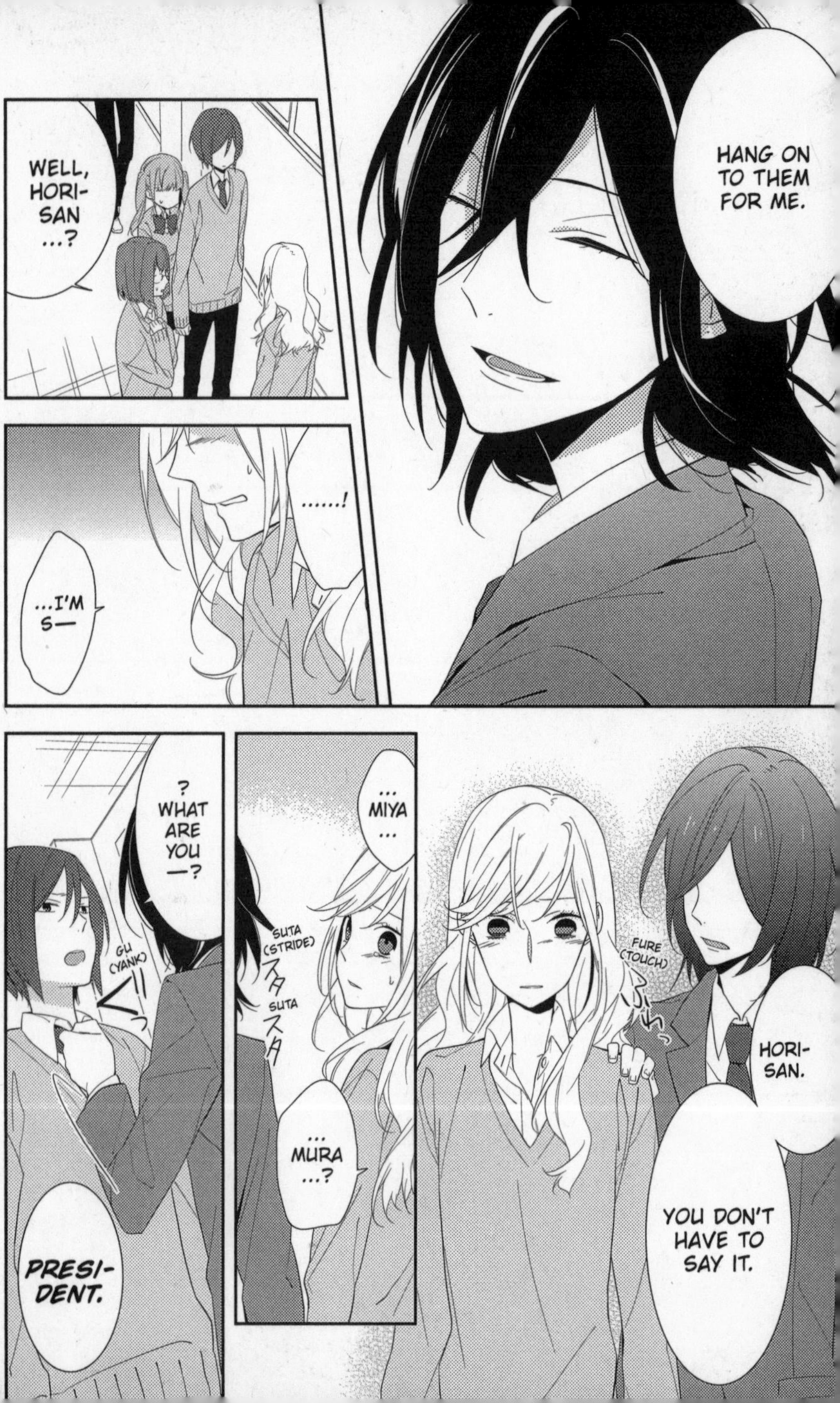
HANG ON TO THEM FOR ME.
WELL, HORI-SAN ...?
......!
...I'M S—
FURE (TOUCH)
HORI-SAN.
YOU DON'T HAVE TO SAY IT.
... MIYA ...
SUTA (STRIDE)
SUTA
... MURA ...?
? WHAT ARE YOU —?
GU (YANK)
PRESI-DENT.

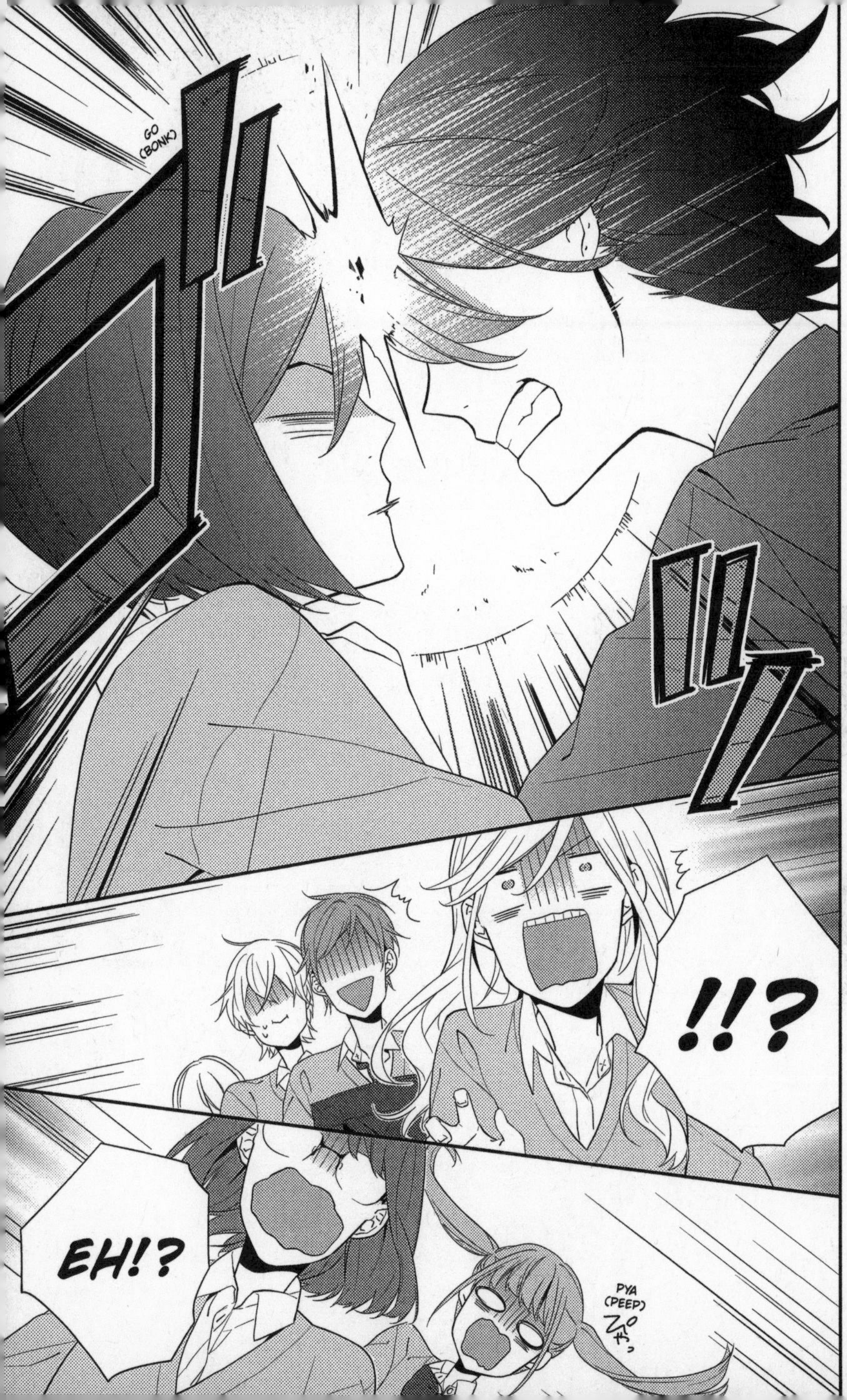
GO
(BONK)
!!?
EH!?
PYA
(PEEP)

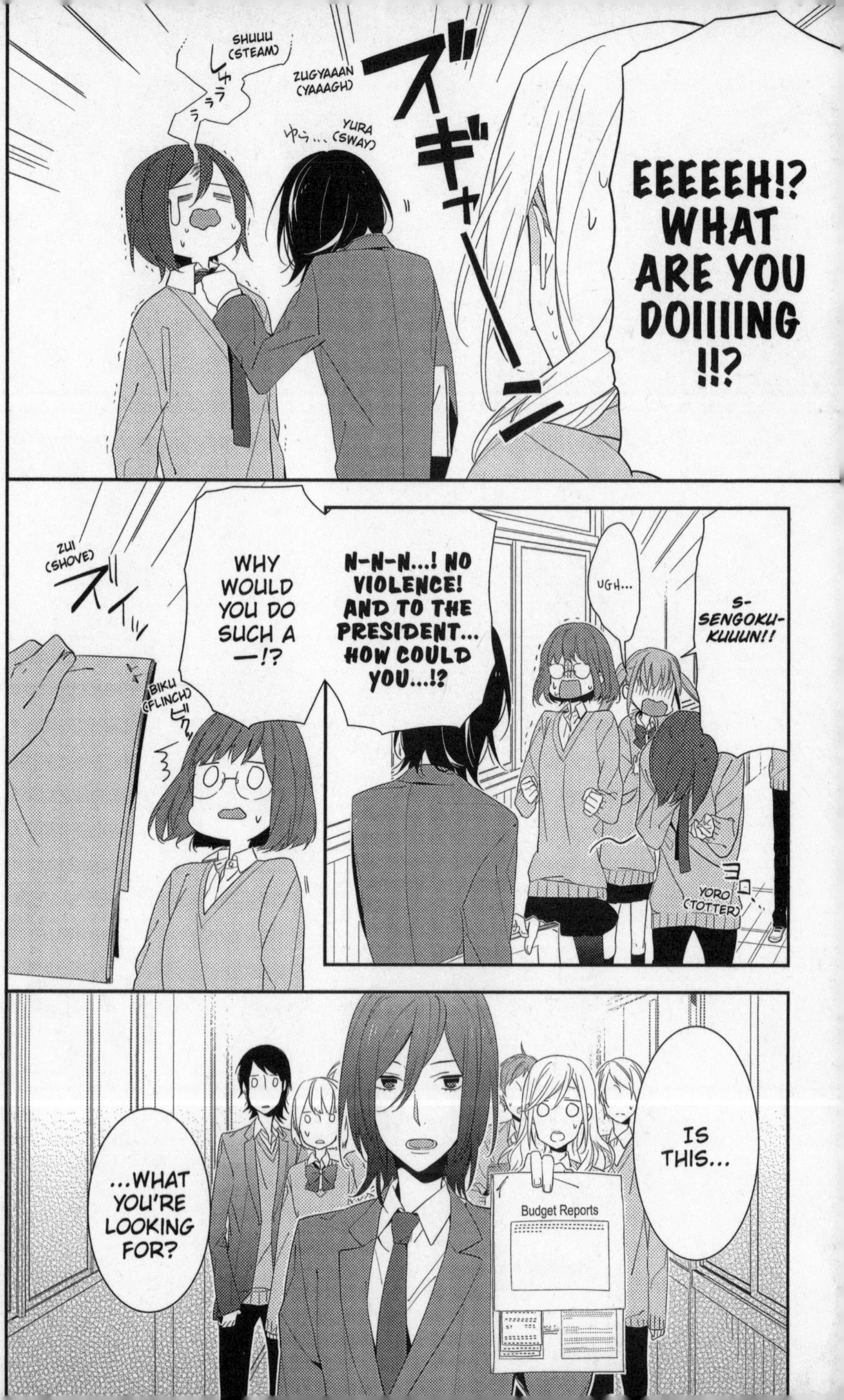
EEEEEH!? WHAT ARE YOU DOIIIIING !!?
ズギャーー
ZUGYAAAN (YAAAGH)
ゆら…
YURA (SWAY)
しゅうう
SHUUU (STEAM)
S-SENGOKU-KUUUN!!
UGH...
ヨロ
YORO (TOTTER)
N-N-N...! NO VIOLENCE! AND TO THE PRESIDENT... HOW COULD YOU...!?
WHY WOULD YOU DO SUCH A ー!?
ズイッ
ZUI (SHOVE)
ビク
BIKU (FLINCH)
IS THIS...
Budget Reports
...WHAT YOU'RE LOOKING FOR?

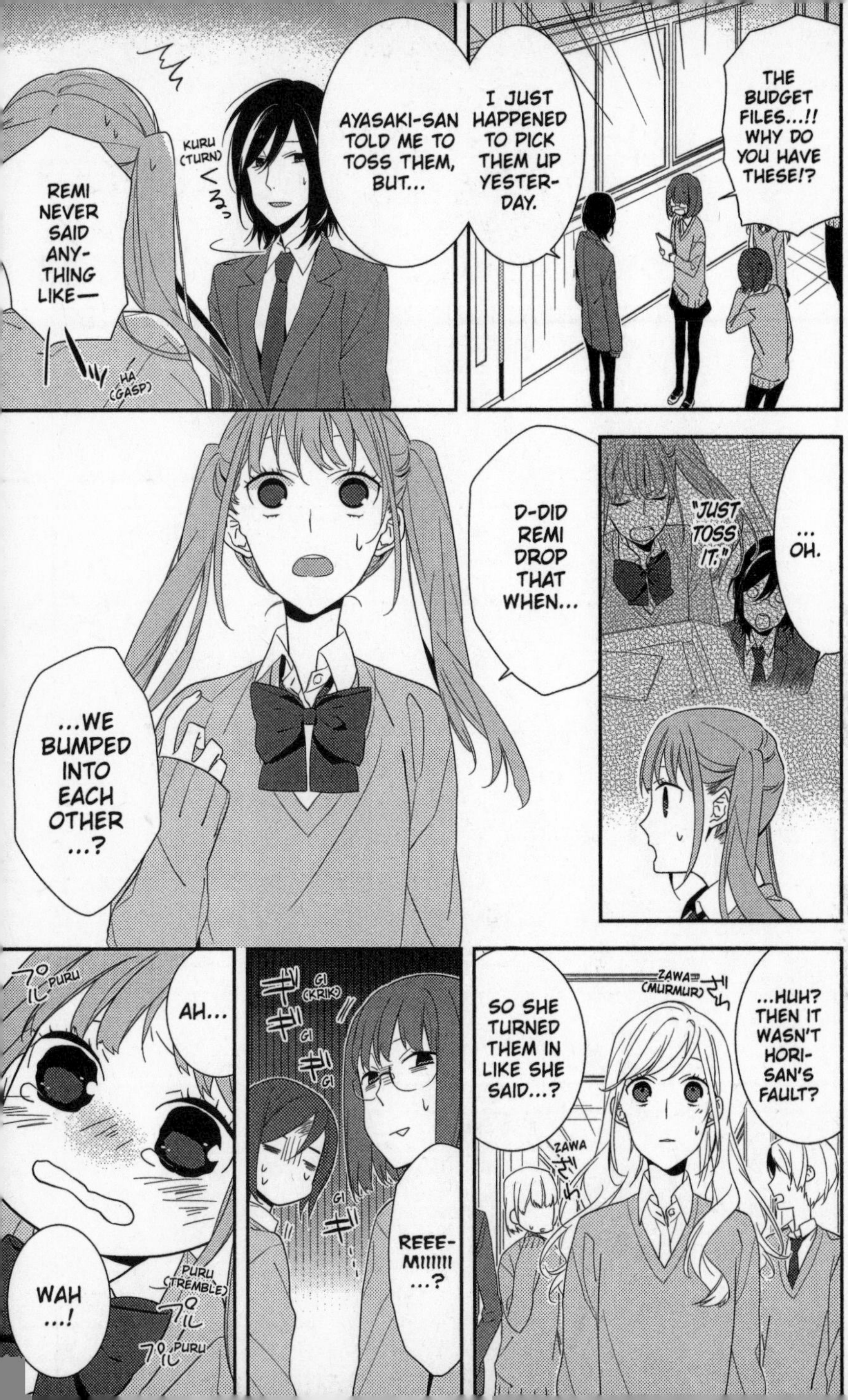
THE BUDGET FILES...!! WHY DO YOU HAVE THESE!?
I JUST HAPPENED TO PICK THEM UP YESTER-DAY.
AYASAKI-SAN TOLD ME TO TOSS THEM, BUT...
KURU (TURN)
REMI NEVER SAID ANY-THING LIKE—
HA (GASP)
...OH.
"JUST TOSS IT."
D-DID REMI DROP THAT WHEN...
...WE BUMPED INTO EACH OTHER...?
...HUH? THEN IT WASN'T HORI-SAN'S FAULT?
ZAWA (MURMUR)
SO SHE TURNED THEM IN LIKE SHE SAID...?
ZAWA
GI (KRIK)
GI
GI
REEE-MI!!!!!! ...?
PURU
AH...
PURU (TREMBLE)
WAH ...!
PURU

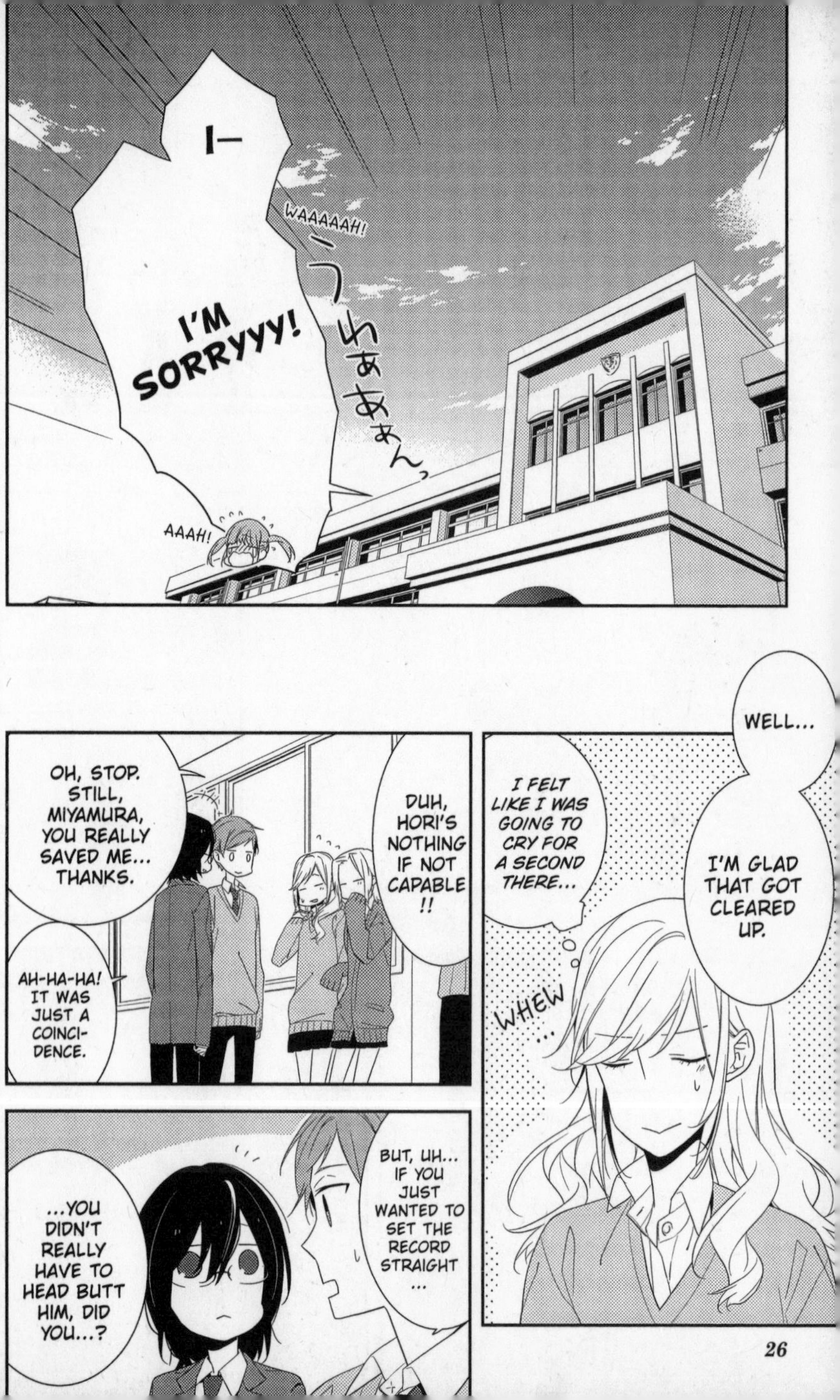
I—
I'M SORRYYY!
WAAAAAH!
うわあああぁんっ
AAAH!
WELL...
I'M GLAD THAT GOT CLEARED UP.
I FELT LIKE I WAS GOING TO CRY FOR A SECOND THERE...
WHEW...
DUH, HORI'S NOTHING IF NOT CAPABLE!!
OH, STOP. STILL, MIYAMURA, YOU REALLY SAVED ME... THANKS.
AH-HA-HA! IT WAS JUST A COINCI-DENCE.
BUT, UH... IF YOU JUST WANTED TO SET THE RECORD STRAIGHT...
...YOU DIDN'T REALLY HAVE TO HEAD BUTT HIM, DID YOU...?

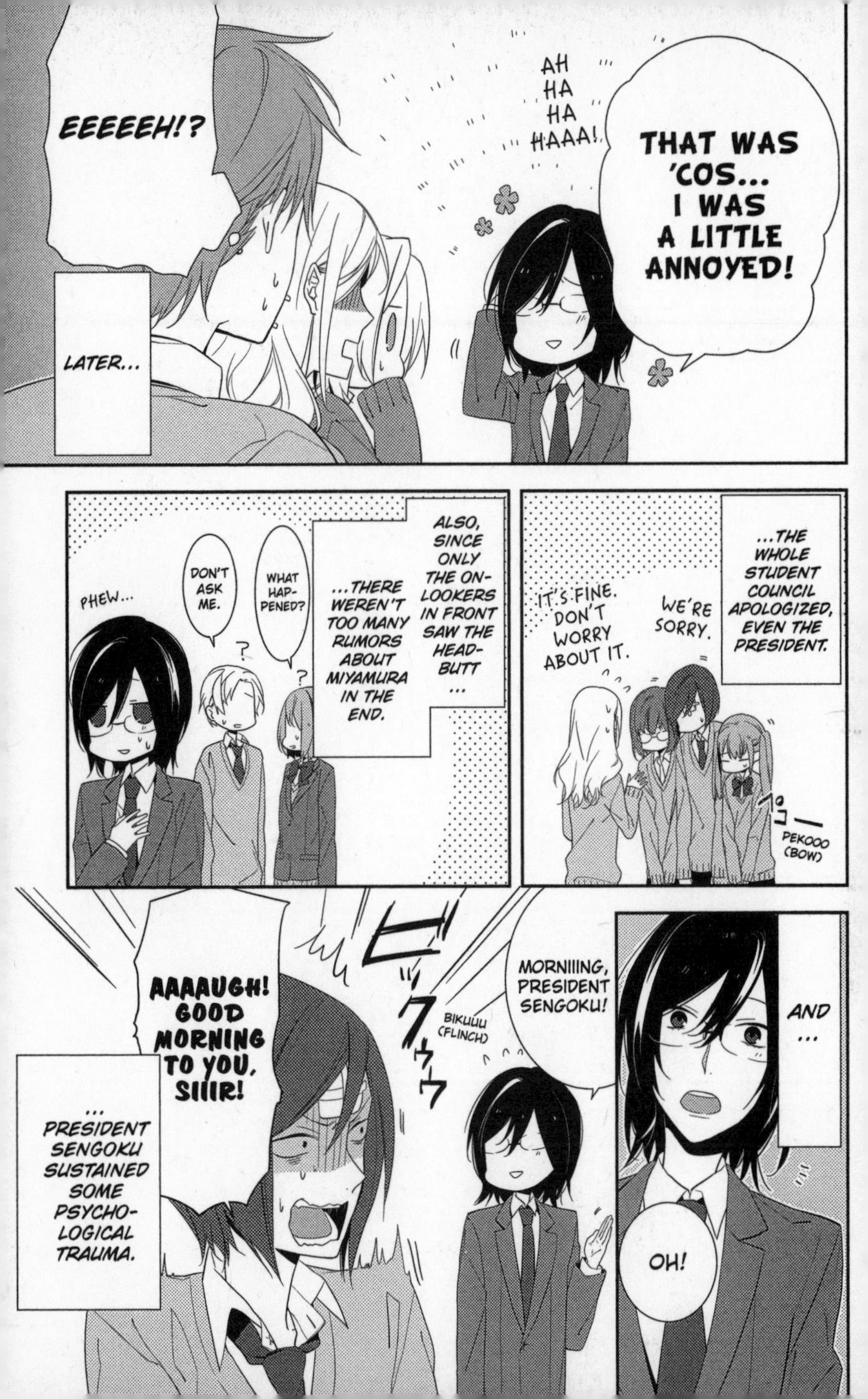
THAT WAS 'COS... I WAS A LITTLE ANNOYED!
AH HA HA HAAA!
EEEEEH!?
LATER...
...THE WHOLE STUDENT COUNCIL APOLOGIZED, EVEN THE PRESIDENT.
WE'RE SORRY.
IT'S FINE. DON'T WORRY ABOUT IT.
PEKOOO (BOW)
ALSO, SINCE ONLY THE ON-LOOKERS IN FRONT SAW THE HEAD-BUTT ...
...THERE WEREN'T TOO MANY RUMORS ABOUT MIYAMURA IN THE END.
WHAT HAP-PENED?
DON'T ASK ME.
PHEW...
AND ...
OH!
MORNIIING, PRESIDENT SENGOKU!
BIKUUU (FLINCH)
AAAAUGH! GOOD MORNING TO YOU, SIIIR!
... PRESIDENT SENGOKU SUSTAINED SOME PSYCHOLOGICAL TRAUMA.

HORIMIYA

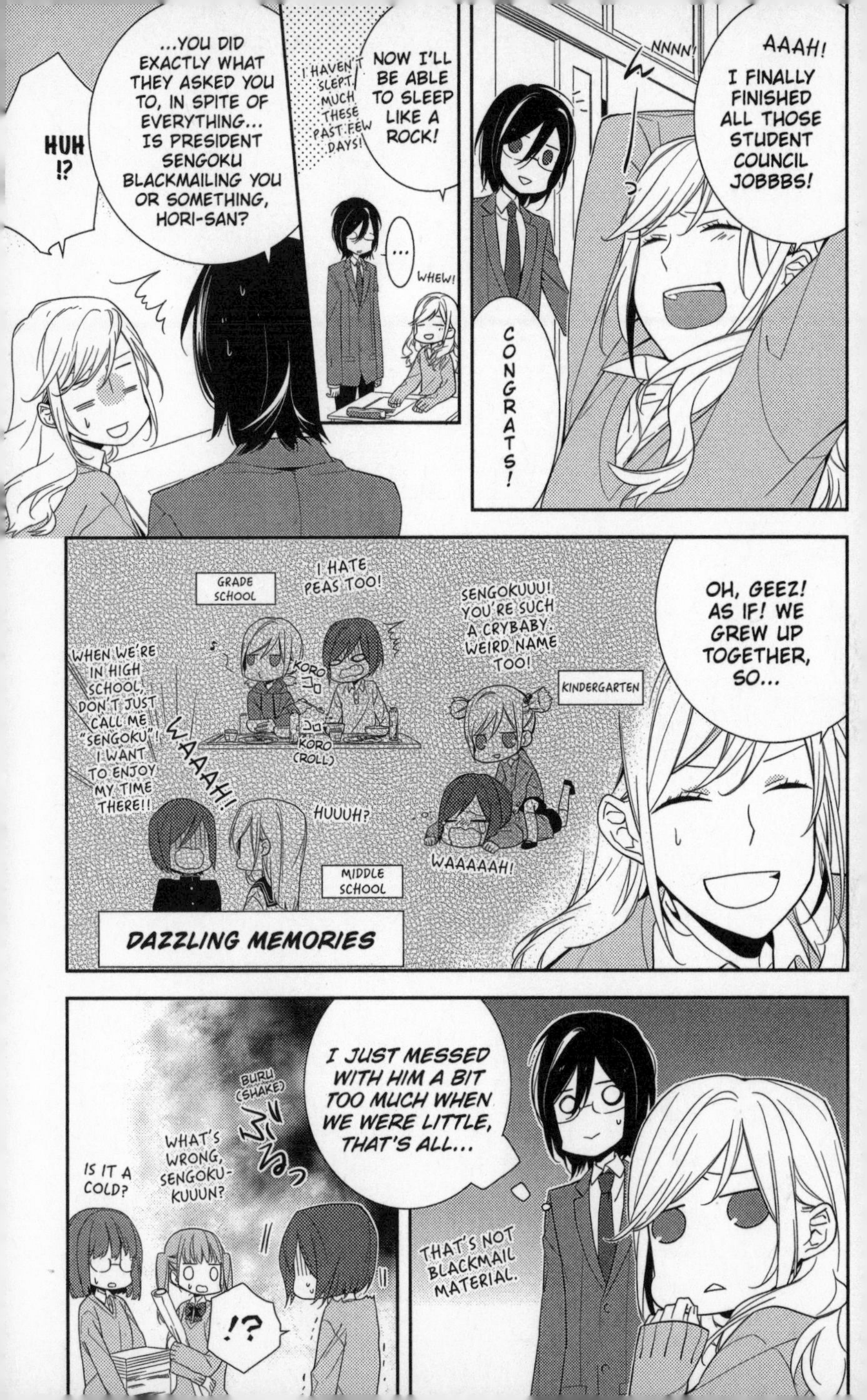
AAAH!
NNNNN!
I FINALLY FINISHED ALL THOSE STUDENT COUNCIL JOBBBS!
CONGRATS!
NOW I'LL BE ABLE TO SLEEP LIKE A ROCK!
I HAVEN'T SLEPT MUCH THESE PAST FEW DAYS!
...
WHEW!
...YOU DID EXACTLY WHAT THEY ASKED YOU TO, IN SPITE OF EVERYTHING... IS PRESIDENT SENGOKU BLACKMAILING YOU OR SOMETHING, HORI-SAN?
HUH!?
OH, GEEZ! AS IF! WE GREW UP TOGETHER, SO...
KINDERGARTEN
SENGOKUUU! YOU'RE SUCH A CRYBABY. WEIRD NAME TOO!
WAAAAAH!
GRADE SCHOOL
I HATE PEAS TOO!
KORO
KORO (ROLL)
MIDDLE SCHOOL
HUUUH?
WAAAAH!
WHEN WE'RE IN HIGH SCHOOL, DON'T JUST CALL ME "SENGOKU"! I WANT TO ENJOY MY TIME THERE!!
DAZZLING MEMORIES
I JUST MESSED WITH HIM A BIT TOO MUCH WHEN WE WERE LITTLE, THAT'S ALL...
THAT'S NOT BLACKMAIL MATERIAL.
BURU (SHAKE)
WHAT'S WRONG, SENGOKU-KUUUN?
IS IT A COLD?
!?

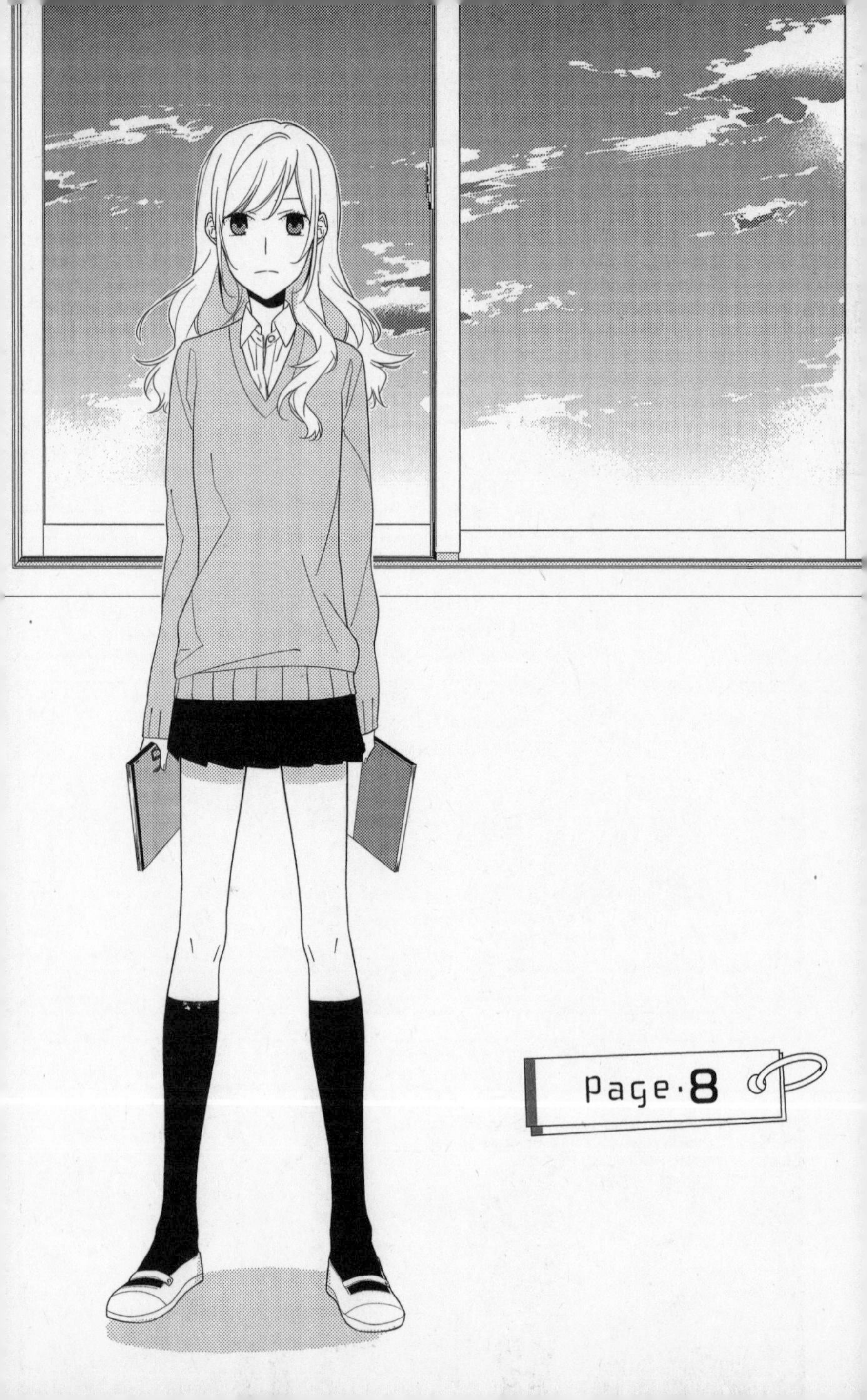
Page·8

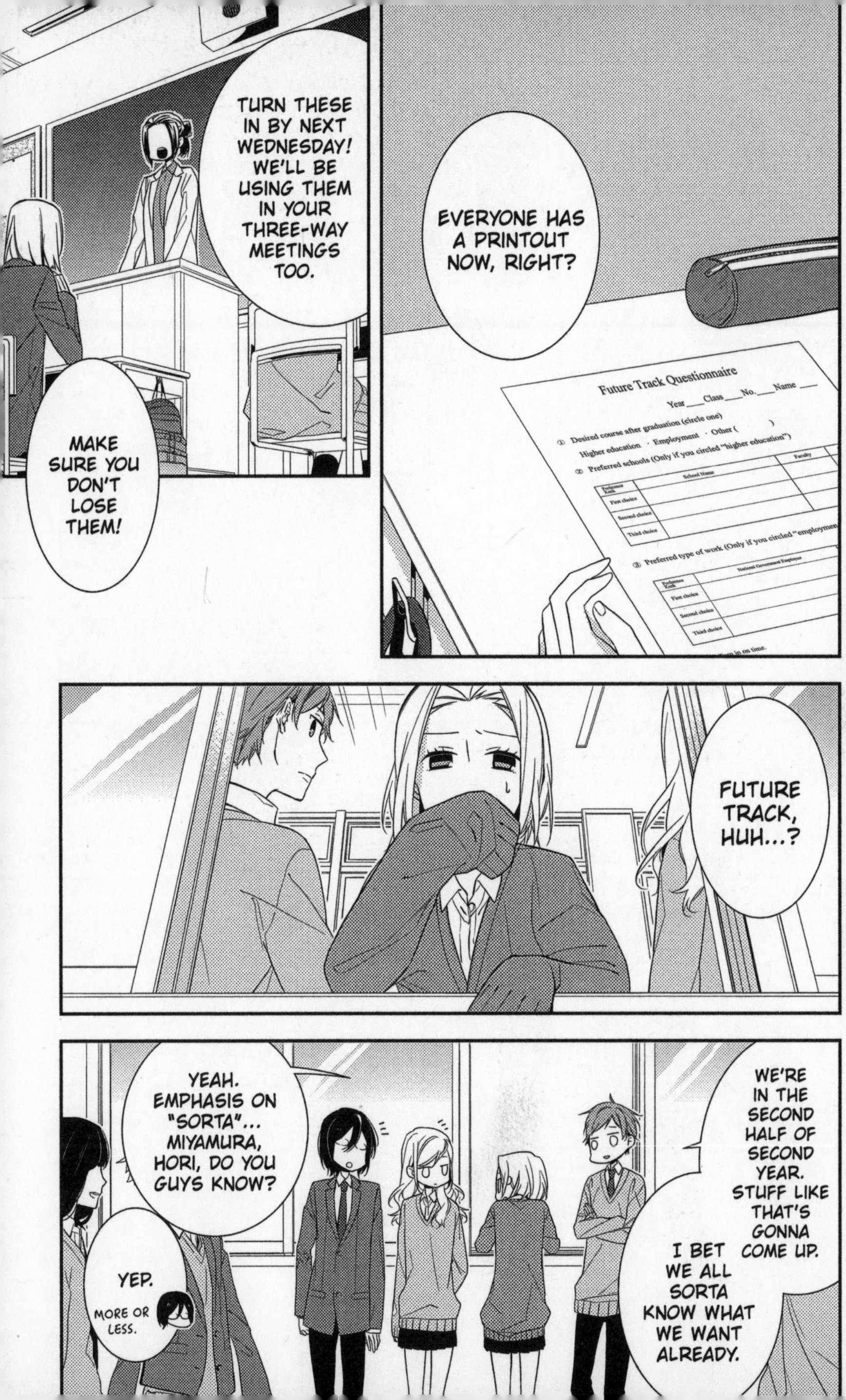
EVERYONE HAS A PRINTOUT NOW, RIGHT?
Future Track Questionnaire
Year___ Class___ No.___ Name ___
① Desired course after graduation (circle one)
Higher education · Employment · Other ( )
② Preferred schools (Only if you circled "higher education")
First choice
Second choice
Third choice
③ Preferred type of work (Only if you circled "employment
First choice
Second choice
Third choice
TURN THESE IN BY NEXT WEDNESDAY! WE'LL BE USING THEM IN YOUR THREE-WAY MEETINGS TOO.
MAKE SURE YOU DON'T LOSE THEM!
FUTURE TRACK, HUH...?
WE'RE IN THE SECOND HALF OF SECOND YEAR. STUFF LIKE THAT'S GONNA COME UP.
I BET WE ALL SORTA KNOW WHAT WE WANT ALREADY.
YEAH. EMPHASIS ON "SORTA"... MIYAMURA, HORI, DO YOU GUYS KNOW?
YEP.
MORE OR LESS.

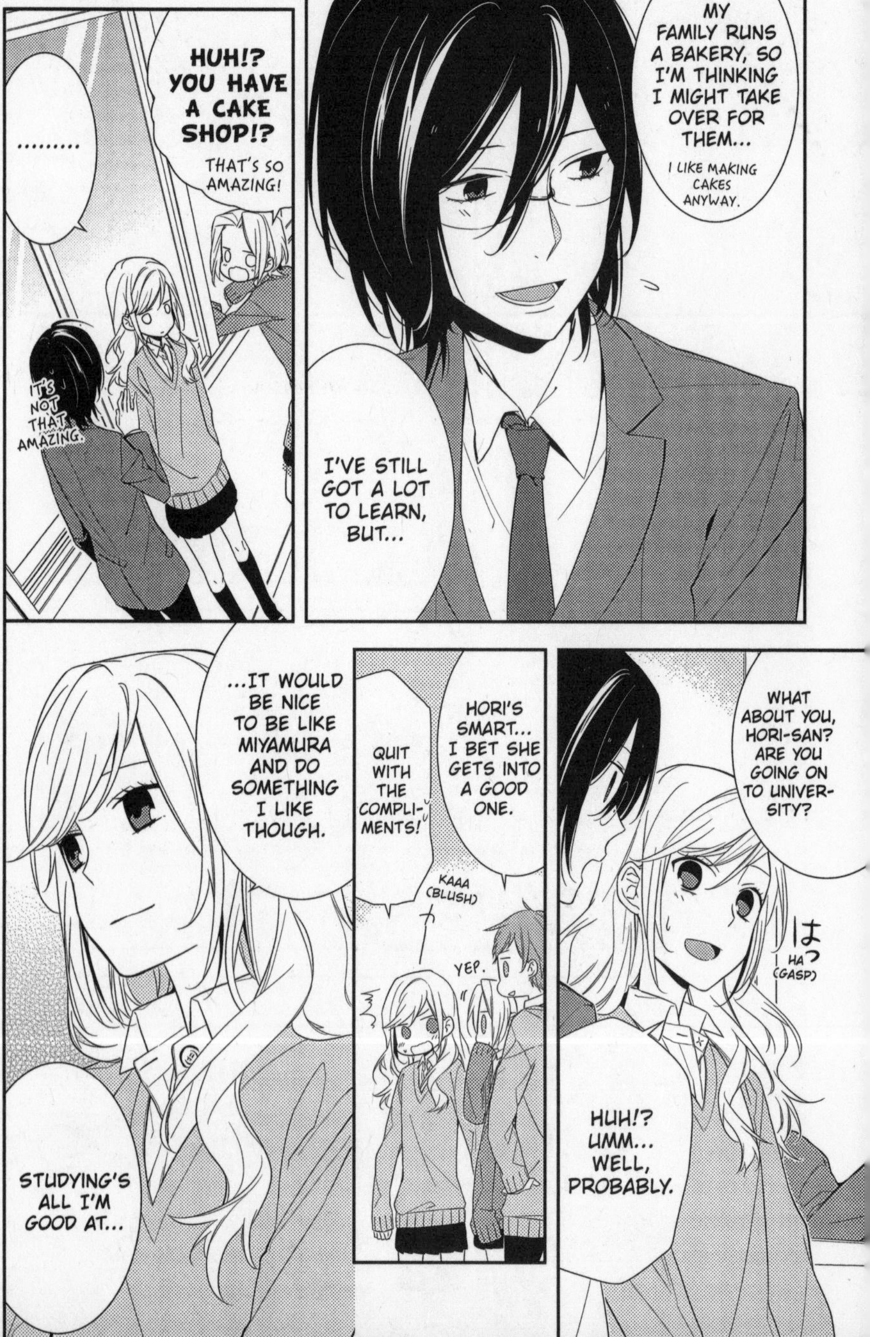
MY FAMILY RUNS A BAKERY, SO I'M THINKING I MIGHT TAKE OVER FOR THEM...
I LIKE MAKING CAKES ANYWAY.
I'VE STILL GOT A LOT TO LEARN, BUT...
HUH!? YOU HAVE A CAKE SHOP!?
THAT'S SO AMAZING!
....
IT'S NOT THAT AMAZING.
WHAT ABOUT YOU, HORI-SAN? ARE YOU GOING ON TO UNIVERSITY?
はっ
HA (GASP)
HUH!? UMM... WELL, PROBABLY.
HORI'S SMART... I BET SHE GETS INTO A GOOD ONE.
QUIT WITH THE COMPLIMENTS!
KAAA (BLUSH)
YEP.
...IT WOULD BE NICE TO BE LIKE MIYAMURA AND DO SOMETHING I LIKE THOUGH.
STUDYING'S ALL I'M GOOD AT...

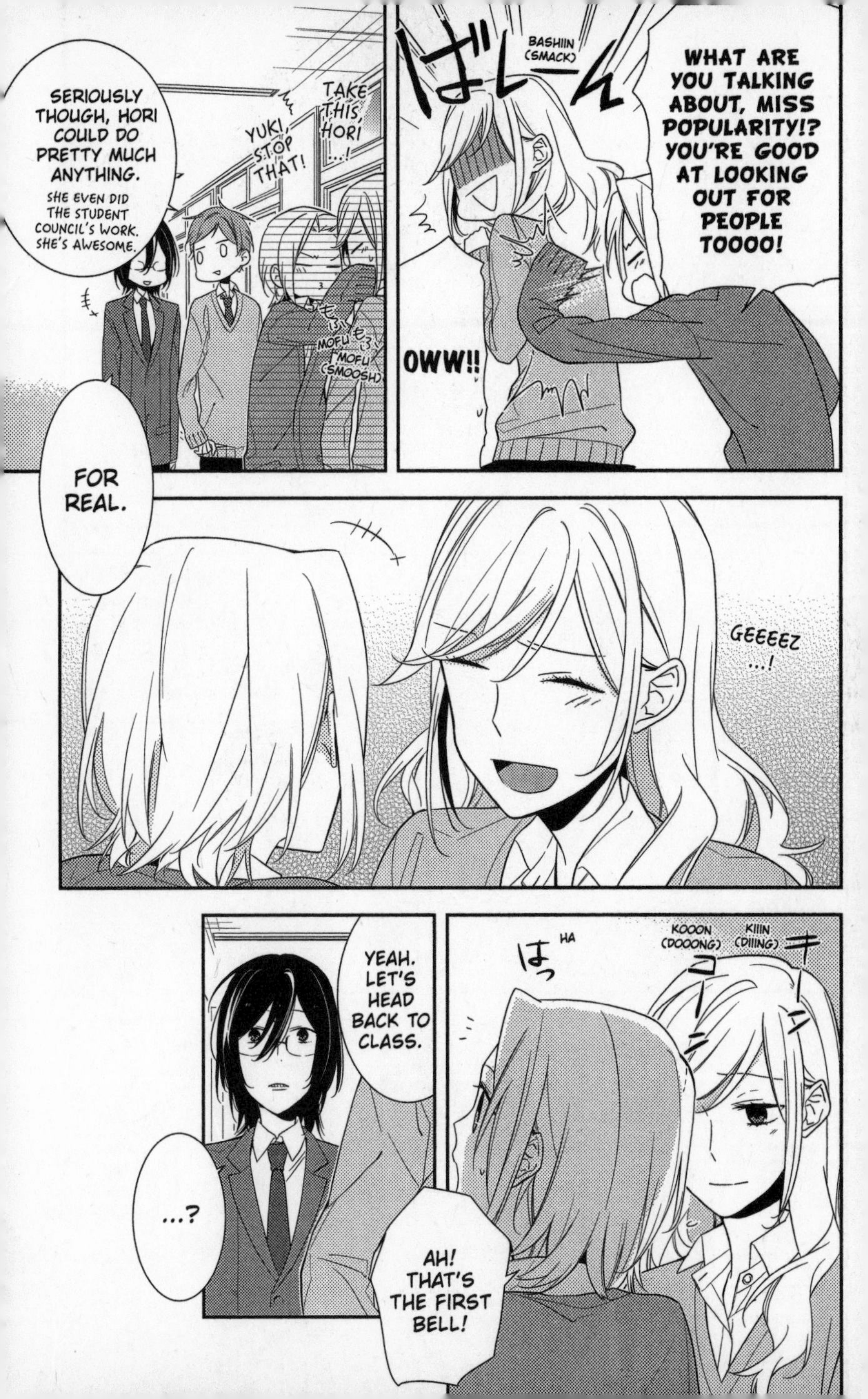

BASHIIN (SMACK)
WHAT ARE YOU TALKING ABOUT, MISS POPULARITY!? YOU'RE GOOD AT LOOKING OUT FOR PEOPLE TOOOO!
OWW!!
TAKE THIS, HORI...!
YUKI, STOP THAT!
SERIOUSLY THOUGH, HORI COULD DO PRETTY MUCH ANYTHING.
SHE EVEN DID THE STUDENT COUNCIL'S WORK. SHE'S AWESOME.
MOFU MOFU (SMOOSH)
FOR REAL.
GEEEEZ ...!
HA
KIIN (DIIING)
KOOON (DOOONG)
AH! THAT'S THE FIRST BELL!
YEAH. LET'S HEAD BACK TO CLASS.
...?

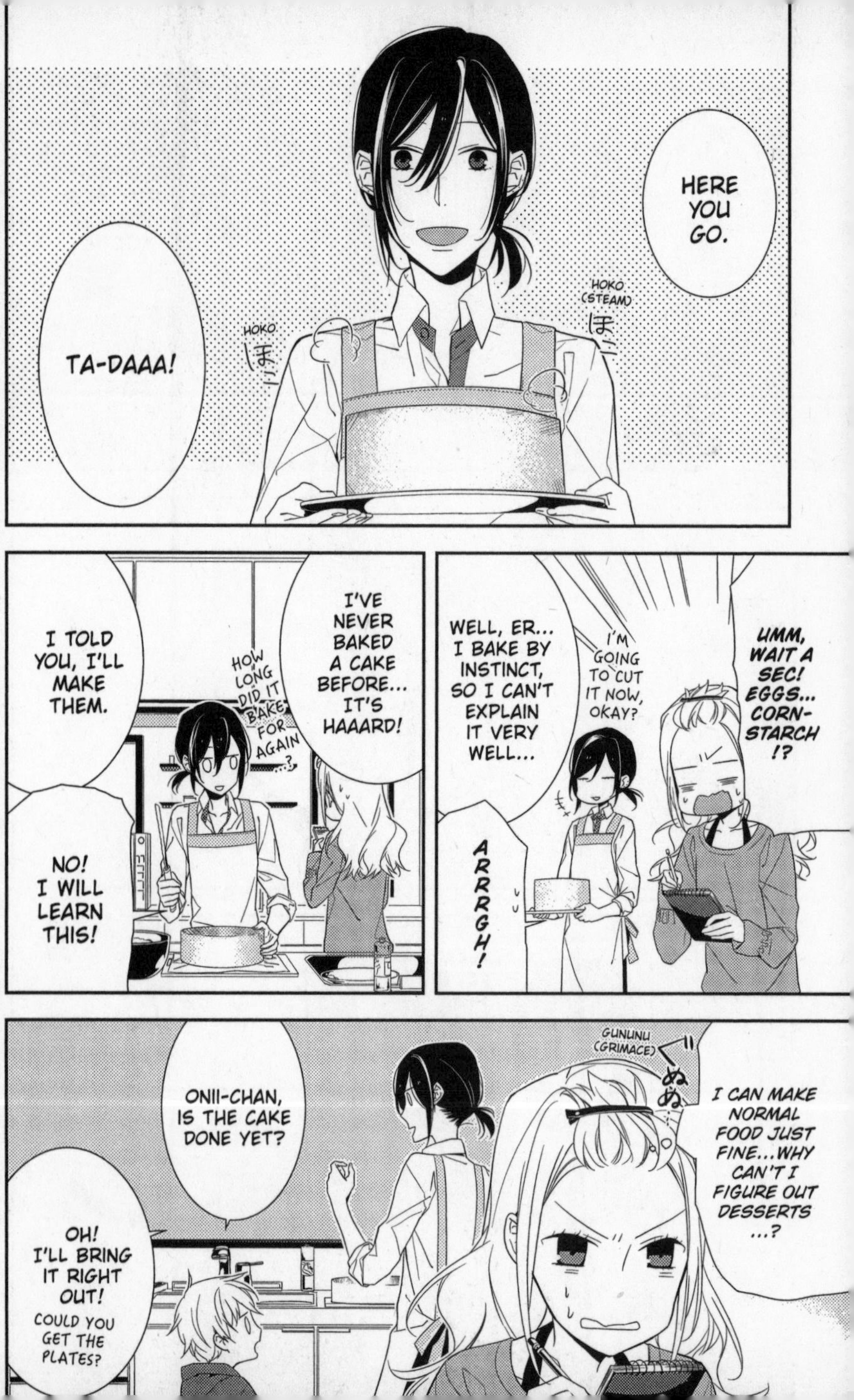
HERE YOU GO.
HOKO (STEAM)
ほこ
HOKO
ほこ
TA-DAAA!
UMM, WAIT A SEC! EGGS... CORN-STARCH!?
I'M GOING TO CUT IT NOW, OKAY?
WELL, ER... I BAKE BY INSTINCT, SO I CAN'T EXPLAIN IT VERY WELL...
ARRRGH!
I'VE NEVER BAKED A CAKE BEFORE... IT'S HAAARD!
HOW LONG DID IT BAKE FOR AGAIN...?
I TOLD YOU, I'LL MAKE THEM.
NO! I WILL LEARN THIS!
GUNUNU (GRIMACE)
ぐぬぬ
I CAN MAKE NORMAL FOOD JUST FINE...WHY CAN'T I FIGURE OUT DESSERTS...?
ONII-CHAN, IS THE CAKE DONE YET?
OH! I'LL BRING IT RIGHT OUT!
COULD YOU GET THE PLATES?

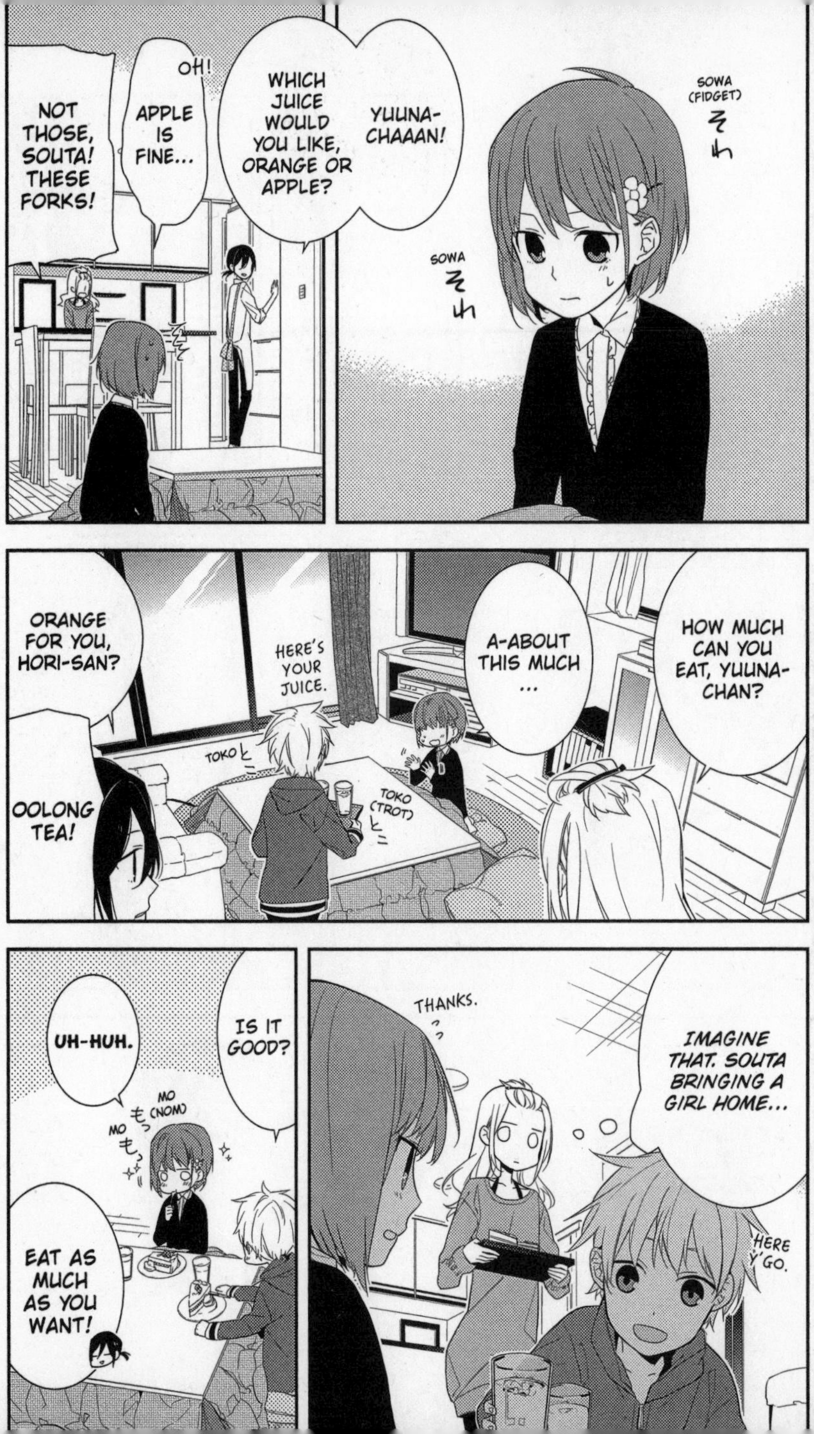
SOWA (FIDGET) そわ
SOWA そわ
YUUNA-CHAAAN!
WHICH JUICE WOULD YOU LIKE, ORANGE OR APPLE?
OH!
APPLE IS FINE...
NOT THOSE, SOUTA! THESE FORKS!
HOW MUCH CAN YOU EAT, YUUNA-CHAN?
A-ABOUT THIS MUCH...
HERE'S YOUR JUICE.
TOKO と
TOKO (TROT) と
ORANGE FOR YOU, HORI-SAN?
OOLONG TEA!
IMAGINE THAT. SOUTA BRINGING A GIRL HOME...
THANKS.
HERE Y'GO.
IS IT GOOD?
UH-HUH.
MO もっ (NOM)
MO もっ
EAT AS MUCH AS YOU WANT!

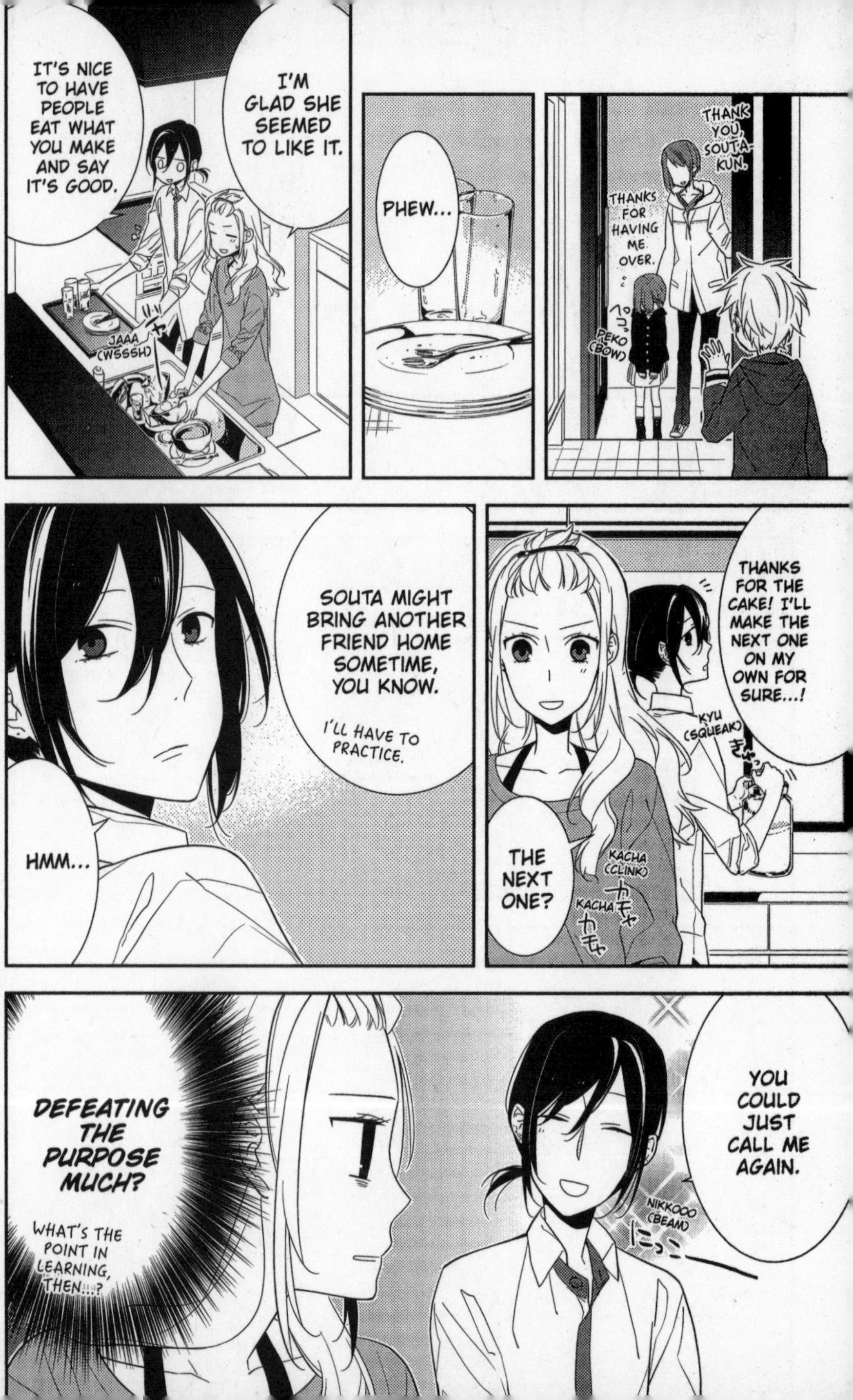
THANK YOU, SOUTA-KUN.
THANKS FOR HAVING ME OVER.
PEKO (BOW)
PHEW...
I'M GLAD SHE SEEMED TO LIKE IT.
IT'S NICE TO HAVE PEOPLE EAT WHAT YOU MAKE AND SAY IT'S GOOD.
JAAA (WSSSH)
THANKS FOR THE CAKE! I'LL MAKE THE NEXT ONE ON MY OWN FOR SURE...!
KYU (SQUEAK)
THE NEXT ONE?
KACHA (CLINK)
KACHA
SOUTA MIGHT BRING ANOTHER FRIEND HOME SOMETIME, YOU KNOW.
I'LL HAVE TO PRACTICE.
HMM...
YOU COULD JUST CALL ME AGAIN.
NIKKOOO (BEAM)
DEFEATING THE PURPOSE MUCH?
WHAT'S THE POINT IN LEARNING, THEN!!?

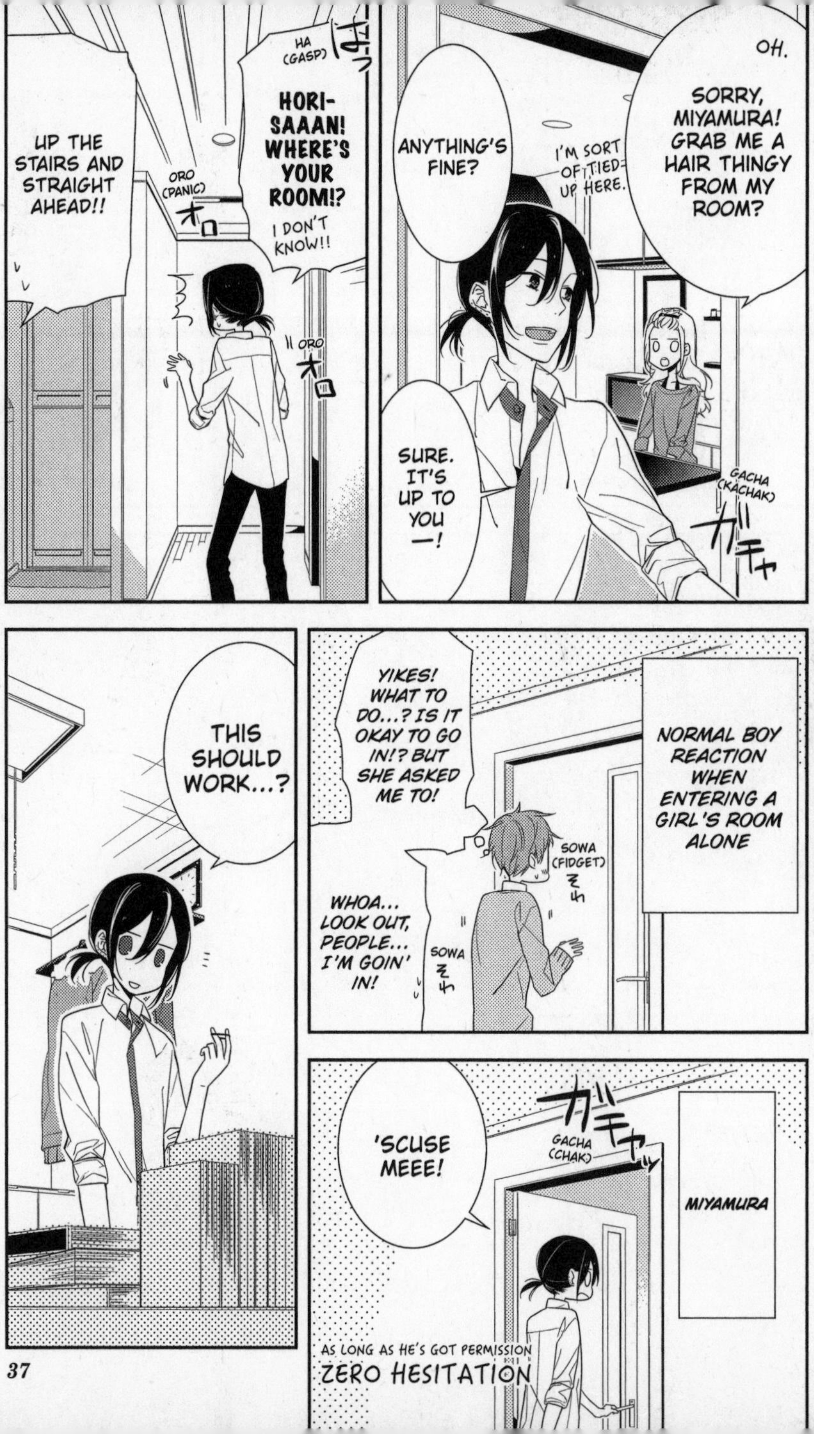
OH.
SORRY, MIYAMURA! GRAB ME A HAIR THINGY FROM MY ROOM?
I'M SORT OF TIED UP HERE.
ANYTHING'S FINE?
SURE. IT'S UP TO YOU—!
GACHA (KACHAK)
HA (GASP)
HORI-SAAAN! WHERE'S YOUR ROOM!?
ORO (PANIC)
UP THE STAIRS AND STRAIGHT AHEAD!!
I DON'T KNOW!!
ORO
NORMAL BOY REACTION WHEN ENTERING A GIRL'S ROOM ALONE
YIKES! WHAT TO DO...? IS IT OKAY TO GO IN!? BUT SHE ASKED ME TO!
SOWA (FIDGET)
WHOA... LOOK OUT, PEOPLE... I'M GOIN' IN!
SOWA
MIYAMURA
GACHA (CHAK)
'SCUSE MEEE!
AS LONG AS HE'S GOT PERMISSION
ZERO HESITATION
THIS SHOULD WORK...?

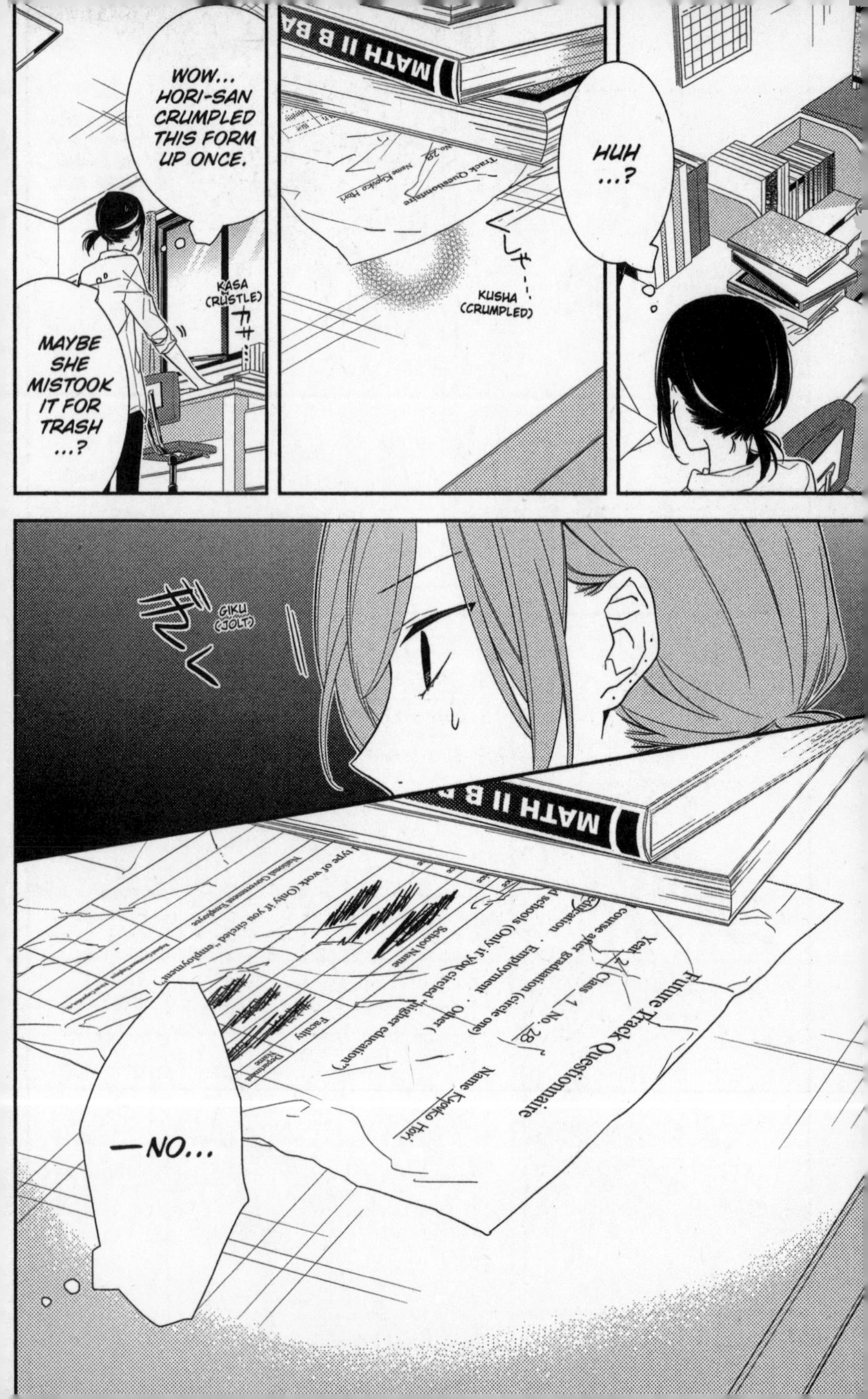
HUH ...?
MATH II B BA
Track Questionnaire
No. 28
Name Kyoko Hori
KUSHA (CRUMPLED)
WOW... HORI-SAN CRUMPLED THIS FORM UP ONCE.
KASA (RUSTLE)
MAYBE SHE MISTOOK IT FOR TRASH ...?
GIKU (JOLT)
MATH II B B
Future Track Questionnaire
Year 2 Class 1 No. 28
Name Kyoko Hori
course after graduation (circle one)
education · Employment · Other ( )
schools (Only if you circled "higher education")
School Name
Faculty
type of work (Only if you circled "employment")
National Government Employee
—NO...

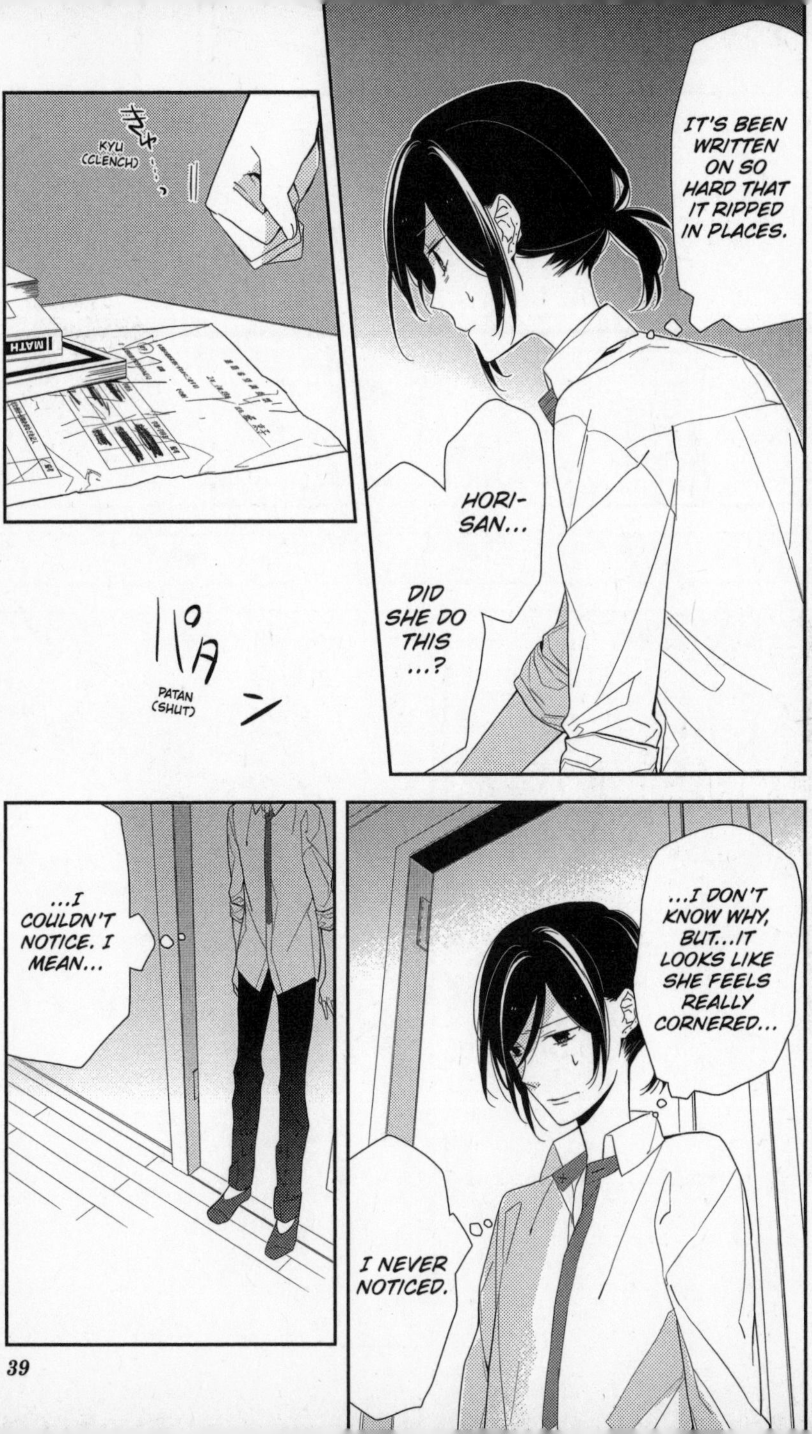
IT'S BEEN WRITTEN ON SO HARD THAT IT RIPPED IN PLACES.
HORI-SAN...
DID SHE DO THIS...?
KYU (CLENCH)
MATH
PATAN (SHUT)
...I DON'T KNOW WHY, BUT...IT LOOKS LIKE SHE FEELS REALLY CORNERED...
I NEVER NOTICED.
...I COULDN'T NOTICE. I MEAN...

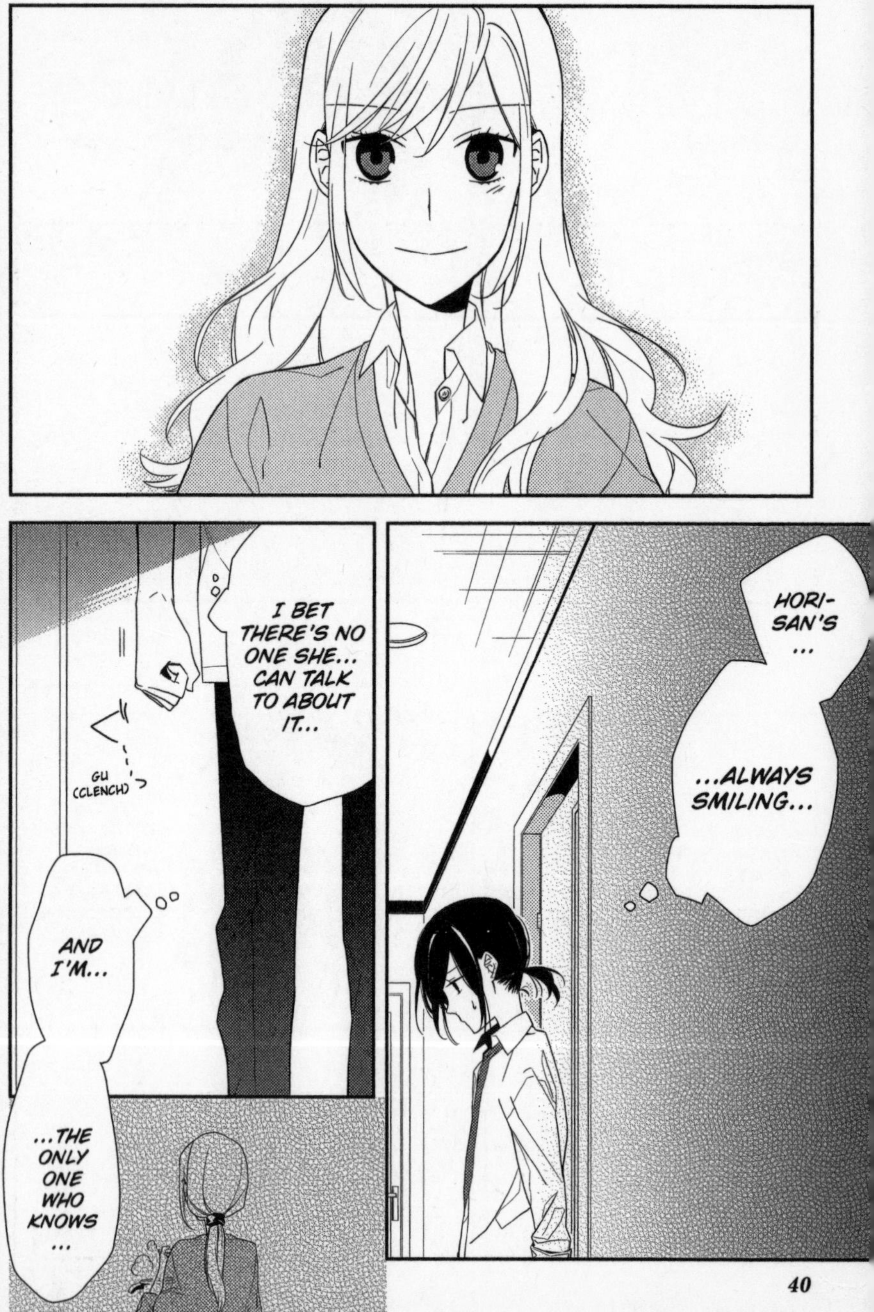
HORI-SAN'S ...
...ALWAYS SMILING...
I BET THERE'S NO ONE SHE... CAN TALK TO ABOUT IT...
GU (CLENCH)
AND I'M...
...THE ONLY ONE WHO KNOWS ...

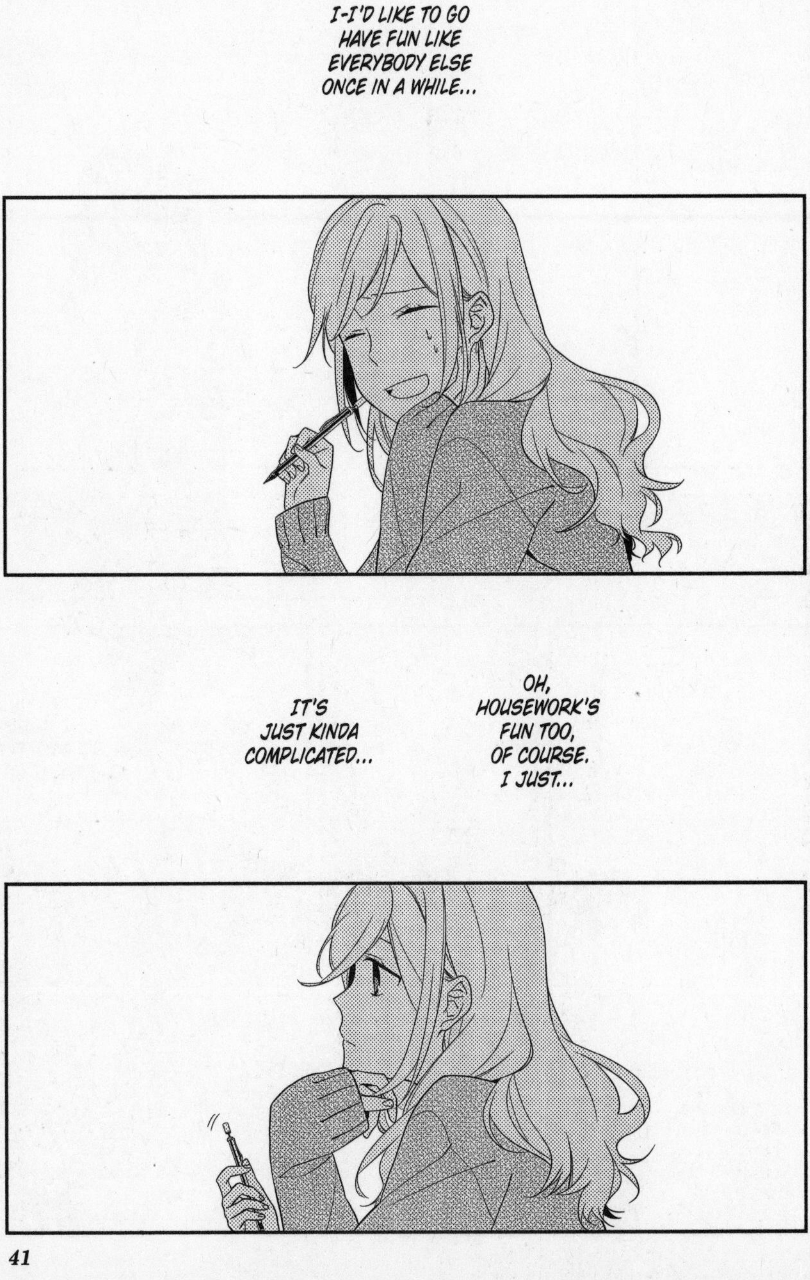
I-I'D LIKE TO GO HAVE FUN LIKE EVERYBODY ELSE ONCE IN A WHILE...
OH, HOUSEWORK'S FUN TOO, OF COURSE. I JUST...
IT'S JUST KINDA COMPLICATED...

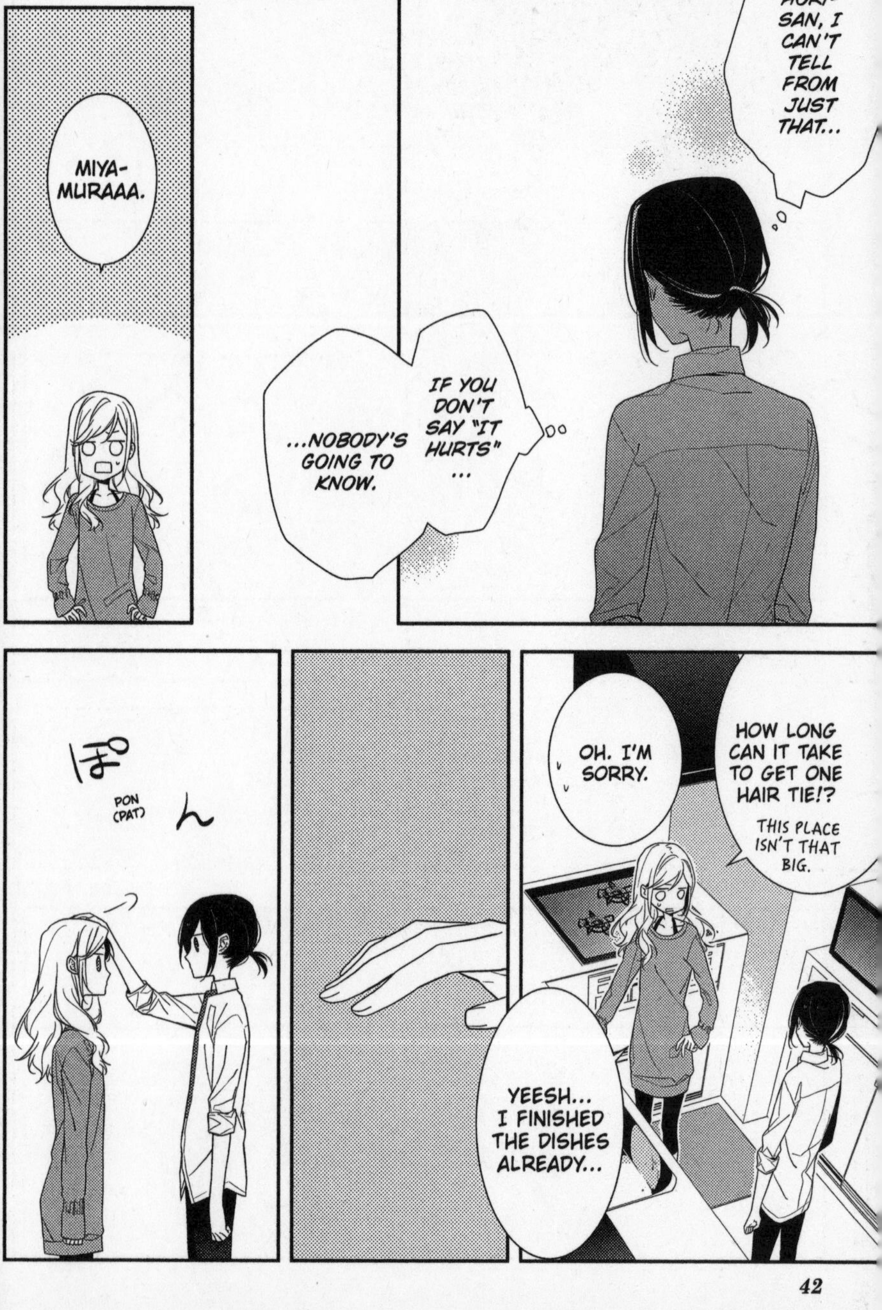
HORI-SAN, I CAN'T TELL FROM JUST THAT...
IF YOU DON'T SAY "IT HURTS"...
...NOBODY'S GOING TO KNOW.
MIYA-MURAAA.
HOW LONG CAN IT TAKE TO GET ONE HAIR TIE!?
THIS PLACE ISN'T THAT BIG.
OH. I'M SORRY.
YEESH... I FINISHED THE DISHES ALREADY...
ぽん
PON (PAT)

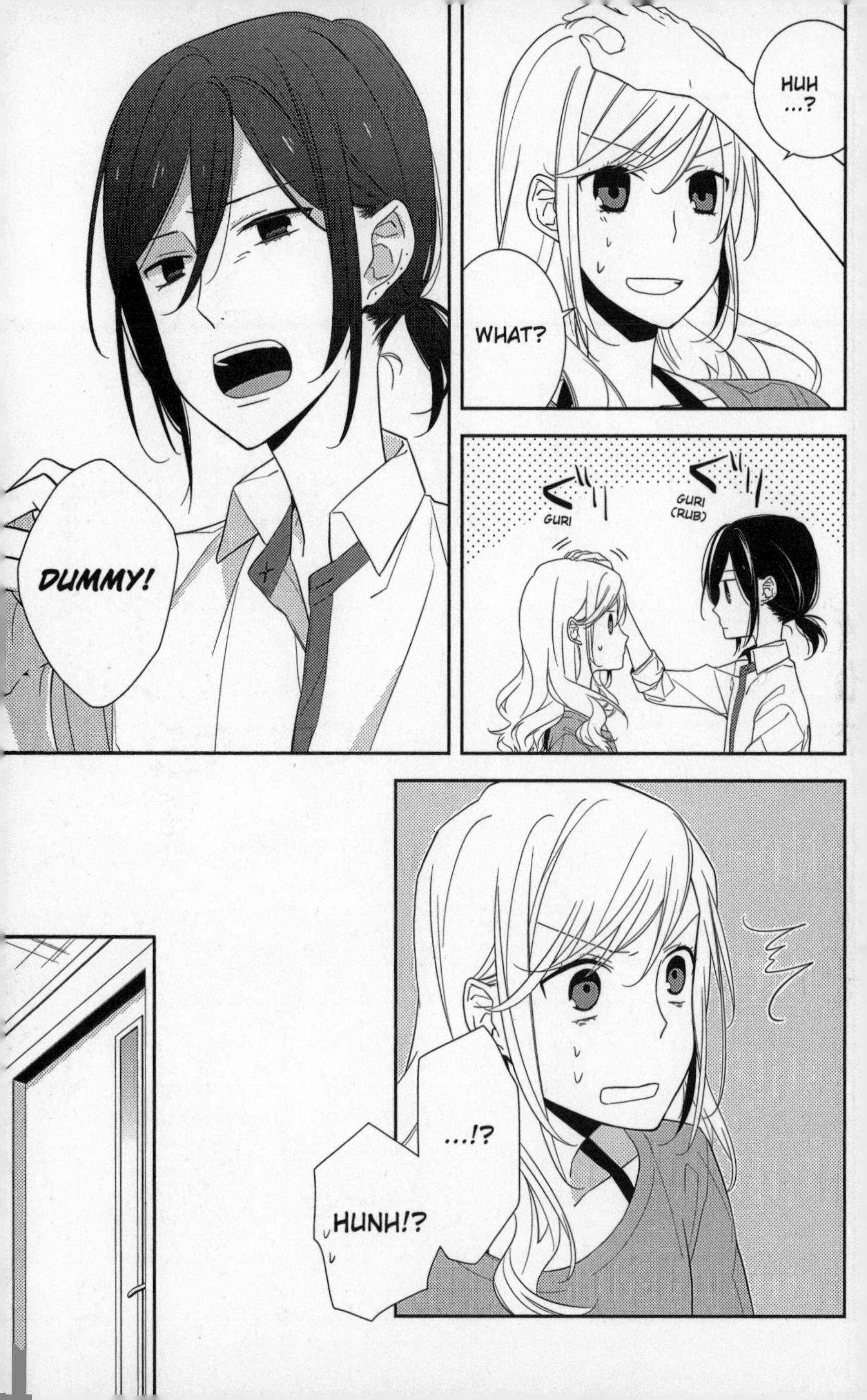
HUH ...?
WHAT?
GURI (RUB)
GURI
DUMMY!
...!?
HUNH!?

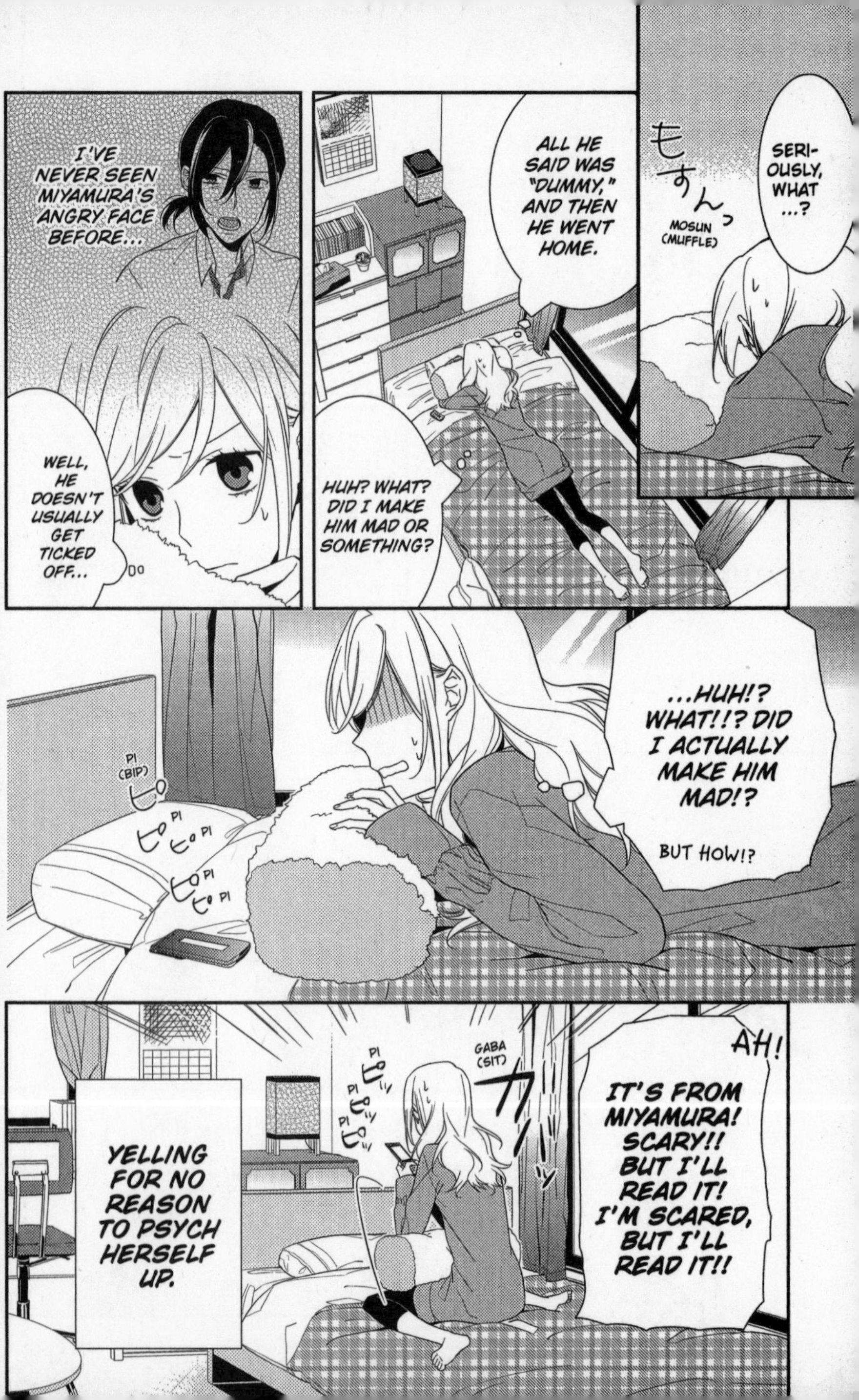
SERI-OUSLY, WHAT ...?
もすんっ
MOSUN (MUFFLE)
ALL HE SAID WAS "DUMMY," AND THEN HE WENT HOME.
HUH? WHAT? DID I MAKE HIM MAD OR SOMETHING?
I'VE NEVER SEEN MIYAMURA'S ANGRY FACE BEFORE...
WELL, HE DOESN'T USUALLY GET TICKED OFF...
...HUH!? WHAT!!? DID I ACTUALLY MAKE HIM MAD!?
BUT HOW!?
PI (BIP)
PI
PI
PI
PI
AH!
IT'S FROM MIYAMURA! SCARY!! BUT I'LL READ IT! I'M SCARED, BUT I'LL READ IT!!
GABA (SIT)
PI
PI
PI
YELLING FOR NO REASON TO PSYCH HERSELF UP.

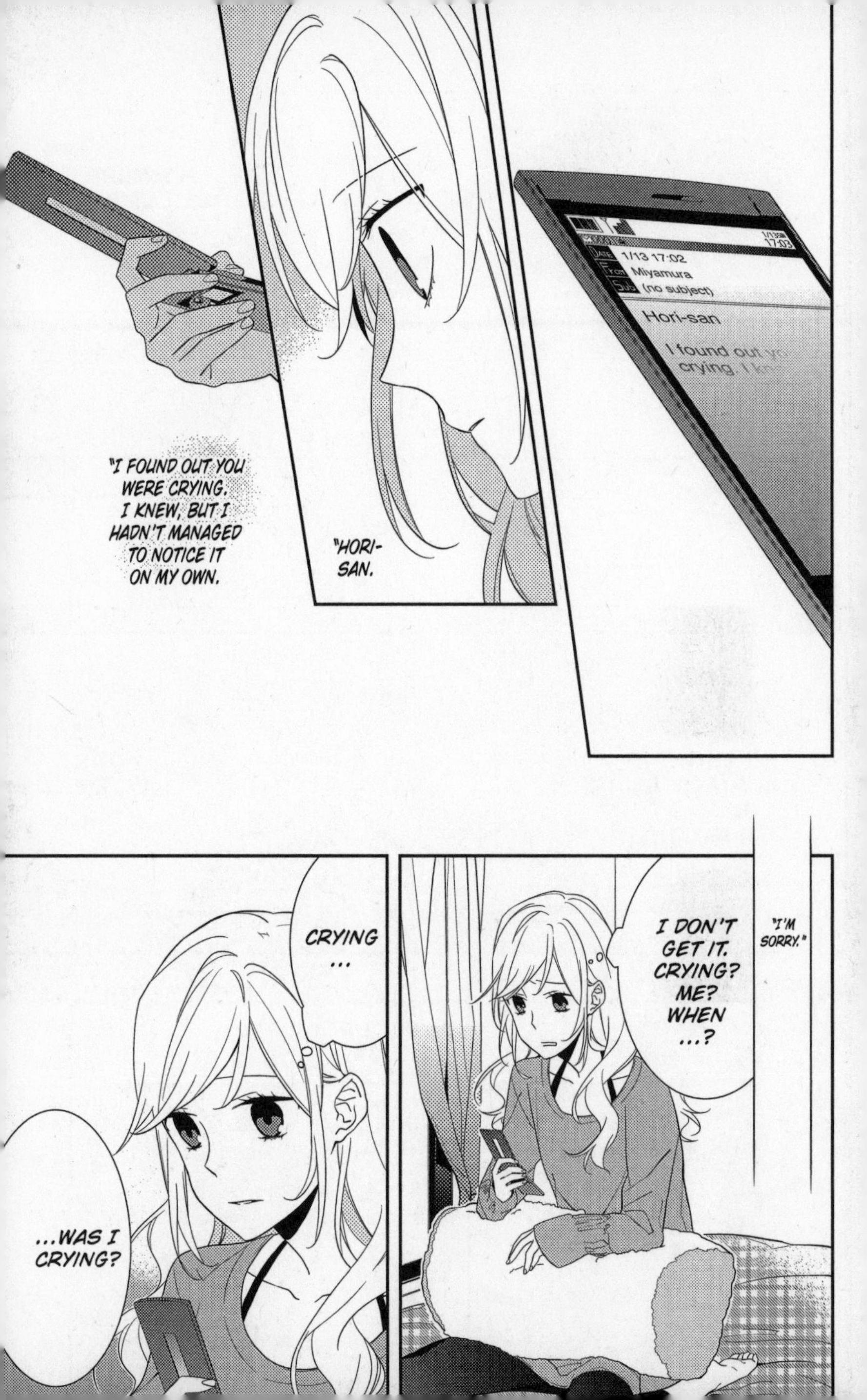
1/13 17:02
Miyamura
(no subject)
Hori-san
"HORI-SAN.
"I FOUND OUT YOU WERE CRYING. I KNEW, BUT I HADN'T MANAGED TO NOTICE IT ON MY OWN.
"I'M SORRY."
I DON'T GET IT. CRYING? ME? WHEN ...?
CRYING ...
...WAS I CRYING?

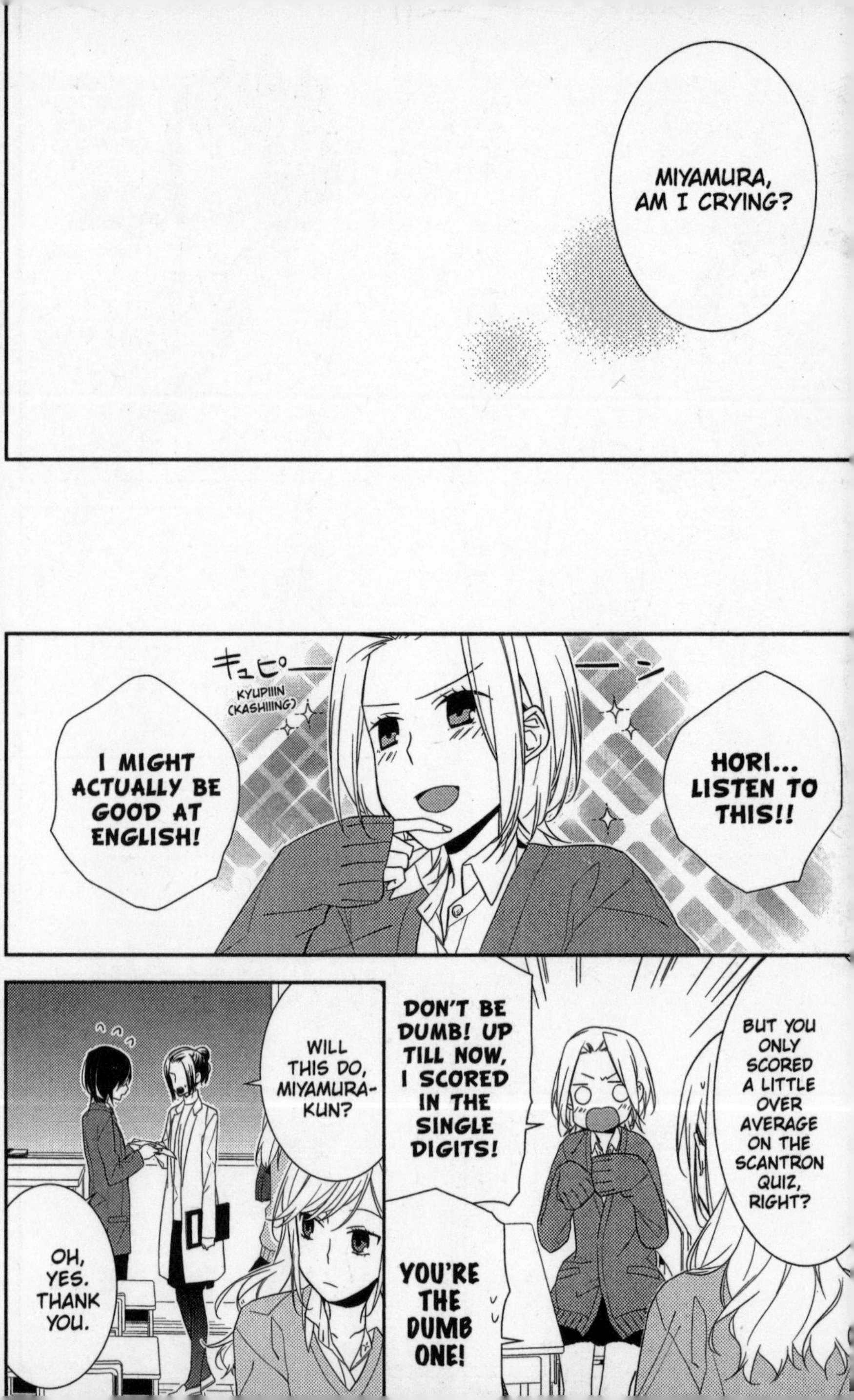
MIYAMURA, AM I CRYING?
キュピーーン
KYUPIIIN (KASHIIING)
HORI... LISTEN TO THIS!!
I MIGHT ACTUALLY BE GOOD AT ENGLISH!
BUT YOU ONLY SCORED A LITTLE OVER AVERAGE ON THE SCANTRON QUIZ, RIGHT?
DON'T BE DUMB! UP TILL NOW, I SCORED IN THE SINGLE DIGITS!
YOU'RE THE DUMB ONE!
WILL THIS DO, MIYAMURA-KUN?
OH, YES. THANK YOU.

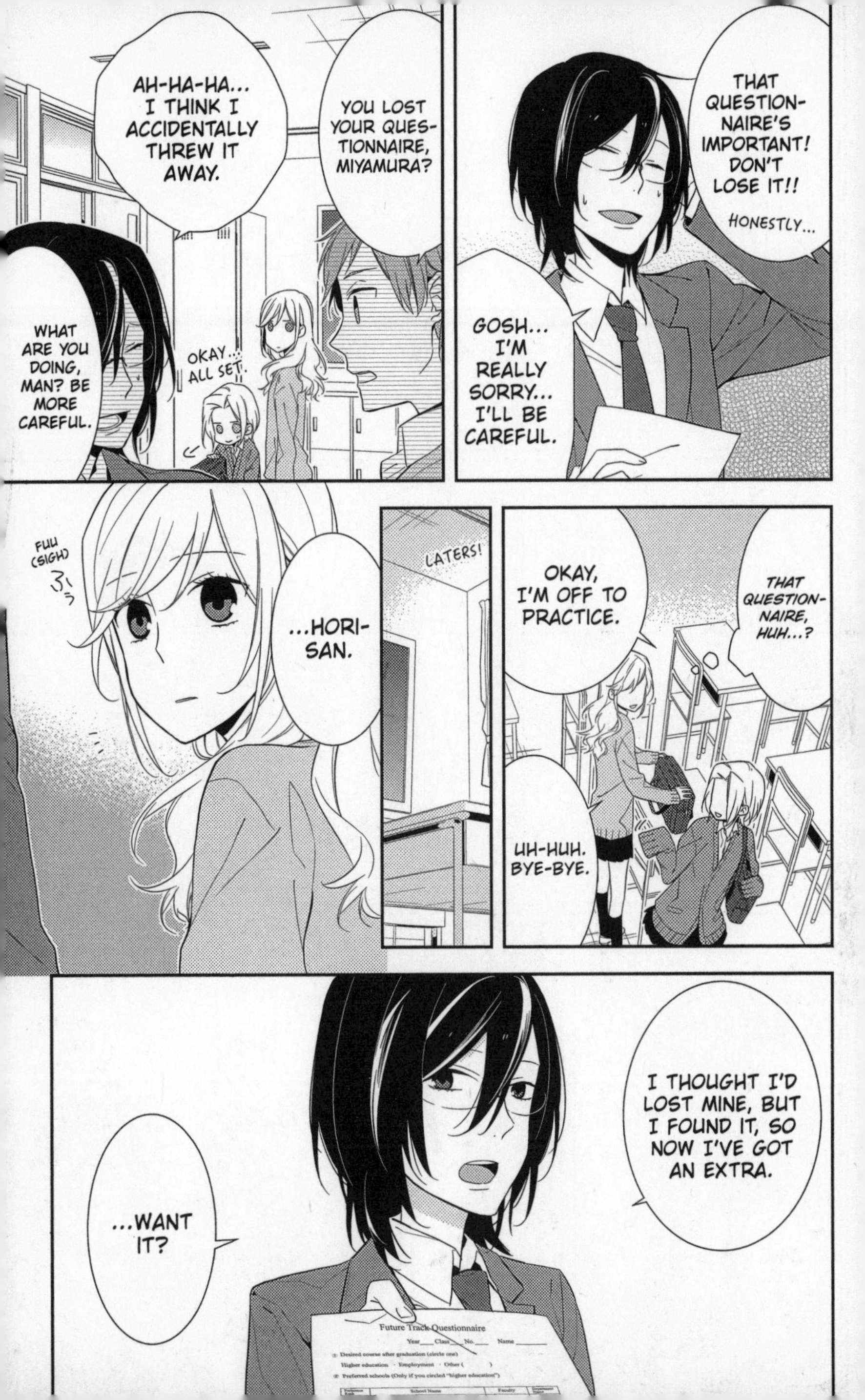
THAT QUESTION-NAIRE'S IMPORTANT! DON'T LOSE IT!!
HONESTLY...
GOSH... I'M REALLY SORRY... I'LL BE CAREFUL.
YOU LOST YOUR QUES-TIONNAIRE, MIYAMURA?
AH-HA-HA... I THINK I ACCIDENTALLY THREW IT AWAY.
OKAY... ALL SET.
WHAT ARE YOU DOING, MAN? BE MORE CAREFUL.
THAT QUESTION-NAIRE, HUH...?
OKAY, I'M OFF TO PRACTICE.
UH-HUH. BYE-BYE.
LATERS!
...HORI-SAN.
FUU (SIGH)
ふぅ
I THOUGHT I'D LOST MINE, BUT I FOUND IT, SO NOW I'VE GOT AN EXTRA.
...WANT IT?
Future Track Questionnaire
Year___ Class___ No.___ Name______
① Desired course after graduation (circle one)
Higher education · Employment · Other ( )
② Preferred schools (Only if you circled "higher education")

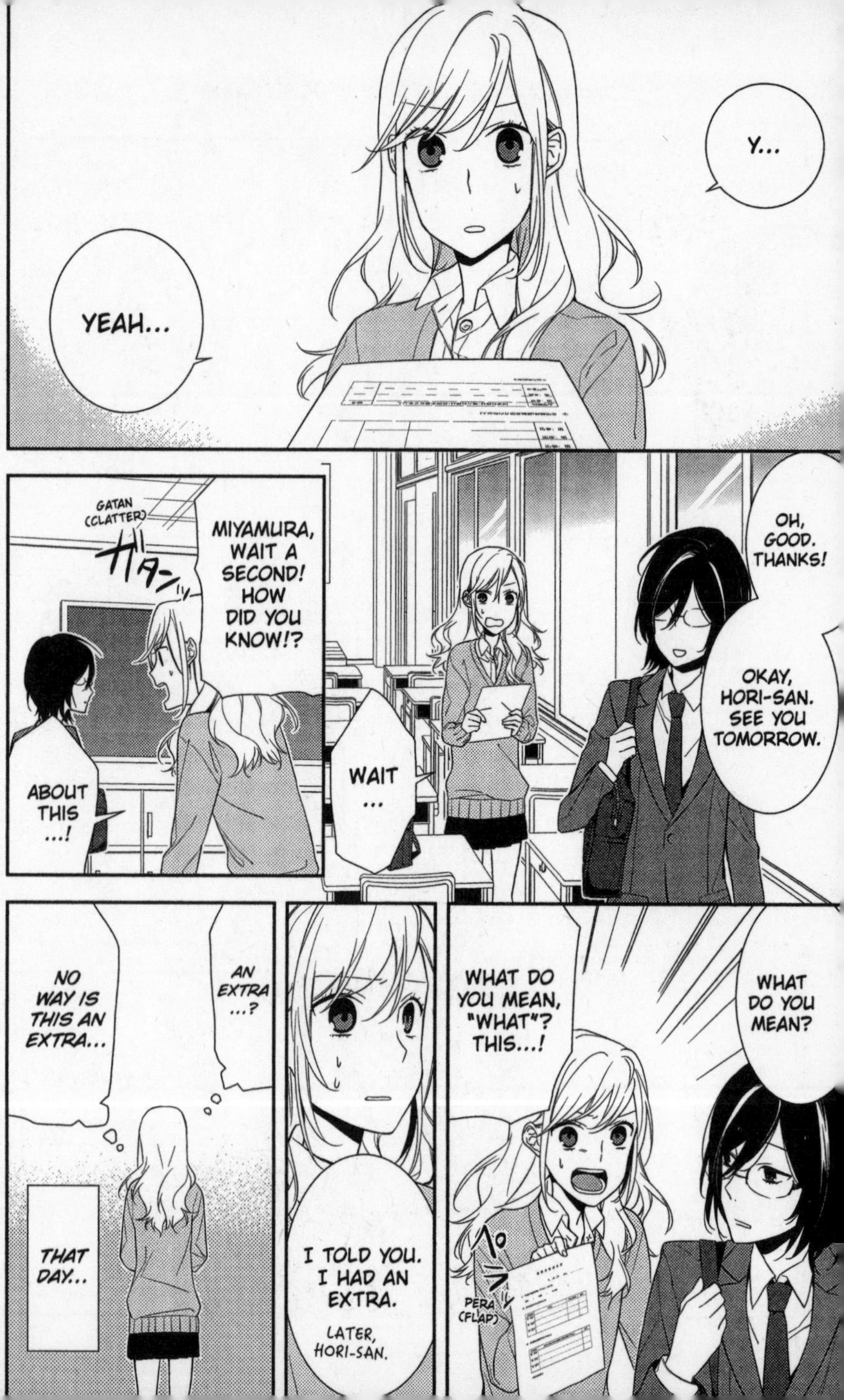

Y...
YEAH...
OH, GOOD. THANKS!
OKAY, HORI-SAN. SEE YOU TOMORROW.
WAIT ...
MIYAMURA, WAIT A SECOND! HOW DID YOU KNOW!?
GATAN (CLATTER)
ABOUT THIS ...!
WHAT DO YOU MEAN?
WHAT DO YOU MEAN, "WHAT"? THIS...!
PERA (FLAP)
I TOLD YOU. I HAD AN EXTRA.
LATER, HORI-SAN.
AN EXTRA ...?
NO WAY IS THIS AN EXTRA...
THAT DAY...

...MIYAMURA SHOWED UP IN MY DREAM.

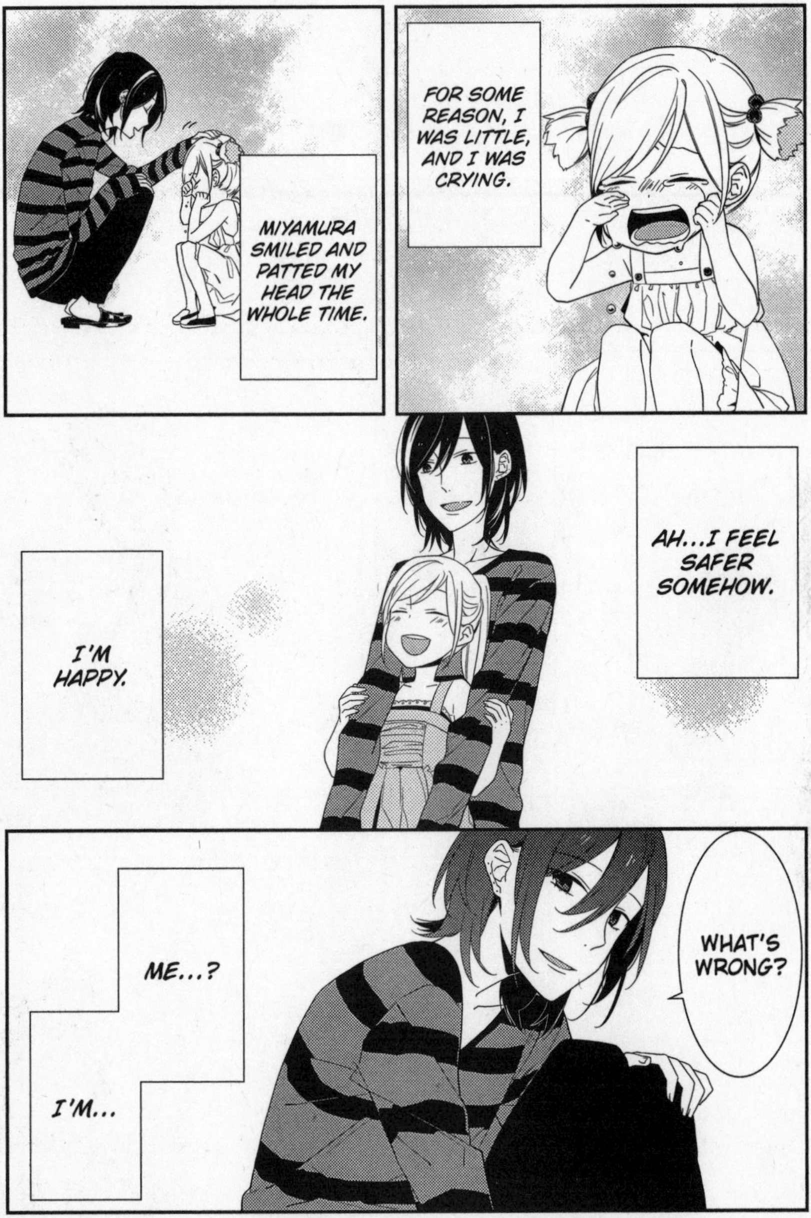
FOR SOME REASON, I WAS LITTLE, AND I WAS CRYING.
MIYAMURA SMILED AND PATTED MY HEAD THE WHOLE TIME.
AH...I FEEL SAFER SOMEHOW.
I'M HAPPY.
WHAT'S WRONG?
ME...?
I'M...

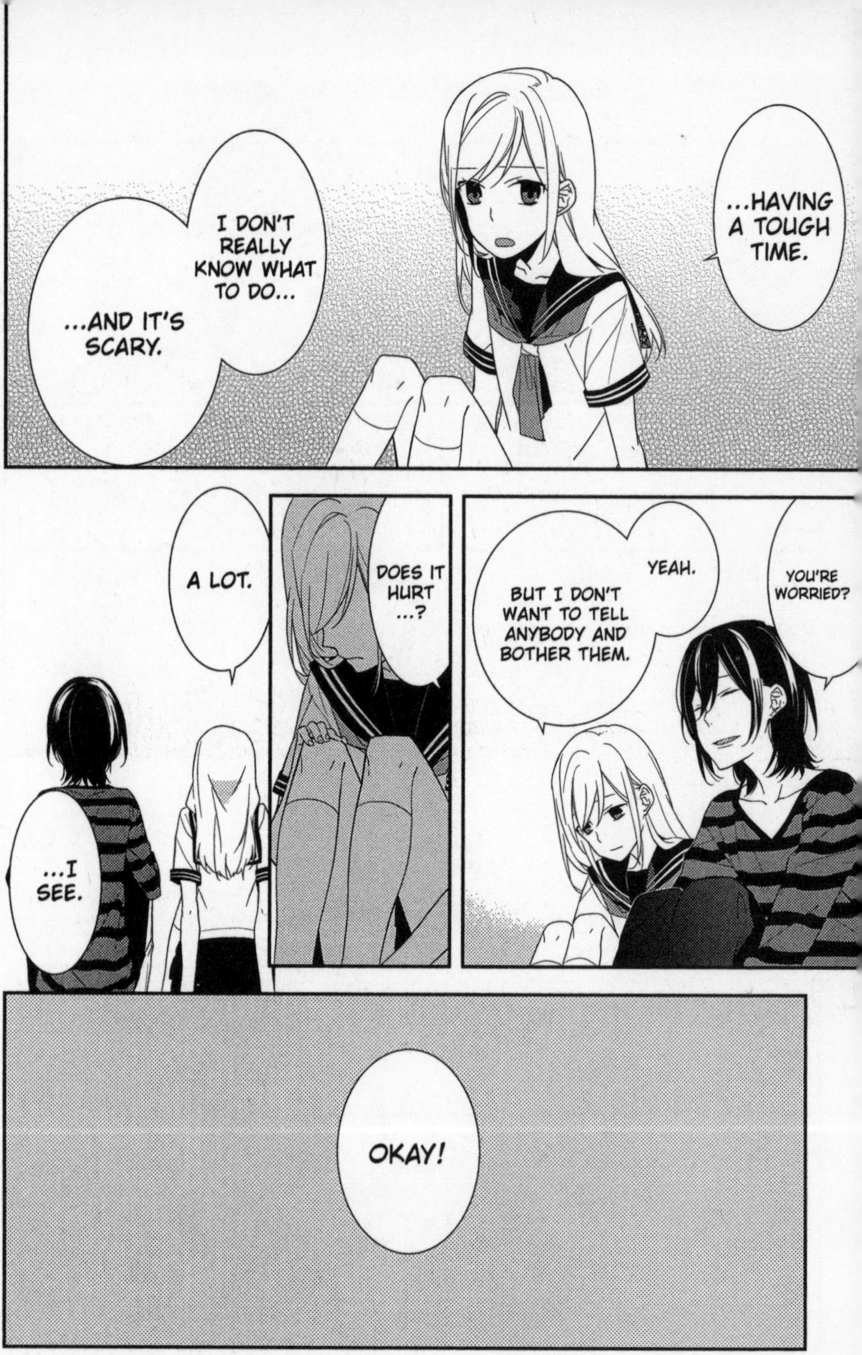
...HAVING A TOUGH TIME.
I DON'T REALLY KNOW WHAT TO DO...
...AND IT'S SCARY.
YOU'RE WORRIED?
YEAH.
BUT I DON'T WANT TO TELL ANYBODY AND BOTHER THEM.
DOES IT HURT ...?
A LOT.
...I SEE.
OKAY!

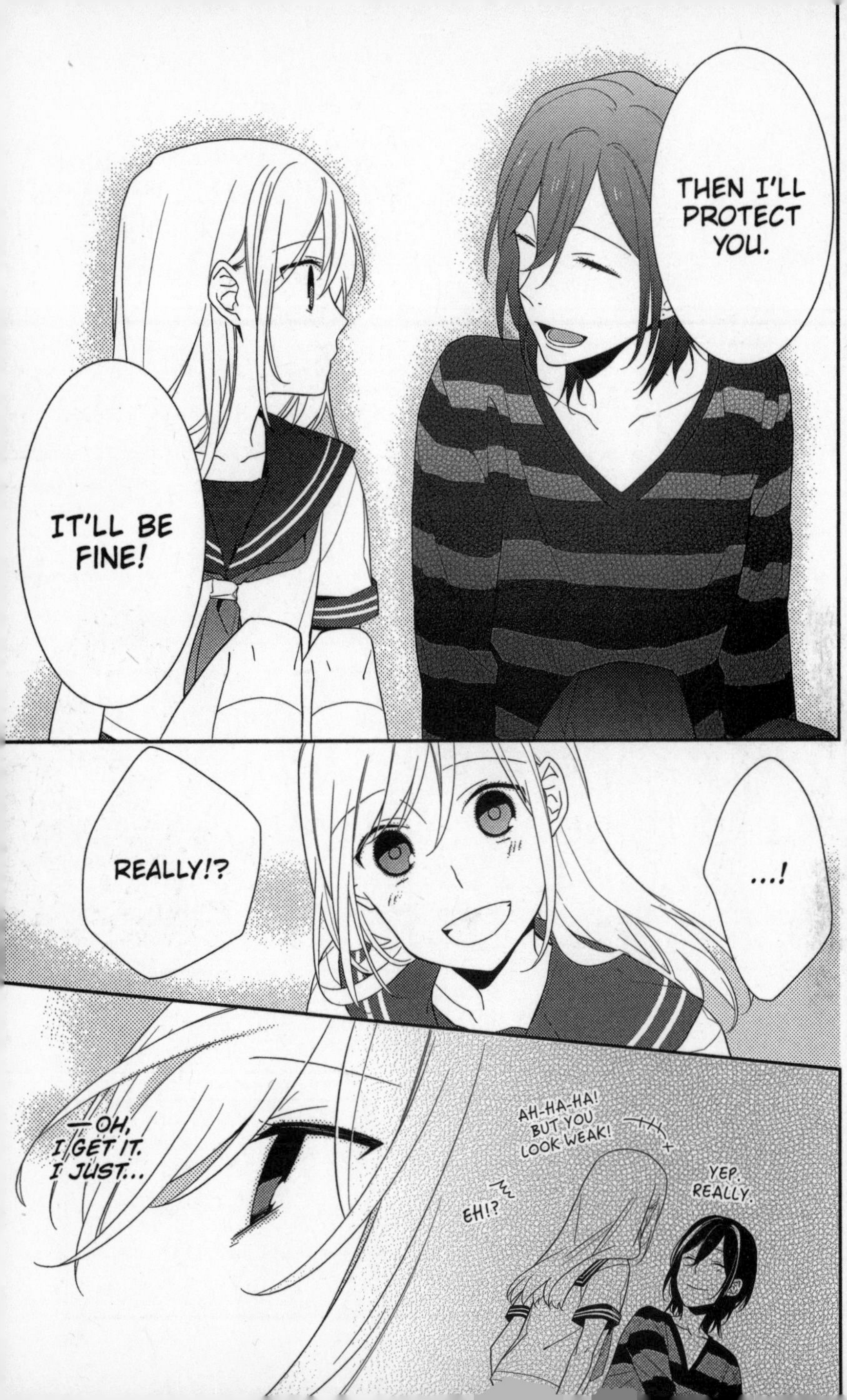
THEN I'LL PROTECT YOU.
IT'LL BE FINE!
...!
REALLY!?
YEP. REALLY.
AH-HA-HA! BUT YOU LOOK WEAK!
EH!?
—OH, I GET IT. I JUST...

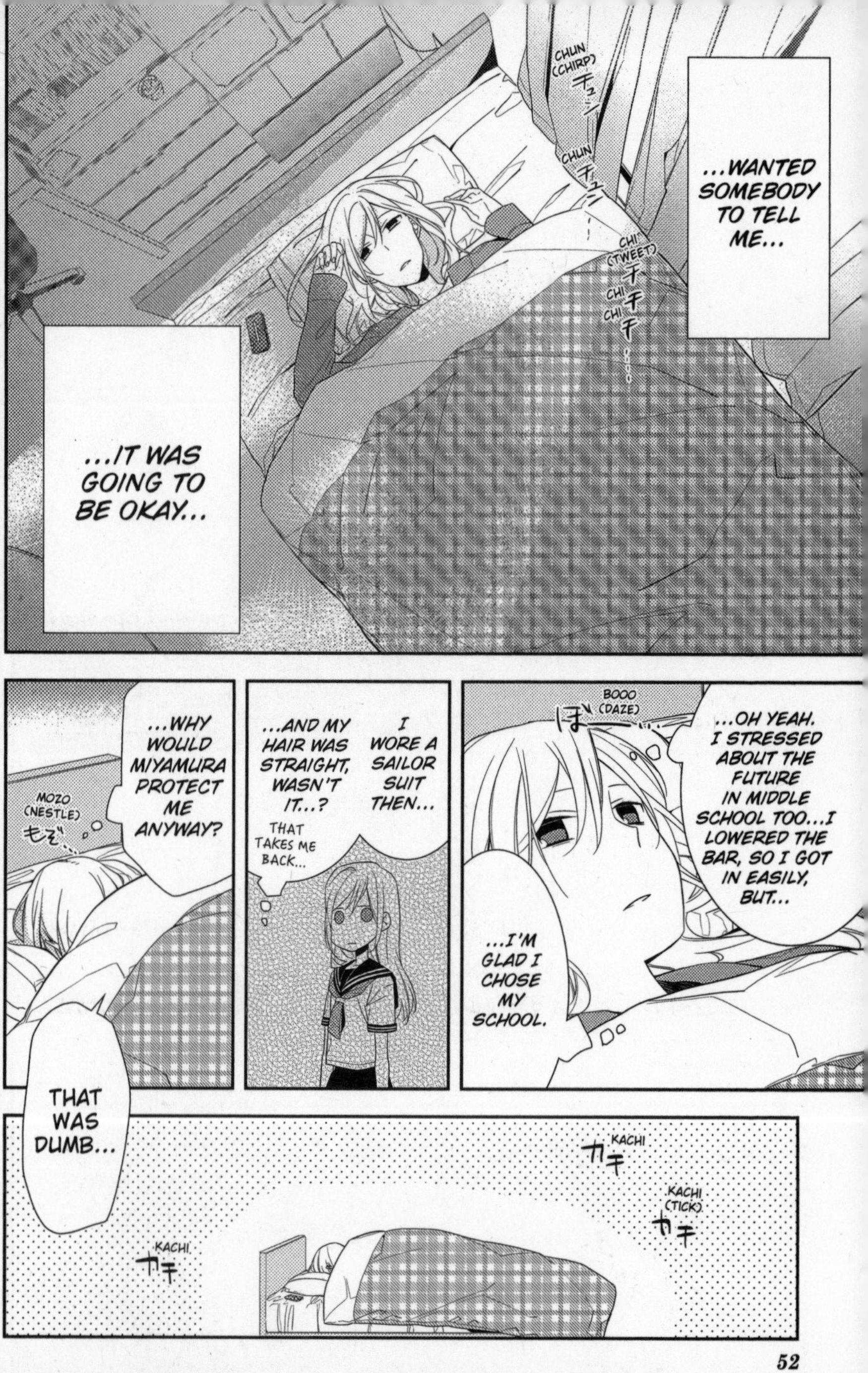
...WANTED SOMEBODY TO TELL ME...
CHUN (CHIRP) チュン
CHUN チュン
CHI (TWEET) チ
CHI チ
CHI チ
...IT WAS GOING TO BE OKAY...
BOOO (DAZE) ぼー
...OH YEAH. I STRESSED ABOUT THE FUTURE IN MIDDLE SCHOOL TOO...I LOWERED THE BAR, SO I GOT IN EASILY, BUT...
...I'M GLAD I CHOSE MY SCHOOL.
I WORE A SAILOR SUIT THEN...
...AND MY HAIR WAS STRAIGHT, WASN'T IT...?
THAT TAKES ME BACK...
...WHY WOULD MIYAMURA PROTECT ME ANYWAY?
MOZO (NESTLE) もぞ
THAT WAS DUMB...
KACHI カチ
KACHI (TICK) カチ
KACHI カチ

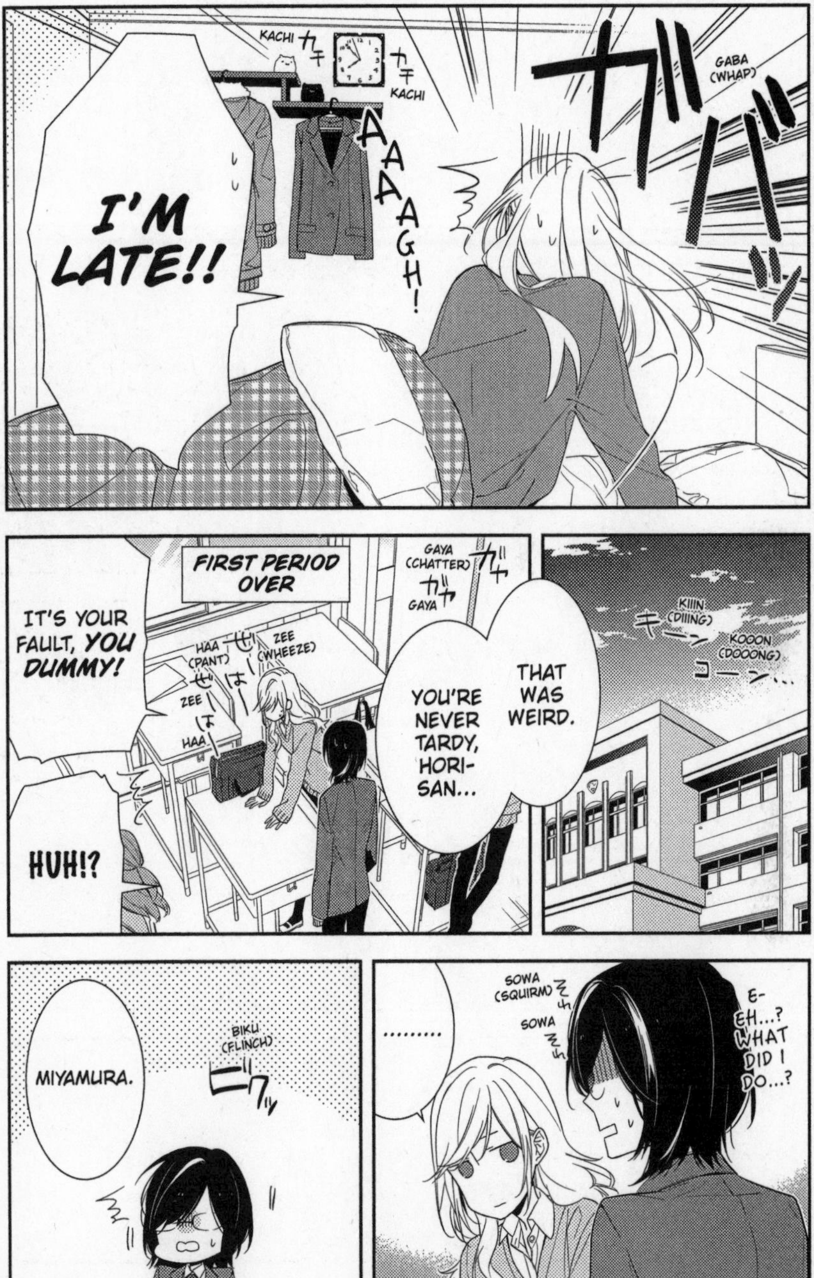

GABA (WHAP)
KACHI
AAAAGH!
KACHI
I'M LATE!!
KIIN (DIIING)
KOOON (DOOONG)
THAT WAS WEIRD.
YOU'RE NEVER TARDY, HORI-SAN...
GAYA (CHATTER)
GAYA
FIRST PERIOD OVER
ZEE (WHEEZE)
HAA (PANT)
ZEE
HAA
IT'S YOUR FAULT, YOU DUMMY!
HUH!?
E-EH...? WHAT DID I DO...?
SOWA (SQUIRM)
SOWA
....
BIKU (FLINCH)
MIYAMURA.

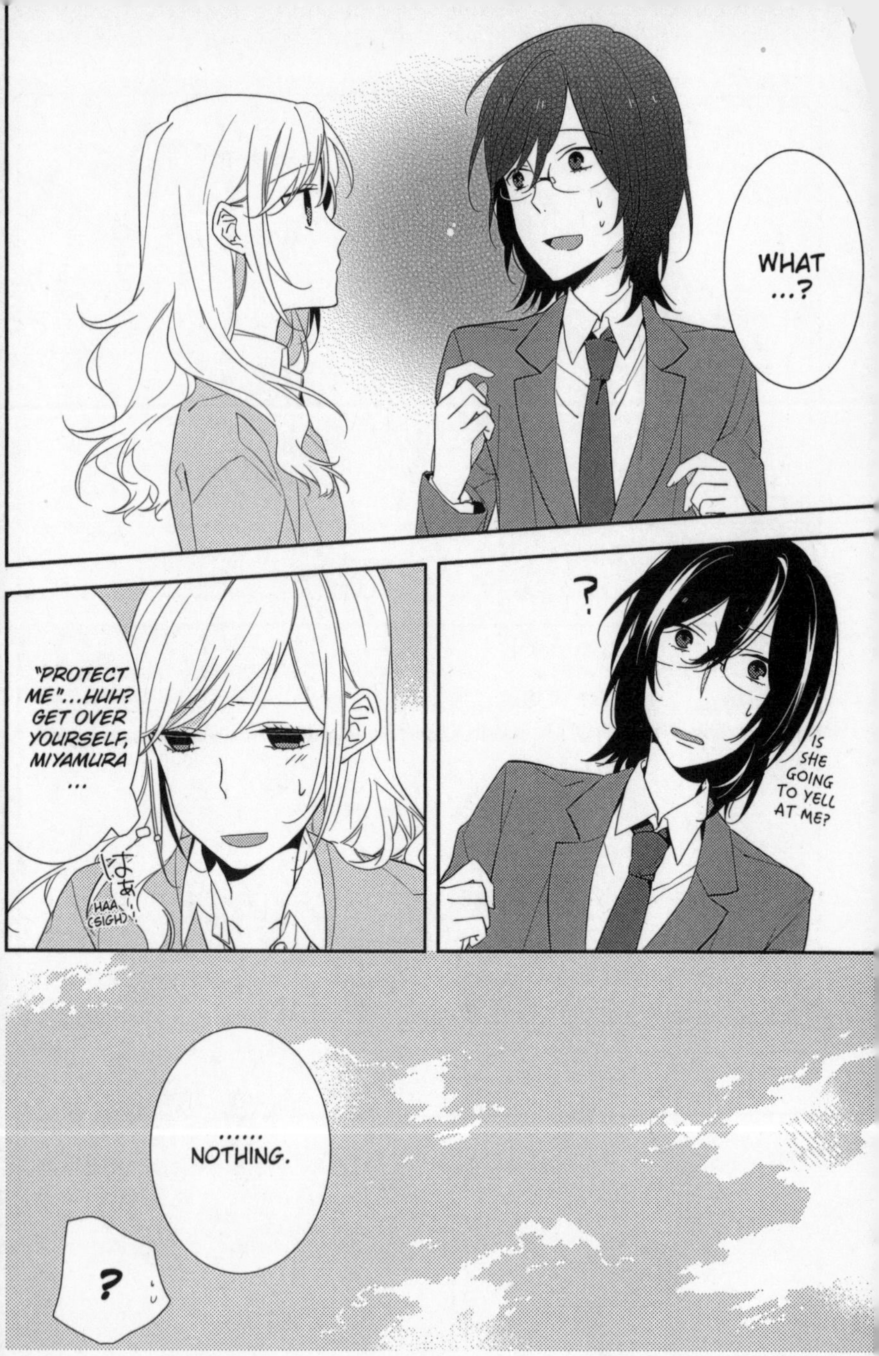
WHAT ...?
?
IS SHE GOING TO YELL AT ME?
"PROTECT ME"...HUH? GET OVER YOURSELF, MIYAMURA ...
はぁ
HAA (SIGH)
...... NOTHING.
?

HORIMIYA

HORIMIYA

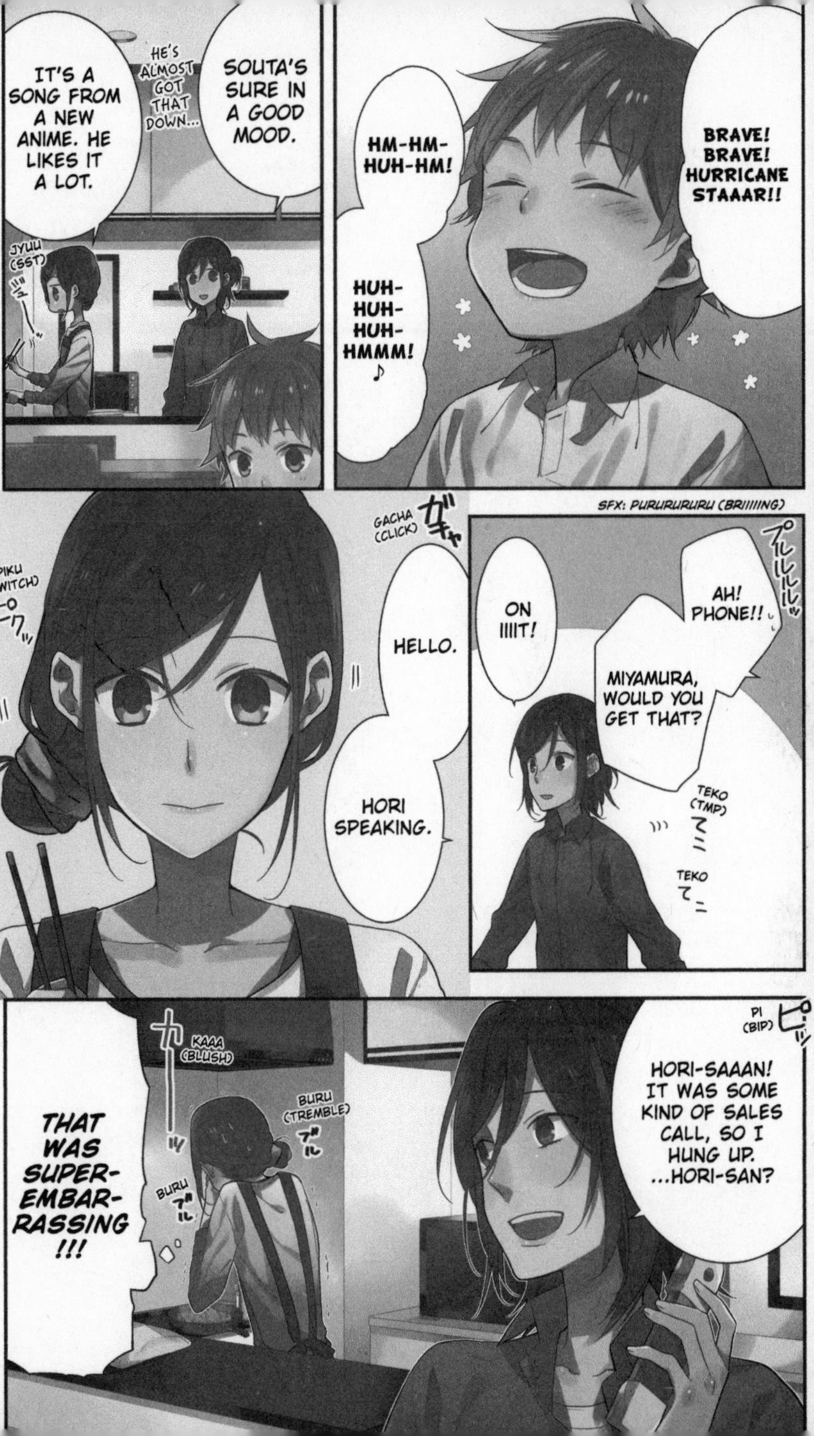
BRAVE! BRAVE! HURRICANE STAAAR!!
HM-HM-HUH-HM!
HUH-HUH-HUH-HMMM! ♪
SOUTA'S SURE IN A GOOD MOOD.
HE'S ALMOST GOT THAT DOWN...
IT'S A SONG FROM A NEW ANIME. HE LIKES IT A LOT.
JYUU (SST)
SFX: PURURURURU (BRIIIIING)
AH! PHONE!!
MIYAMURA, WOULD YOU GET THAT?
ON IIIIT!
TEKO (TMP)
TEKO
GACHA (CLICK)
HELLO.
HORI SPEAKING.
PIKU (TWITCH)
PI (BIP)
HORI-SAAAN! IT WAS SOME KIND OF SALES CALL, SO I HUNG UP. ...HORI-SAN?
KAAA (BLUSH)
BURU (TREMBLE)
BURU
THAT WAS SUPER-EMBARRASSING!!!

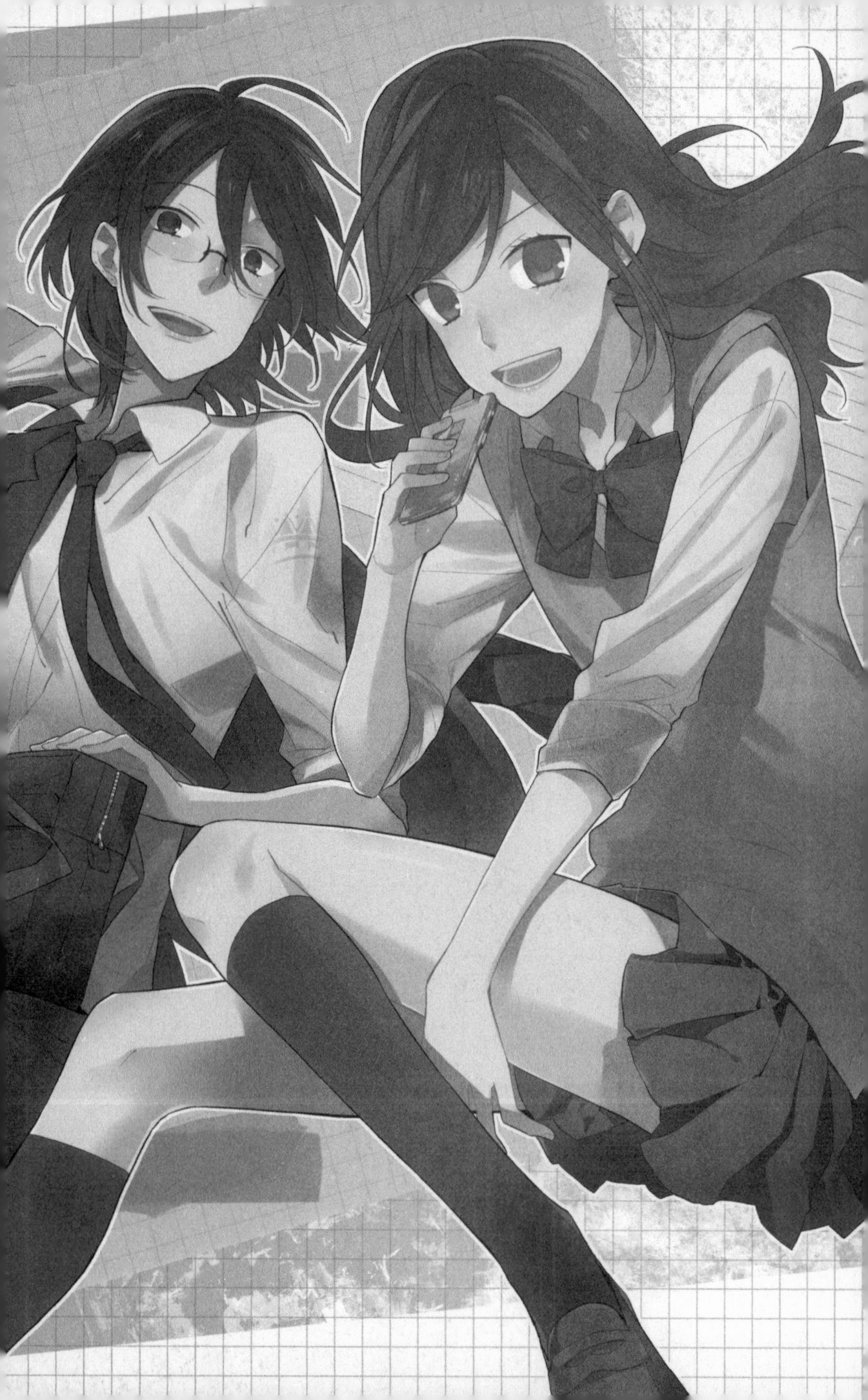

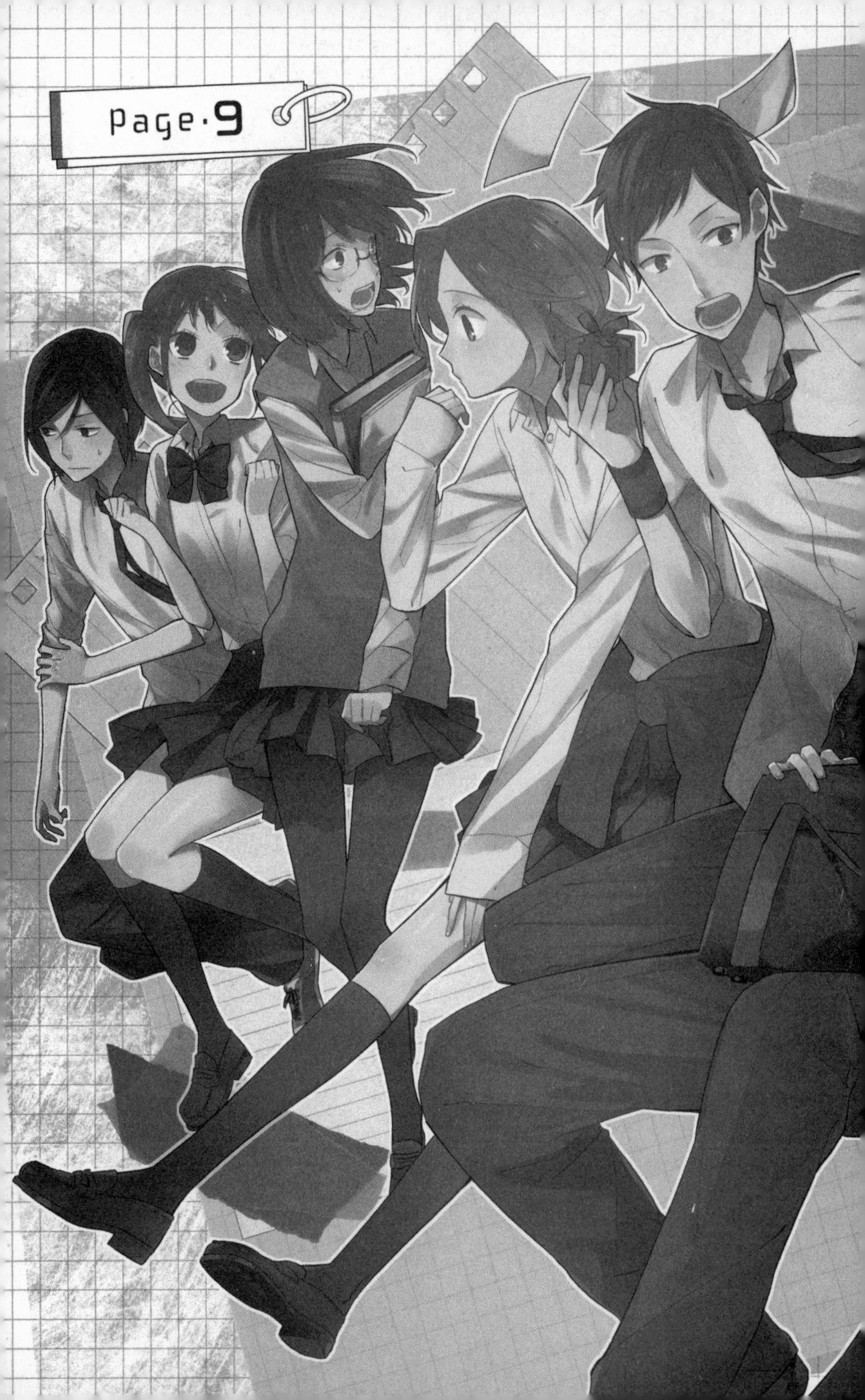
Page·9

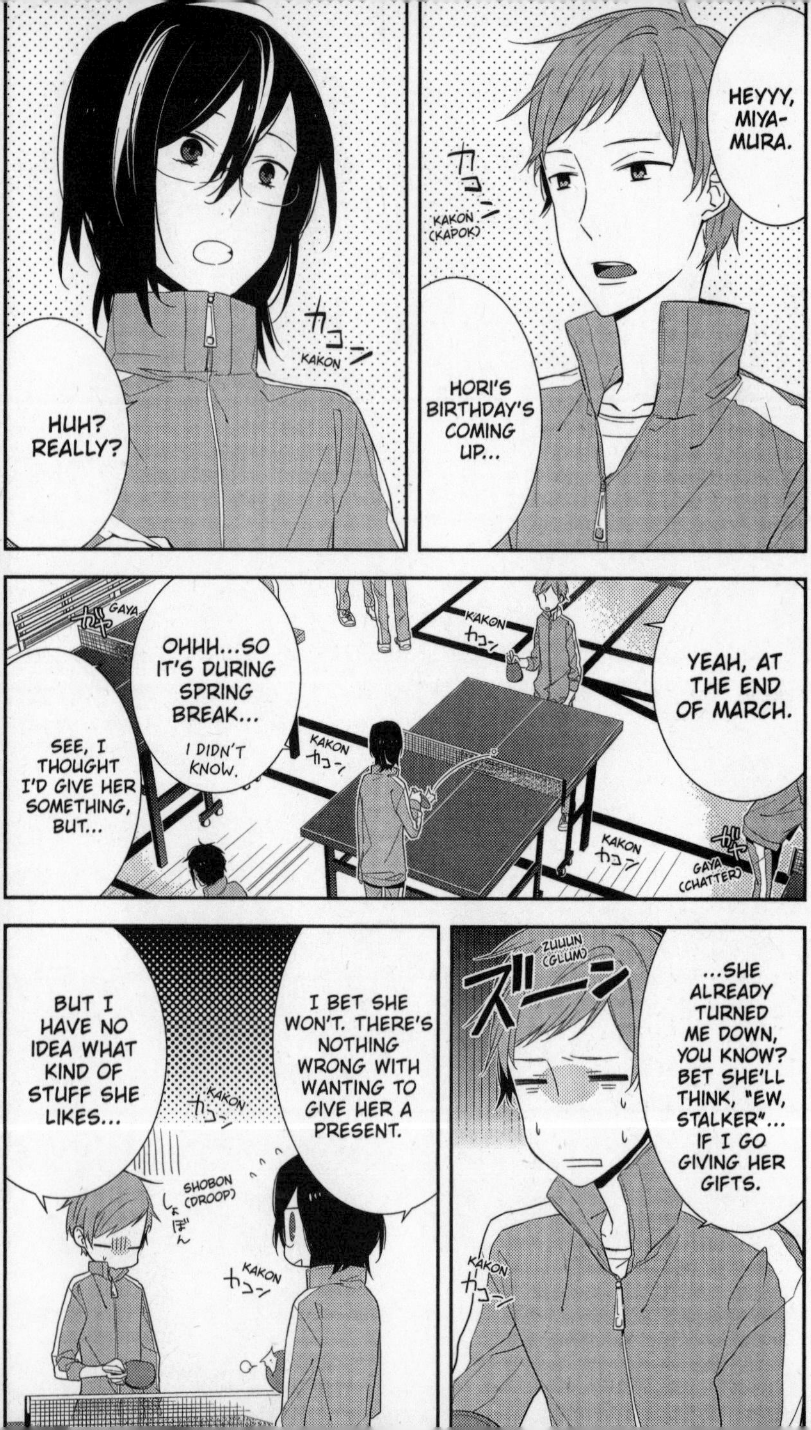

HEYYY, MIYAMURA.
KAKON (KAPOK)
HORI'S BIRTHDAY'S COMING UP...
KAKON
HUH? REALLY?
YEAH, AT THE END OF MARCH.
KAKON
GAYA (CHATTER)
KAKON
KAKON
OHHH...SO IT'S DURING SPRING BREAK...
I DIDN'T KNOW.
GAYA
SEE, I THOUGHT I'D GIVE HER SOMETHING, BUT...
ZUUUN (GLUM)
...SHE ALREADY TURNED ME DOWN, YOU KNOW? BET SHE'LL THINK, "EW, STALKER"... IF I GO GIVING HER GIFTS.
KAKON
I BET SHE WON'T. THERE'S NOTHING WRONG WITH WANTING TO GIVE HER A PRESENT.
BUT I HAVE NO IDEA WHAT KIND OF STUFF SHE LIKES...
KAKON
SHOBON (DROOP)
KAKON

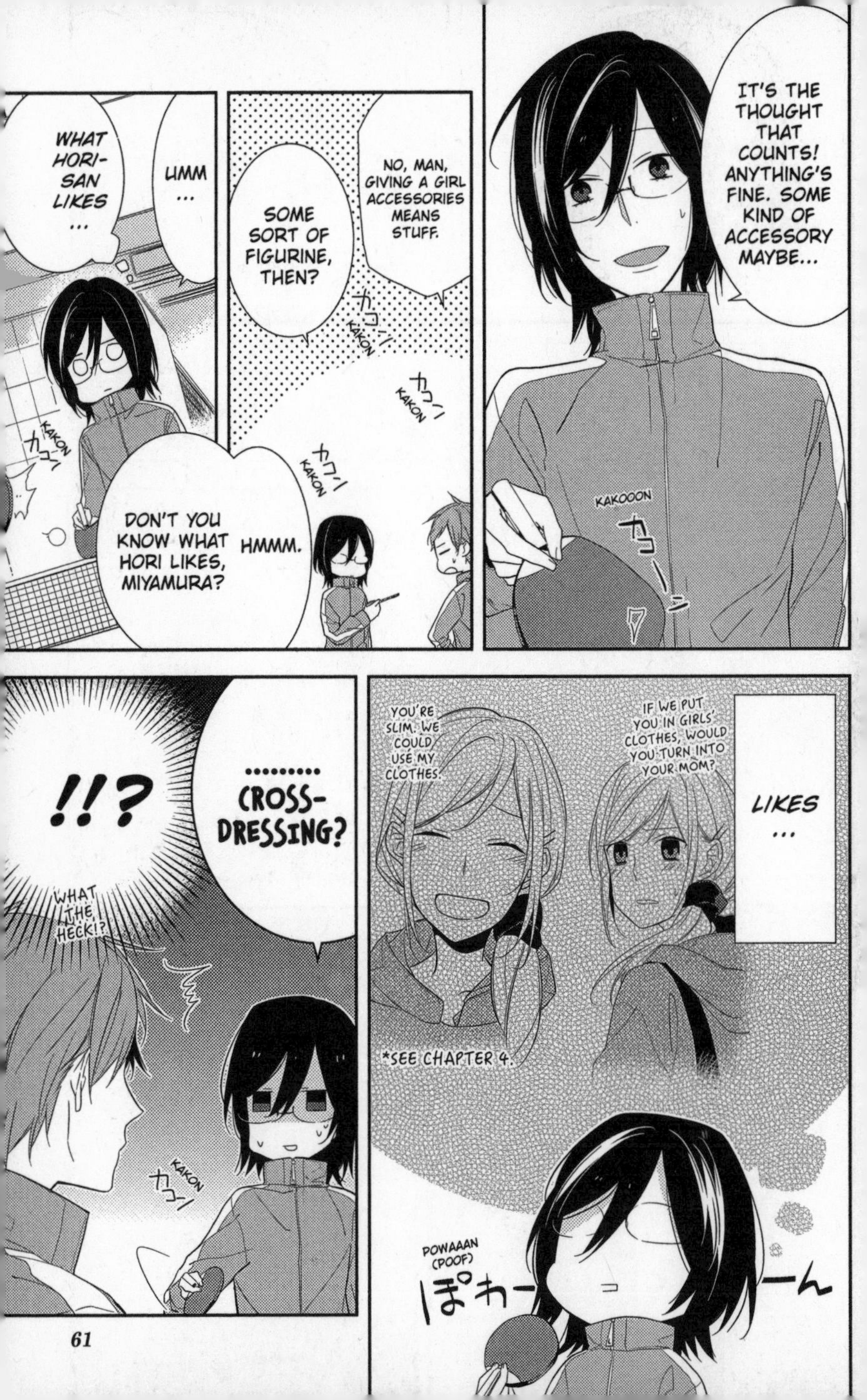
IT'S THE THOUGHT THAT COUNTS! ANYTHING'S FINE. SOME KIND OF ACCESSORY MAYBE...
KAKOOON
NO, MAN, GIVING A GIRL ACCESSORIES MEANS STUFF.
SOME SORT OF FIGURINE, THEN?
KAKON
KAKON
KAKON
HMMM.
DON'T YOU KNOW WHAT HORI LIKES, MIYAMURA?
UMM ...
WHAT HORI-SAN LIKES ...
KAKON
LIKES ...
IF WE PUT YOU IN GIRLS' CLOTHES, WOULD YOU TURN INTO YOUR MOM?
YOU'RE SLIM. WE COULD USE MY CLOTHES.
*SEE CHAPTER 4.
POWAAAN (POOF)
..........CROSS-DRESSING?
!!?
WHAT THE HECK!?
KAKON

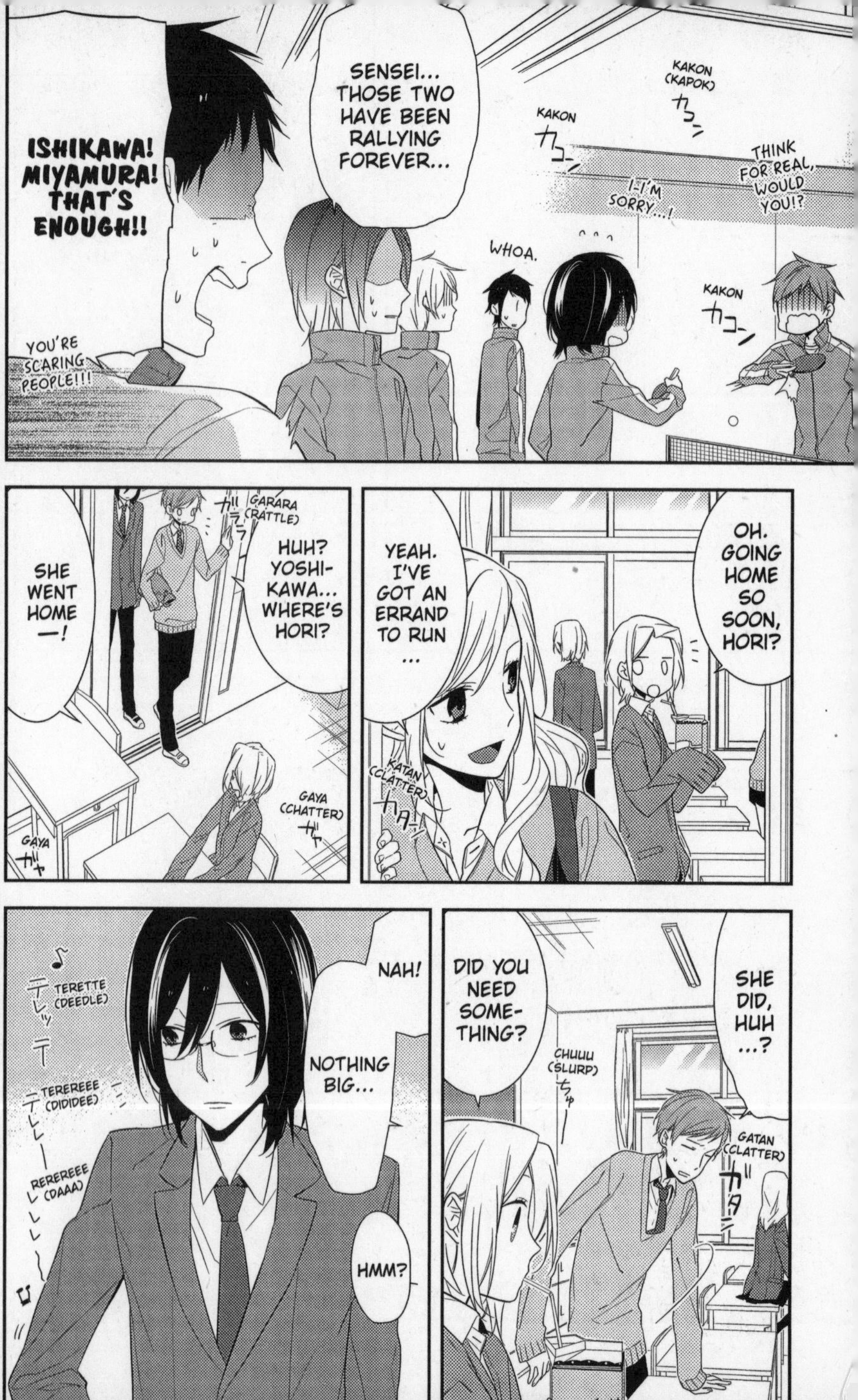
KAKON (KAPOK)
THINK FOR REAL, WOULD YOU!?
I-I'M SORRY...!
KAKON
SENSEI... THOSE TWO HAVE BEEN RALLYING FOREVER...
WHOA.
KAKON
ISHIKAWA! MIYAMURA! THAT'S ENOUGH!!
YOU'RE SCARING PEOPLE!!!
OH. GOING HOME SO SOON, HORI?
YEAH. I'VE GOT AN ERRAND TO RUN ...
KATAN (CLATTER)
GARARA (RATTLE)
HUH? YOSHIKAWA... WHERE'S HORI?
SHE WENT HOME—!
GAYA (CHATTER)
GAYA
SHE DID, HUH ...?
DID YOU NEED SOMETHING?
CHUUU (SLURP)
GATAN (CLATTER)
NAH!
NOTHING BIG...
HMM?
TERETTE (DEEDLE)
TEREREEE (DIDIDEE)
REREREEE (DAAA)

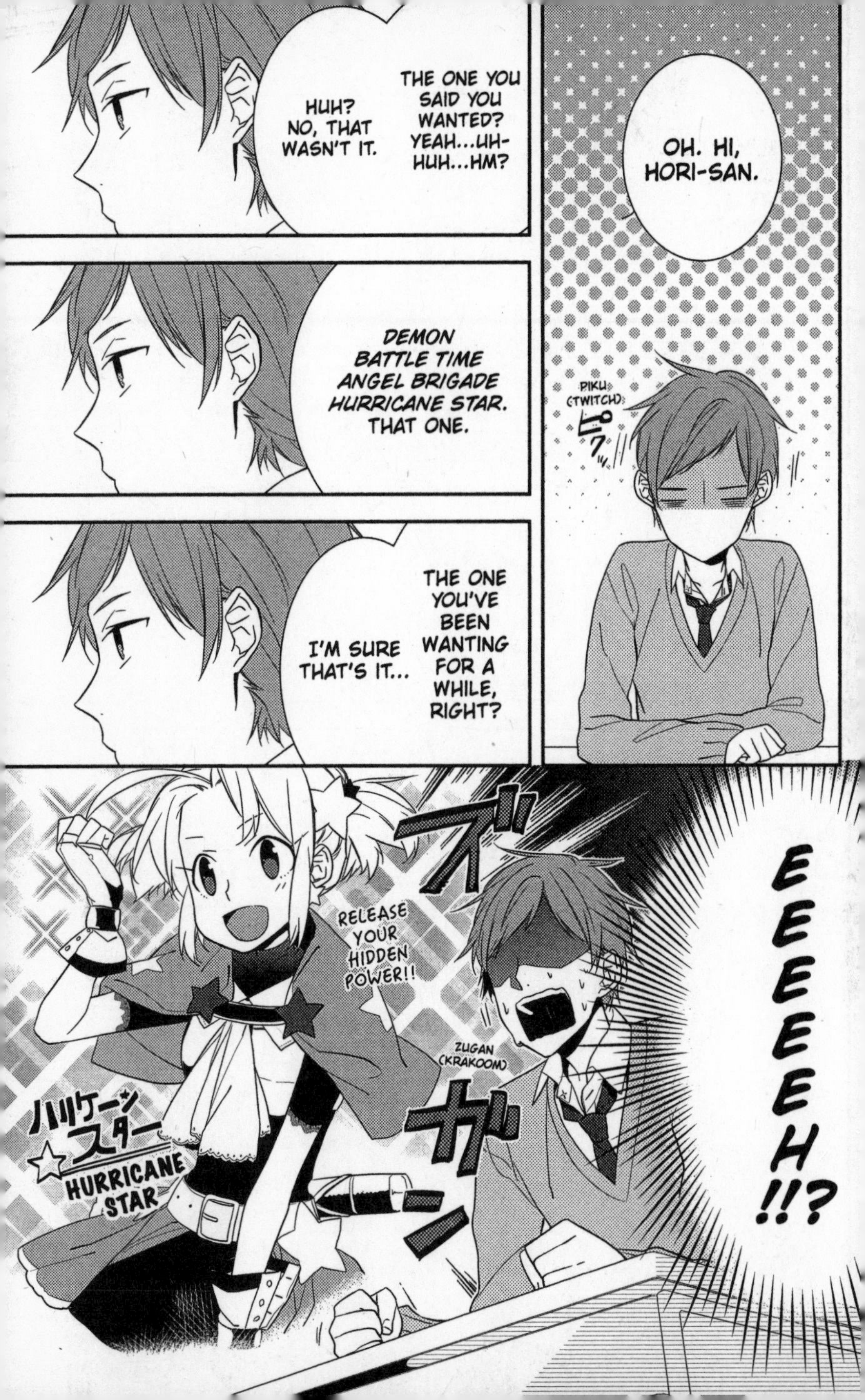
OH. HI, HORI-SAN.
PIKU (TWITCH)
ピク
THE ONE YOU SAID YOU WANTED? YEAH...UH-HUH...HM?
HUH? NO, THAT WASN'T IT.
DEMON BATTLE TIME ANGEL BRIGADE HURRICANE STAR. THAT ONE.
THE ONE YOU'VE BEEN WANTING FOR A WHILE, RIGHT?
I'M SURE THAT'S IT...
EEEEEEH!!?
ズ
RELEASE YOUR HIDDEN POWER!!
ZUGAN (KRAKOOM)
ガン
ハリケーンスター
☆HURRICANE STAR

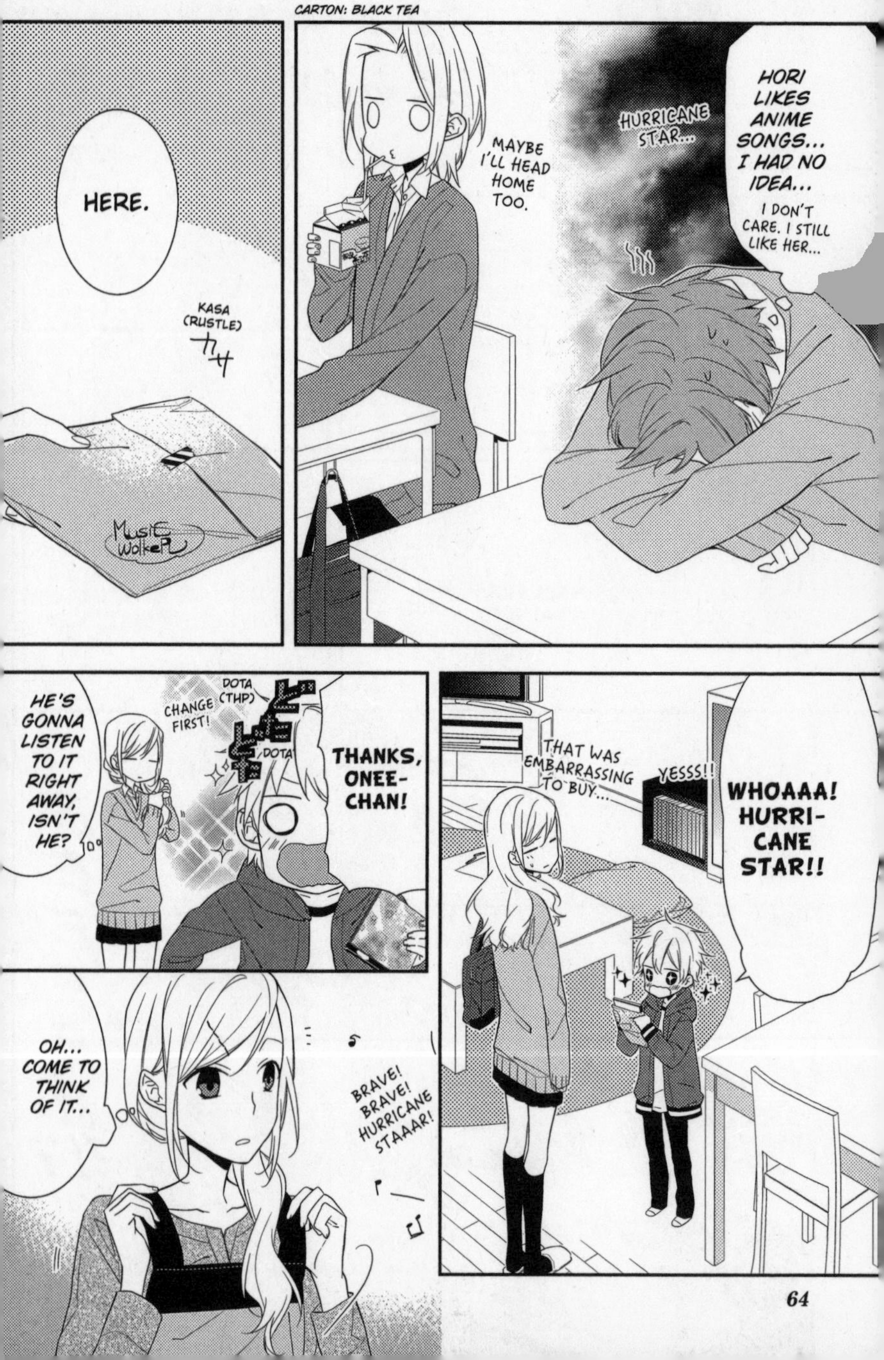
CARTON: BLACK TEA
HORI LIKES ANIME SONGS... I HAD NO IDEA...
I DON'T CARE. I STILL LIKE HER...
HURRICANE STAR...
MAYBE I'LL HEAD HOME TOO.
HERE.
KASA (RUSTLE)
WHOAAA! HURRI-CANE STAR!!
YESSS!!
THAT WAS EMBARRASSING TO BUY...
THANKS, ONEE-CHAN!
DOTA (THP)
DOTA
CHANGE FIRST!
HE'S GONNA LISTEN TO IT RIGHT AWAY, ISN'T HE?
BRAVE! BRAVE! HURRICANE STAAAR!
OH... COME TO THINK OF IT...

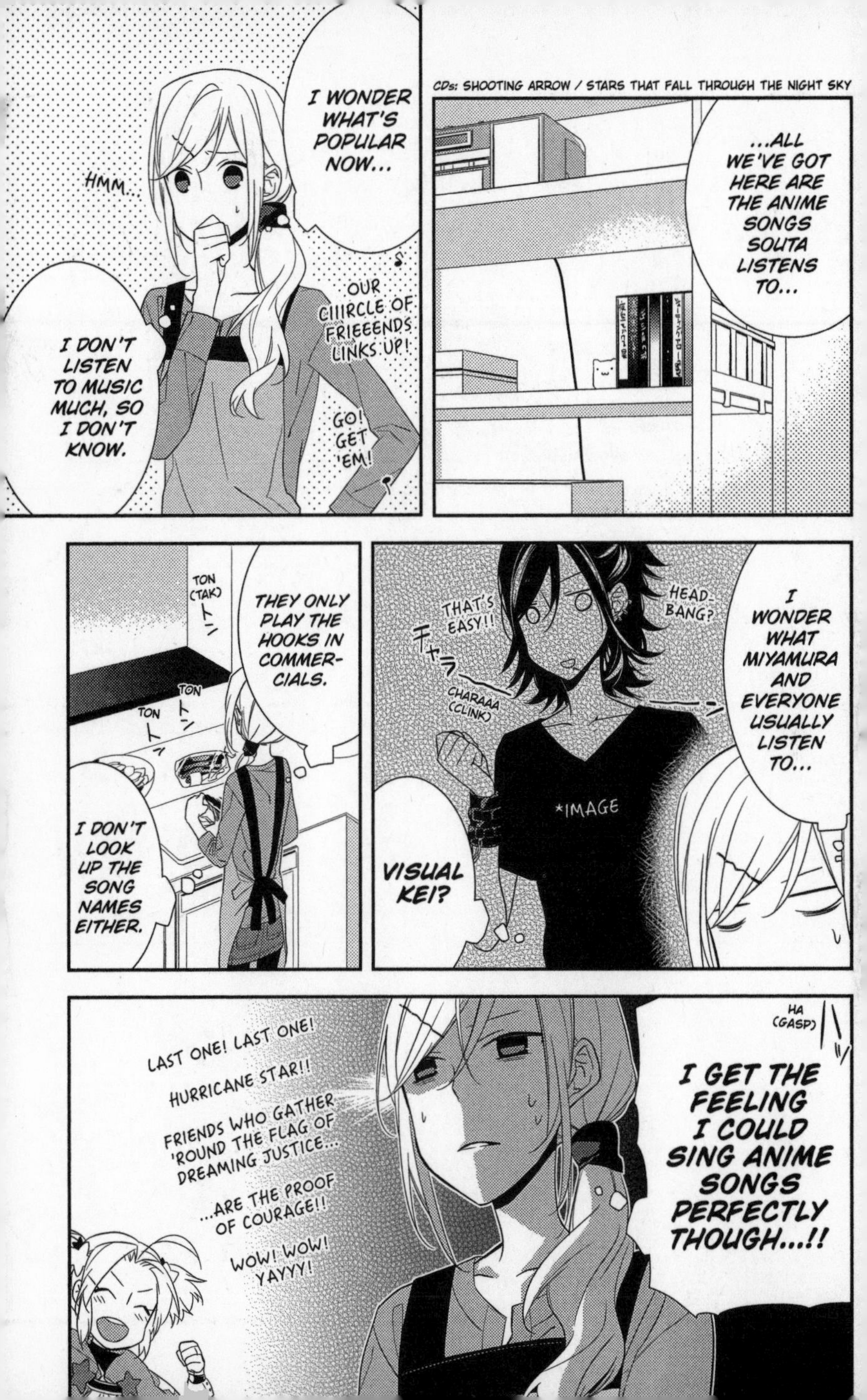
CDs: SHOOTING ARROW / STARS THAT FALL THROUGH THE NIGHT SKY
...ALL WE'VE GOT HERE ARE THE ANIME SONGS SOUTA LISTENS TO...
I WONDER WHAT'S POPULAR NOW...
HMM..
OUR CIIIRCLE OF FRIEEEENDS LINKS UP!
GO! GET 'EM!
I DON'T LISTEN TO MUSIC MUCH, SO I DON'T KNOW.
I WONDER WHAT MIYAMURA AND EVERYONE USUALLY LISTEN TO...
HEAD-BANG?
THAT'S EASY!!
チャラ
CHARAAA (CLINK)
*IMAGE
VISUAL KEI?
THEY ONLY PLAY THE HOOKS IN COMMERCIALS.
TON (TAK)
TON
TON
I DON'T LOOK UP THE SONG NAMES EITHER.
HA (GASP)
I GET THE FEELING I COULD SING ANIME SONGS PERFECTLY THOUGH...!!
LAST ONE! LAST ONE!
HURRICANE STAR!!
FRIENDS WHO GATHER 'ROUND THE FLAG OF DREAMING JUSTICE...
...ARE THE PROOF OF COURAGE!!
WOW! WOW! YAYYY!

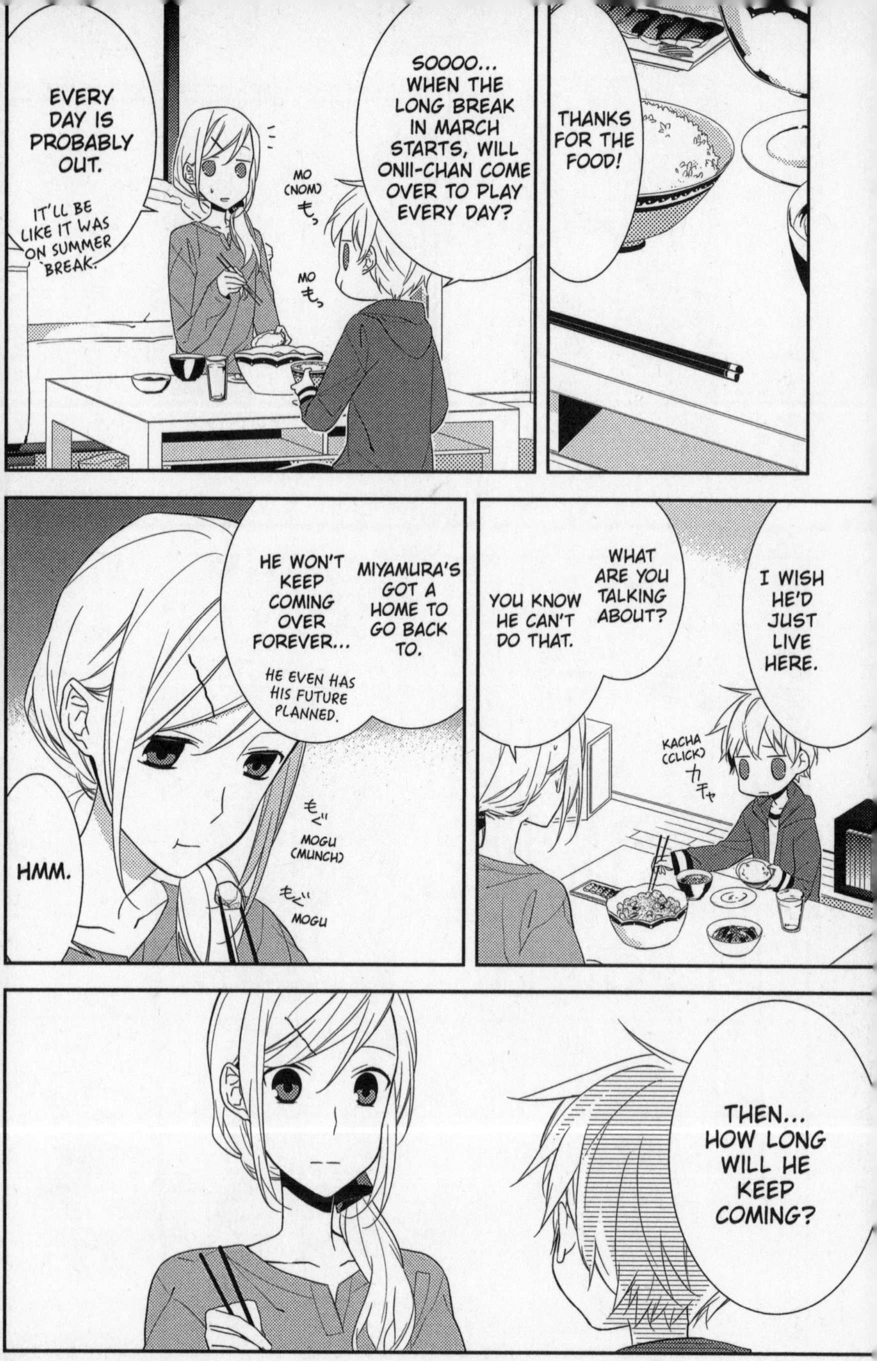
THANKS FOR THE FOOD!
SOOOO... WHEN THE LONG BREAK IN MARCH STARTS, WILL ONII-CHAN COME OVER TO PLAY EVERY DAY?
MO (NOM) もっ
MO もっ
EVERY DAY IS PROBABLY OUT.
IT'LL BE LIKE IT WAS ON SUMMER BREAK.
I WISH HE'D JUST LIVE HERE.
KACHA (CLICK) カチャ
WHAT ARE YOU TALKING ABOUT?
YOU KNOW HE CAN'T DO THAT.
MIYAMURA'S GOT A HOME TO GO BACK TO.
HE WON'T KEEP COMING OVER FOREVER...
HE EVEN HAS HIS FUTURE PLANNED.
もぐ MOGU (MUNCH)
もぐ MOGU
HMM.
THEN... HOW LONG WILL HE KEEP COMING?

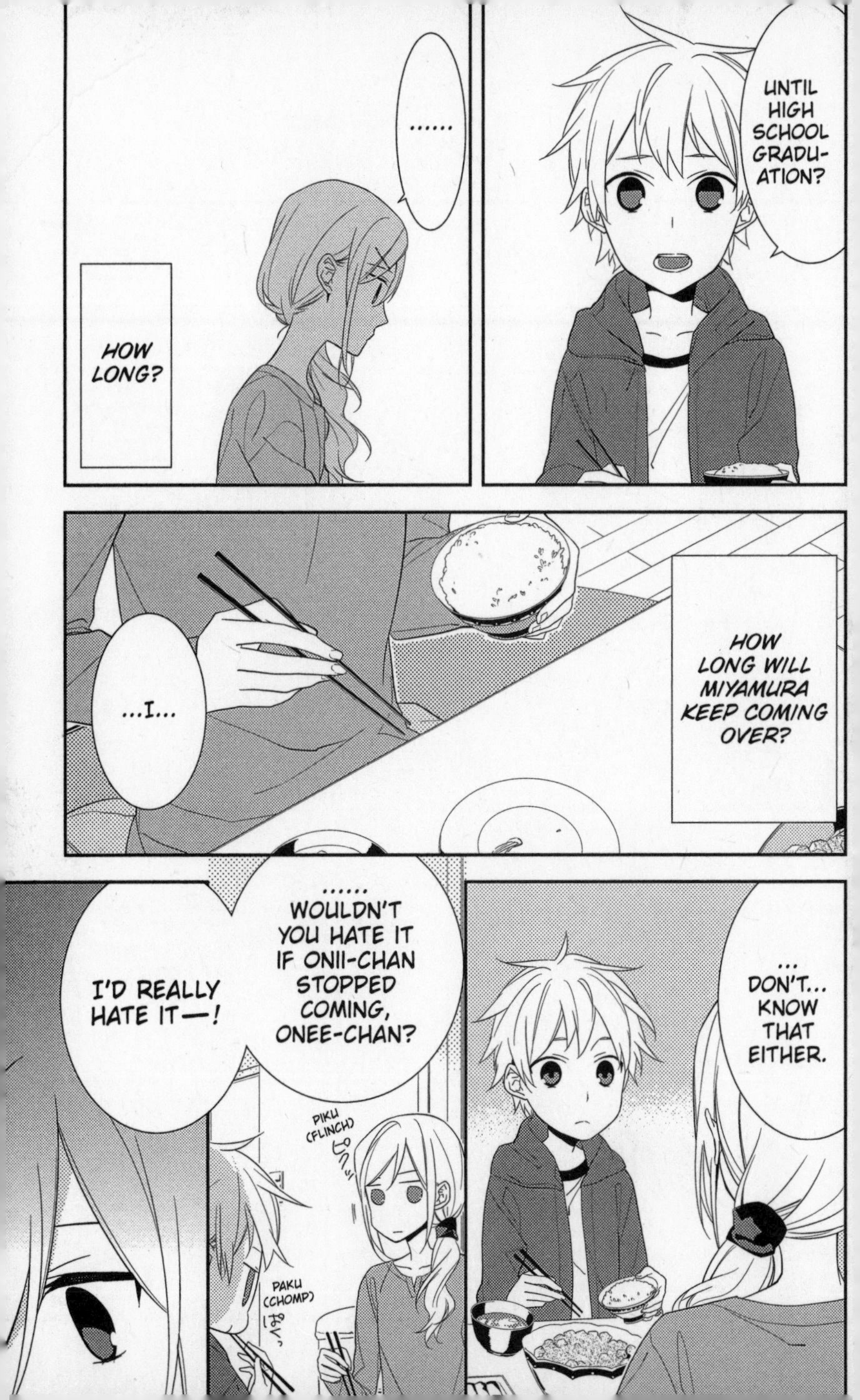
UNTIL HIGH SCHOOL GRADUATION?
......
HOW LONG?
HOW LONG WILL MIYAMURA KEEP COMING OVER?
...I...
... DON'T... KNOW THAT EITHER.
...... WOULDN'T YOU HATE IT IF ONII-CHAN STOPPED COMING, ONEE-CHAN?
I'D REALLY HATE IT—!
PIKU (FLINCH)
PAKU (CHOMP)

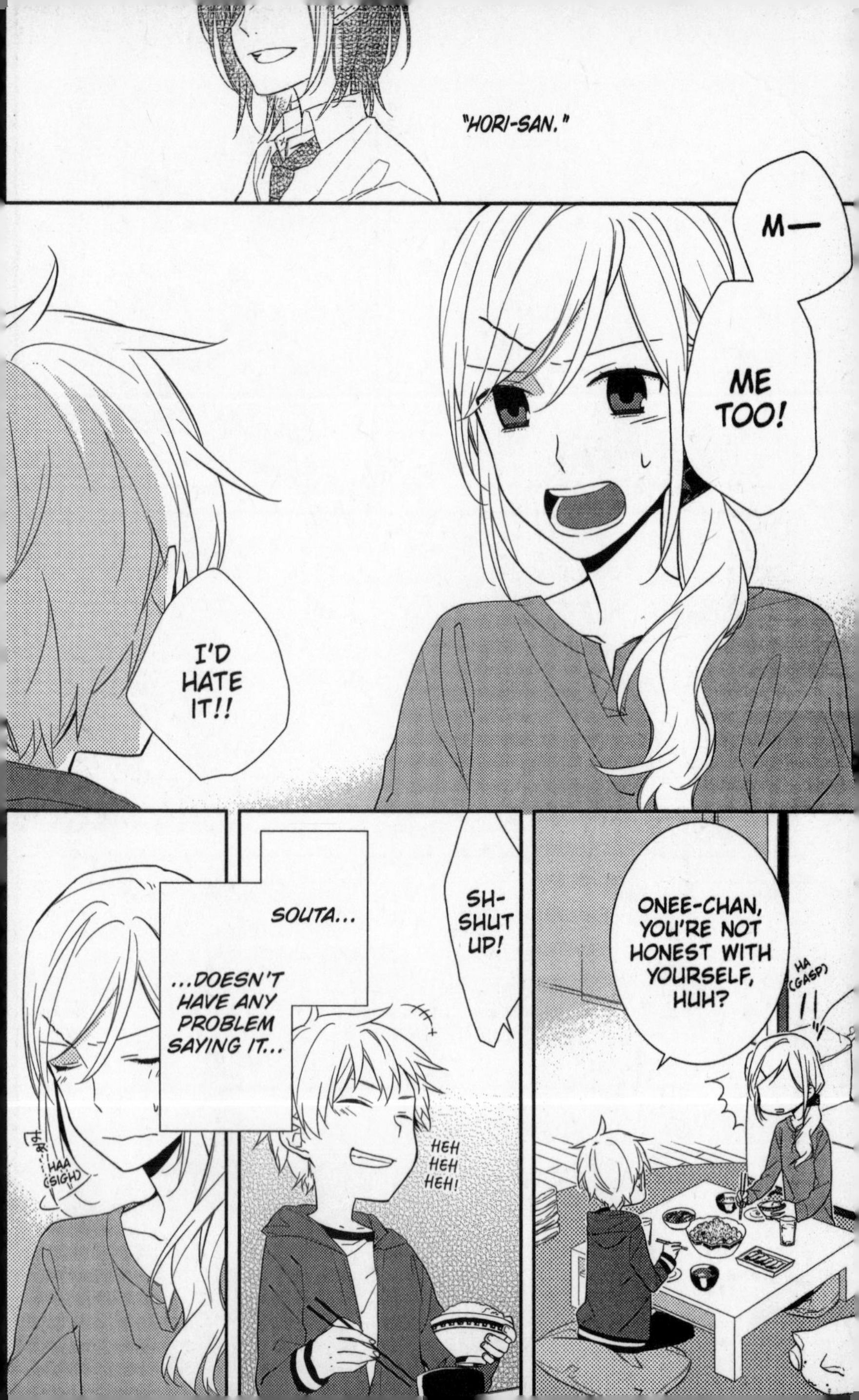
"HORI-SAN."
M—
ME TOO!
I'D HATE IT!!
ONEE-CHAN, YOU'RE NOT HONEST WITH YOURSELF, HUH?
HA (GASP)
SH-SHUT UP!
HEH HEH HEH!
SOUTA...
...DOESN'T HAVE ANY PROBLEM SAYING IT...
HAA (SIGH)

I JUST KEEP TRYING TO HIDE IT...

EAT YOUR CARROTS!

YUCK!!

HMM...

3

SUN	MON	TUE	WED	THU	FRI	SAT
1	2	3	4	5	6	7
8	9	10	11	12	13	14
15	16	17	18	19	20	21
22	23	24	25	26	27	28
29	30	31	1	2	3	4

SO HORI-SAN'S BIRTHDAY IS THE TWENTY-FIFTH...

GUNIIIN (STRETCH)

THAT'S SPRING, ALL RIGHT...

I'D LIKE TO GIVE HER SOMETHING TOO.

GORON (ROLL)
ゴロン

I CAN'T COPY ISHIKAWA-KUN'S GIFT THOUGH. WHAT WOULD BE GOOD?

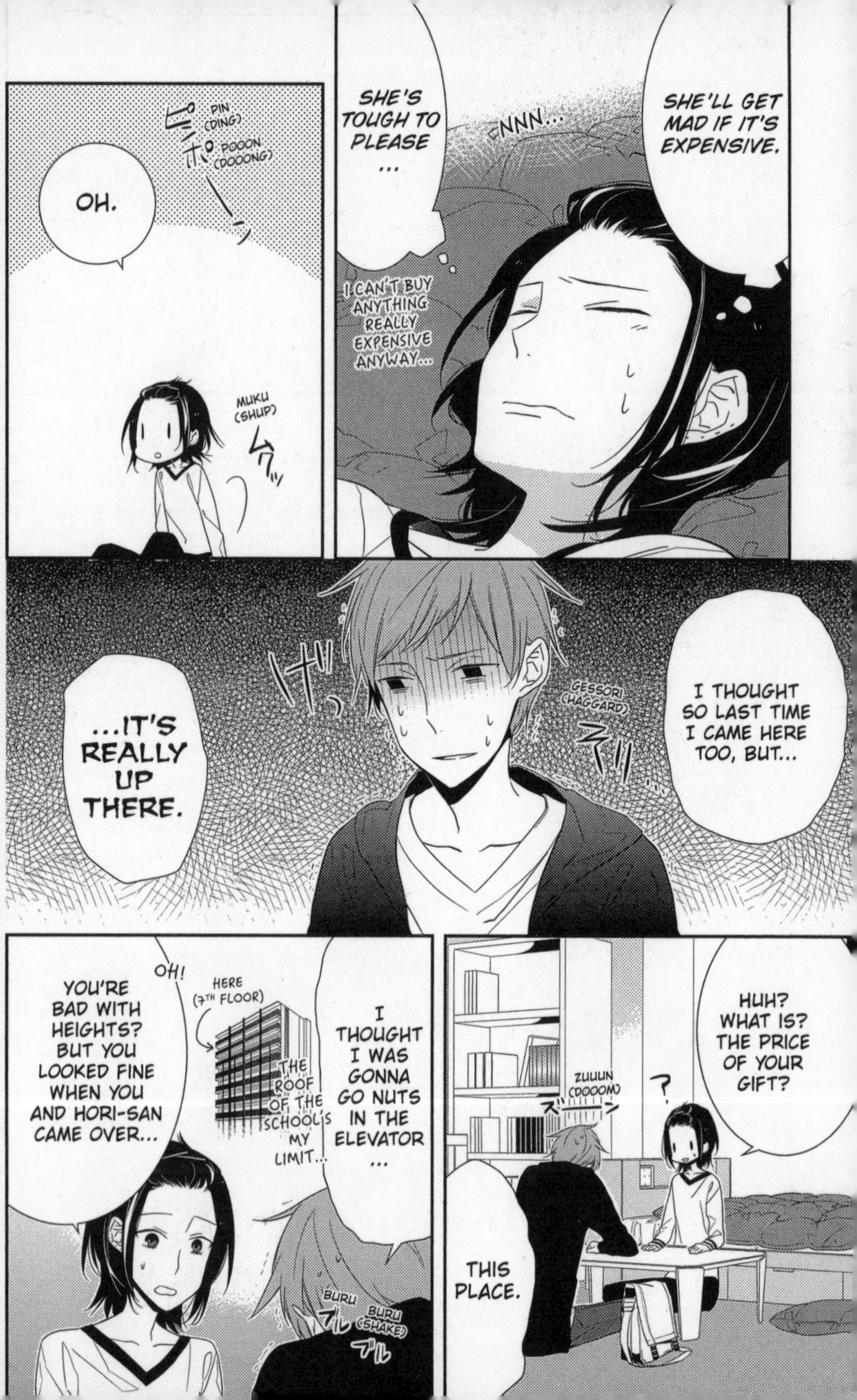
SHE'LL GET MAD IF IT'S EXPENSIVE.
NNN...
SHE'S TOUGH TO PLEASE ...
I CAN'T BUY ANYTHING REALLY EXPENSIVE ANYWAY...
PIN (DING)
POOON (DOOONG)
OH.
MUKU (SHUP)
I THOUGHT SO LAST TIME I CAME HERE TOO, BUT...
GESSORI (HAGGARD)
...IT'S REALLY UP THERE.
HUH? WHAT IS? THE PRICE OF YOUR GIFT?
ZUUUN (DOOOM)
?
THIS PLACE.
I THOUGHT I WAS GONNA GO NUTS IN THE ELEVATOR ...
THE ROOF OF THE SCHOOL'S MY LIMIT...
HERE (7TH FLOOR)
OH!
YOU'RE BAD WITH HEIGHTS? BUT YOU LOOKED FINE WHEN YOU AND HORI-SAN CAME OVER...
BURU
BURU (SHAKE)

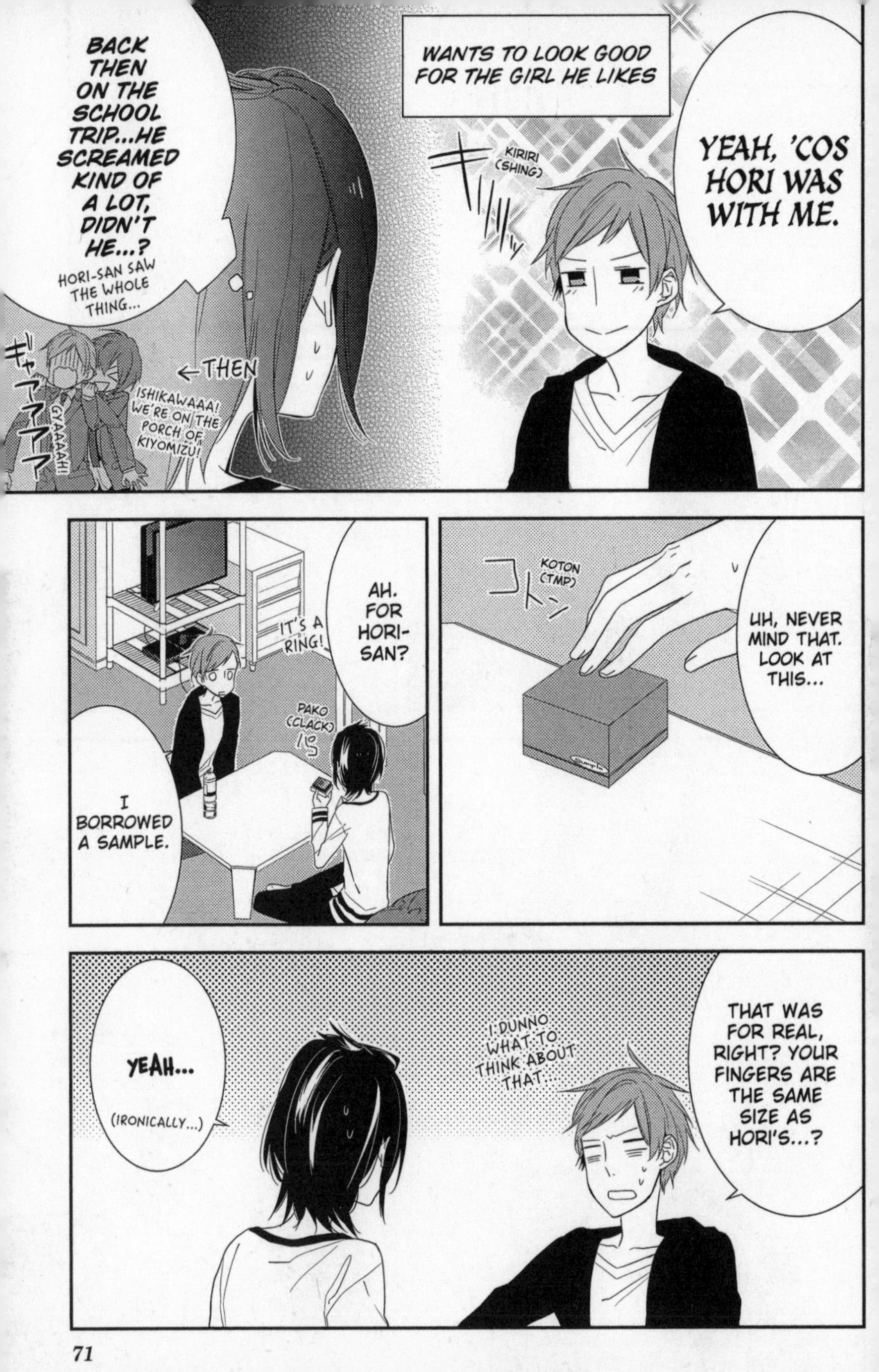
WANTS TO LOOK GOOD FOR THE GIRL HE LIKES
KIRIRI (SHING)
YEAH, 'COS HORI WAS WITH ME.
BACK THEN ON THE SCHOOL TRIP...HE SCREAMED KIND OF A LOT, DIDN'T HE...?
HORI-SAN SAW THE WHOLE THING...
←THEN
ISHIKAWAAA! WE'RE ON THE PORCH OF KIYOMIZU!
GYAAAAH!
KOTON (TMP)
UH, NEVER MIND THAT. LOOK AT THIS...
AH. FOR HORI-SAN?
IT'S A RING!
PAKO (CLACK)
I BORROWED A SAMPLE.
THAT WAS FOR REAL, RIGHT? YOUR FINGERS ARE THE SAME SIZE AS HORI'S...?
I DUNNO WHAT TO THINK ABOUT THAT.
YEAH...
(IRONICALLY...)

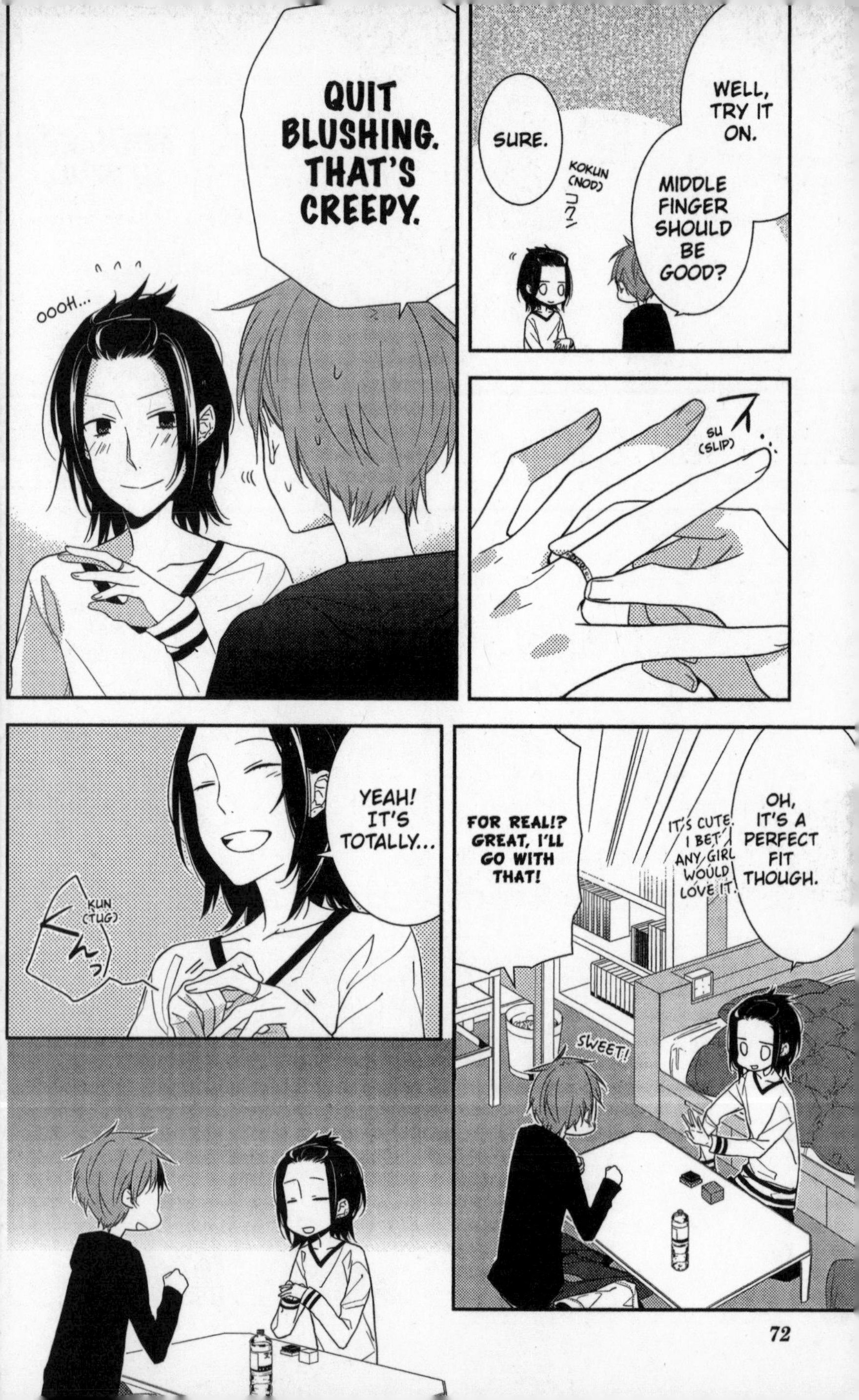
WELL, TRY IT ON.
MIDDLE FINGER SHOULD BE GOOD?
SURE.
KOKUN (NOD)
SU (SLIP)
QUIT BLUSHING. THAT'S CREEPY.
OOOH...
OH, IT'S A PERFECT FIT THOUGH.
IT'S CUTE. I BET ANY GIRL WOULD LOVE IT.
FOR REAL!? GREAT, I'LL GO WITH THAT!
SWEET!
YEAH! IT'S TOTALLY...
KUN (TUG)

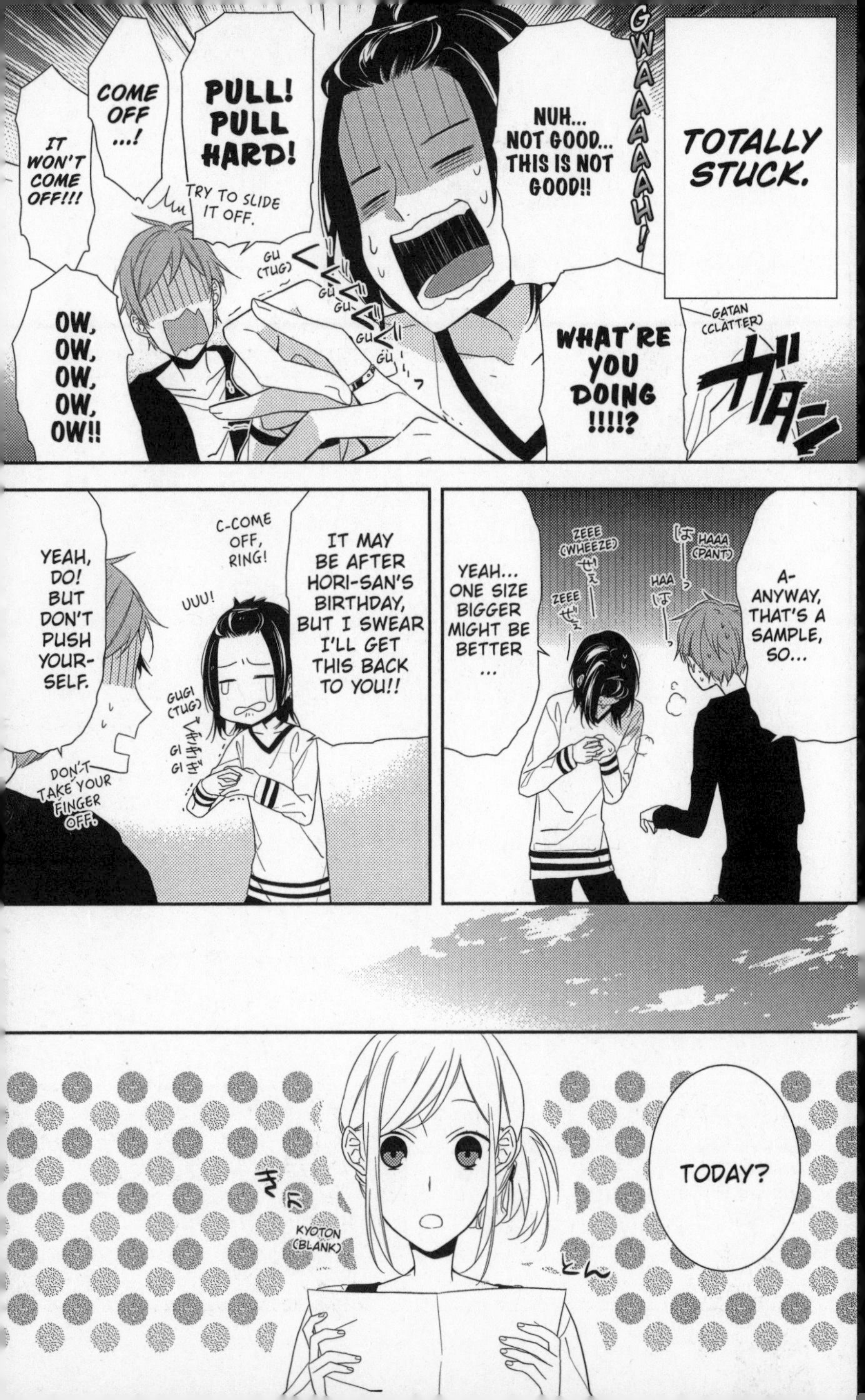
TOTALLY STUCK.
GWAAAAAH!
NUH... NOT GOOD... THIS IS NOT GOOD!!
PULL! PULL HARD!
COME OFF ...!
IT WON'T COME OFF!!!
TRY TO SLIDE IT OFF.
GU (TUG)
GU
GU
GU
GU
GATAN (CLATTER)
WHAT'RE YOU DOING !!!!?
OW, OW, OW, OW, OW!!
A- ANYWAY, THAT'S A SAMPLE, SO...
HAAA (PANT)
HAA
ZEEE (WHEEZE)
ZEEE
YEAH... ONE SIZE BIGGER MIGHT BE BETTER ...
IT MAY BE AFTER HORI-SAN'S BIRTHDAY, BUT I SWEAR I'LL GET THIS BACK TO YOU!!
C-COME OFF, RING!
UUU!
GUGI (TUG)
GI GI
YEAH, DO! BUT DON'T PUSH YOURSELF.
DON'T TAKE YOUR FINGER OFF.
TODAY?
KYOTON (BLANK)

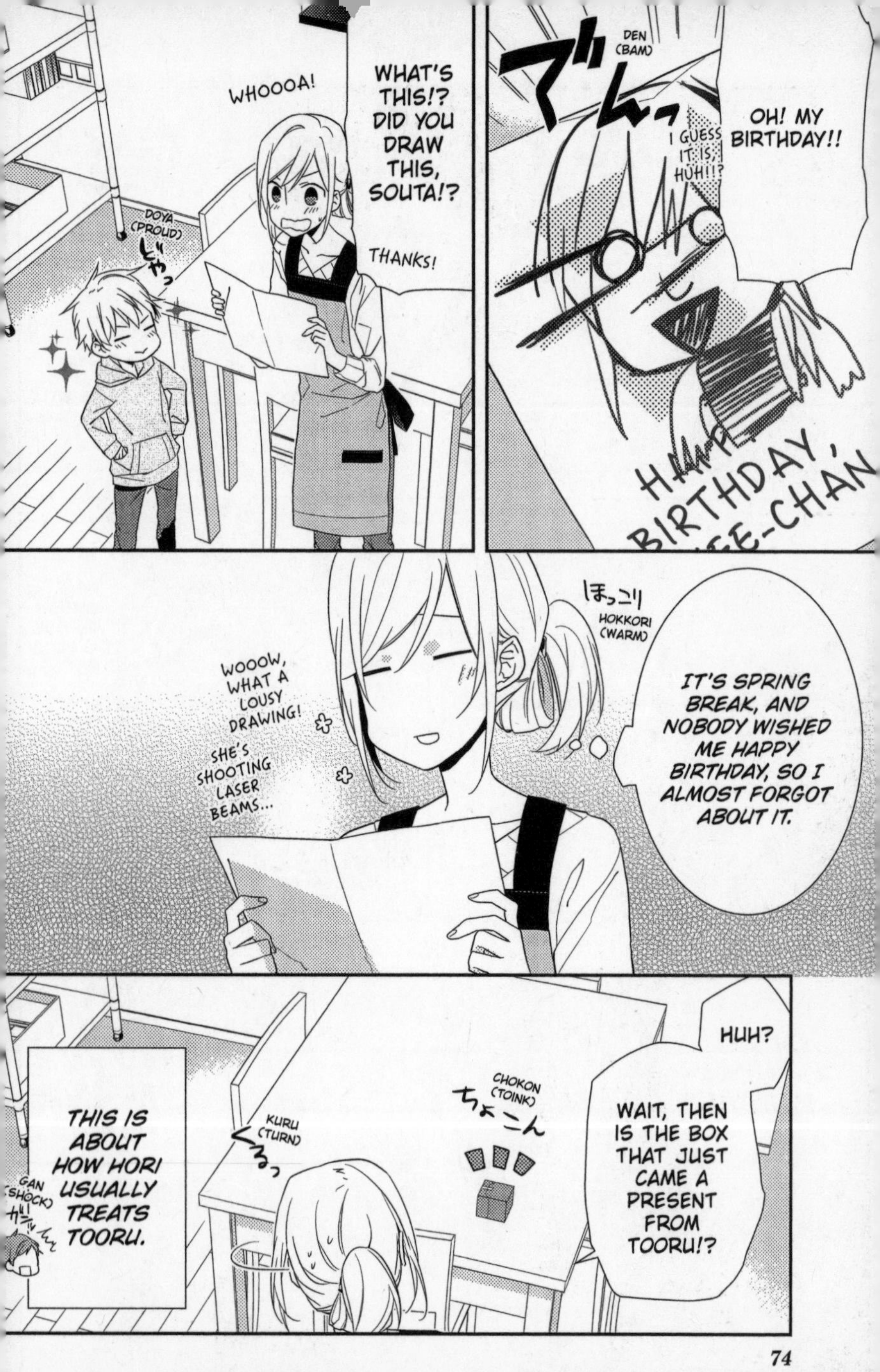
DEN (BAM)
でんっ
OH! MY BIRTHDAY!!
I GUESS IT IS, HUH!!?
BIRTHDAY,
WHAT'S THIS!? DID YOU DRAW THIS, SOUTA!?
WHOOOA!
THANKS!
DOYA (PROUD)
ほっこり
HOKKORI (WARM)
IT'S SPRING BREAK, AND NOBODY WISHED ME HAPPY BIRTHDAY, SO I ALMOST FORGOT ABOUT IT.
WOOOW, WHAT A LOUSY DRAWING!
SHE'S SHOOTING LASER BEAMS...
HUH?
WAIT, THEN IS THE BOX THAT JUST CAME A PRESENT FROM TOORU!?
CHOKON (TOINK)
ちょこん
KURU (TURN)
くるっ
THIS IS ABOUT HOW HORI USUALLY TREATS TOORU.
GAN (SHOCK)
ガーン

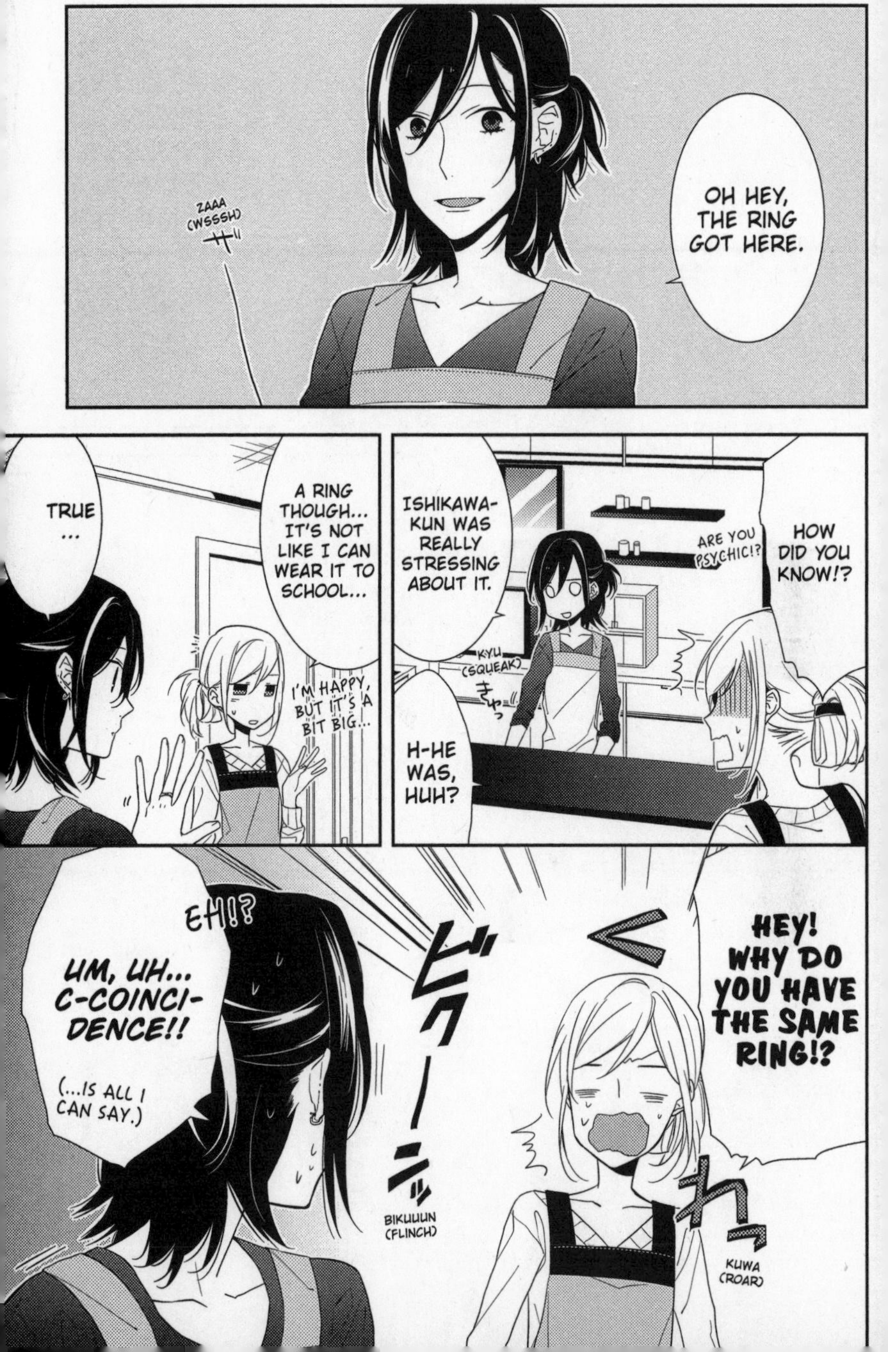
OH HEY, THE RING GOT HERE.
ZAAA (WSSSH)
HOW DID YOU KNOW!?
ARE YOU PSYCHIC!?
ISHIKAWA-KUN WAS REALLY STRESSING ABOUT IT.
KYU (SQUEAK)
H-HE WAS, HUH?
A RING THOUGH... IT'S NOT LIKE I CAN WEAR IT TO SCHOOL...
TRUE ...
I'M HAPPY, BUT IT'S A BIT BIG...
HEY! WHY DO YOU HAVE THE SAME RING!?
KUWA (ROAR)
BIKUUUN (FLINCH)
EH!?
UM, UH... C-COINCIDENCE!!
(...IS ALL I CAN SAY.)

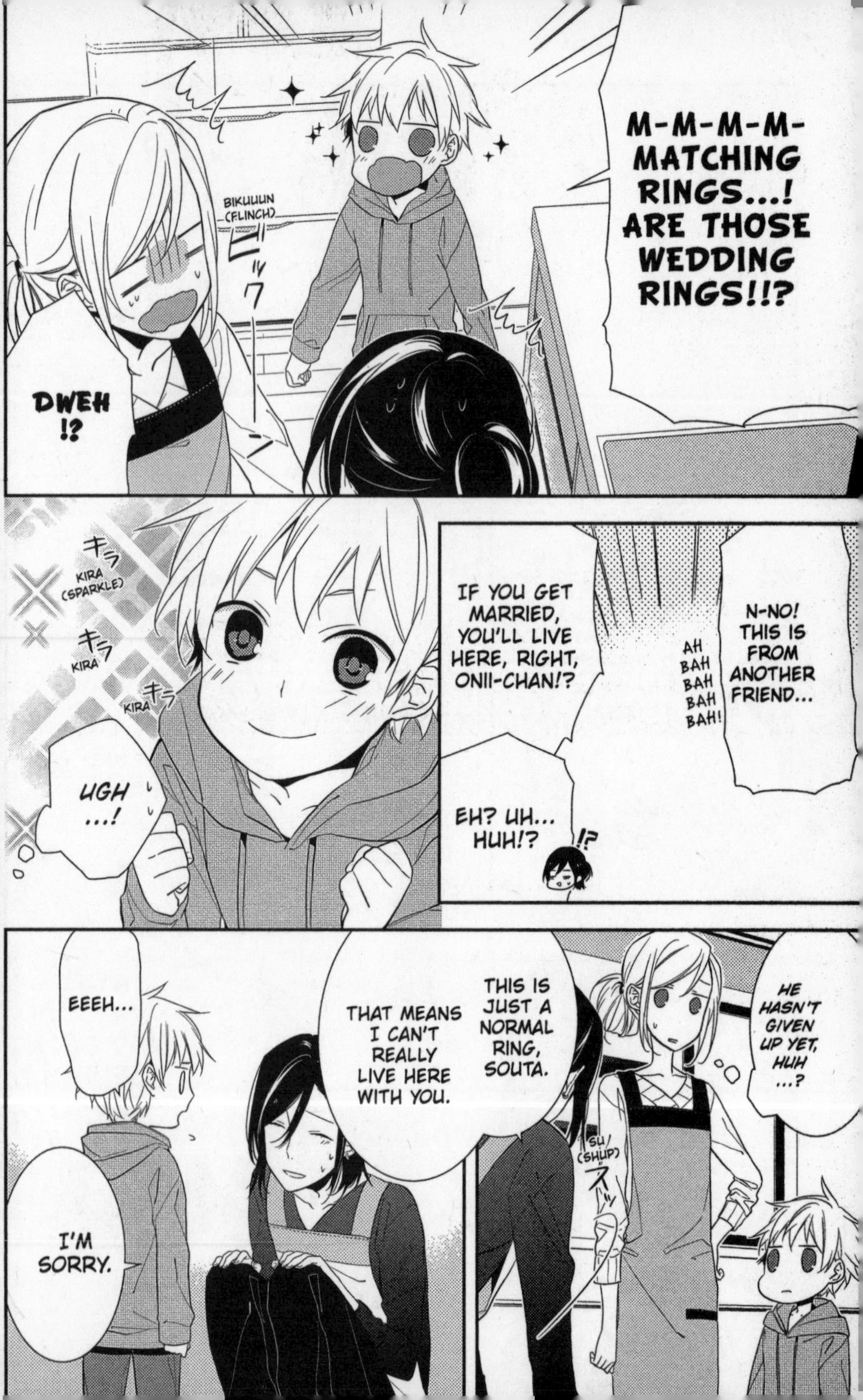
M-M-M-M-MATCHING RINGS...! ARE THOSE WEDDING RINGS!!?
BIKUUUN (FLINCH)
DWEH !?
N-NO! THIS IS FROM ANOTHER FRIEND...
AH BAH BAH BAH BAH!
IF YOU GET MARRIED, YOU'LL LIVE HERE, RIGHT, ONII-CHAN!?
EH? UH... HUH!?
!?
KIRA (SPARKLE)
KIRA
KIRA
UGH ...!
HE HASN'T GIVEN UP YET, HUH ...?
SU (SHUP)
THIS IS JUST A NORMAL RING, SOUTA.
THAT MEANS I CAN'T REALLY LIVE HERE WITH YOU.
EEEH...
I'M SORRY.

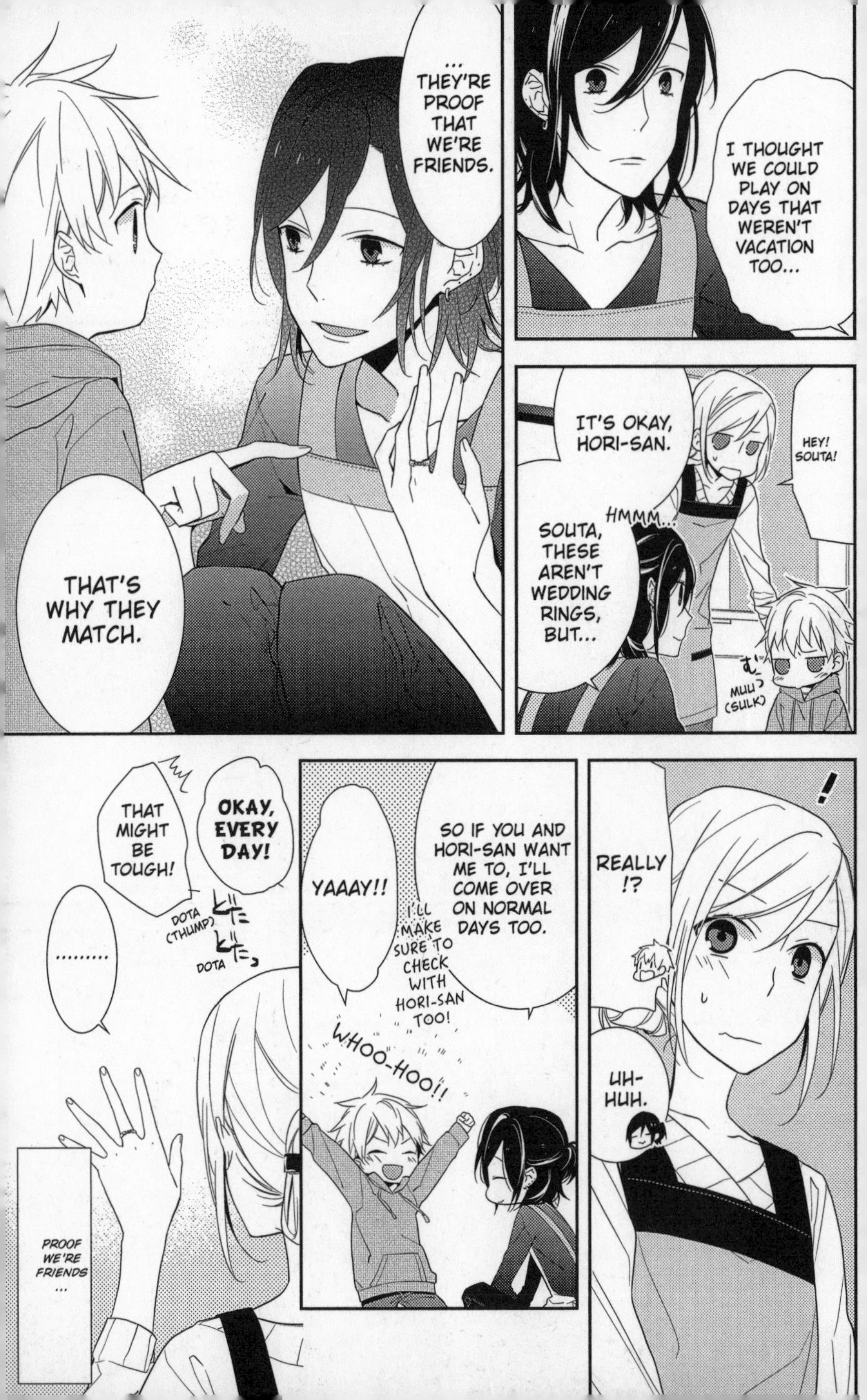
I THOUGHT WE COULD PLAY ON DAYS THAT WEREN'T VACATION TOO...
HEY! SOUTA!
IT'S OKAY, HORI-SAN.
HMMM...
SOUTA, THESE AREN'T WEDDING RINGS, BUT...
むー MUU (SULK)
... THEY'RE PROOF THAT WE'RE FRIENDS.
THAT'S WHY THEY MATCH.
!
REALLY !?
UH-HUH.
SO IF YOU AND HORI-SAN WANT ME TO, I'LL COME OVER ON NORMAL DAYS TOO.
I'LL MAKE SURE TO CHECK WITH HORI-SAN TOO!
YAAAY!!
WHOO-HOO!!
OKAY, EVERY DAY!
THAT MIGHT BE TOUGH!
どてっ DOTA (THUMP)
どてっ DOTA
....
PROOF WE'RE FRIENDS ...

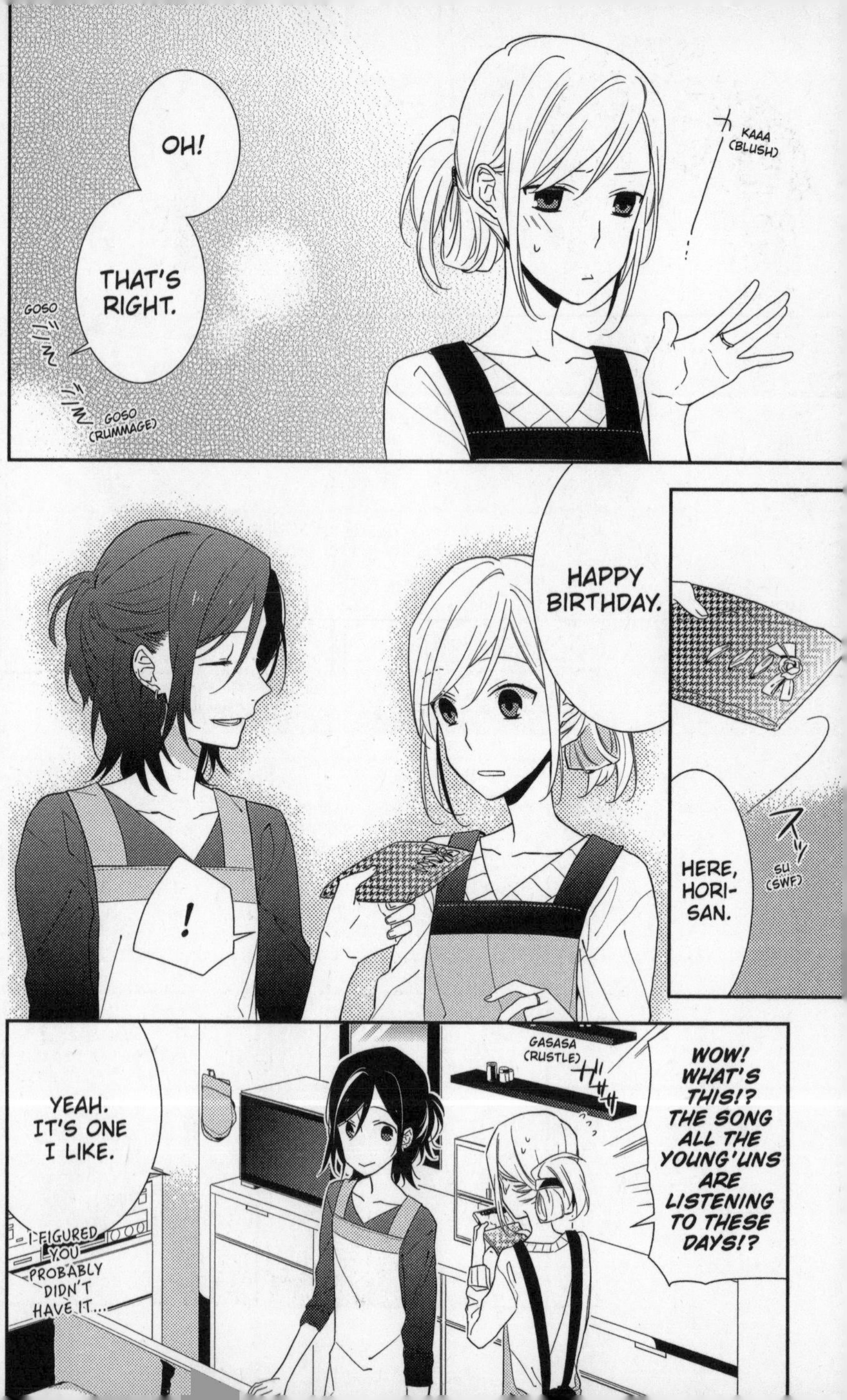
KAAA (BLUSH)
OH!
THAT'S RIGHT.
GOSO
GOSO (RUMMAGE)
SU (SWF)
HERE, HORI-SAN.
HAPPY BIRTHDAY.
!
WOW! WHAT'S THIS!? THE SONG ALL THE YOUNG'UNS ARE LISTENING TO THESE DAYS!?
GASASA (RUSTLE)
YEAH. IT'S ONE I LIKE.
I FIGURED YOU PROBABLY DIDN'T HAVE IT...

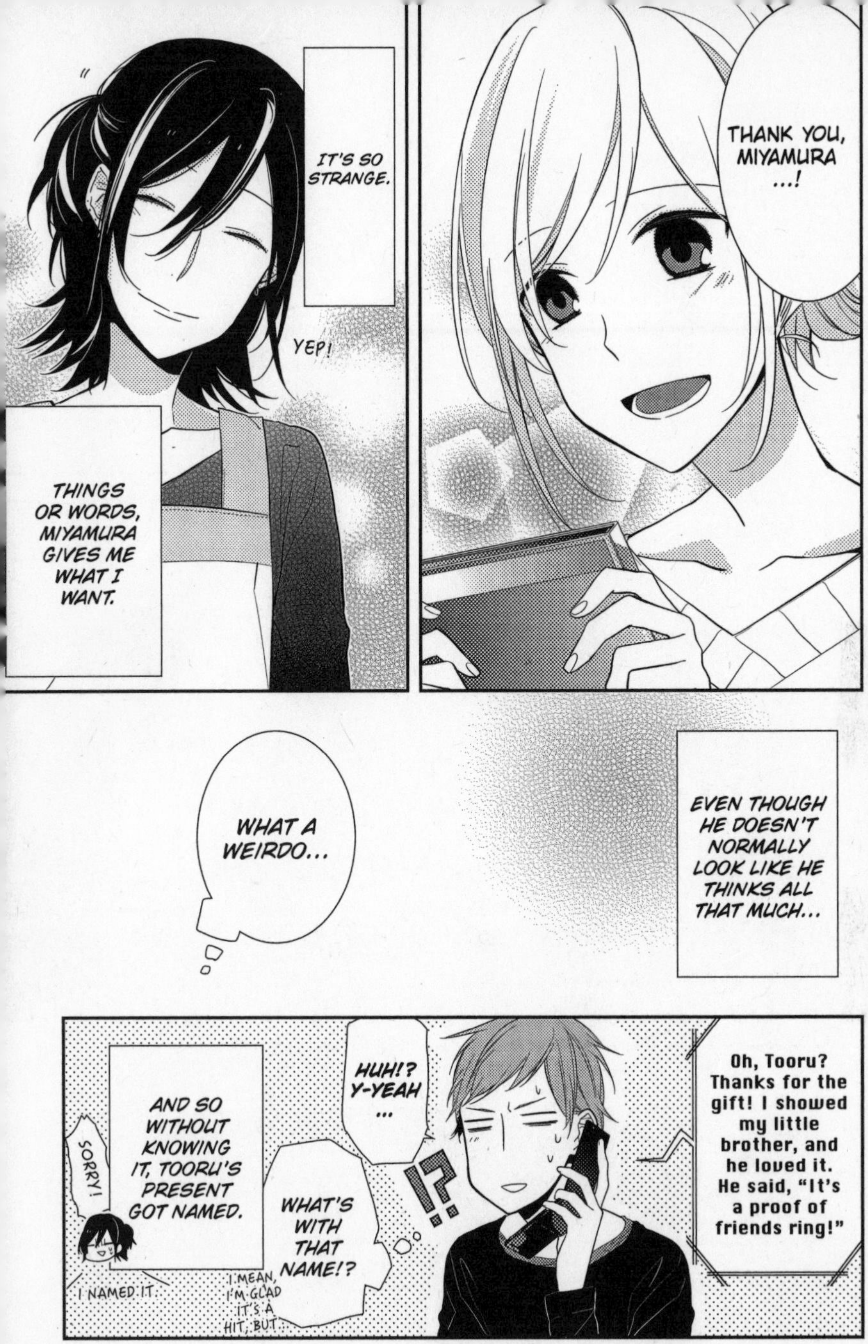
THANK YOU, MIYAMURA ...!
IT'S SO STRANGE.
YEP!
THINGS OR WORDS, MIYAMURA GIVES ME WHAT I WANT.
EVEN THOUGH HE DOESN'T NORMALLY LOOK LIKE HE THINKS ALL THAT MUCH...
WHAT A WEIRDO...
Oh, Tooru? Thanks for the gift! I showed my little brother, and he loved it. He said, "It's a proof of friends ring!"
HUH!? Y-YEAH ...
!?
AND SO WITHOUT KNOWING IT, TOORU'S PRESENT GOT NAMED.
SORRY!
WHAT'S WITH THAT NAME!?
I MEAN, I'M GLAD IT'S A HIT, BUT
I NAMED IT.

HORIMIYA

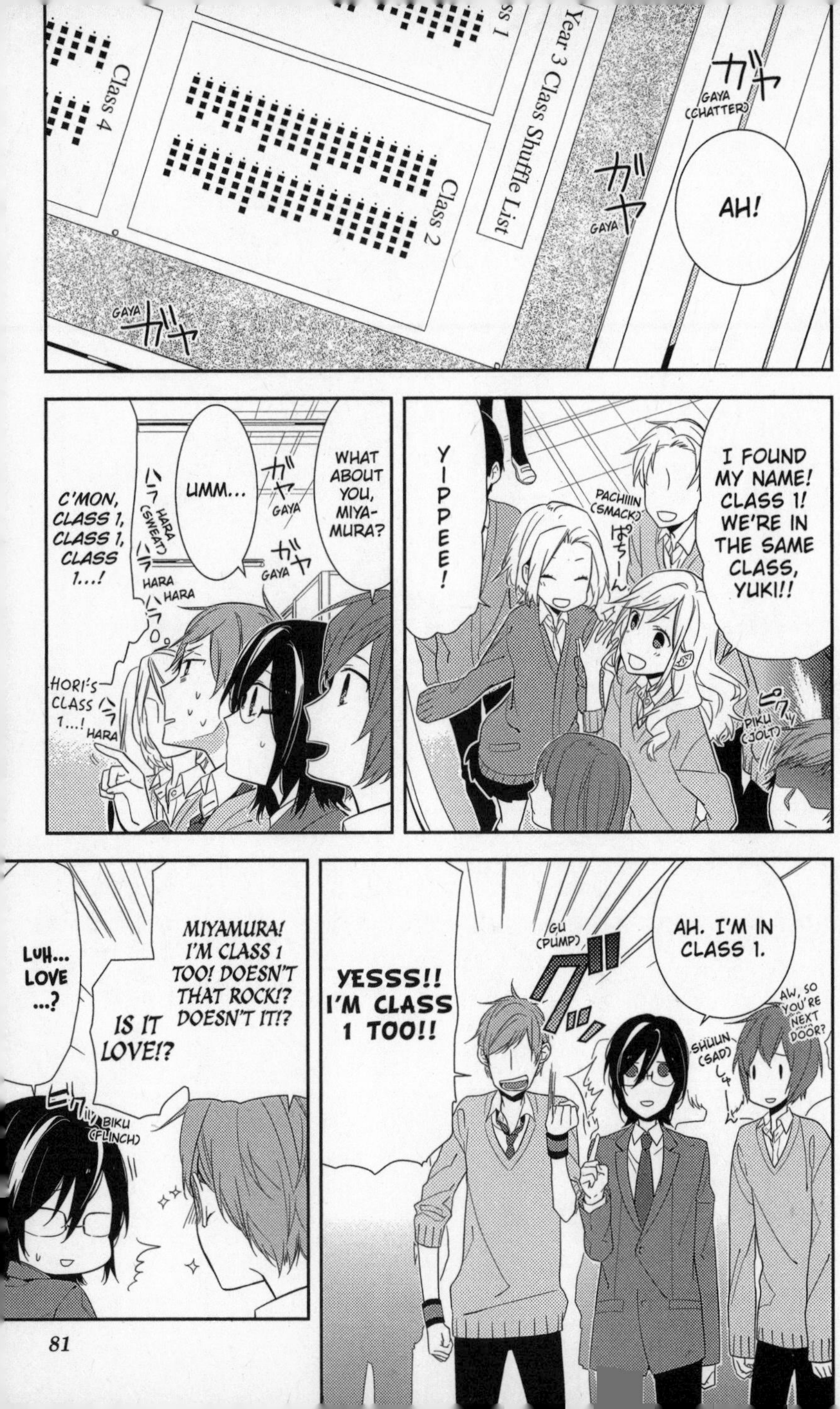
Year 3 Class Shuffle List
Class 2
Class 4
ガヤ GAYA (CHATTER)
ガヤ GAYA
AH!
ガヤ GAYA
I FOUND MY NAME! CLASS 1! WE'RE IN THE SAME CLASS, YUKI!!
ぱちーん PACHIIIN (SMACK)
YIPPEE!
ピクッ PIKU (JOLT)
WHAT ABOUT YOU, MIYAMURA?
ガヤ GAYA
ガヤ GAYA
UMM...
ハラ HARA (SWEAT)
ハラ HARA
C'MON, CLASS 1, CLASS 1, CLASS 1...!
HORI'S CLASS 1...!
ハラ HARA
AH. I'M IN CLASS 1.
AW, SO YOU'RE NEXT DOOR?
しゅーん SHUUN (SAD)
グッ GU (PUMP)
YESSS!! I'M CLASS 1 TOO!!
MIYAMURA! I'M CLASS 1 TOO! DOESN'T THAT ROCK!? DOESN'T IT!?
IS IT LOVE!?
LUH... LOVE ...?
ビクッ BIKU (FLINCH)

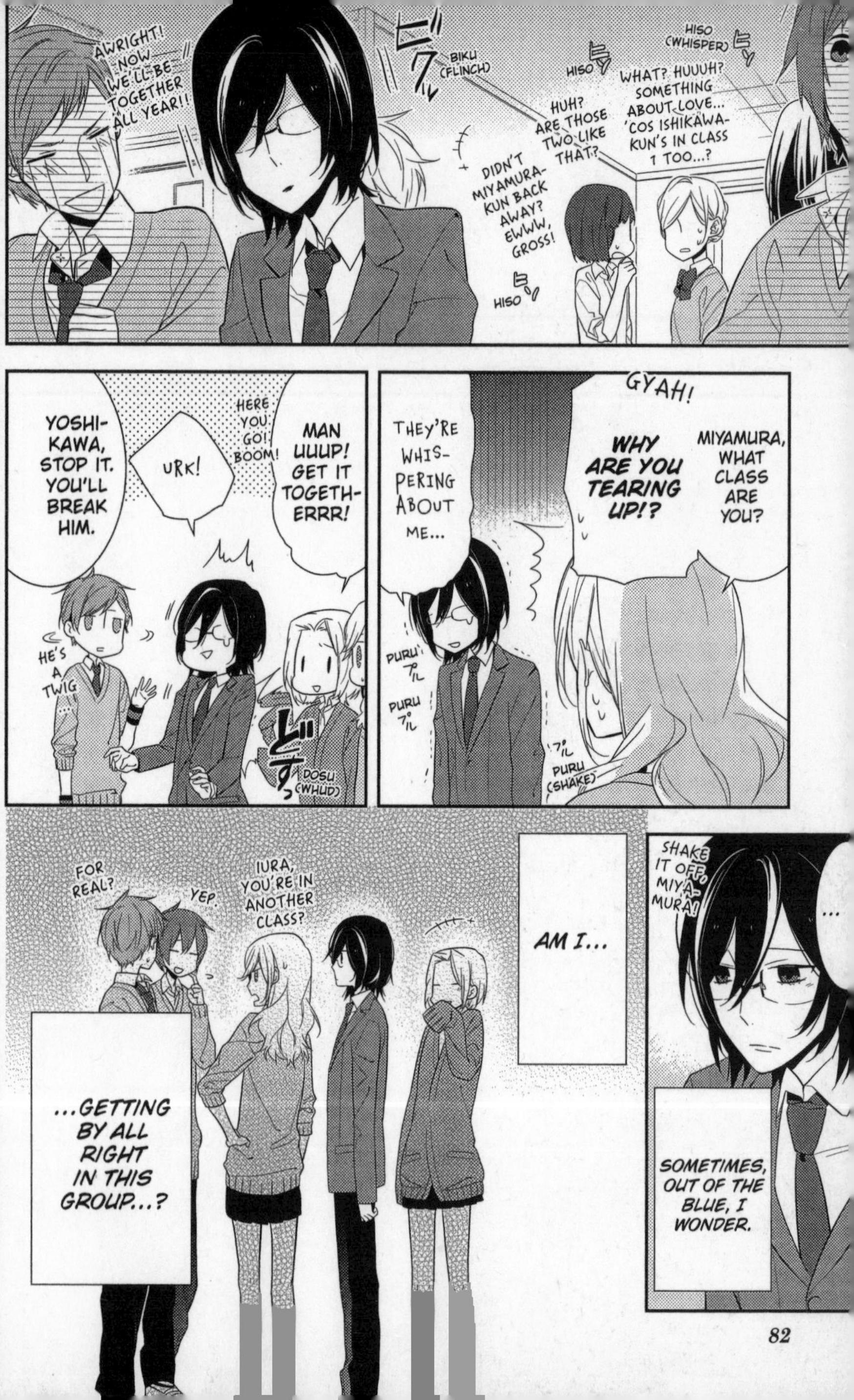
HISO (WHISPER)
WHAT? HUUUH? SOMETHING ABOUT LOVE... 'COS ISHIKAWA-KUN'S IN CLASS 1 TOO...?
HISO
HUH? ARE THOSE TWO LIKE THAT?
DIDN'T MIYAMURA-KUN BACK AWAY? EWWW, GROSS!
HISO
BIKU (FLINCH)
AWRIGHT! NOW WE'LL BE TOGETHER ALL YEAR!!
GYAH!
MIYAMURA, WHAT CLASS ARE YOU?
WHY ARE YOU TEARING UP!?
THEY'RE WHISPERING ABOUT ME...
PURU
PURU
PURU (SHAKE)
MAN UUUP! GET IT TOGETHERRR!
HERE YOU GO! BOOM!
URK!
YOSHIKAWA, STOP IT. YOU'LL BREAK HIM.
HE'S A TWIG...
DOSU (WHUD)
SHAKE IT OFF, MIYAMURA!
...
SOMETIMES, OUT OF THE BLUE, I WONDER.
AM I...
IURA, YOU'RE IN ANOTHER CLASS?
YEP.
FOR REAL?
...GETTING BY ALL RIGHT IN THIS GROUP...?

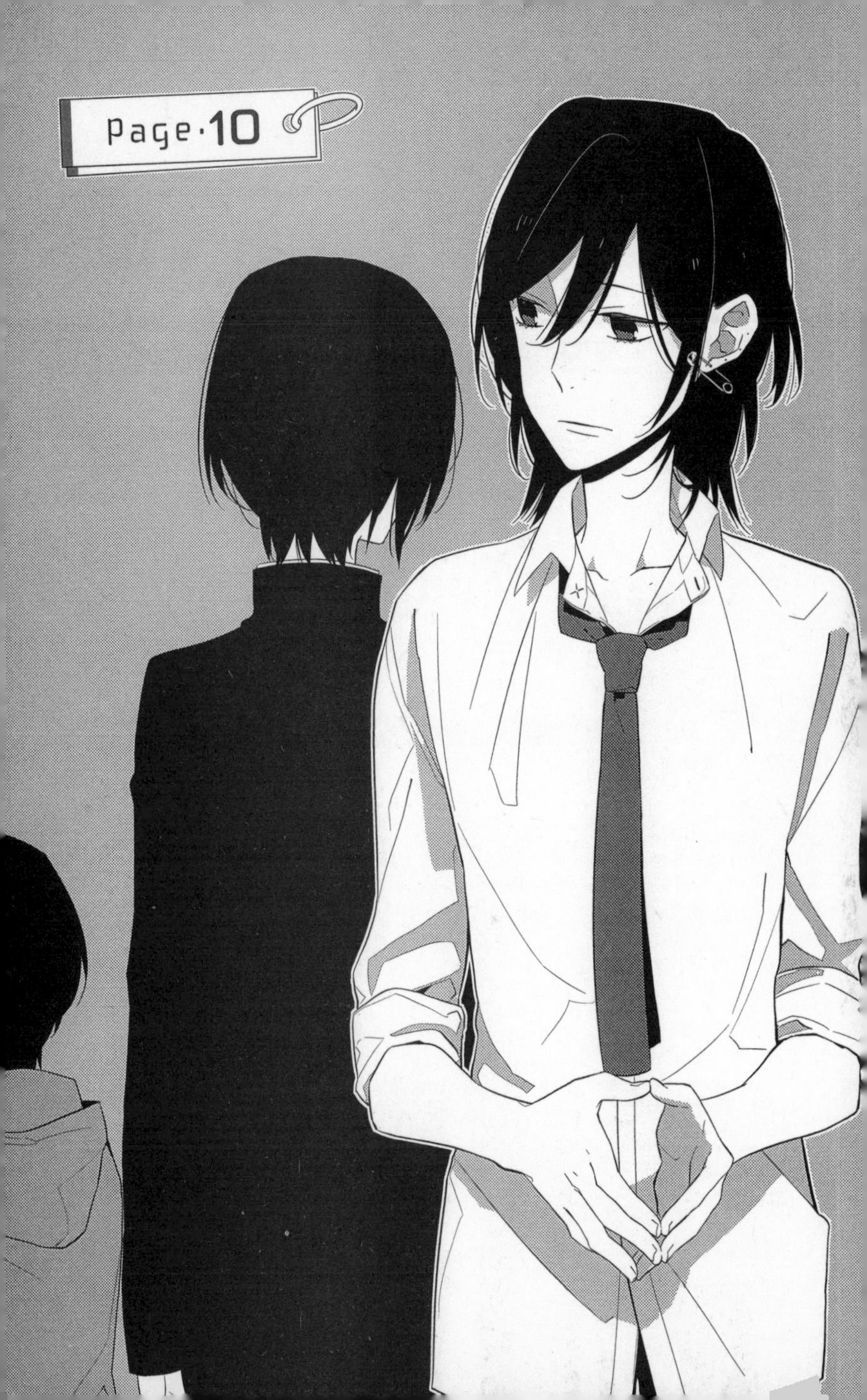
Page·10

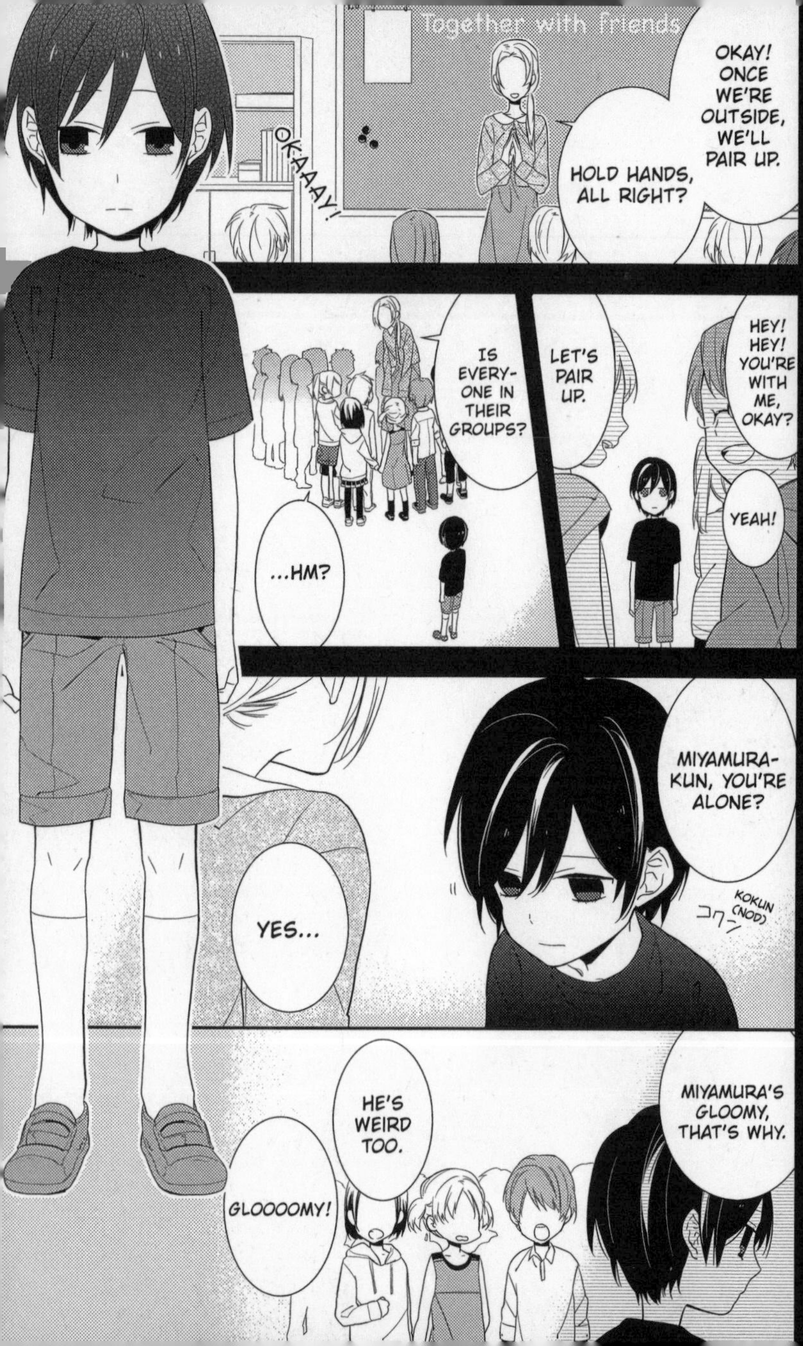
Together with friends
OKAY! ONCE WE'RE OUTSIDE, WE'LL PAIR UP.
HOLD HANDS, ALL RIGHT?
OKAAAAY!
HEY! HEY! YOU'RE WITH ME, OKAY?
YEAH!
LET'S PAIR UP.
IS EVERY-ONE IN THEIR GROUPS?
...HM?
MIYAMURA-KUN, YOU'RE ALONE?
KOKUN (NOD)
コクン
YES...
MIYAMURA'S GLOOMY, THAT'S WHY.
HE'S WEIRD TOO.
GLOOOOMY!

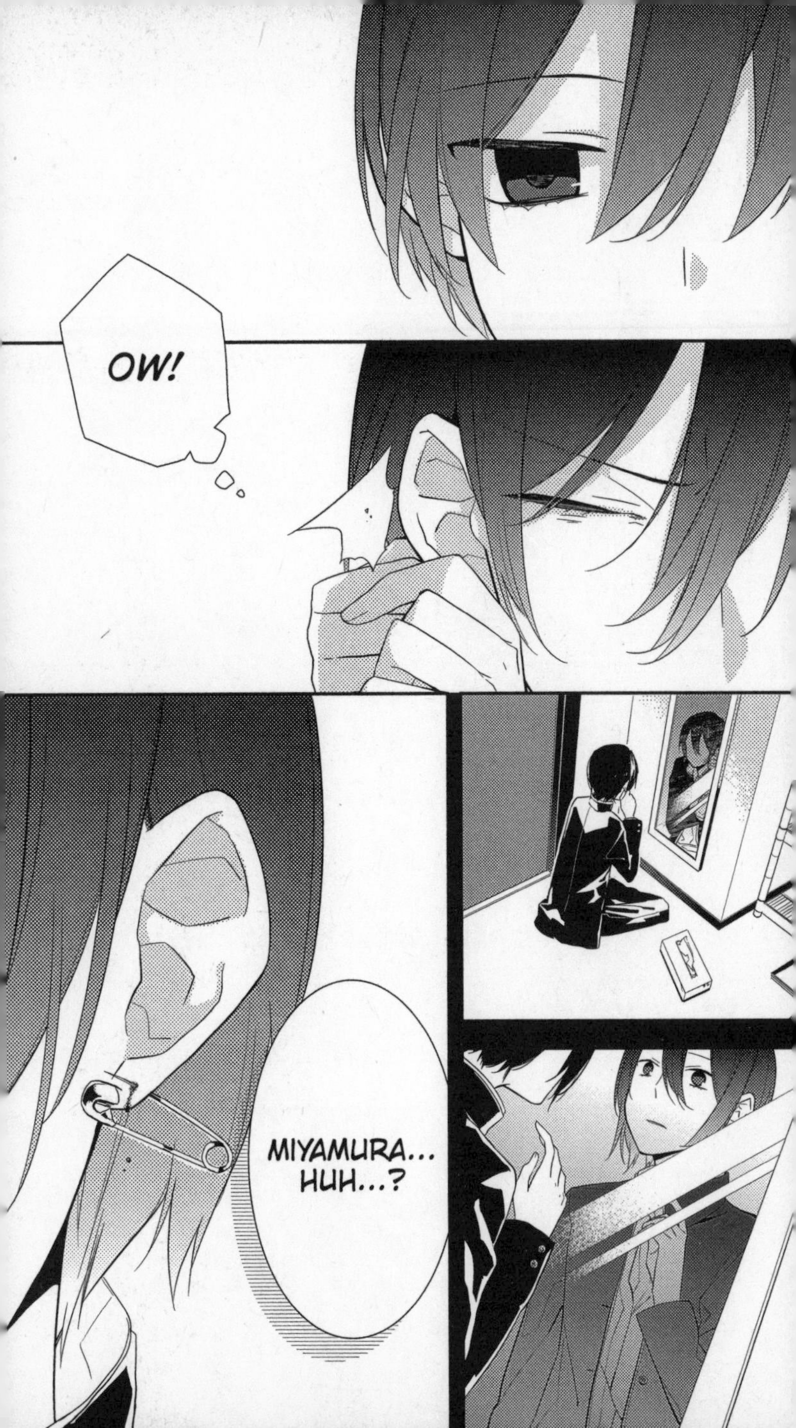
OW!
MIYAMURA... HUH...?

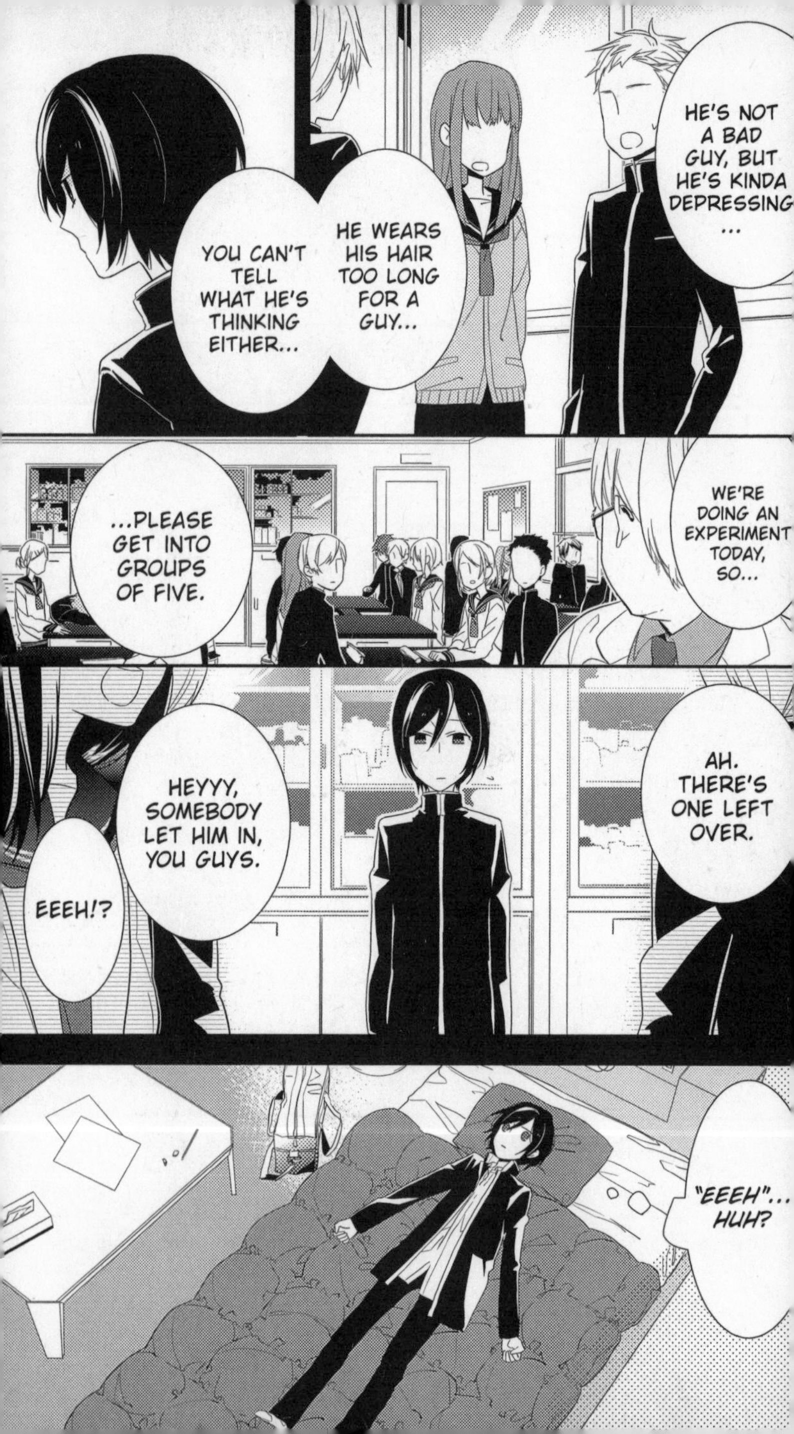
HE'S NOT A BAD GUY, BUT HE'S KINDA DEPRESSING...
HE WEARS HIS HAIR TOO LONG FOR A GUY...
YOU CAN'T TELL WHAT HE'S THINKING EITHER...
WE'RE DOING AN EXPERIMENT TODAY, SO...
...PLEASE GET INTO GROUPS OF FIVE.
AH. THERE'S ONE LEFT OVER.
HEYYY, SOMEBODY LET HIM IN, YOU GUYS.
EEEH!?
"EEEH"... HUH?

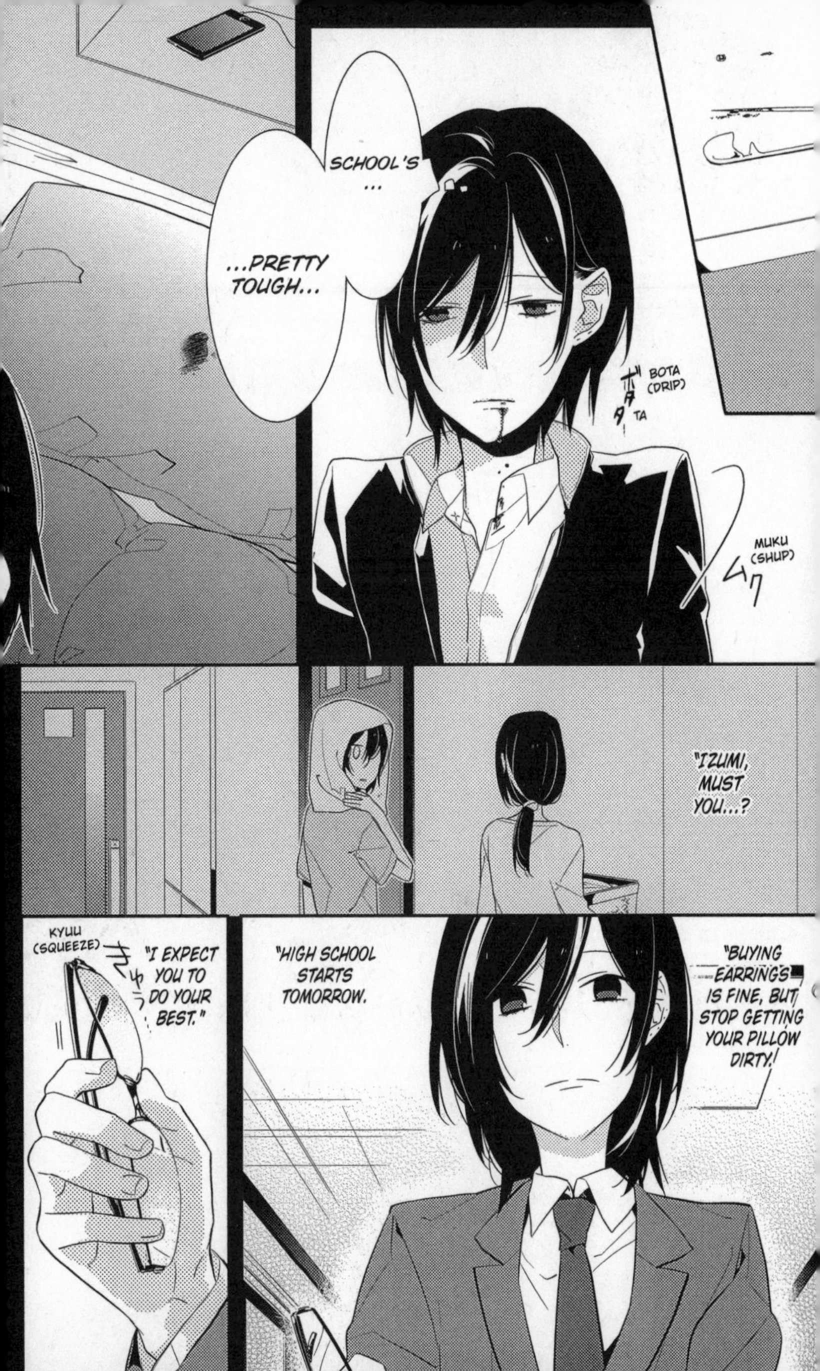
SCHOOL'S ...
...PRETTY TOUGH...
BOTA (DRIP)
TA
MUKU (SHUP)
"IZUMI, MUST YOU...?
"BUYING EARRINGS IS FINE, BUT STOP GETTING YOUR PILLOW DIRTY!
"HIGH SCHOOL STARTS TOMORROW.
"I EXPECT YOU TO DO YOUR BEST."
KYUU (SQUEEZE)

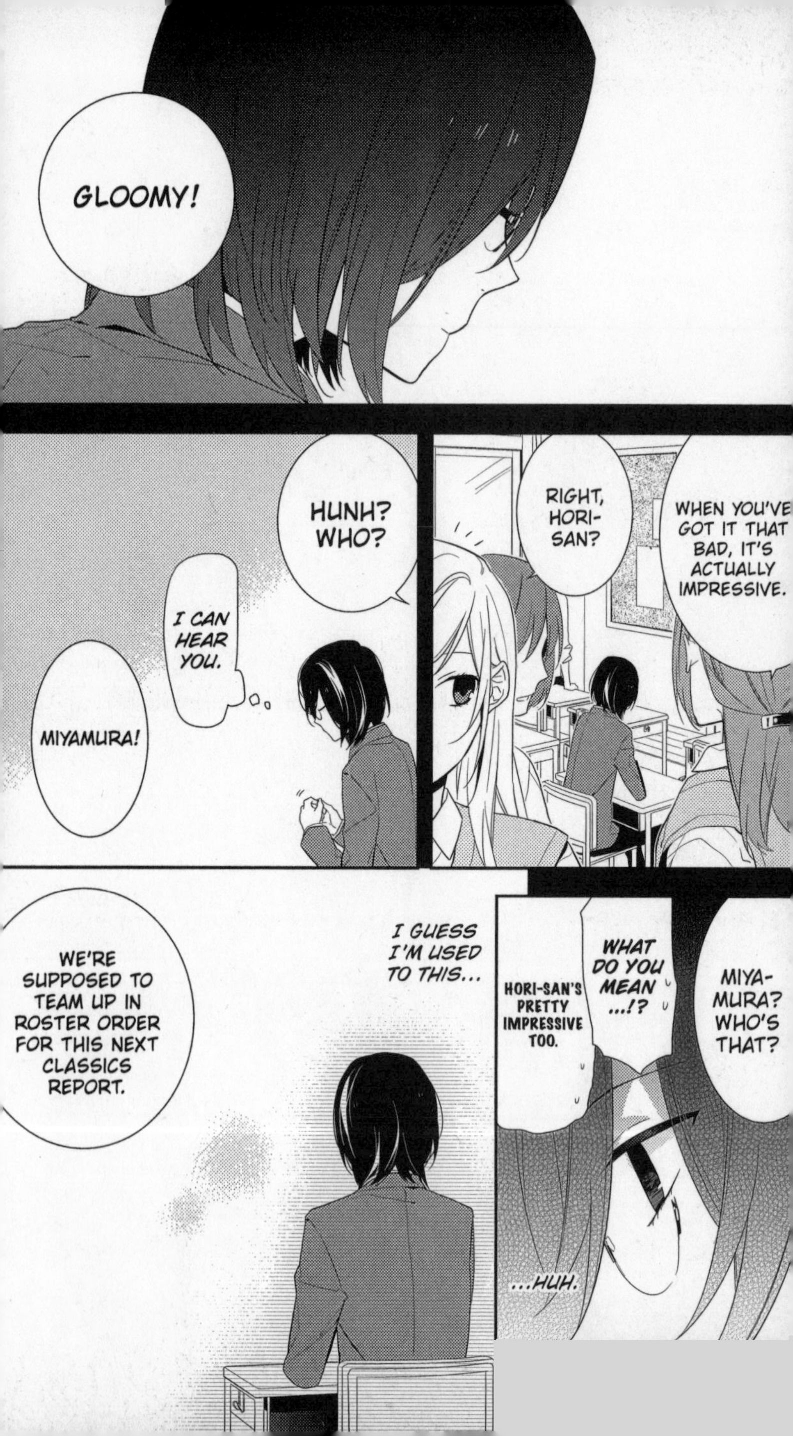
GLOOMY!
WHEN YOU'VE GOT IT THAT BAD, IT'S ACTUALLY IMPRESSIVE.
RIGHT, HORI-SAN?
HUNH? WHO?
I CAN HEAR YOU.
MIYAMURA!
MIYA-MURA? WHO'S THAT?
WHAT DO YOU MEAN ...!?
HORI-SAN'S PRETTY IMPRESSIVE TOO.
...HUH.
I GUESS I'M USED TO THIS...
WE'RE SUPPOSED TO TEAM UP IN ROSTER ORDER FOR THIS NEXT CLASSICS REPORT.

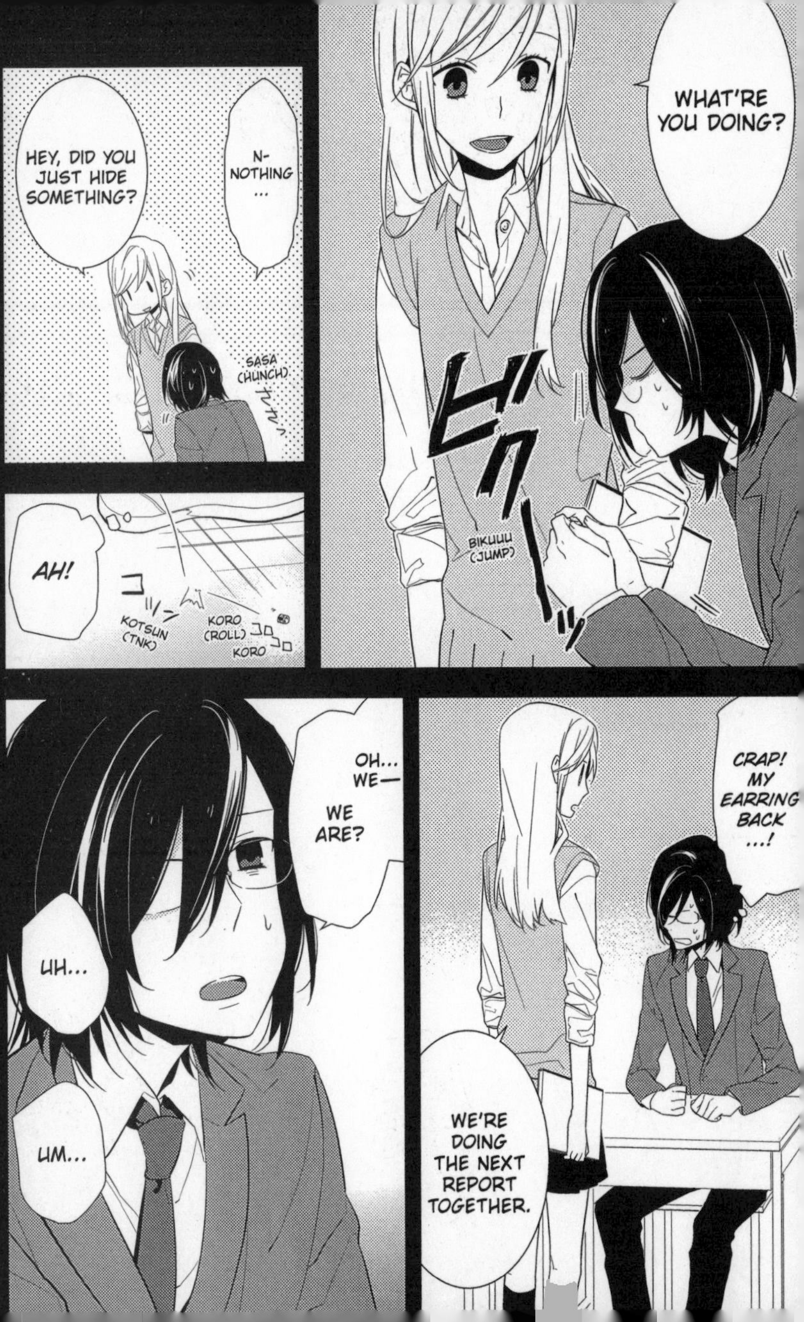
WHAT'RE YOU DOING?
BIKUUU (JUMP)
N-NOTHING ...
HEY, DID YOU JUST HIDE SOMETHING?
SASA (HUNCH)
AH!
KORO (ROLL)
KORO
KOTSUN (TNK)
CRAP! MY EARRING BACK ...!
WE'RE DOING THE NEXT REPORT TOGETHER.
OH... WE—
WE ARE?
UH...
UM...

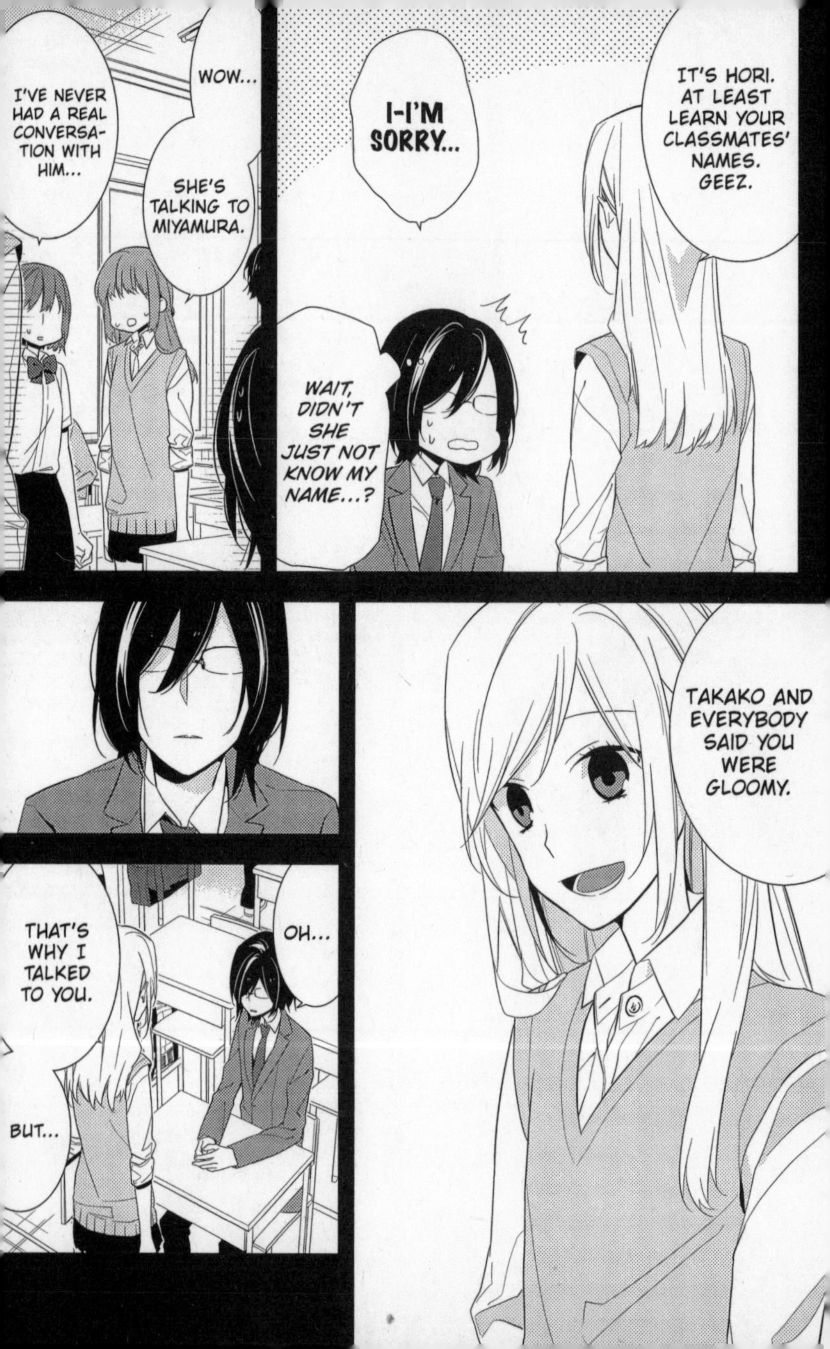
IT'S HORI. AT LEAST LEARN YOUR CLASSMATES' NAMES. GEEZ.
I-I'M SORRY...
WAIT, DIDN'T SHE JUST NOT KNOW MY NAME...?
WOW...
SHE'S TALKING TO MIYAMURA.
I'VE NEVER HAD A REAL CONVERSATION WITH HIM...
TAKAKO AND EVERYBODY SAID YOU WERE GLOOMY.
OH...
THAT'S WHY I TALKED TO YOU.
BUT...

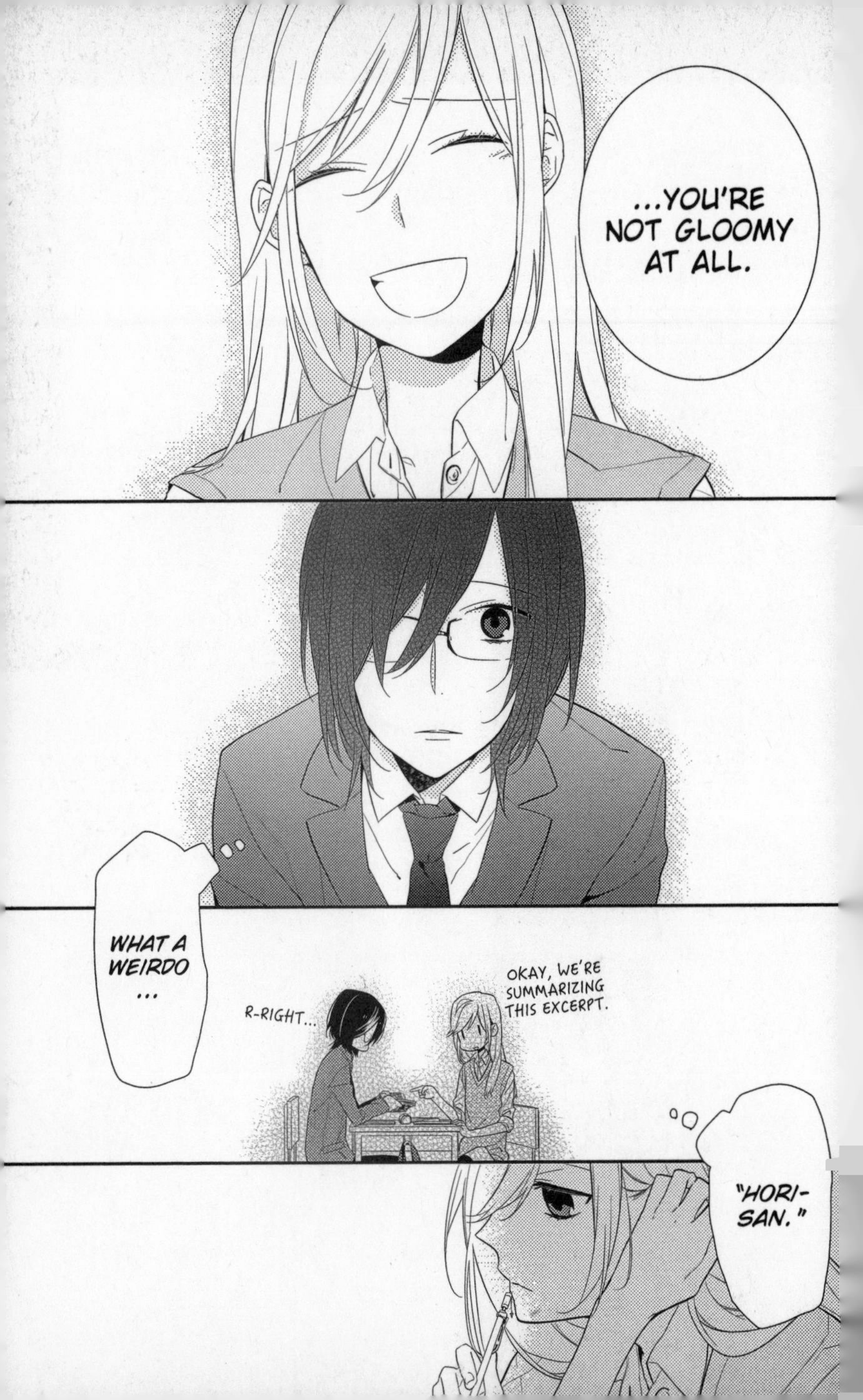
...YOU'RE NOT GLOOMY AT ALL.
OKAY, WE'RE SUMMARIZING THIS EXCERPT.
R-RIGHT...
WHAT A WEIRDO...
"HORI-SAN."

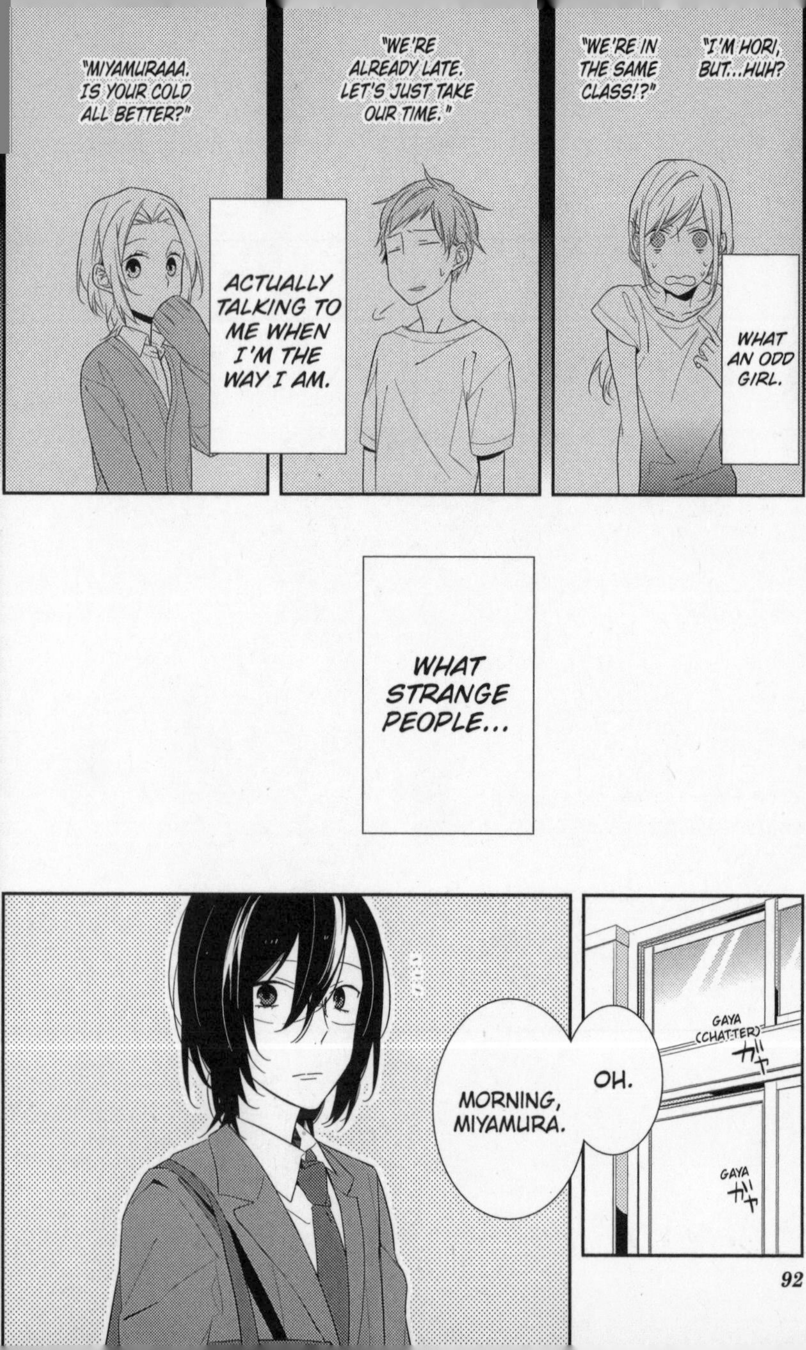
"I'M HORI, BUT...HUH?
"WE'RE IN THE SAME CLASS!?"
WHAT AN ODD GIRL.
"WE'RE ALREADY LATE. LET'S JUST TAKE OUR TIME."
"MIYAMURAAA. IS YOUR COLD ALL BETTER?"
ACTUALLY TALKING TO ME WHEN I'M THE WAY I AM.
WHAT STRANGE PEOPLE...
GAYA (CHAT-TER)
ガヤ
GAYA
ガヤ
OH.
MORNING, MIYAMURA.

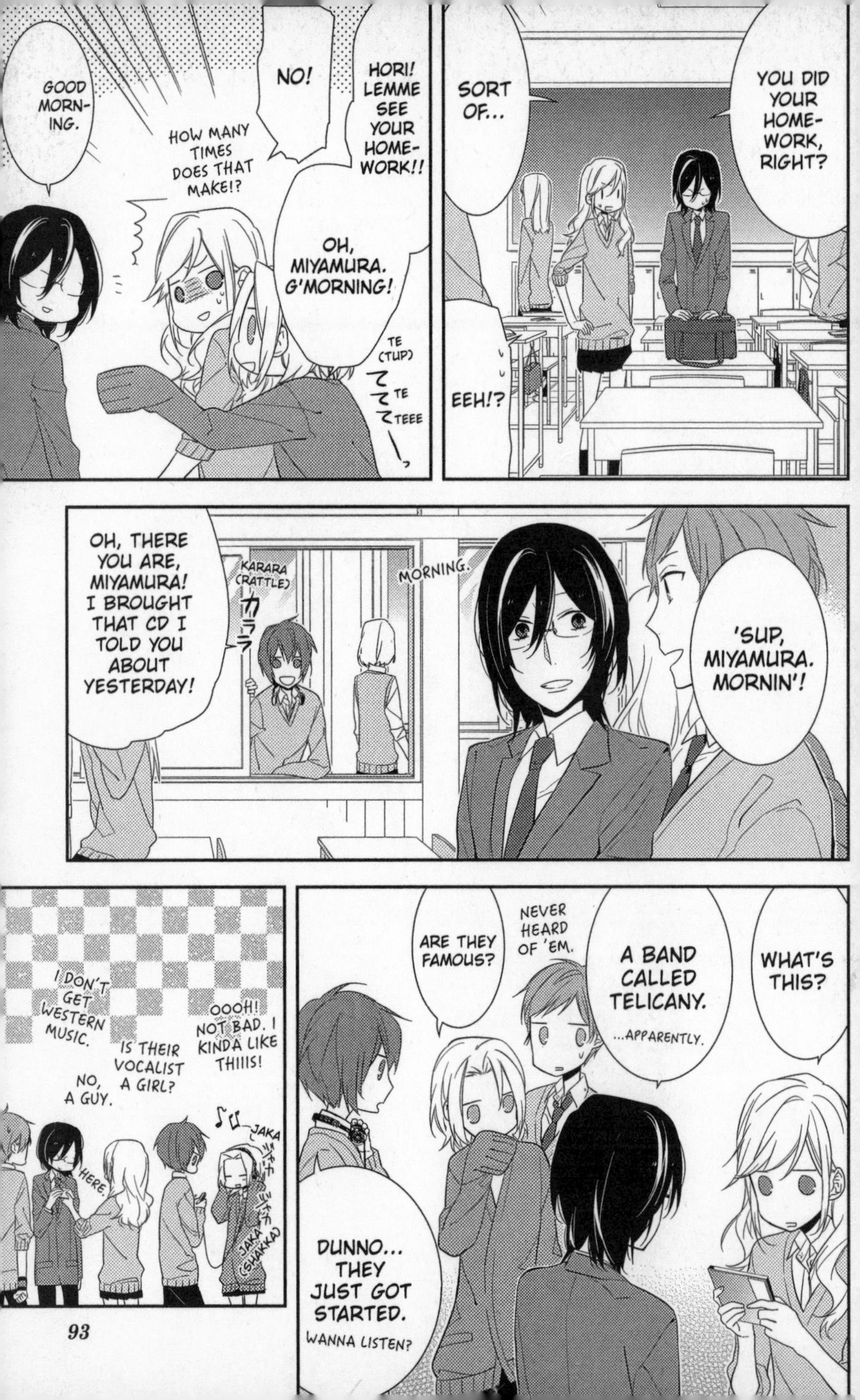
YOU DID YOUR HOMEWORK, RIGHT?
SORT OF...
EEH!?
HORI! LEMME SEE YOUR HOMEWORK!!
NO!
HOW MANY TIMES DOES THAT MAKE!?
GOOD MORNING.
OH, MIYAMURA. G'MORNING!
TE (TUP) TE TEEE
'SUP, MIYAMURA. MORNIN'!
MORNING.
KARARA (RATTLE)
OH, THERE YOU ARE, MIYAMURA! I BROUGHT THAT CD I TOLD YOU ABOUT YESTERDAY!
WHAT'S THIS?
A BAND CALLED TELICANY.
...APPARENTLY.
NEVER HEARD OF 'EM.
ARE THEY FAMOUS?
DUNNO... THEY JUST GOT STARTED.
WANNA LISTEN?
OOOH! NOT BAD. I KINDA LIKE THIIIS!
I DON'T GET WESTERN MUSIC.
IS THEIR VOCALIST A GIRL?
NO, A GUY.
JAKA
JAKA (SHAKKA)
HERE.

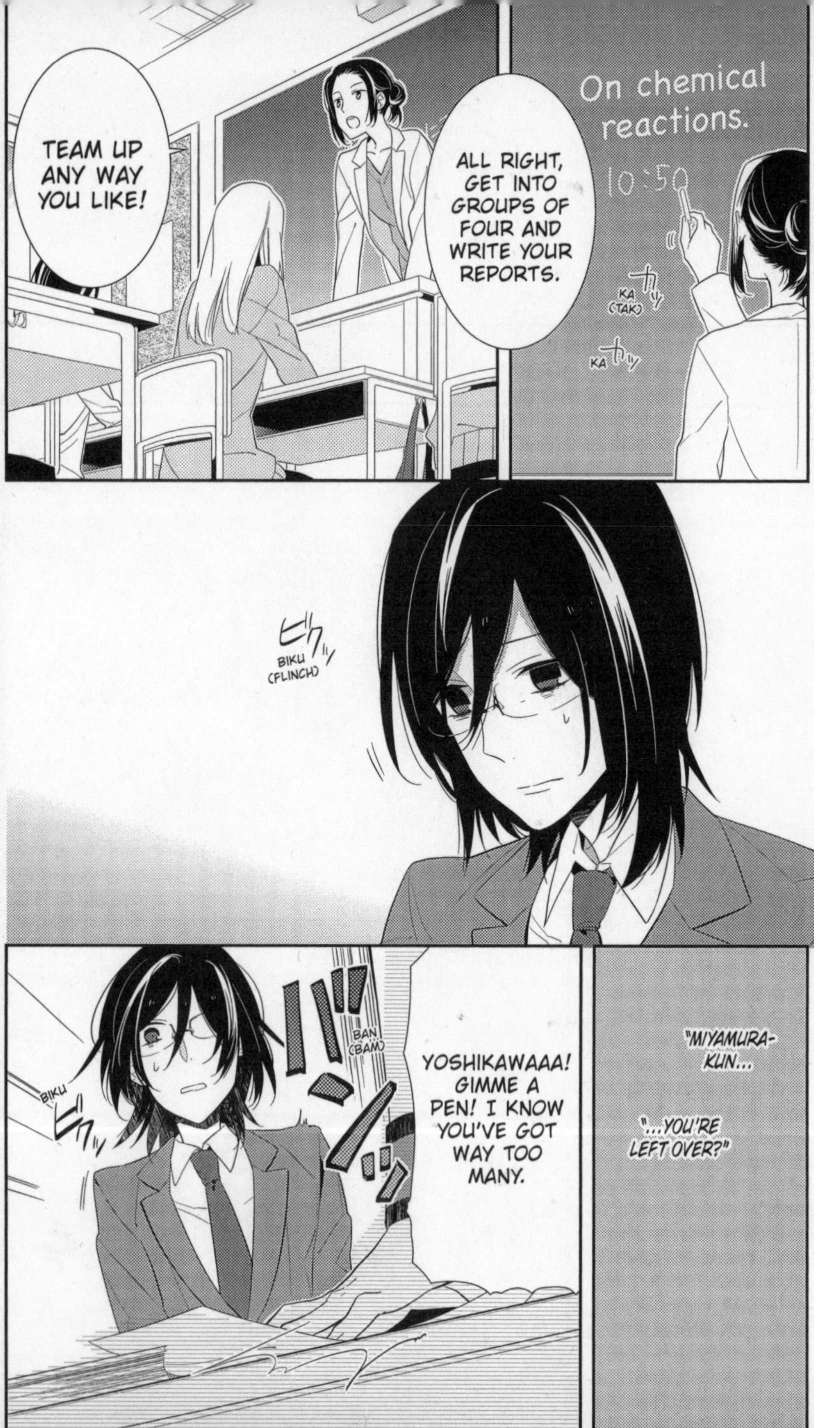
On chemical reactions.
10:50
KA (TAK)
KA
ALL RIGHT, GET INTO GROUPS OF FOUR AND WRITE YOUR REPORTS.
TEAM UP ANY WAY YOU LIKE!
BIKU (FLINCH)
"MIYAMURA-KUN...
"...YOU'RE LEFT OVER?"
YOSHIKAWAAA! GIMME A PEN! I KNOW YOU'VE GOT WAY TOO MANY.
BAN (BAM)
BIKU

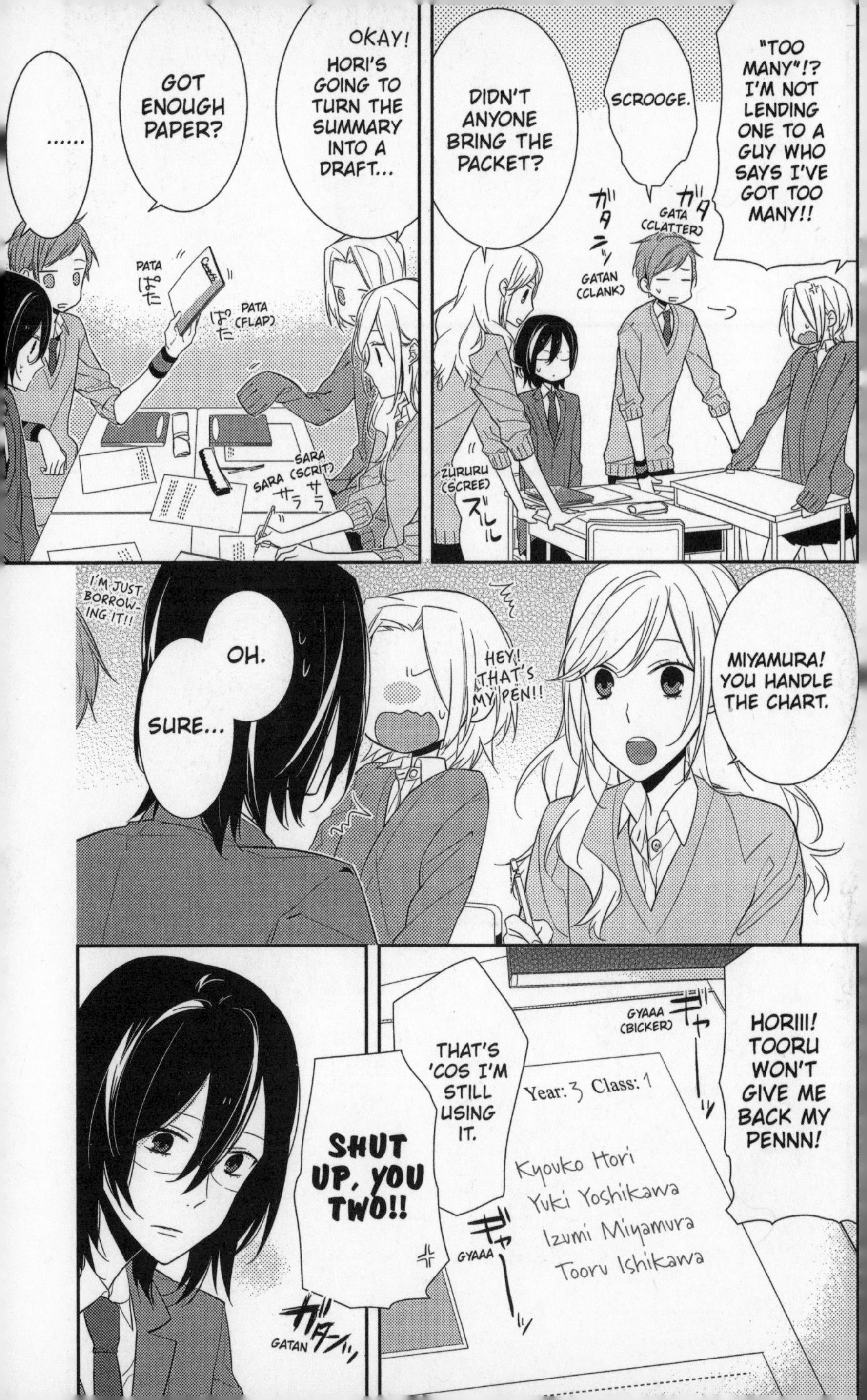
"TOO MANY"!? I'M NOT LENDING ONE TO A GUY WHO SAYS I'VE GOT TOO MANY!!
GATA (CLATTER)
SCROOGE.
DIDN'T ANYONE BRING THE PACKET?
GATAN (CLANK)
ZURURU (SCREE)
OKAY! HORI'S GOING TO TURN THE SUMMARY INTO A DRAFT...
GOT ENOUGH PAPER?
......
PATA (FLAP)
PATA
SARA (SCRIT)
SARA
MIYAMURA! YOU HANDLE THE CHART.
HEY! THAT'S MY PEN!!
I'M JUST BORROWING IT!!
OH.
SURE...
HORIII! TOORU WON'T GIVE ME BACK MY PENNN!
GYAAA (BICKER)
THAT'S 'COS I'M STILL USING IT.
Year: 3 Class: 1
Kyouko Hori
Yuki Yoshikawa
Izumi Miyamura
Tooru Ishikawa
SHUT UP, YOU TWO!!
GYAAA
GATAN

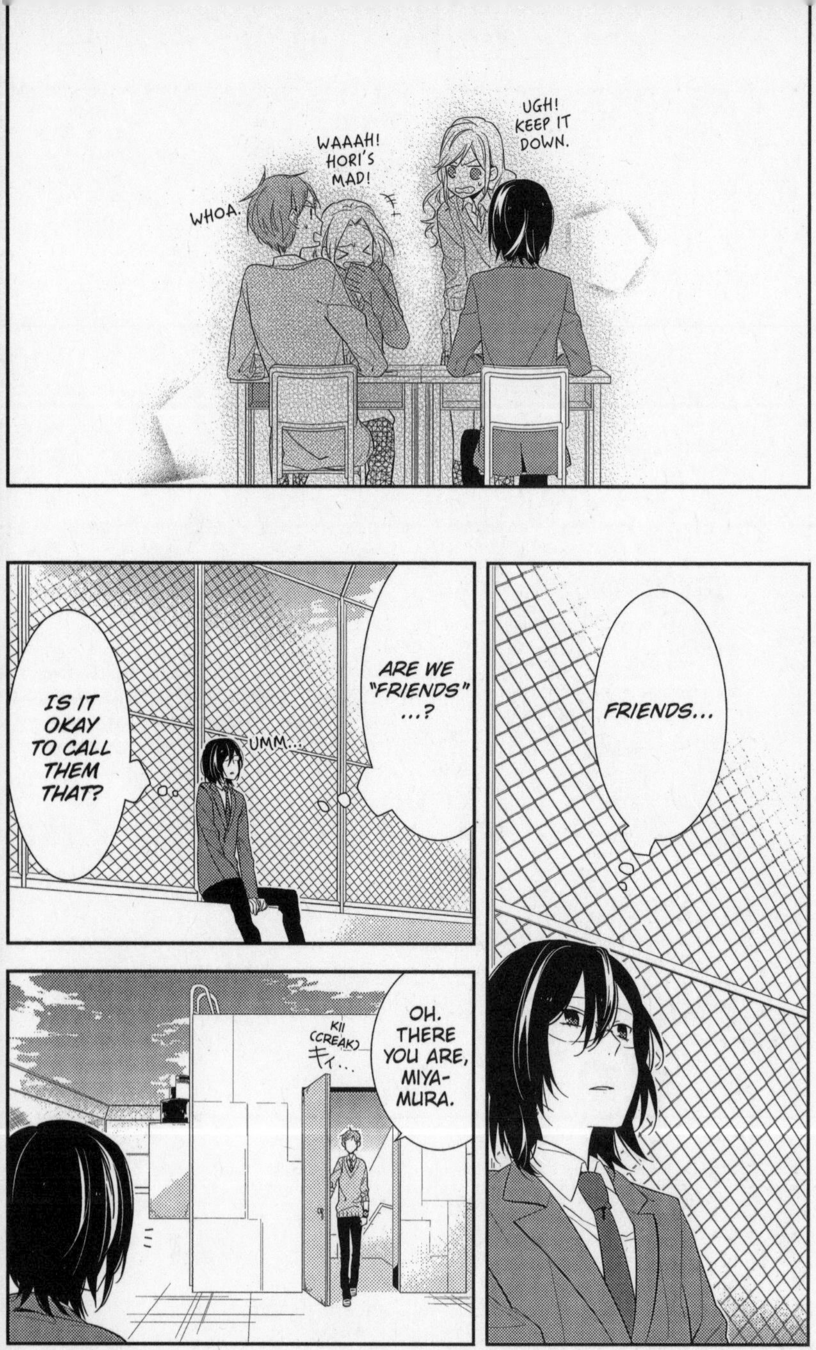
UGH! KEEP IT DOWN.
WAAAH! HORI'S MAD!
WHOA.
FRIENDS...
ARE WE "FRIENDS" ...?
UMM...
IS IT OKAY TO CALL THEM THAT?
OH. THERE YOU ARE, MIYA-MURA.
KII (CREAK)
キィ…

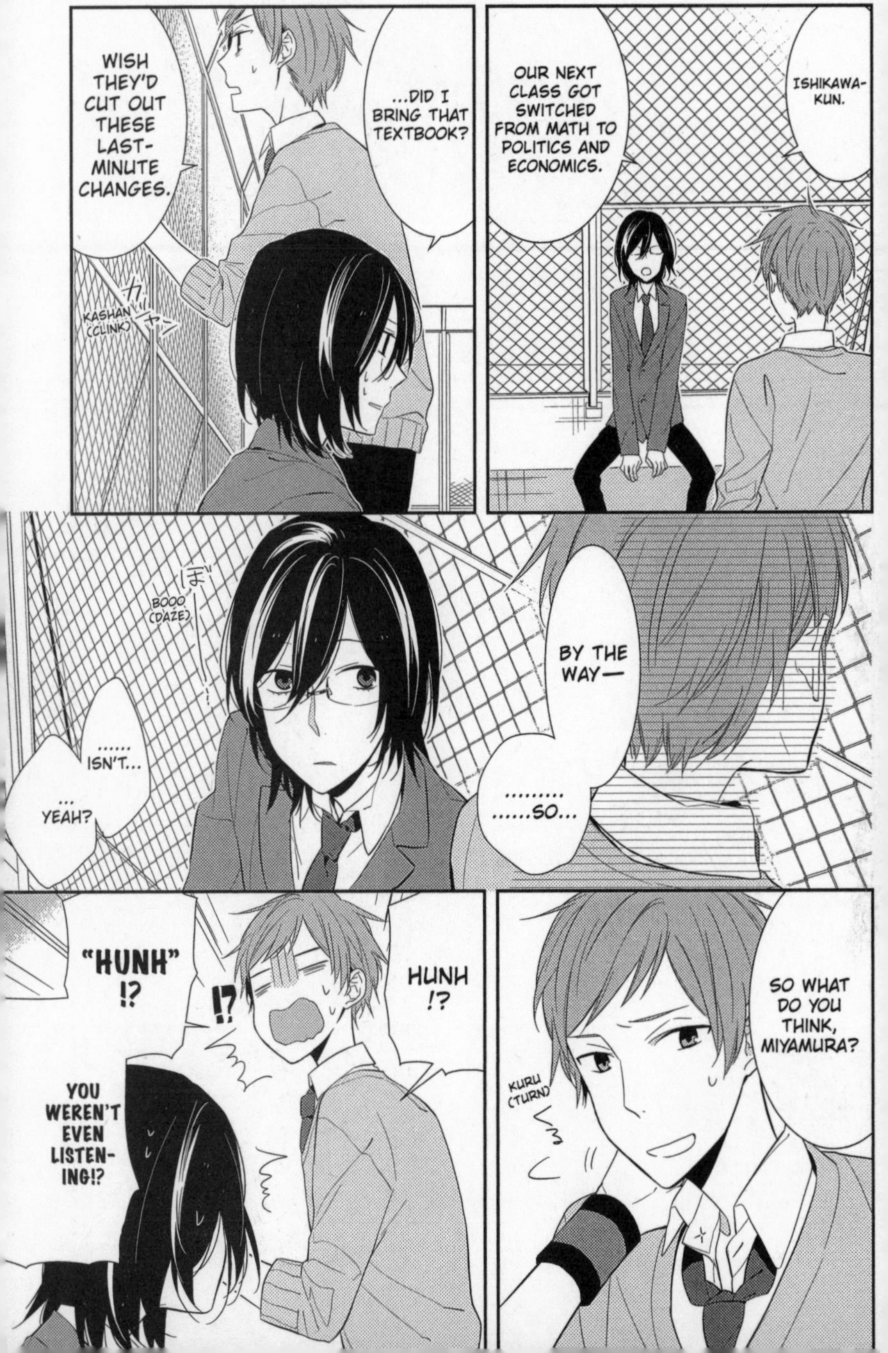
ISHIKAWA-KUN.
OUR NEXT CLASS GOT SWITCHED FROM MATH TO POLITICS AND ECONOMICS.
...DID I BRING THAT TEXTBOOK?
WISH THEY'D CUT OUT THESE LAST-MINUTE CHANGES.
KASHAN (CLINK)
BY THE WAY—
....SO...
BOOO (DAZE)
...... ISN'T...
... YEAH?
SO WHAT DO YOU THINK, MIYAMURA?
KURU (TURN)
HUNH !?
!?
"HUNH" !?
YOU WEREN'T EVEN LISTENING!?

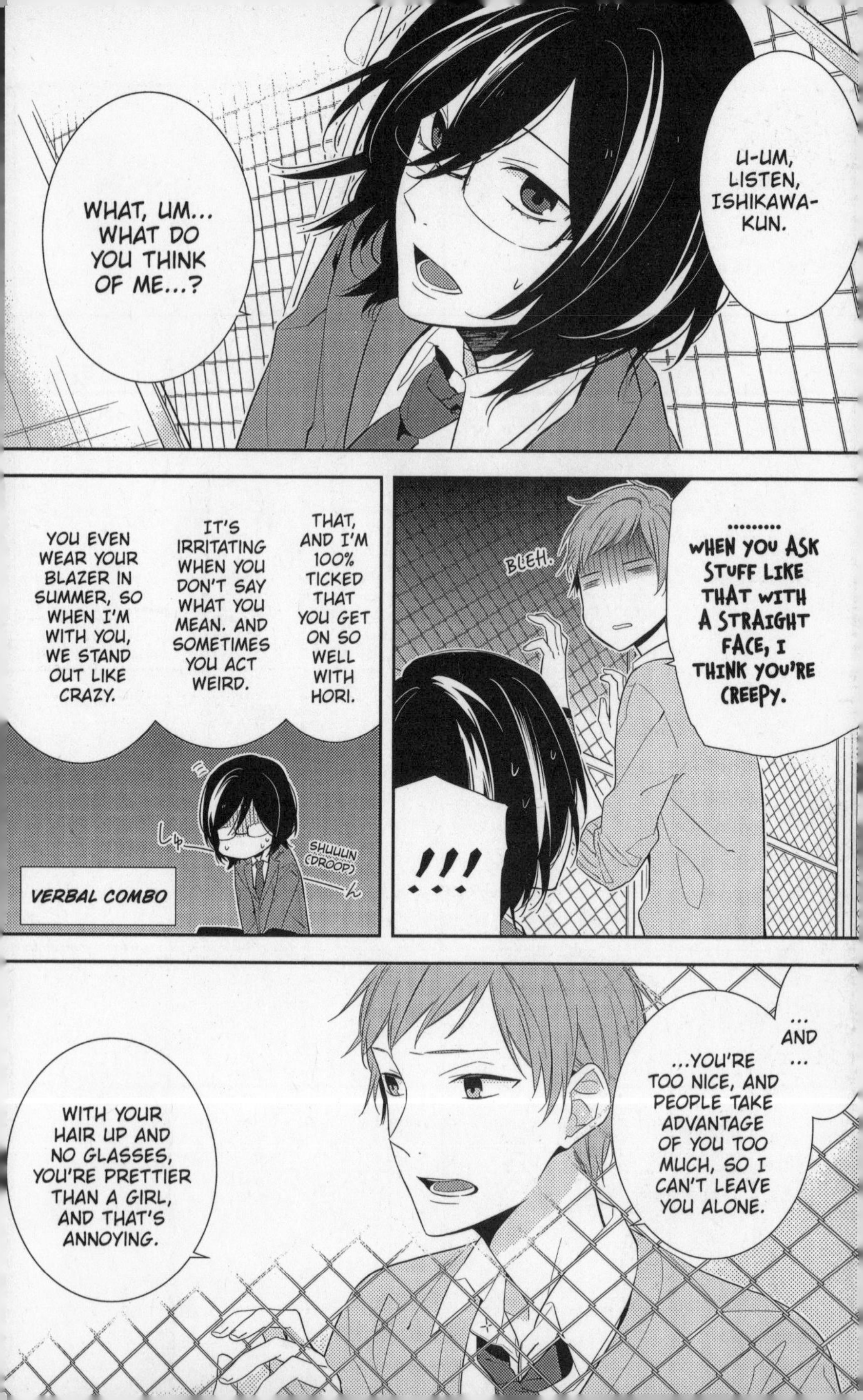

U-UM, LISTEN, ISHIKAWA-KUN.
WHAT, UM... WHAT DO YOU THINK OF ME...?
.... WHEN YOU ASK STUFF LIKE THAT WITH A STRAIGHT FACE, I THINK YOU'RE CREEPY.
BLEH.
!!!
THAT, AND I'M 100% TICKED THAT YOU GET ON SO WELL WITH HORI.
IT'S IRRITATING WHEN YOU DON'T SAY WHAT YOU MEAN. AND SOMETIMES YOU ACT WEIRD.
YOU EVEN WEAR YOUR BLAZER IN SUMMER, SO WHEN I'M WITH YOU, WE STAND OUT LIKE CRAZY.
SHUUUN (DROOP)
VERBAL COMBO
... AND ...
...YOU'RE TOO NICE, AND PEOPLE TAKE ADVANTAGE OF YOU TOO MUCH, SO I CAN'T LEAVE YOU ALONE.
WITH YOUR HAIR UP AND NO GLASSES, YOU'RE PRETTIER THAN A GIRL, AND THAT'S ANNOYING.

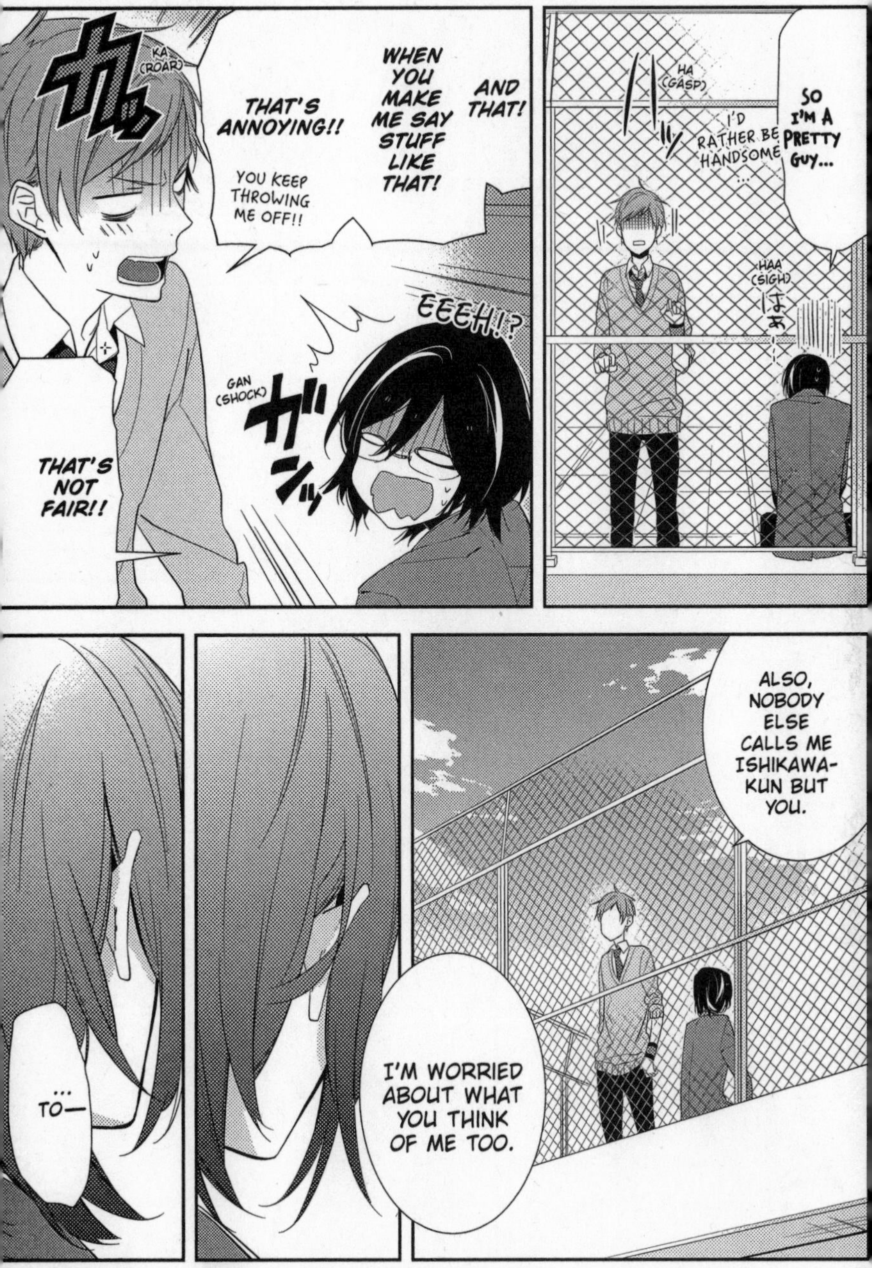

SO I'M A PRETTY GUY...
HA (GASP)
I'D RATHER BE HANDSOME...
HAA (SIGH)
はぁ…
AND THAT!
WHEN YOU MAKE ME SAY STUFF LIKE THAT!
THAT'S ANNOYING!!
KA (ROAR)
YOU KEEP THROWING ME OFF!!
EEEH!?
GAN (SHOCK)
THAT'S NOT FAIR!!
ALSO, NOBODY ELSE CALLS ME ISHIKAWA-KUN BUT YOU.
I'M WORRIED ABOUT WHAT YOU THINK OF ME TOO.
...TO—

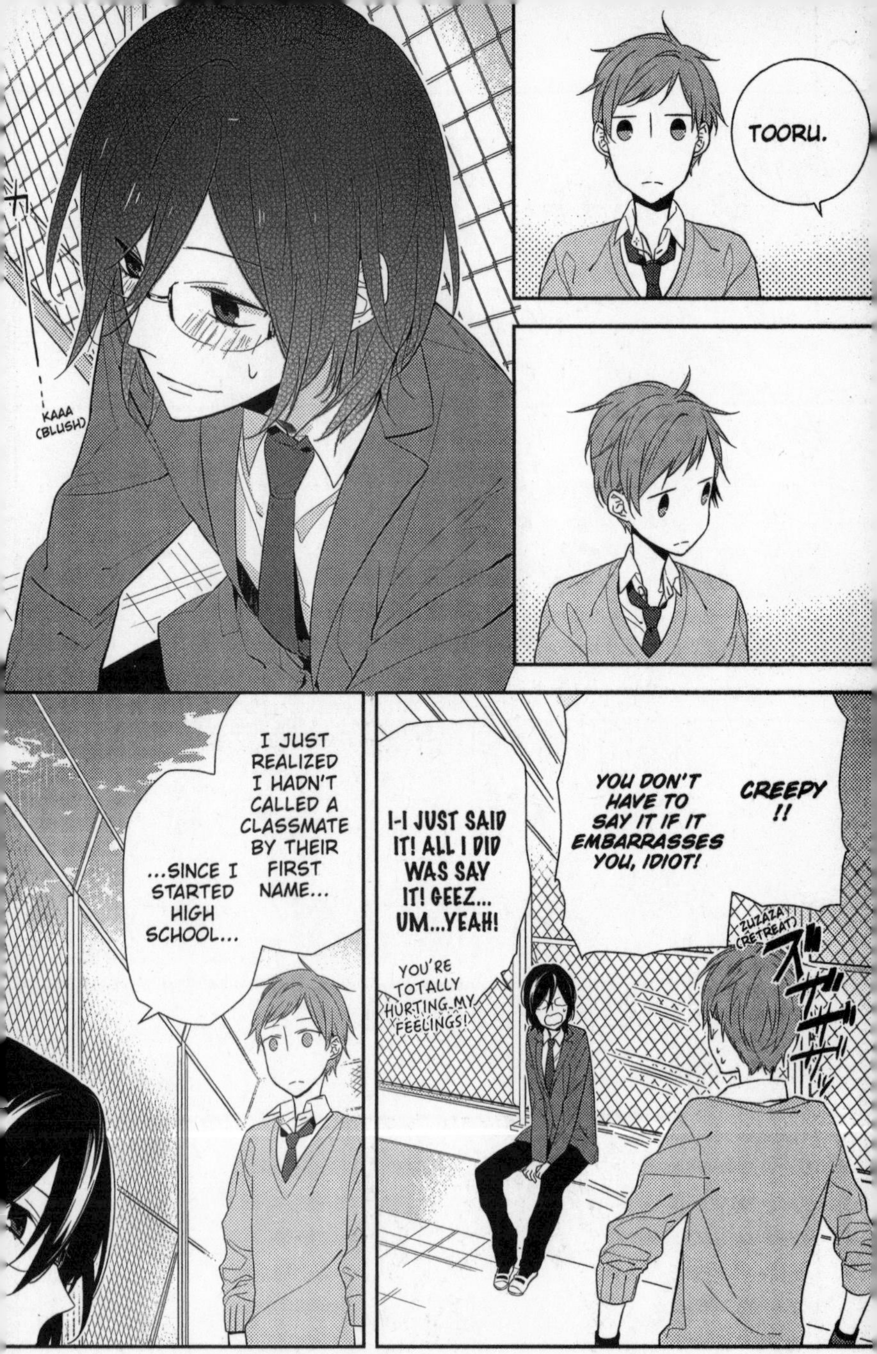
TOORU.
KAAA (BLUSH)
CREEPY !!
YOU DON'T HAVE TO SAY IT IF IT EMBARRASSES YOU, IDIOT!
ZUZAZA (RETREAT)
I-I JUST SAID IT! ALL I DID WAS SAY IT! GEEZ... UM...YEAH!
YOU'RE TOTALLY HURTING MY FEELINGS!
I JUST REALIZED I HADN'T CALLED A CLASSMATE BY THEIR FIRST NAME...
...SINCE I STARTED HIGH SCHOOL...

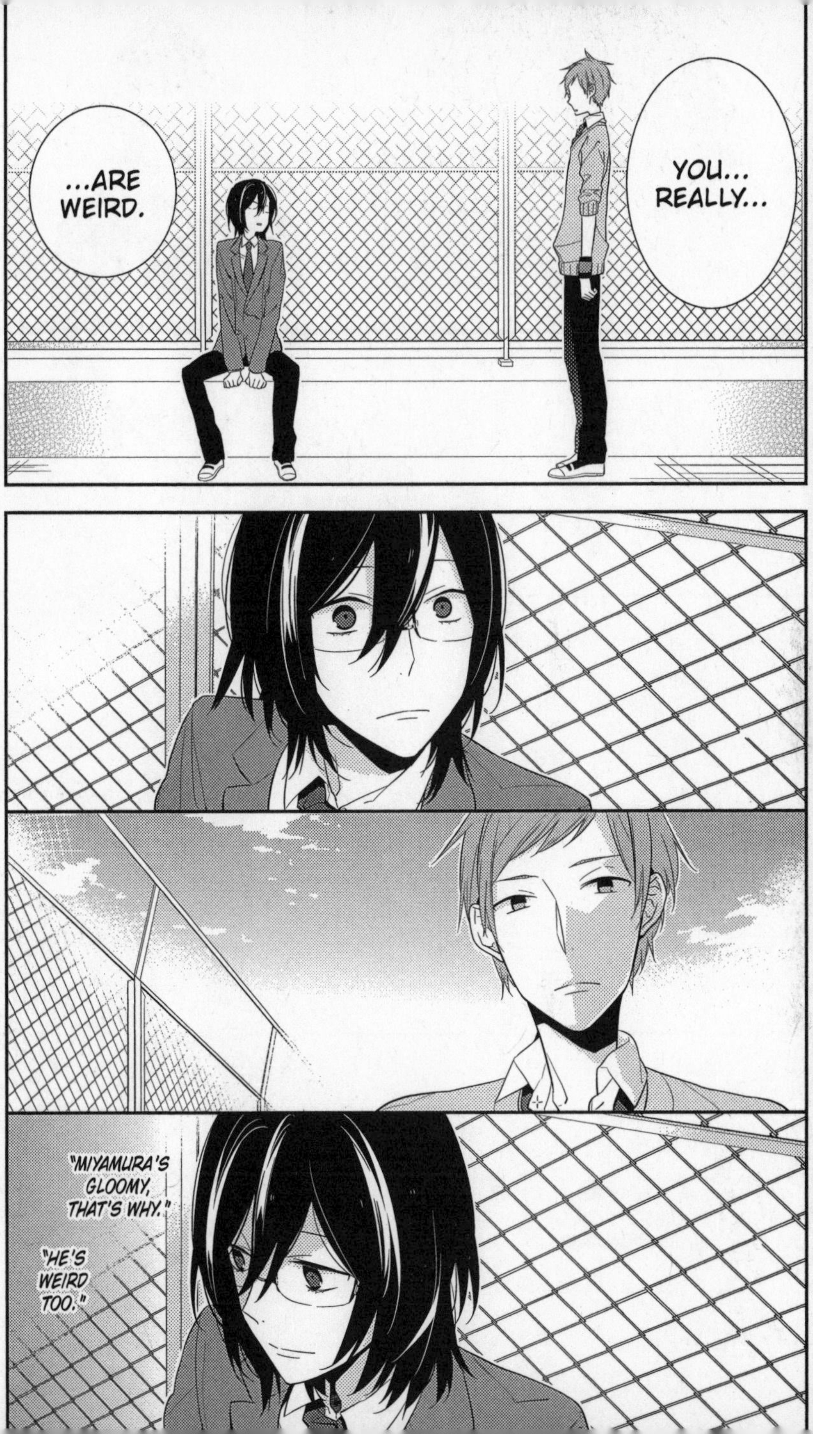
YOU... REALLY...
...ARE WEIRD.
"MIYAMURA'S GLOOMY, THAT'S WHY."
"HE'S WEIRD TOO."

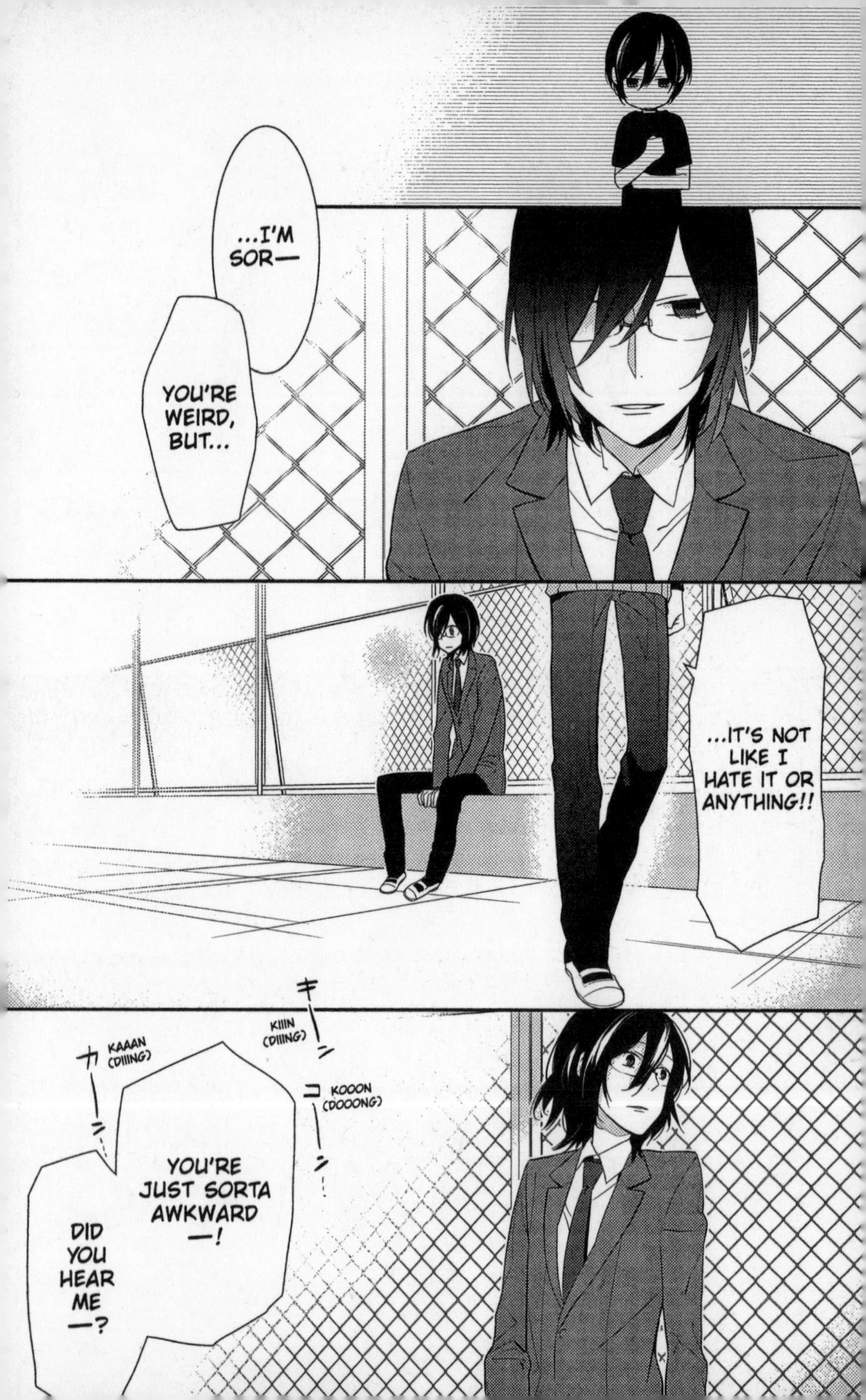
...I'M SOR—
YOU'RE WEIRD, BUT...
...IT'S NOT LIKE I HATE IT OR ANYTHING!!
キーン
KIIIN (DIIING)
カーン
KAAAN (DIIING)
コーン
KOOON (DOOONG)
YOU'RE JUST SORTA AWKWARD—!
DID YOU HEAR ME—?

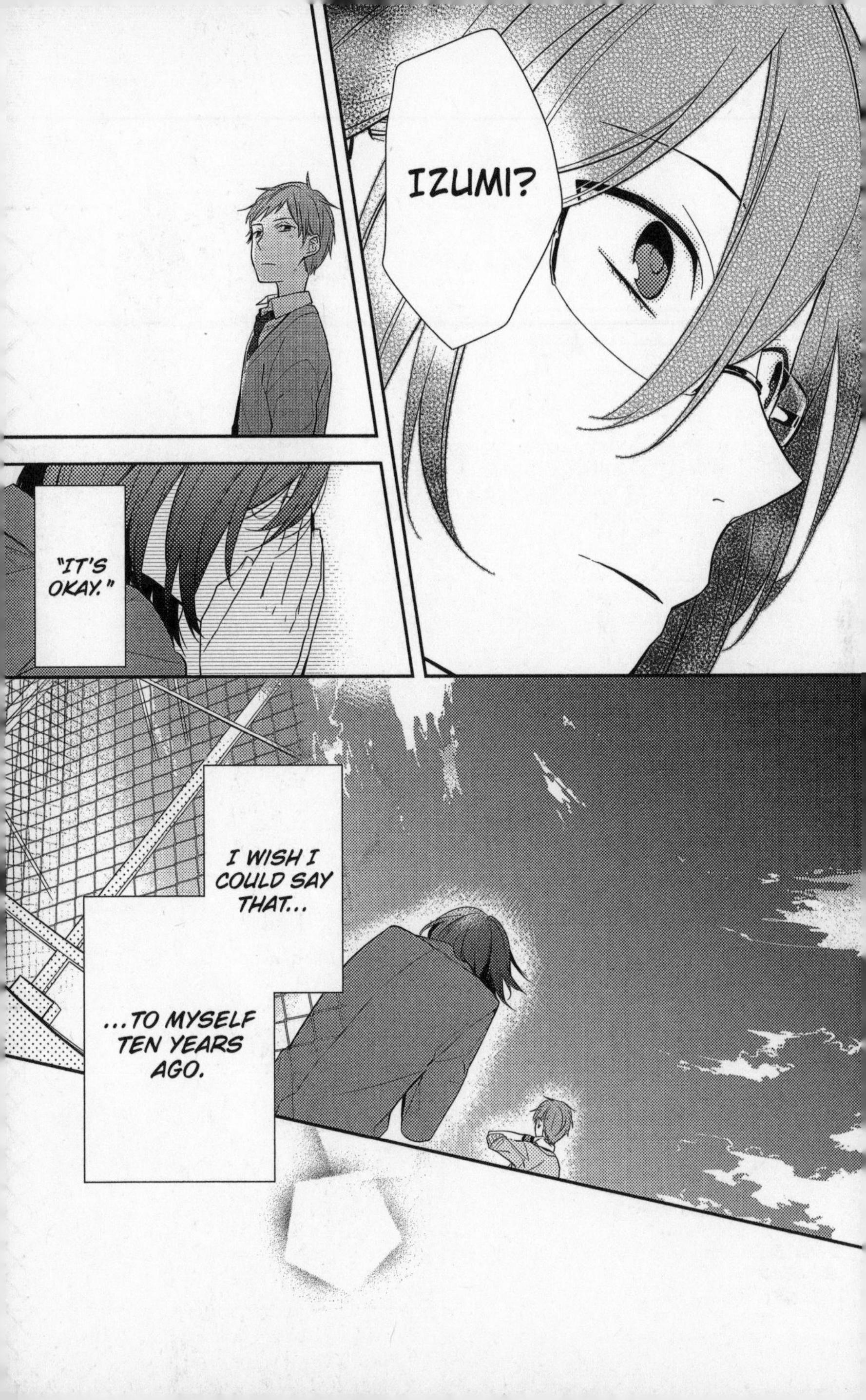
IZUMI?
"IT'S OKAY."
I WISH I COULD SAY THAT...
...TO MYSELF TEN YEARS AGO.

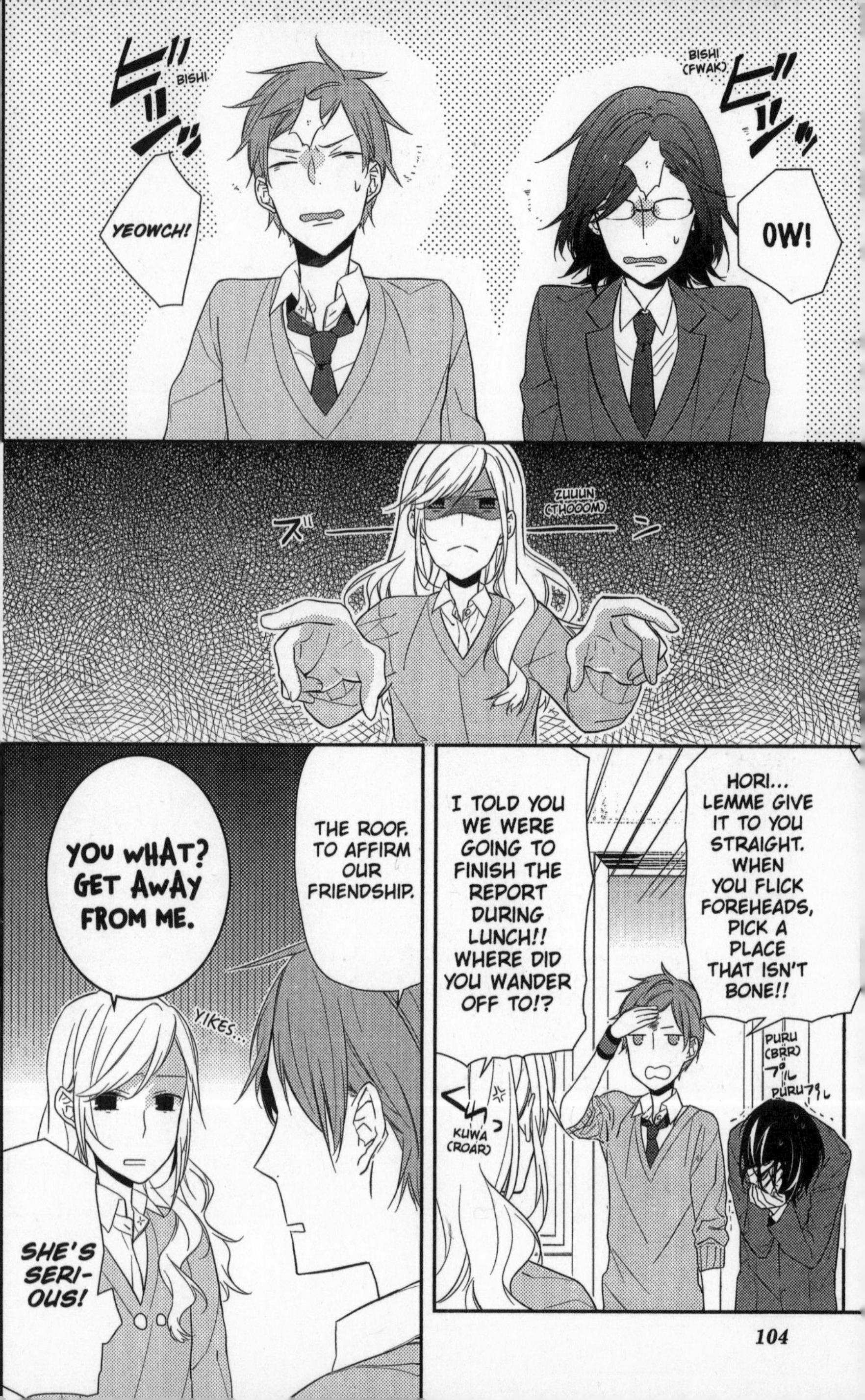
BISHI (FWAK)
OW!
BISHI
YEOWCH!
ZUUUN (THOOOM)
HORI... LEMME GIVE IT TO YOU STRAIGHT. WHEN YOU FLICK FOREHEADS, PICK A PLACE THAT ISN'T BONE!!
I TOLD YOU WE WERE GOING TO FINISH THE REPORT DURING LUNCH!! WHERE DID YOU WANDER OFF TO!?
PURU (BRR) PURU
KUWA (ROAR)
THE ROOF. TO AFFIRM OUR FRIENDSHIP.
YOU WHAT? GET AWAY FROM ME.
YIKES...
SHE'S SERI-OUS!

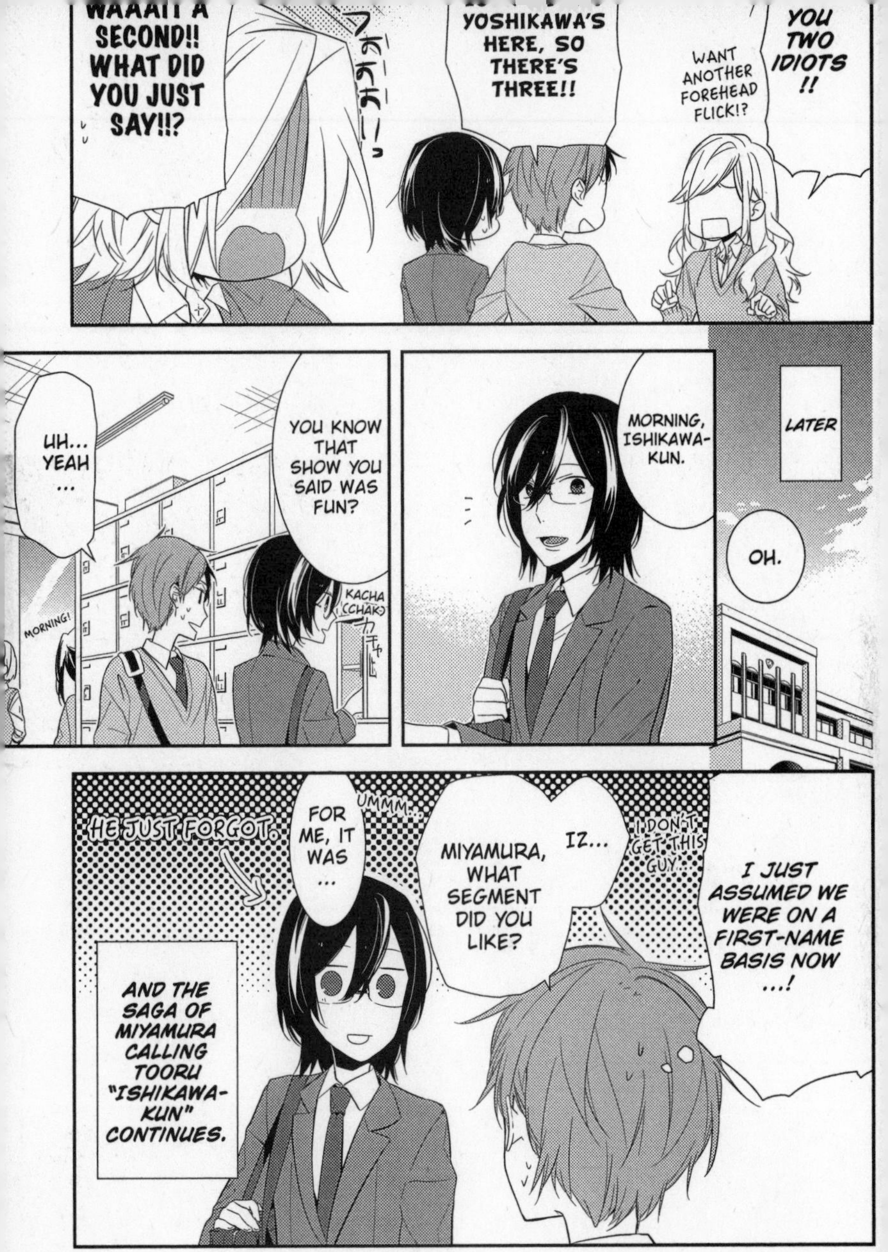
YOU TWO IDIOTS!!
WANT ANOTHER FOREHEAD FLICK!?
YOSHIKAWA'S HERE, SO THERE'S THREE!!
WAAAIT A SECOND!! WHAT DID YOU JUST SAY!!?
LATER
OH.
MORNING, ISHIKAWA-KUN.
YOU KNOW THAT SHOW YOU SAID WAS FUN?
KACHA (CHAK)
MORNING!
UH... YEAH ...
I JUST ASSUMED WE WERE ON A FIRST-NAME BASIS NOW ...!
I DON'T GET THIS GUY...
IZ...
MIYAMURA, WHAT SEGMENT DID YOU LIKE?
UMMM...
FOR ME, IT WAS ...
HE JUST FORGOT.
AND THE SAGA OF MIYAMURA CALLING TOORU "ISHIKAWA-KUN" CONTINUES.

HORIMIYA

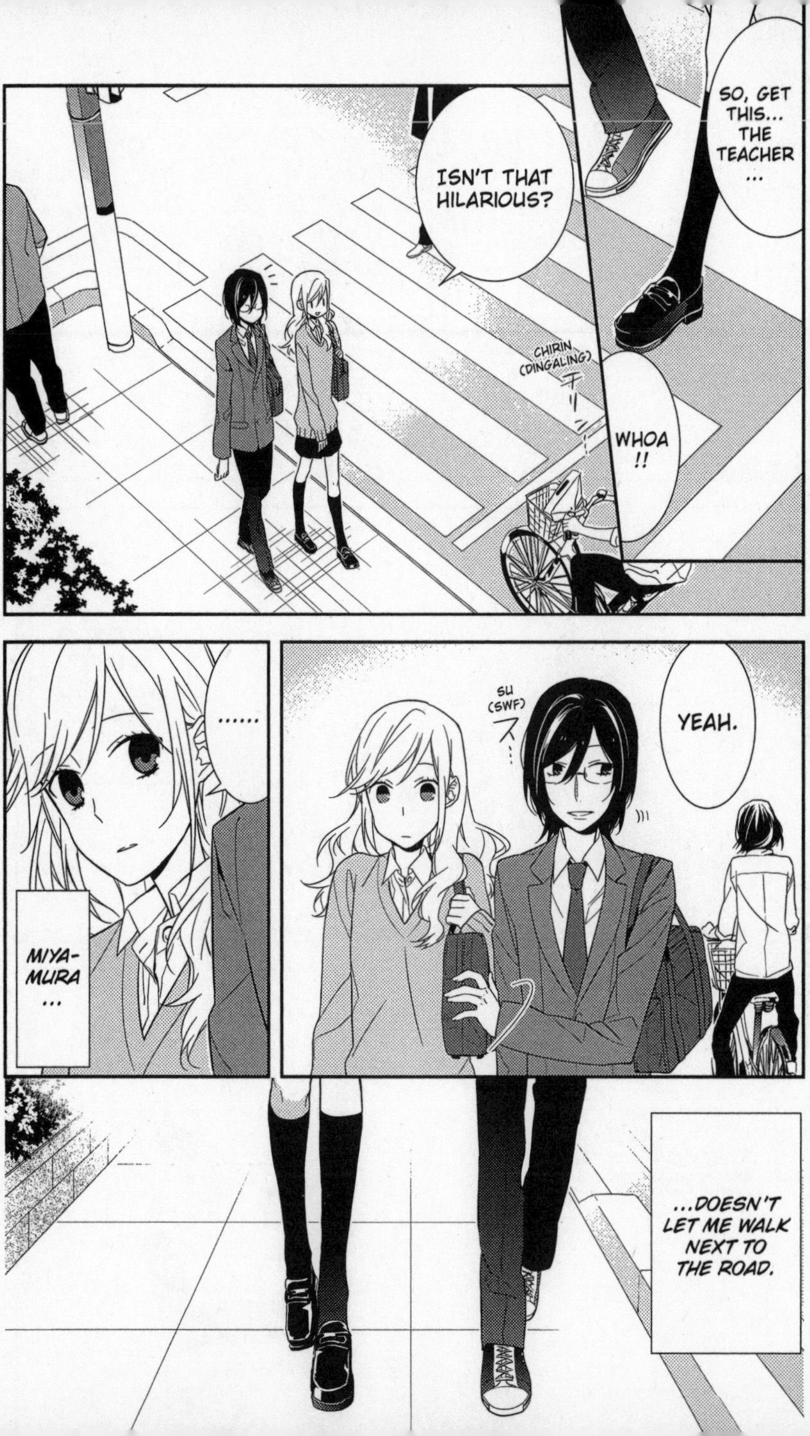
SO, GET THIS... THE TEACHER ...
ISN'T THAT HILARIOUS?
CHIRIN (DINGALING)
WHOA !!
SU (SWF)
YEAH.
......
MIYA-MURA ...
...DOESN'T LET ME WALK NEXT TO THE ROAD.

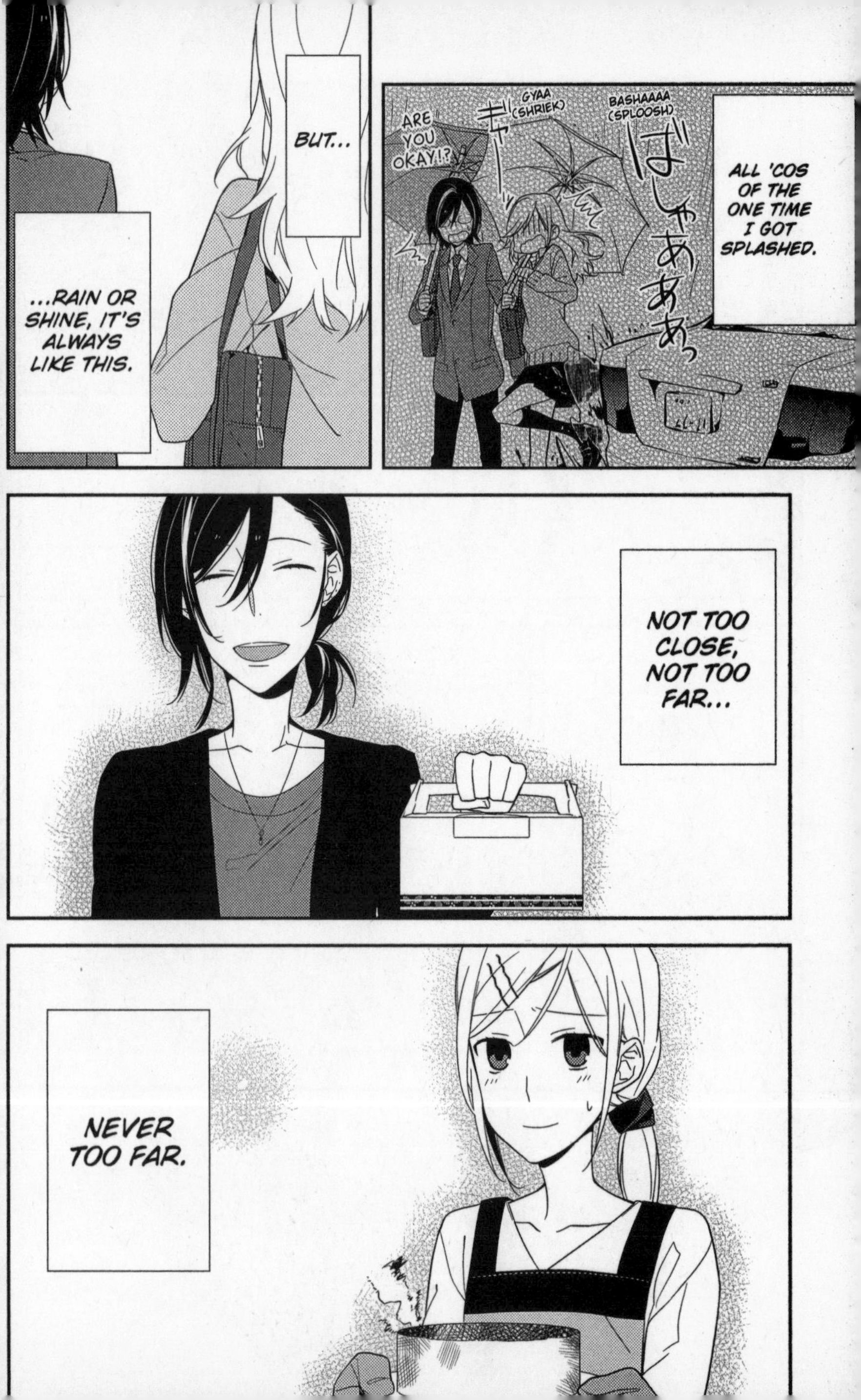
ALL 'COS OF THE ONE TIME I GOT SPLASHED.
BASHAAAA (SPLOOSH)
GYAA (SHRIEK)
ARE YOU OKAY!?
BUT...
...RAIN OR SHINE, IT'S ALWAYS LIKE THIS.
NOT TOO CLOSE, NOT TOO FAR...
NEVER TOO FAR.

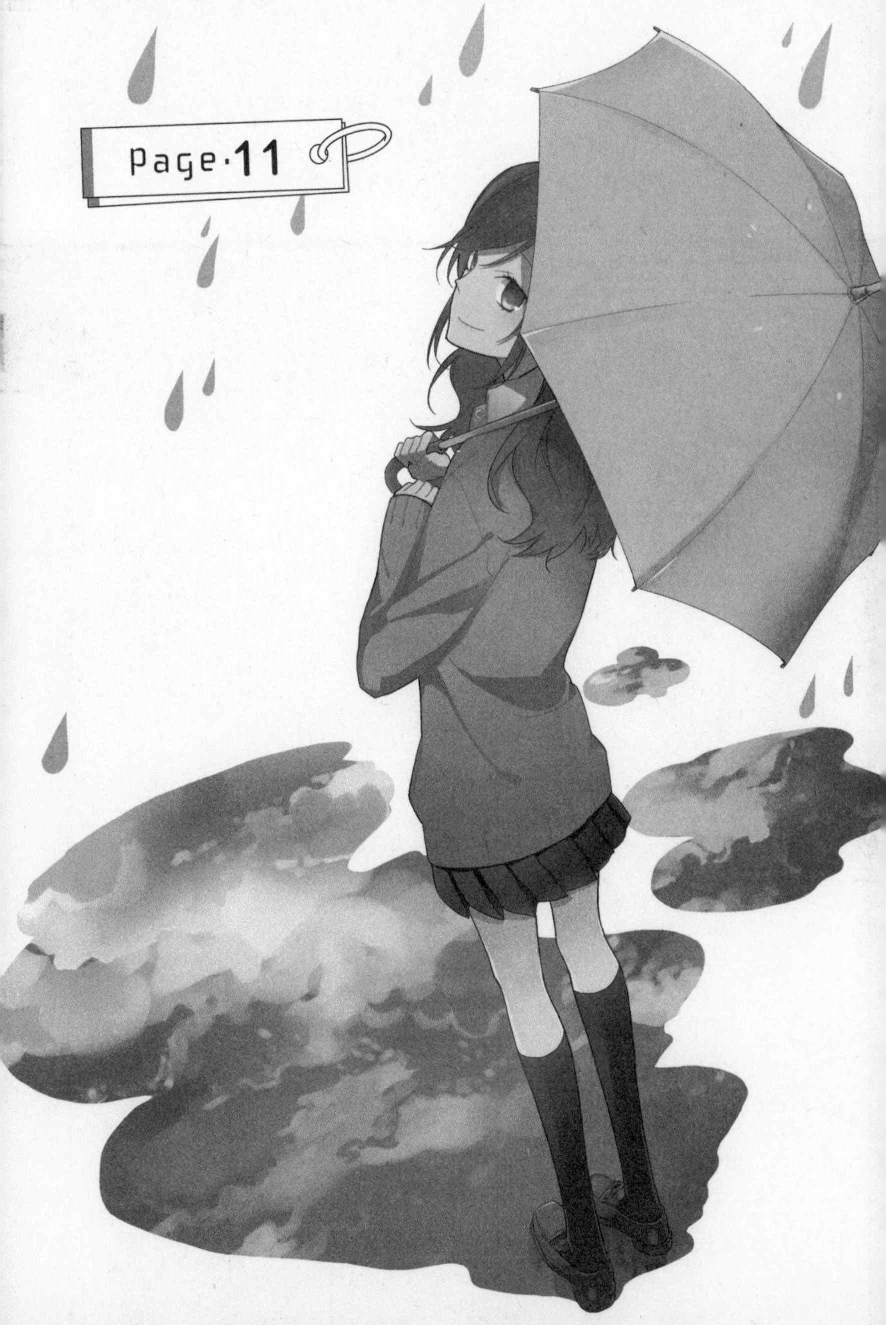
page·11

HORIMIYA

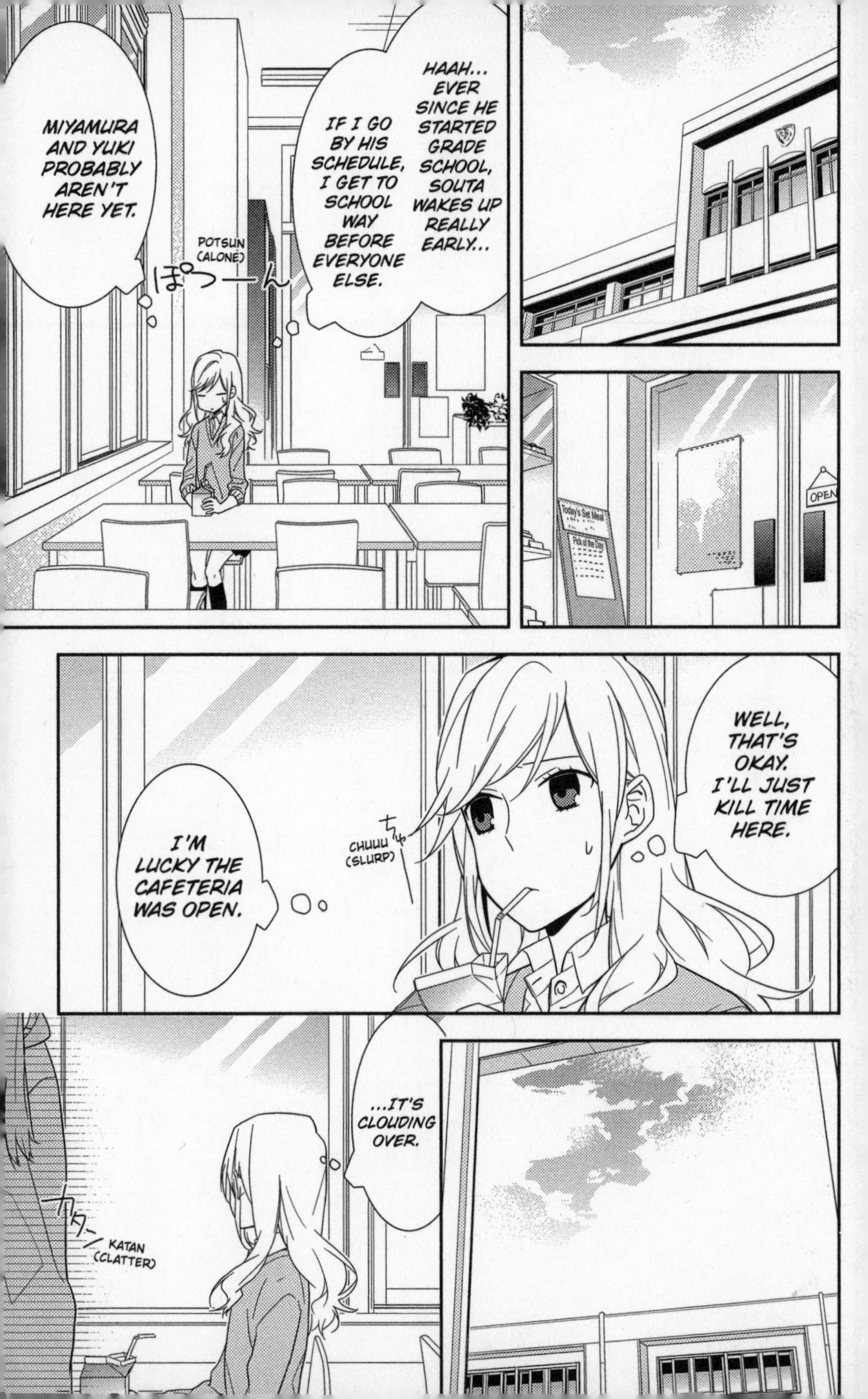
Today's Set Meal
Pick of the Day
OPEN
HAAH... EVER SINCE HE STARTED GRADE SCHOOL, SOUTA WAKES UP REALLY EARLY...
IF I GO BY HIS SCHEDULE, I GET TO SCHOOL WAY BEFORE EVERYONE ELSE.
ぽつーん
POTSUN (ALONE)
MIYAMURA AND YUKI PROBABLY AREN'T HERE YET.
WELL, THAT'S OKAY. I'LL JUST KILL TIME HERE.
CHUUU (SLURP)
I'M LUCKY THE CAFETERIA WAS OPEN.
...IT'S CLOUDING OVER.
KATAN (CLATTER)

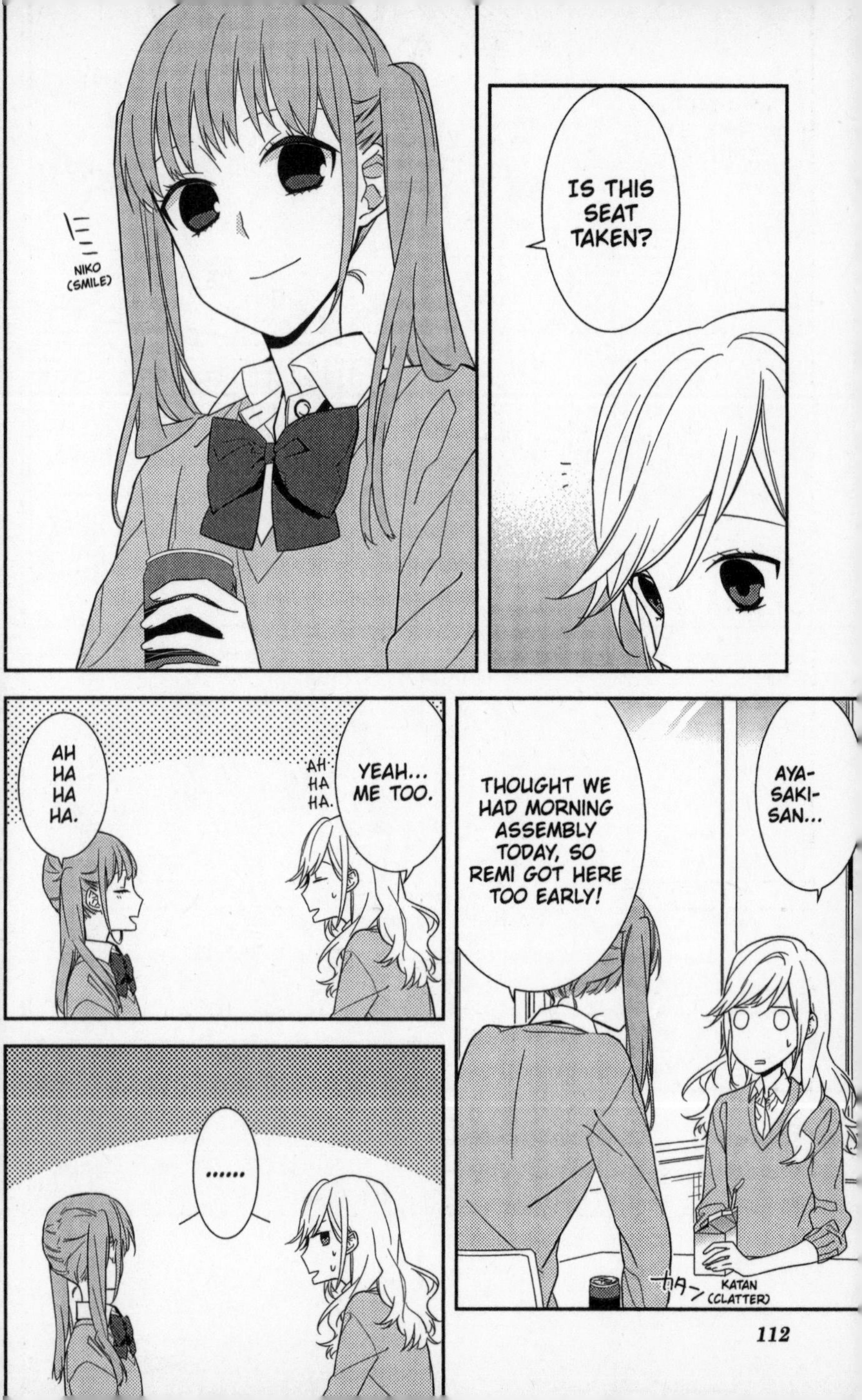
IS THIS SEAT TAKEN?
NIKO (SMILE)
AYA-SAKI-SAN...
THOUGHT WE HAD MORNING ASSEMBLY TODAY, SO REMI GOT HERE TOO EARLY!
KATAN (CLATTER)
YEAH... ME TOO.
AH HA HA.
AH HA HA HA.
......

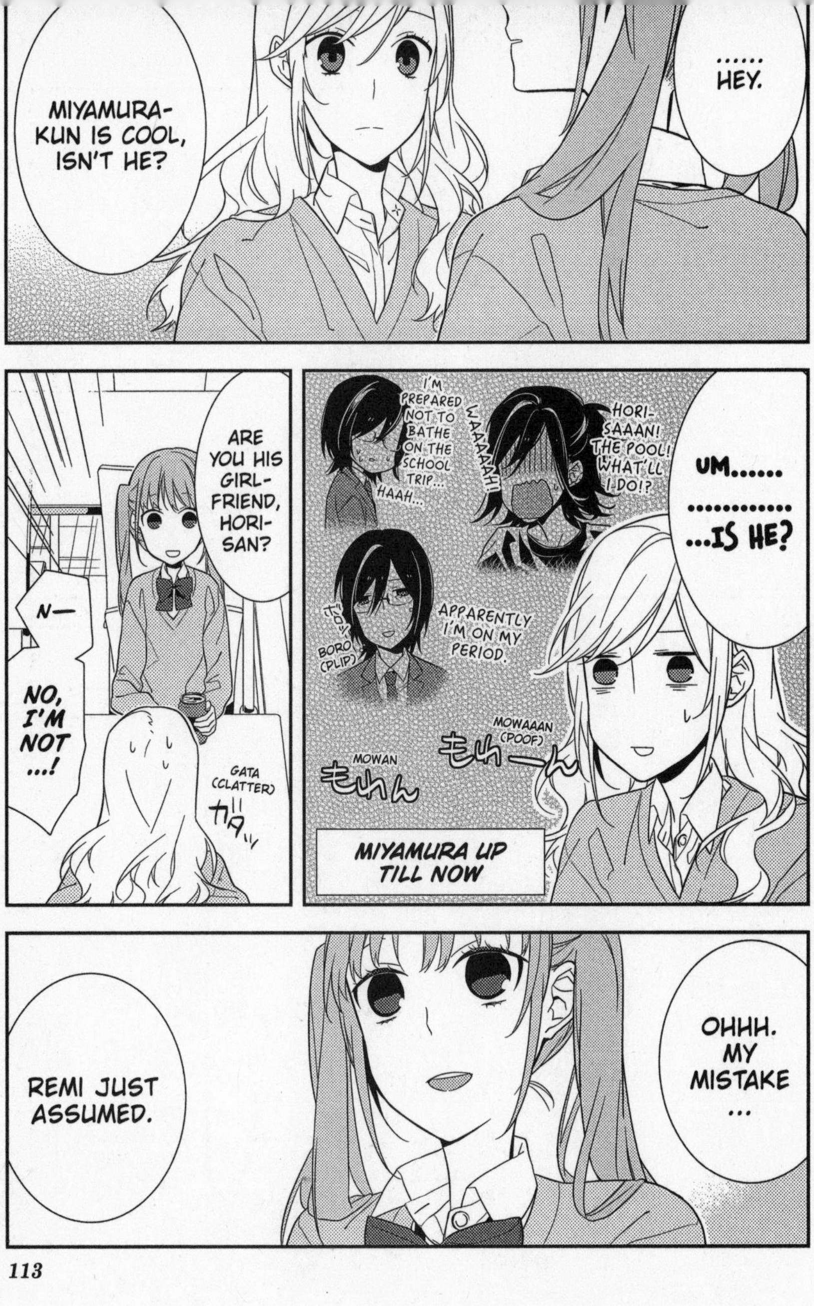

...... HEY.
MIYAMURA-KUN IS COOL, ISN'T HE?
UM...... ....IS HE?
HORI-SAAAN! THE POOL! WHAT'LL I DO!?
WAAAAAH!
I'M PREPARED NOT TO BATHE ON THE SCHOOL TRIP... HAAH...
APPARENTLY I'M ON MY PERIOD.
BORO (PLIP)
MOWAAAN (POOF)
もわーん
MOWAN
もわん
MIYAMURA UP TILL NOW
ARE YOU HIS GIRLFRIEND, HORI-SAN?
N—
NO, I'M NOT ...!
GATA (CLATTER)
OHHH. MY MISTAKE ...
REMI JUST ASSUMED.

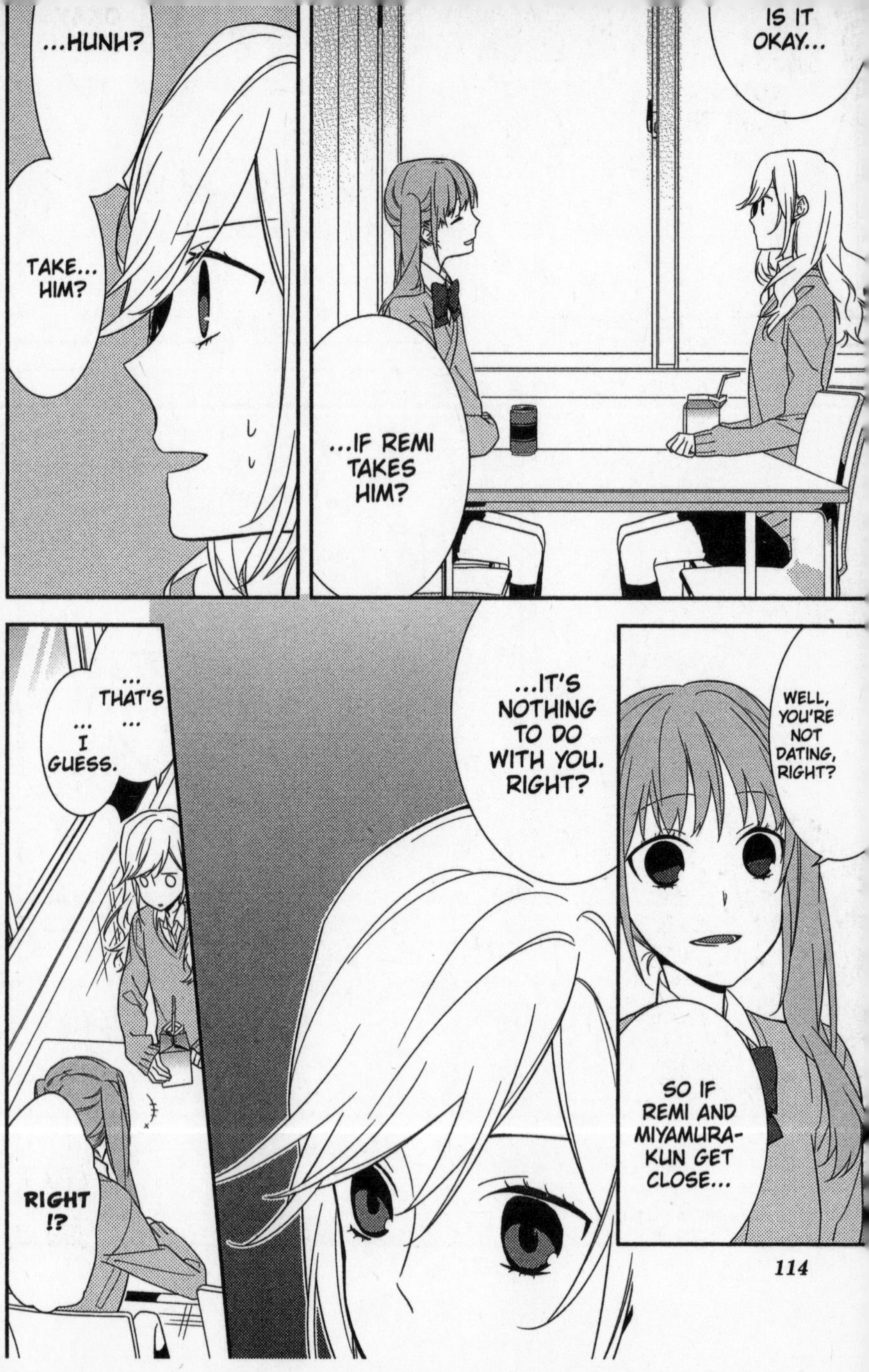
IS IT OKAY...
...IF REMI TAKES HIM?
...HUNH?
TAKE... HIM?
WELL, YOU'RE NOT DATING, RIGHT?
SO IF REMI AND MIYAMURA-KUN GET CLOSE...
...IT'S NOTHING TO DO WITH YOU. RIGHT?
... THAT'S ... ... I GUESS.
RIGHT!?

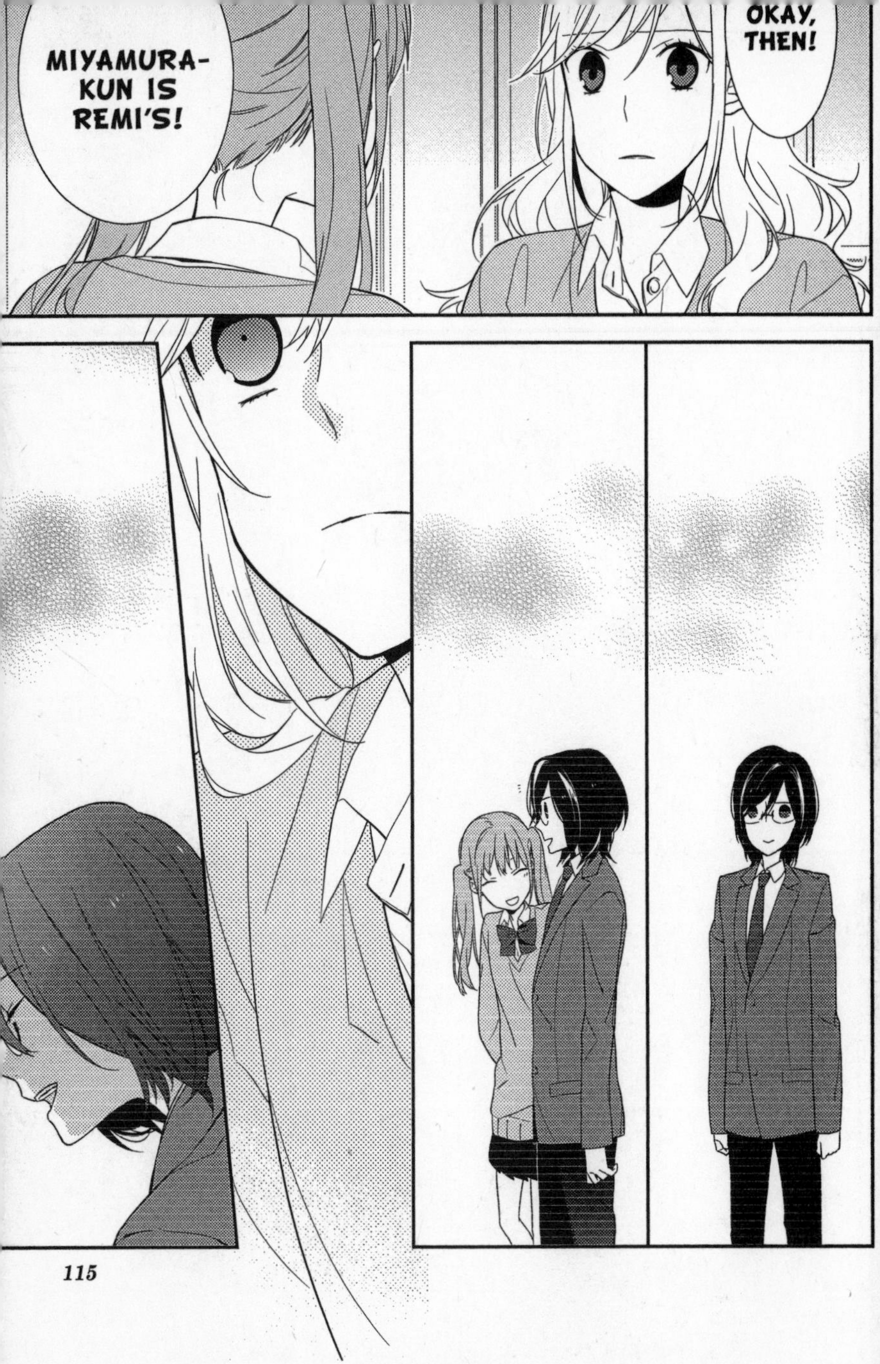
OKAY, THEN!
MIYAMURA-KUN IS REMI'S!

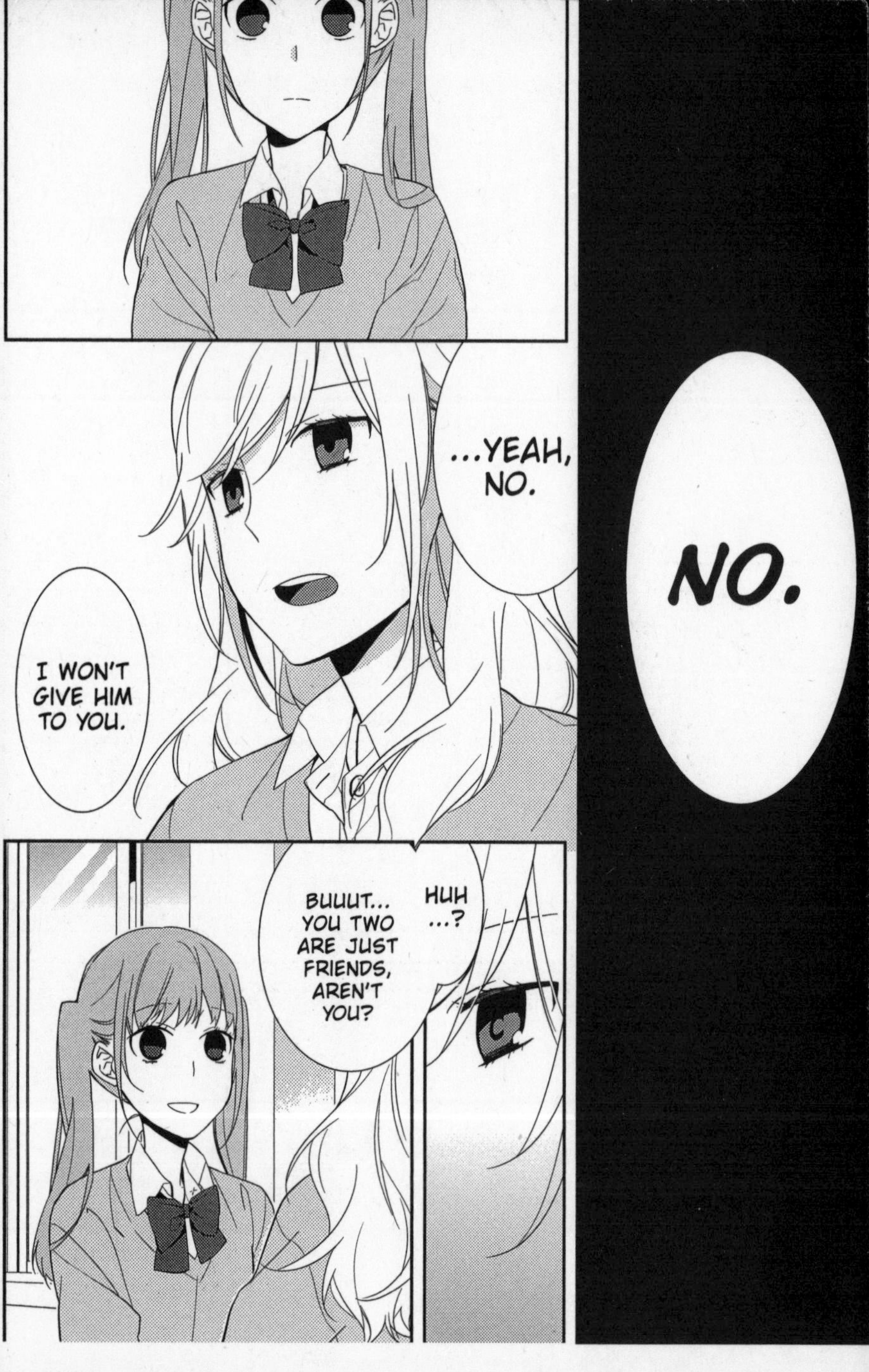
NO.
...YEAH, NO.
I WON'T GIVE HIM TO YOU.
HUH ...?
BUUUT... YOU TWO ARE JUST FRIENDS, AREN'T YOU?

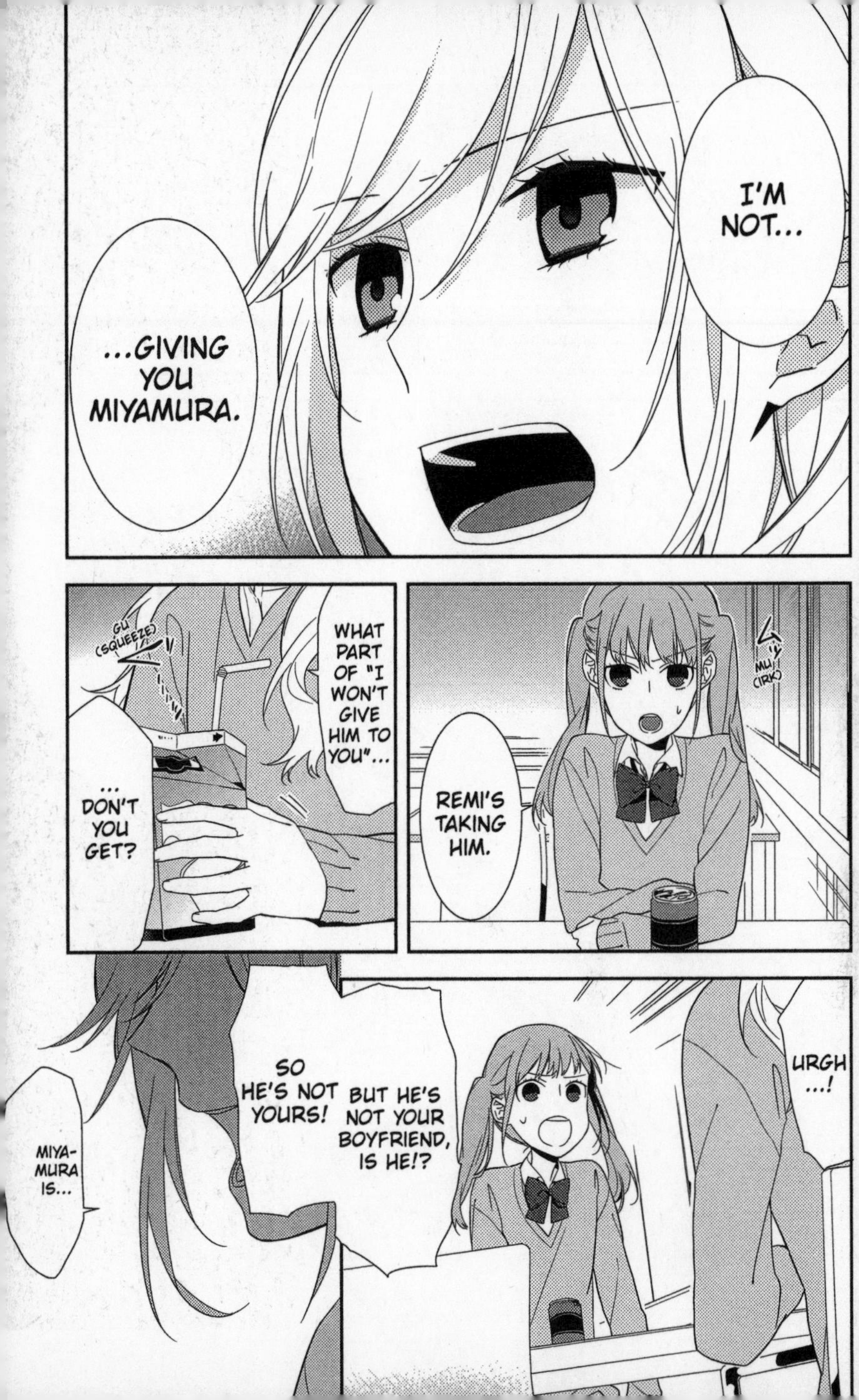
I'M NOT...
...GIVING YOU MIYAMURA.
MU (IRK)
REMI'S TAKING HIM.
WHAT PART OF "I WON'T GIVE HIM TO YOU"...
GU (SQUEEZE)
...DON'T YOU GET?
URGH ...!
BUT HE'S NOT YOUR BOYFRIEND, IS HE!?
SO HE'S NOT YOURS!
MIYA-MURA IS...

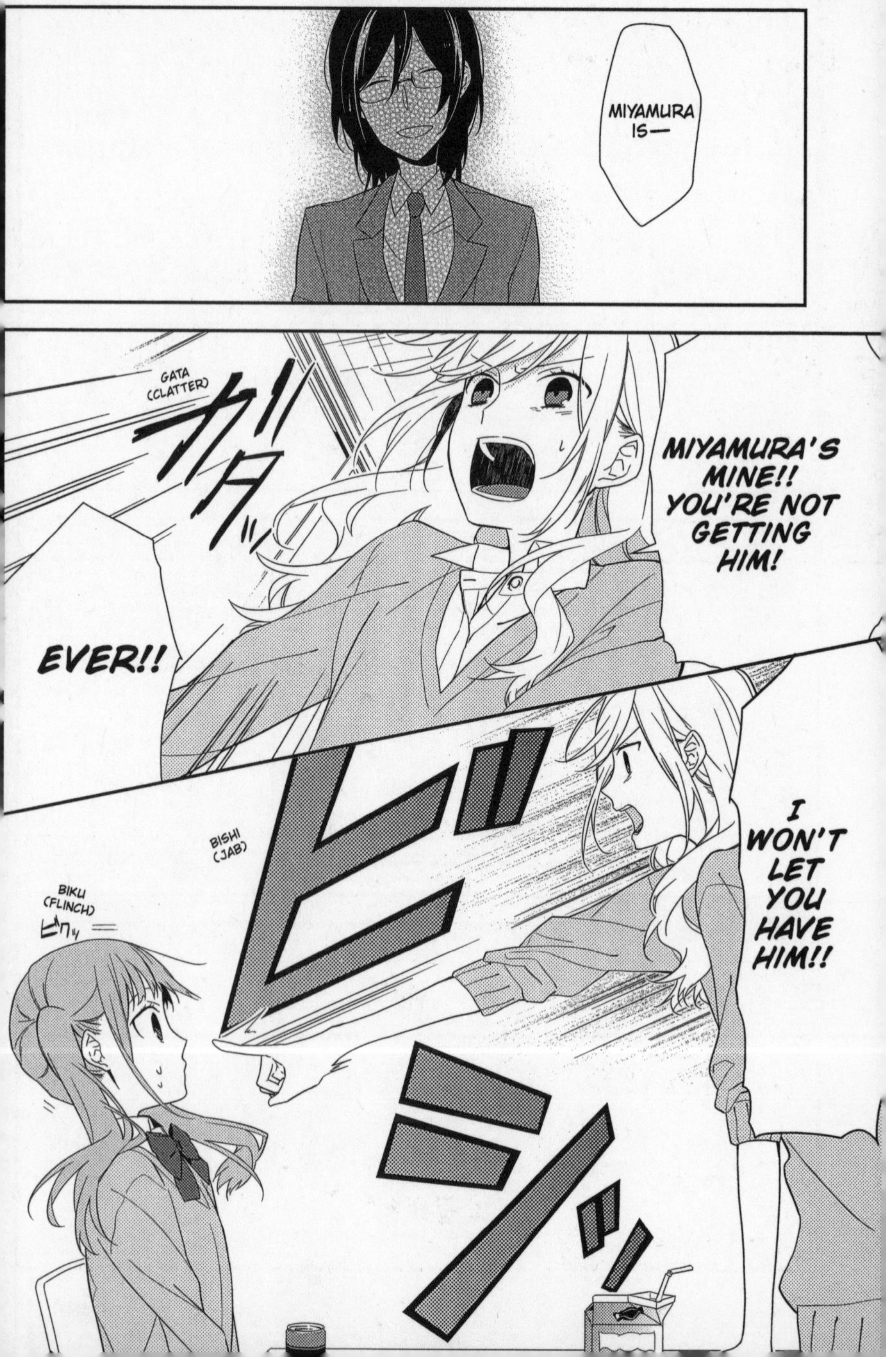
MIYAMURA IS—
MIYAMURA'S MINE!! YOU'RE NOT GETTING HIM!
GATA (CLATTER)
EVER!!
I WON'T LET YOU HAVE HIM!!
BISHI (JAB)
BIKU (FLINCH)

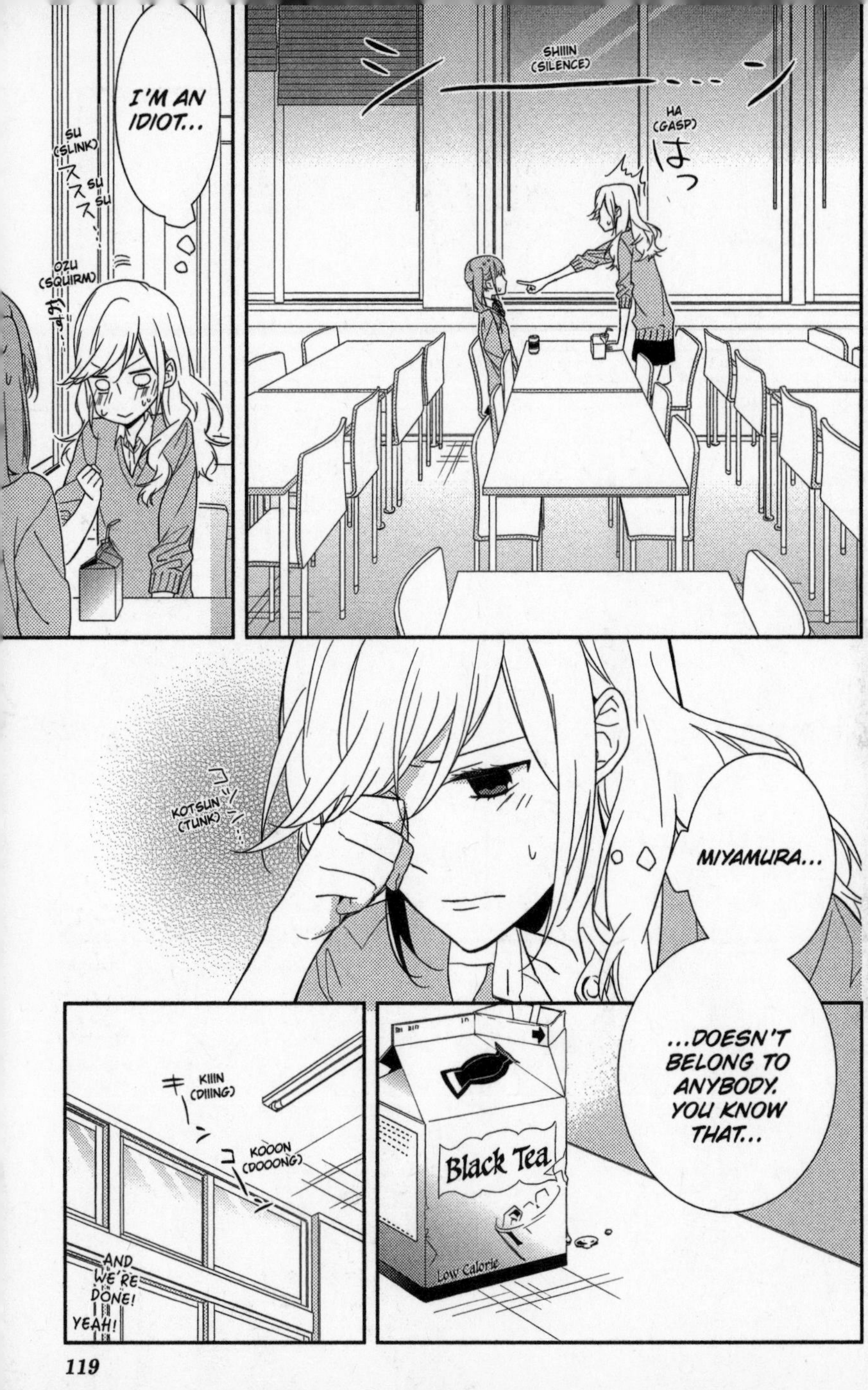
SHIIIN (SILENCE)
HA (GASP)
I'M AN IDIOT...
SU (SLINK)
SU SU
OZU (SQUIRM)
MIYAMURA...
KOTSUN (TUNK)
...DOESN'T BELONG TO ANYBODY. YOU KNOW THAT...
Black Tea
Low Calorie
KIIIN (DIIING)
KOOON (DOOONG)
AND WE'RE DONE! YEAH!

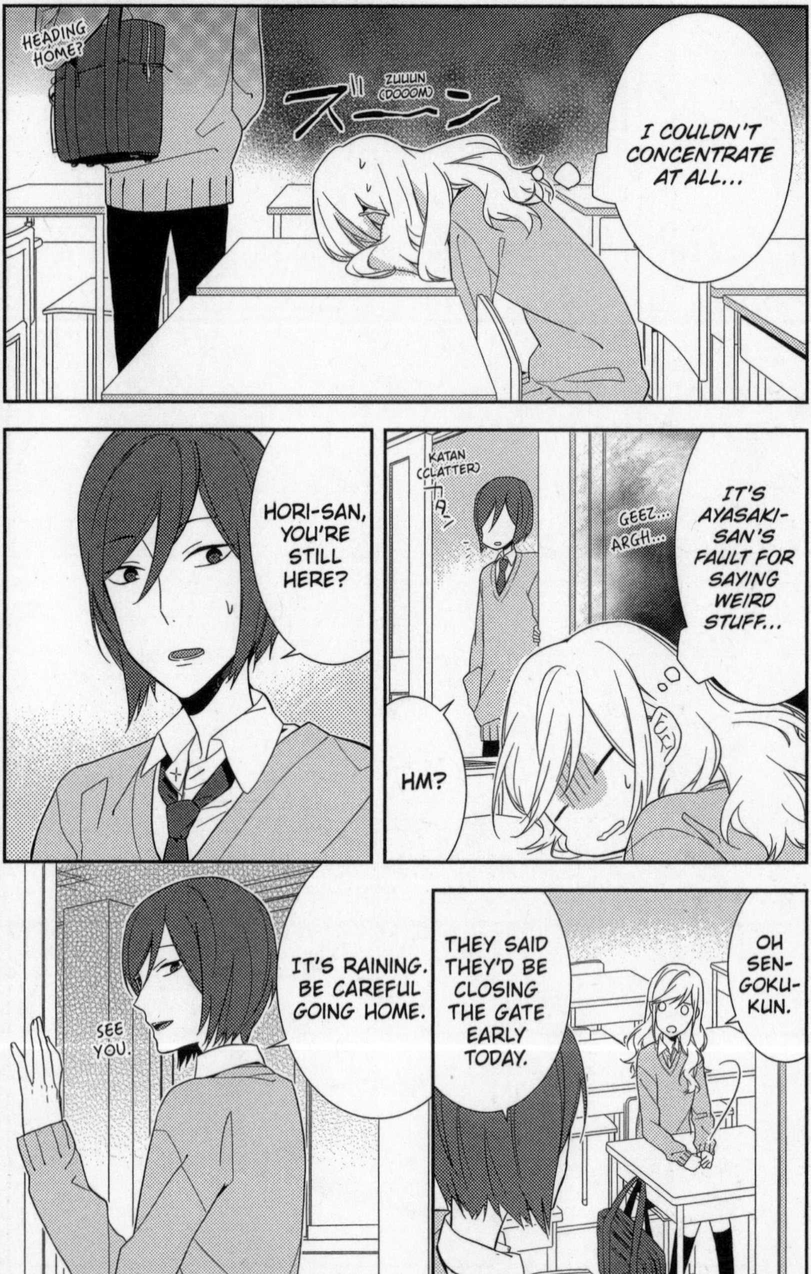
I COULDN'T CONCENTRATE AT ALL...
ZUUUN (DOOOM)
HEADING HOME?
IT'S AYASAKI-SAN'S FAULT FOR SAYING WEIRD STUFF...
GEEZ... ARGH...
KATAN (CLATTER)
HM?
HORI-SAN, YOU'RE STILL HERE?
OH SEN-GOKU-KUN.
THEY SAID THEY'D BE CLOSING THE GATE EARLY TODAY.
IT'S RAINING. BE CAREFUL GOING HOME.
SEE YOU.

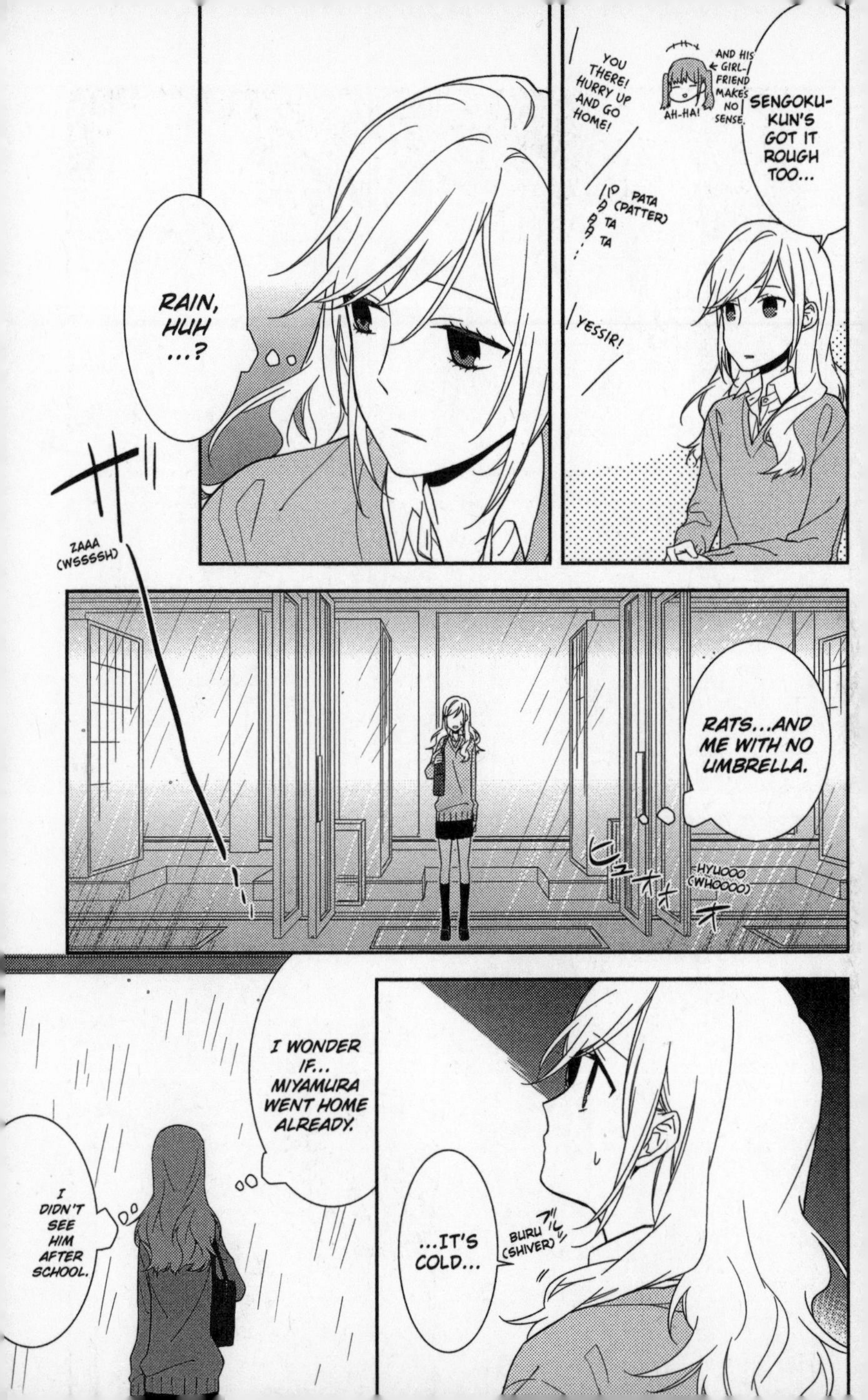
SENGOKU-KUN'S GOT IT ROUGH TOO...
AND HIS GIRLFRIEND MAKES NO SENSE.
AH-HA!
YOU THERE! HURRY UP AND GO HOME!
PATA (PATTER) TA TA
YESSIR!
RAIN, HUH ...?
ZAAA (WSSSSH)
RATS...AND ME WITH NO UMBRELLA.
HYUOOO (WHOOOO)
...IT'S COLD...
BURU (SHIVER)
I WONDER IF... MIYAMURA WENT HOME ALREADY.
I DIDN'T SEE HIM AFTER SCHOOL.

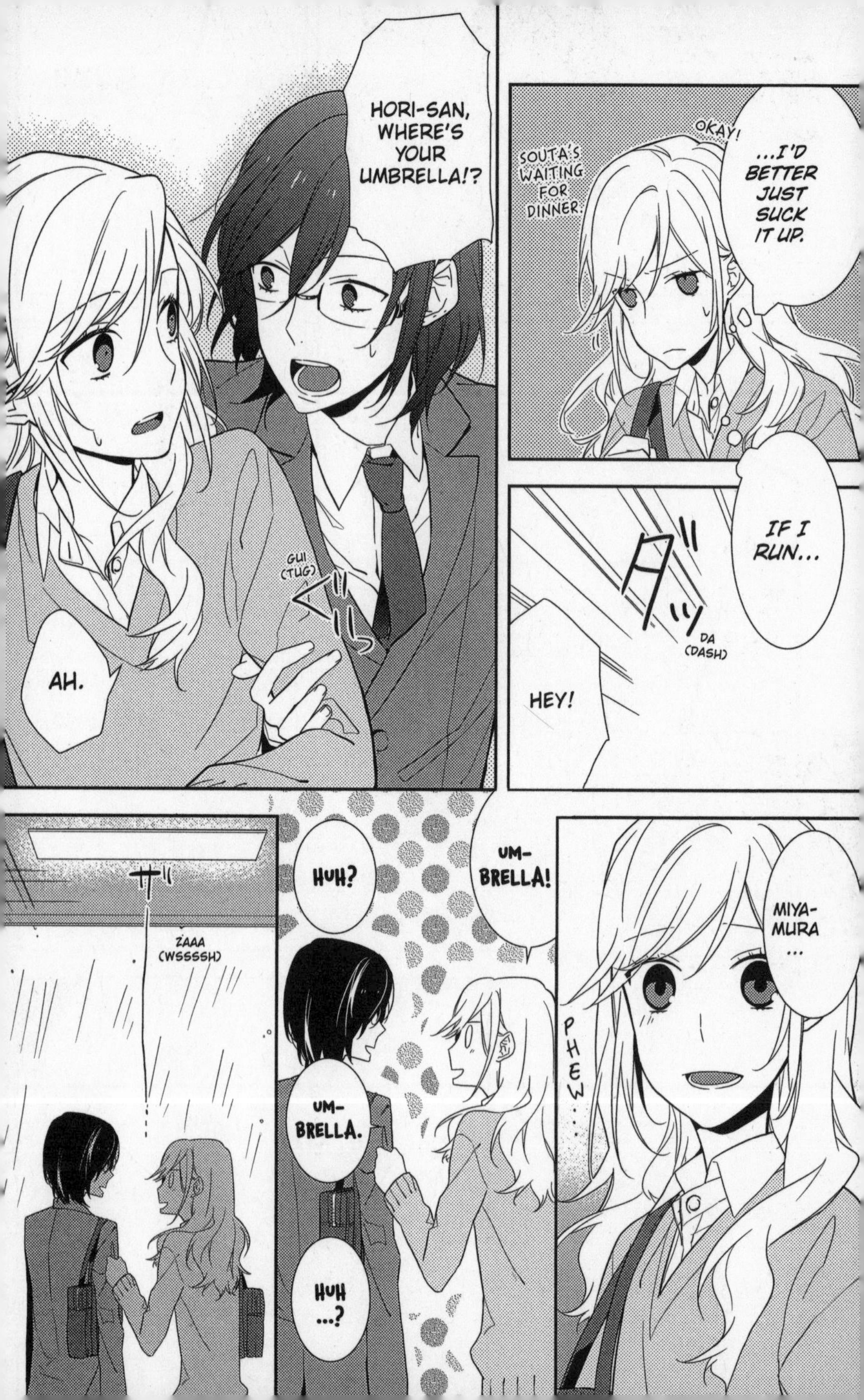
...I'D BETTER JUST SUCK IT UP.
OKAY!
SOUTA'S WAITING FOR DINNER.
IF I RUN...
DA (DASH)
HEY!
HORI-SAN, WHERE'S YOUR UMBRELLA!?
GUI (TUG)
AH.
MIYA-MURA ...
PHEW...
UM-BRELLA!
HUH?
UM-BRELLA.
HUH ...?
ZAAA (WSSSSH)

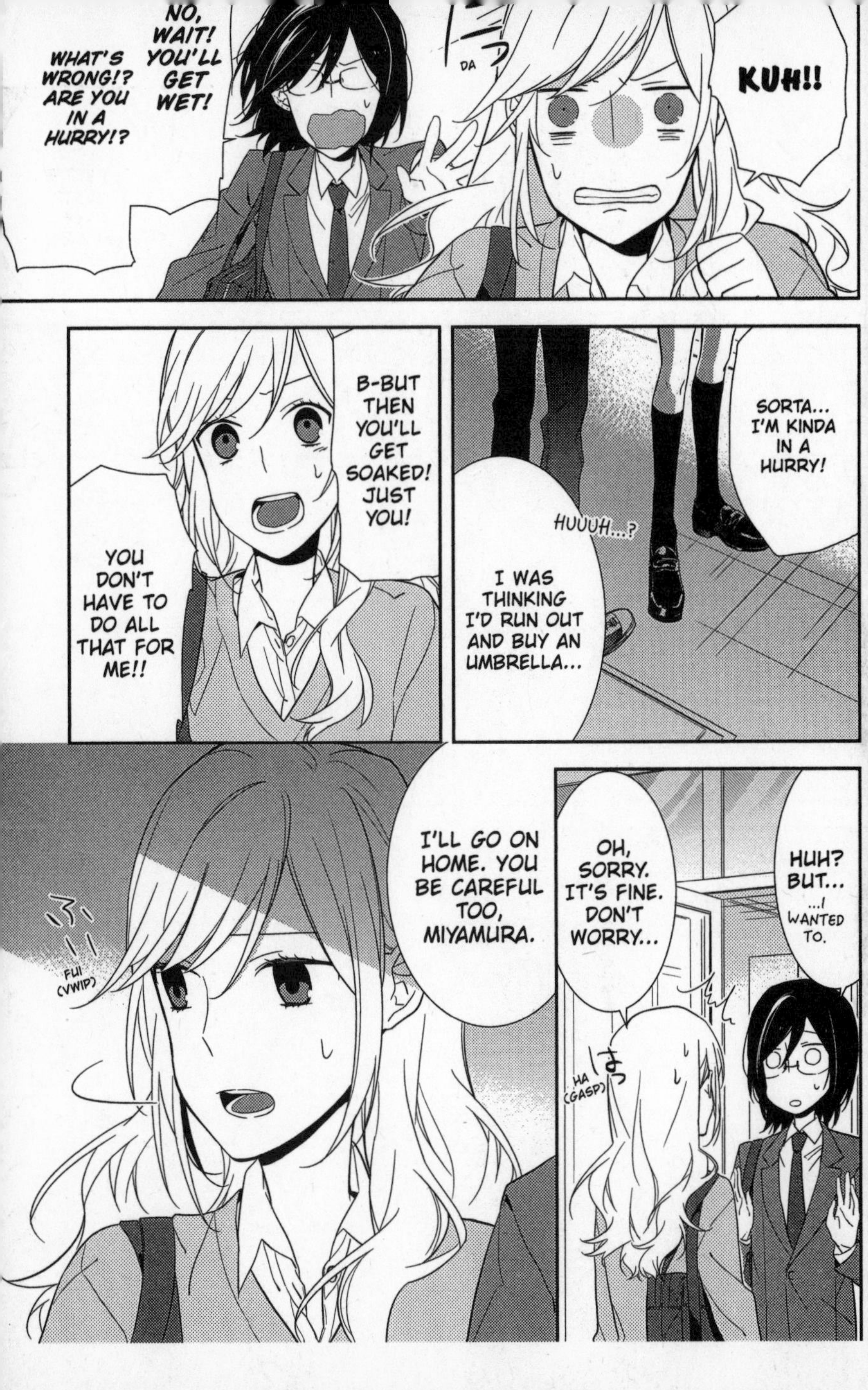
KUH!!
DA
NO, WAIT! YOU'LL GET WET!
WHAT'S WRONG!? ARE YOU IN A HURRY!?
SORTA... I'M KINDA IN A HURRY!
HUUUH...?
I WAS THINKING I'D RUN OUT AND BUY AN UMBRELLA...
B-BUT THEN YOU'LL GET SOAKED! JUST YOU!
YOU DON'T HAVE TO DO ALL THAT FOR ME!!
HUH? BUT...
...I WANTED TO.
OH, SORRY. IT'S FINE. DON'T WORRY...
HA (GASP)
I'LL GO ON HOME. YOU BE CAREFUL TOO, MIYAMURA.
ふい
FUI (VWIP)

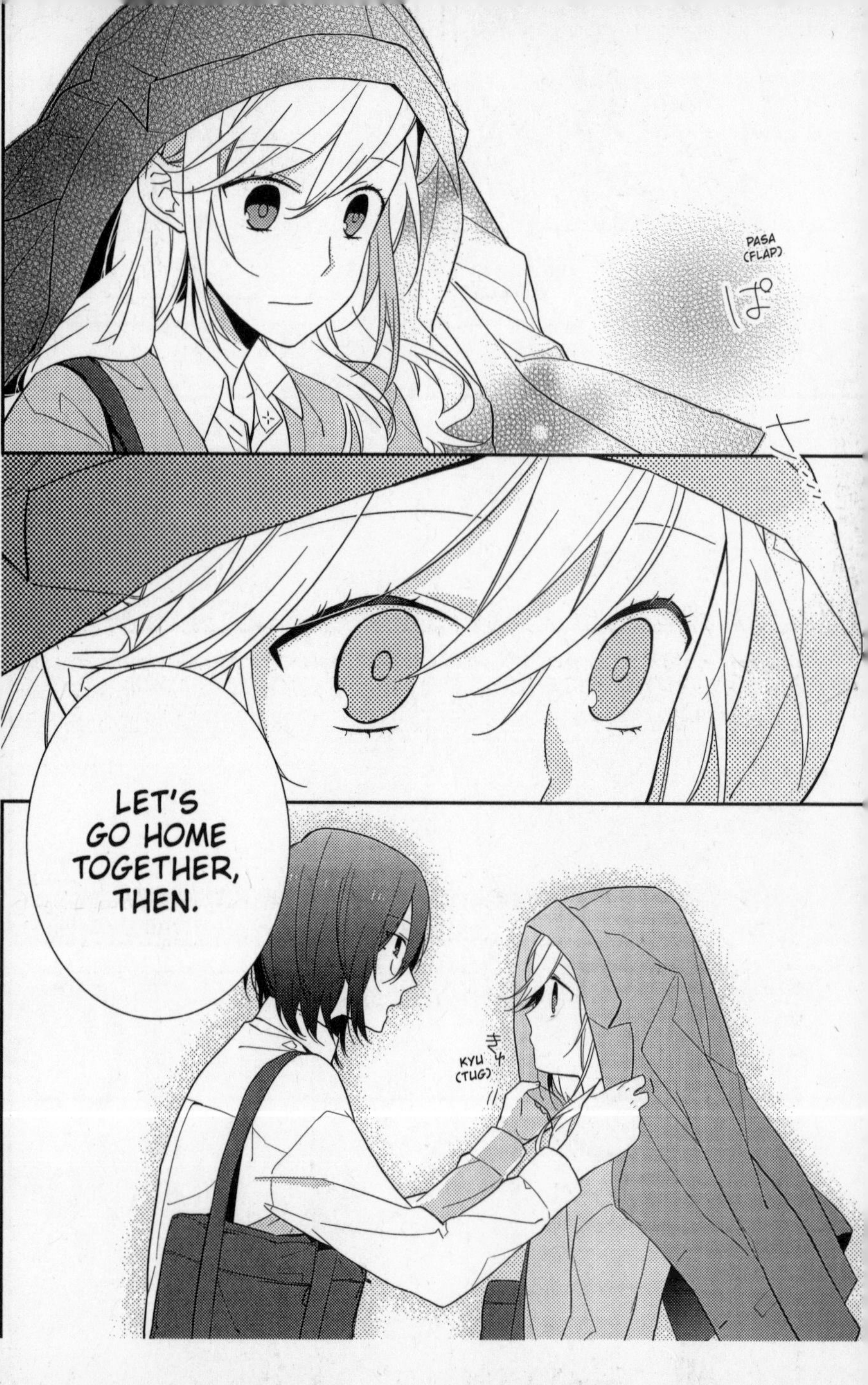
PASA (FLAP)
ぱ
LET'S GO HOME TOGETHER, THEN.
KYU (TUG)
きゅ

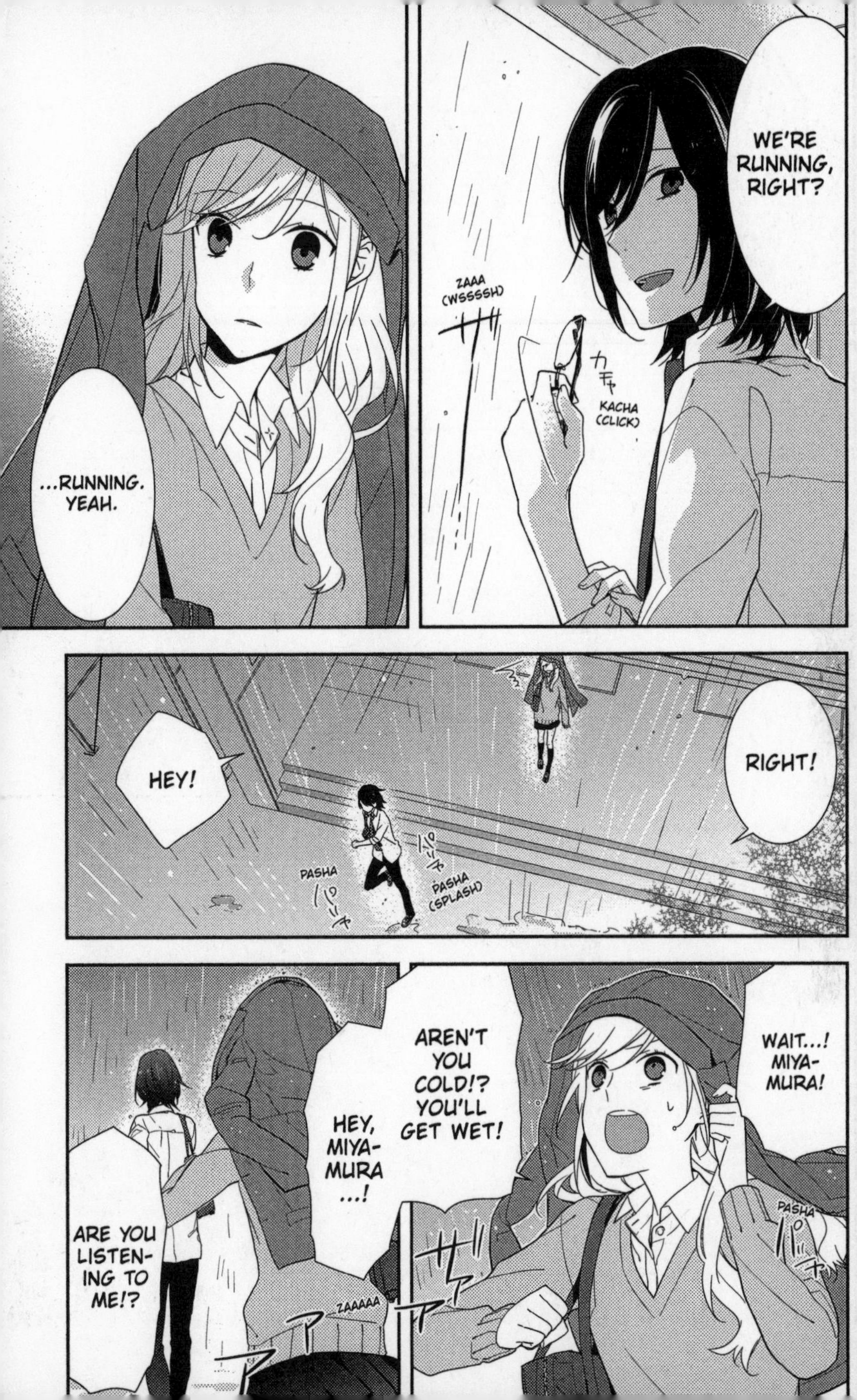
WE'RE RUNNING, RIGHT?
ZAAA (WSSSSH)
KACHA (CLICK)
...RUNNING. YEAH.
RIGHT!
HEY!
PASHA (SPLASH)
PASHA
WAIT...! MIYA-MURA!
AREN'T YOU COLD!? YOU'LL GET WET!
HEY, MIYA-MURA ...!
PASHA
ARE YOU LISTEN-ING TO ME!?
ZAAAAA

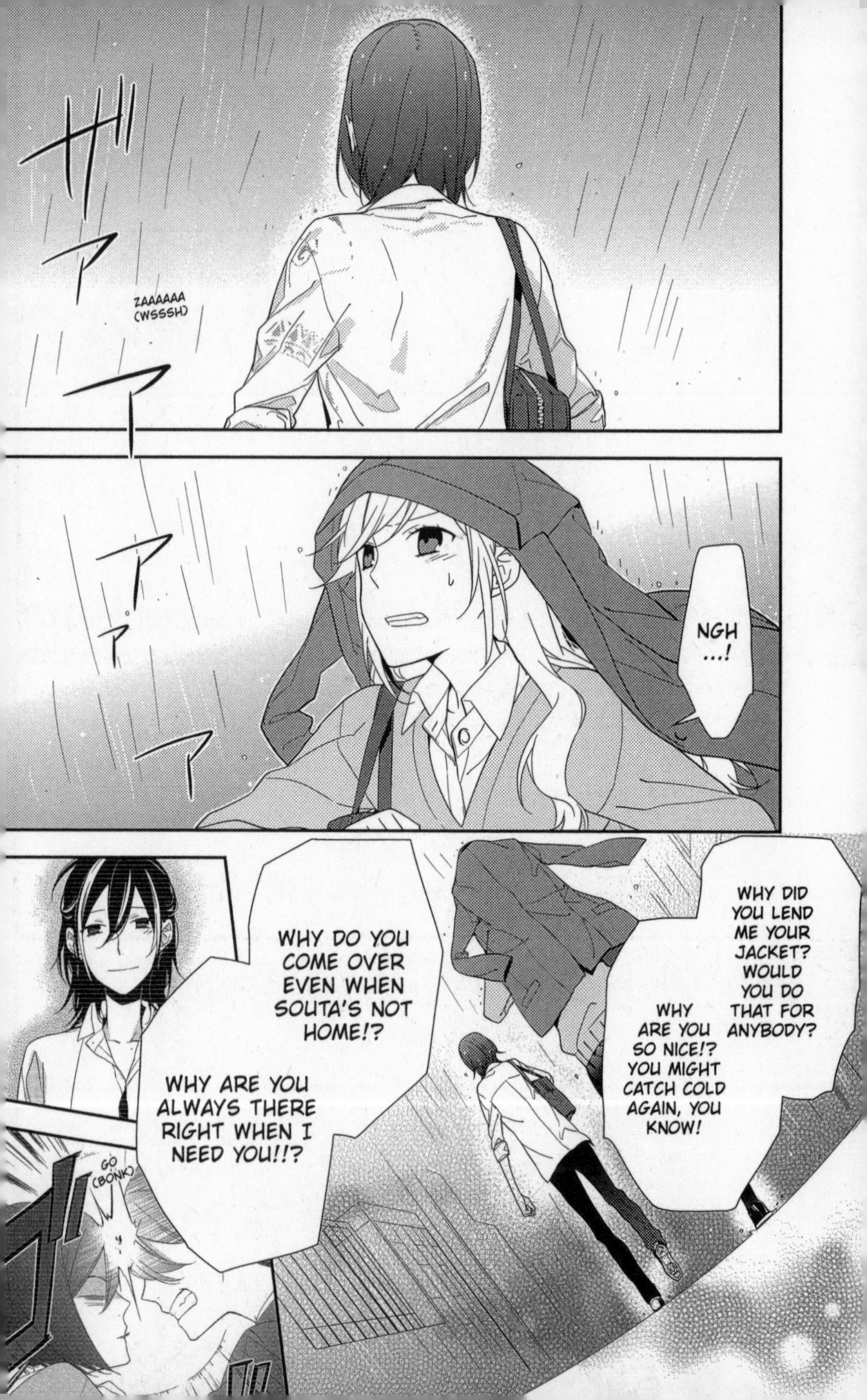
ZAAAAAA (WSSSH)
NGH ...!
WHY DID YOU LEND ME YOUR JACKET? WOULD YOU DO THAT FOR ANYBODY?
WHY ARE YOU SO NICE!? YOU MIGHT CATCH COLD AGAIN, YOU KNOW!
WHY DO YOU COME OVER EVEN WHEN SOUTA'S NOT HOME!?
WHY ARE YOU ALWAYS THERE RIGHT WHEN I NEED YOU!!?
GO (BONK)

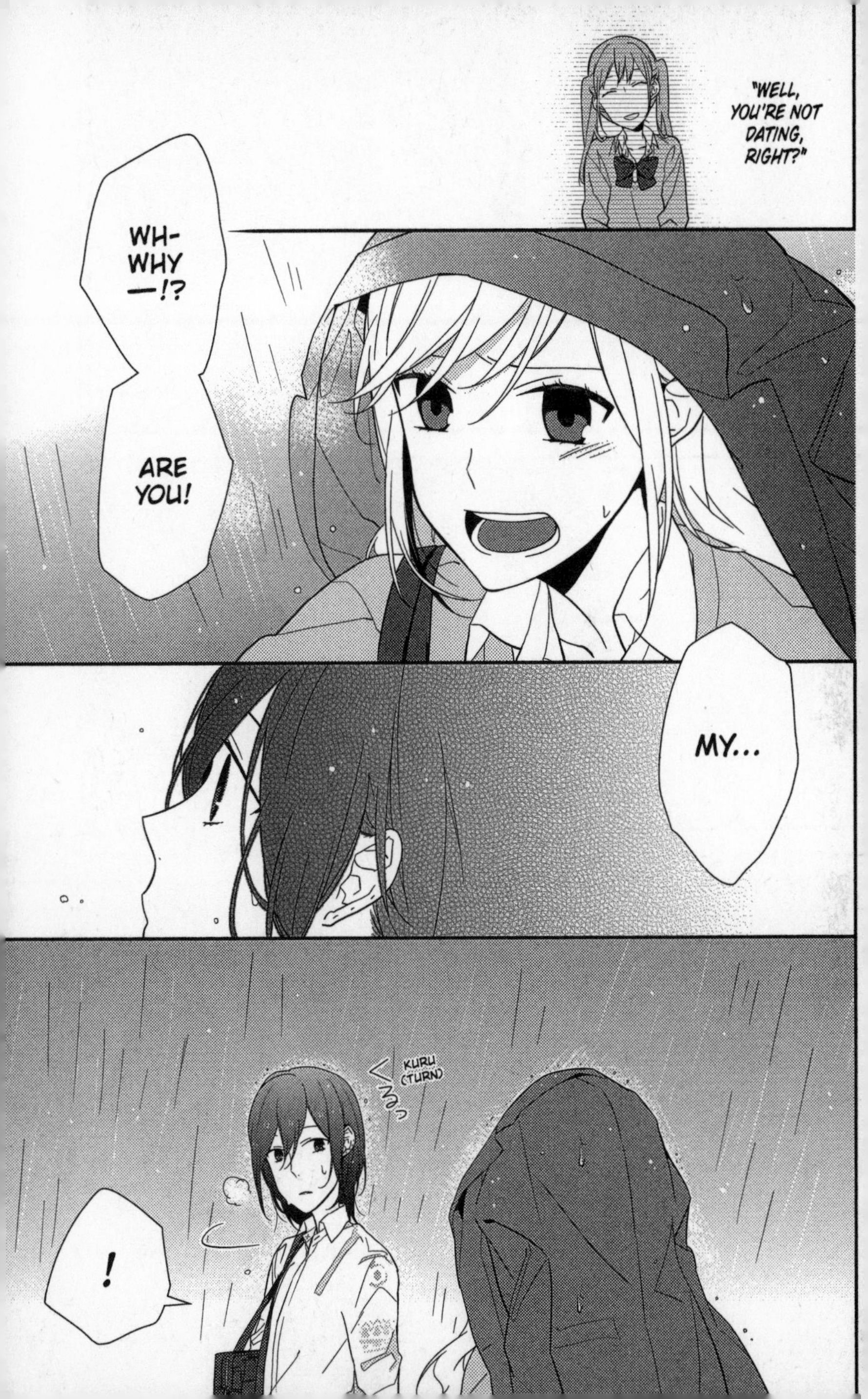
"WELL, YOU'RE NOT DATING, RIGHT?"
WH- WHY ー!?
ARE YOU!
MY...
KURU (TURN)
!

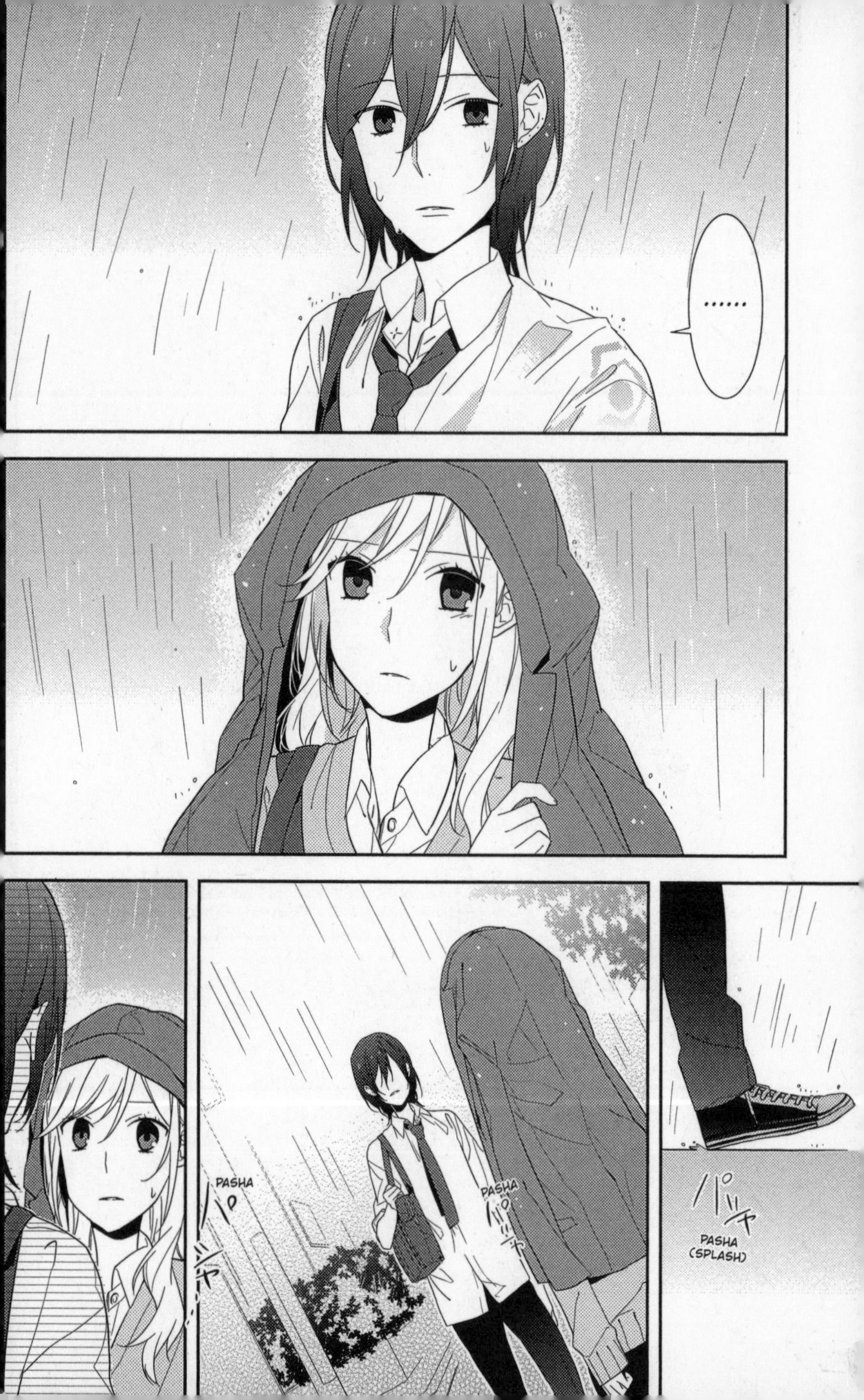

......
パシャ
PASHA
(SPLASH)
PASHA
パシャ
PASHA
パシャ

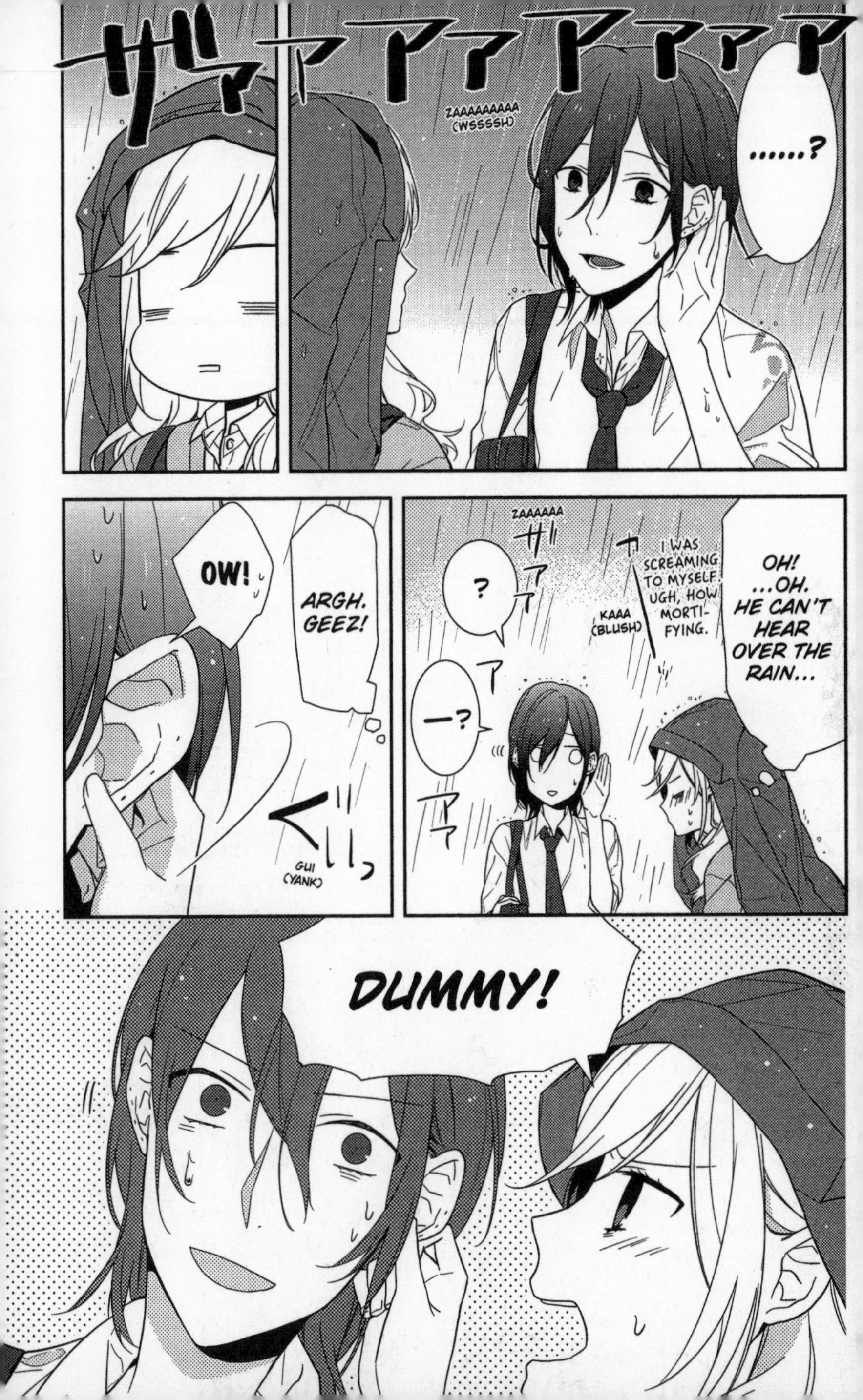
ZAAAAAAAAA (WSSSSH)
......?
OH! ...OH. HE CAN'T HEAR OVER THE RAIN...
I WAS SCREAMING TO MYSELF. UGH, HOW MORTI-FYING.
KAAA (BLUSH)
ZAAAAAAA
?
—?
ARGH. GEEZ!
OW!
GUI (YANK)
DUMMY!

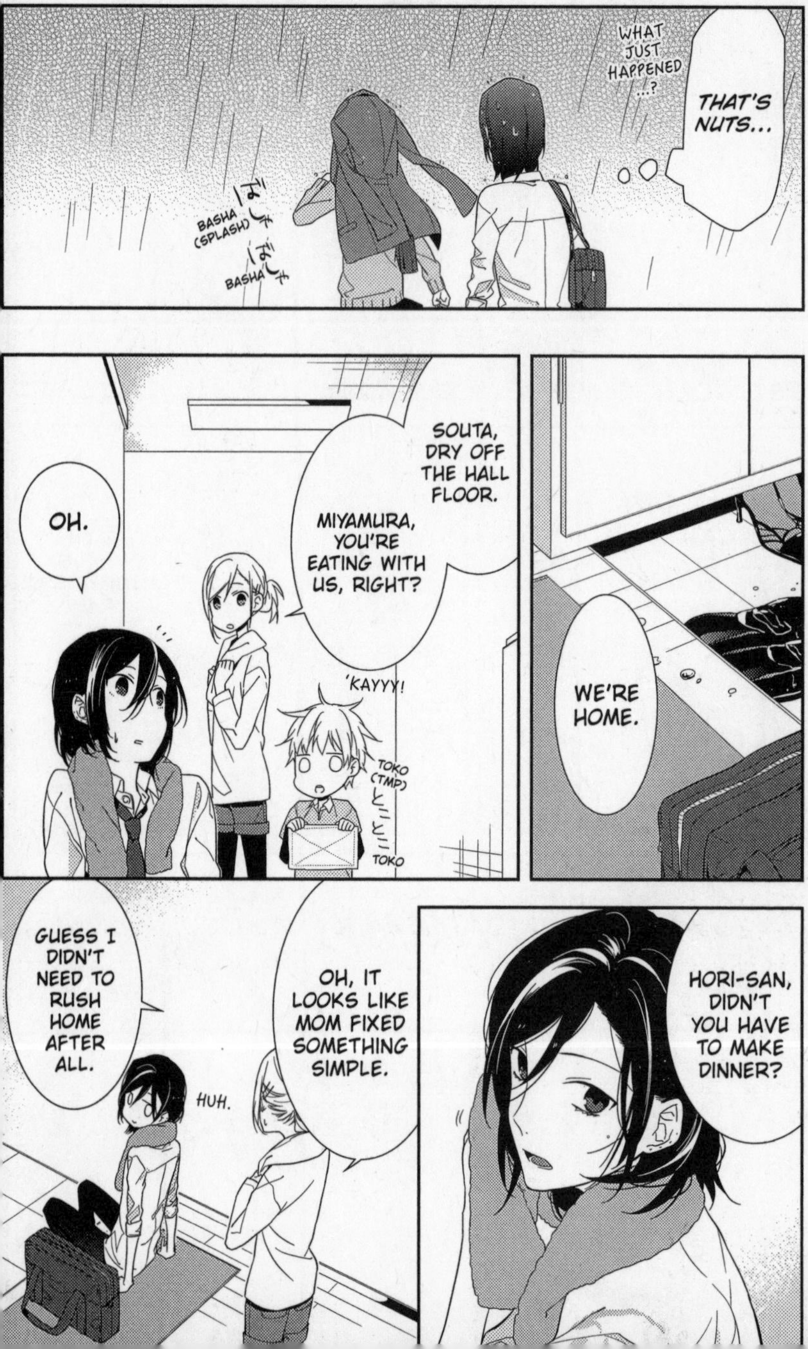
THAT'S NUTS...
WHAT JUST HAPPENED ...?
BASHA (SPLASH)
BASHA
WE'RE HOME.
SOUTA, DRY OFF THE HALL FLOOR.
MIYAMURA, YOU'RE EATING WITH US, RIGHT?
OH.
'KAYYY!
TOKO (TMP)
TOKO
HORI-SAN, DIDN'T YOU HAVE TO MAKE DINNER?
OH, IT LOOKS LIKE MOM FIXED SOMETHING SIMPLE.
GUESS I DIDN'T NEED TO RUSH HOME AFTER ALL.
HUH.

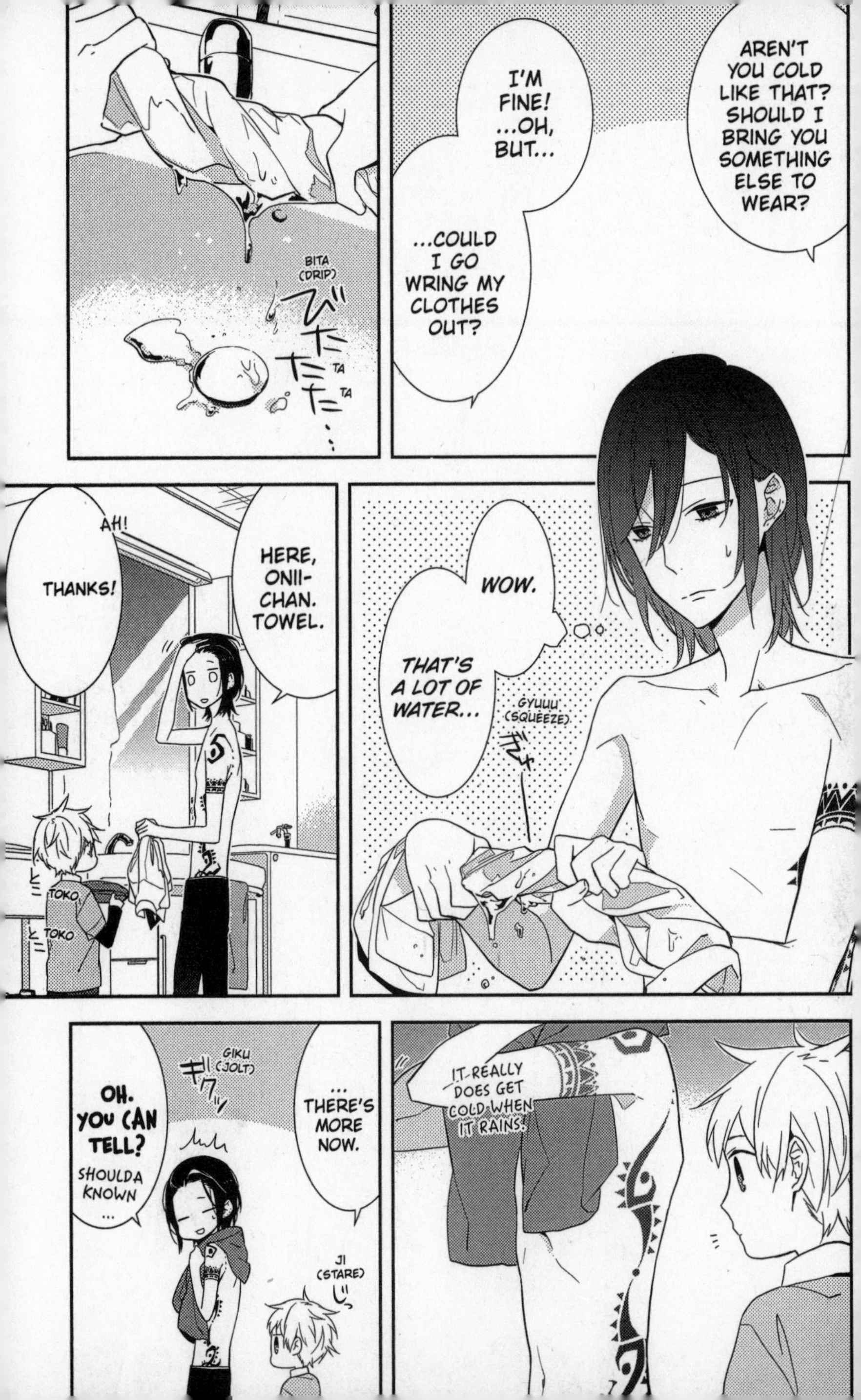
AREN'T YOU COLD LIKE THAT? SHOULD I BRING YOU SOMETHING ELSE TO WEAR?
I'M FINE! ...OH, BUT...
...COULD I GO WRING MY CLOTHES OUT?
BITA (DRIP)
TA
TA
WOW.
THAT'S A LOT OF WATER...
GYUUU (SQUEEZE)
HERE, ONII-CHAN. TOWEL.
AH!
THANKS!
TOKO
TOKO
IT REALLY DOES GET COLD WHEN IT RAINS.
...THERE'S MORE NOW.
GIKU (JOLT)
OH. YOU CAN TELL?
SHOULDA KNOWN...
JI (STARE)

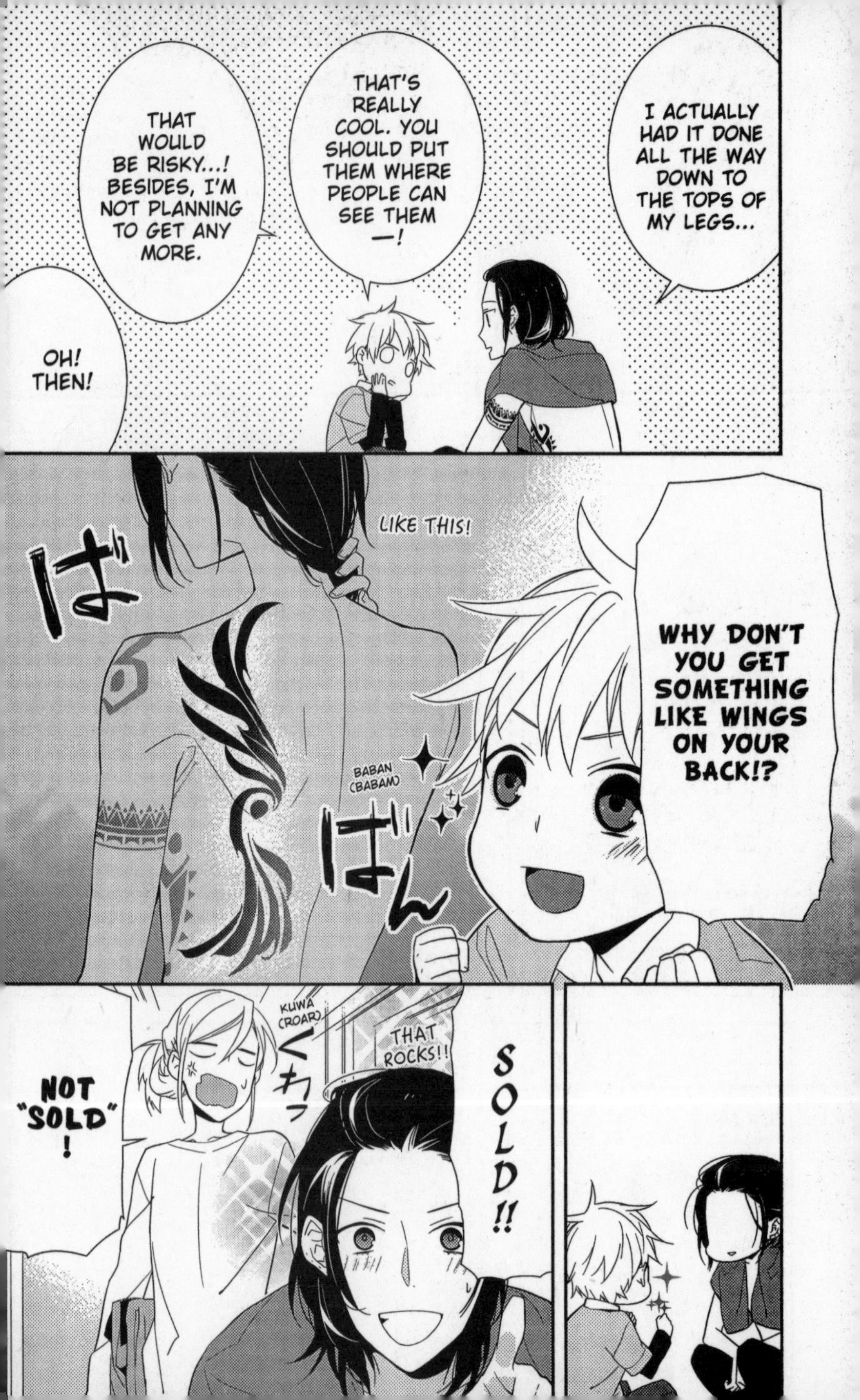
I ACTUALLY HAD IT DONE ALL THE WAY DOWN TO THE TOPS OF MY LEGS...
THAT'S REALLY COOL. YOU SHOULD PUT THEM WHERE PEOPLE CAN SEE THEM—!
THAT WOULD BE RISKY...! BESIDES, I'M NOT PLANNING TO GET ANY MORE.
OH! THEN!
WHY DON'T YOU GET SOMETHING LIKE WINGS ON YOUR BACK!?
LIKE THIS!
ばばん
BABAN (BABAM)
SOLD!!
THAT ROCKS!!
くわっ
KUWA (ROAR)
NOT "SOLD"!

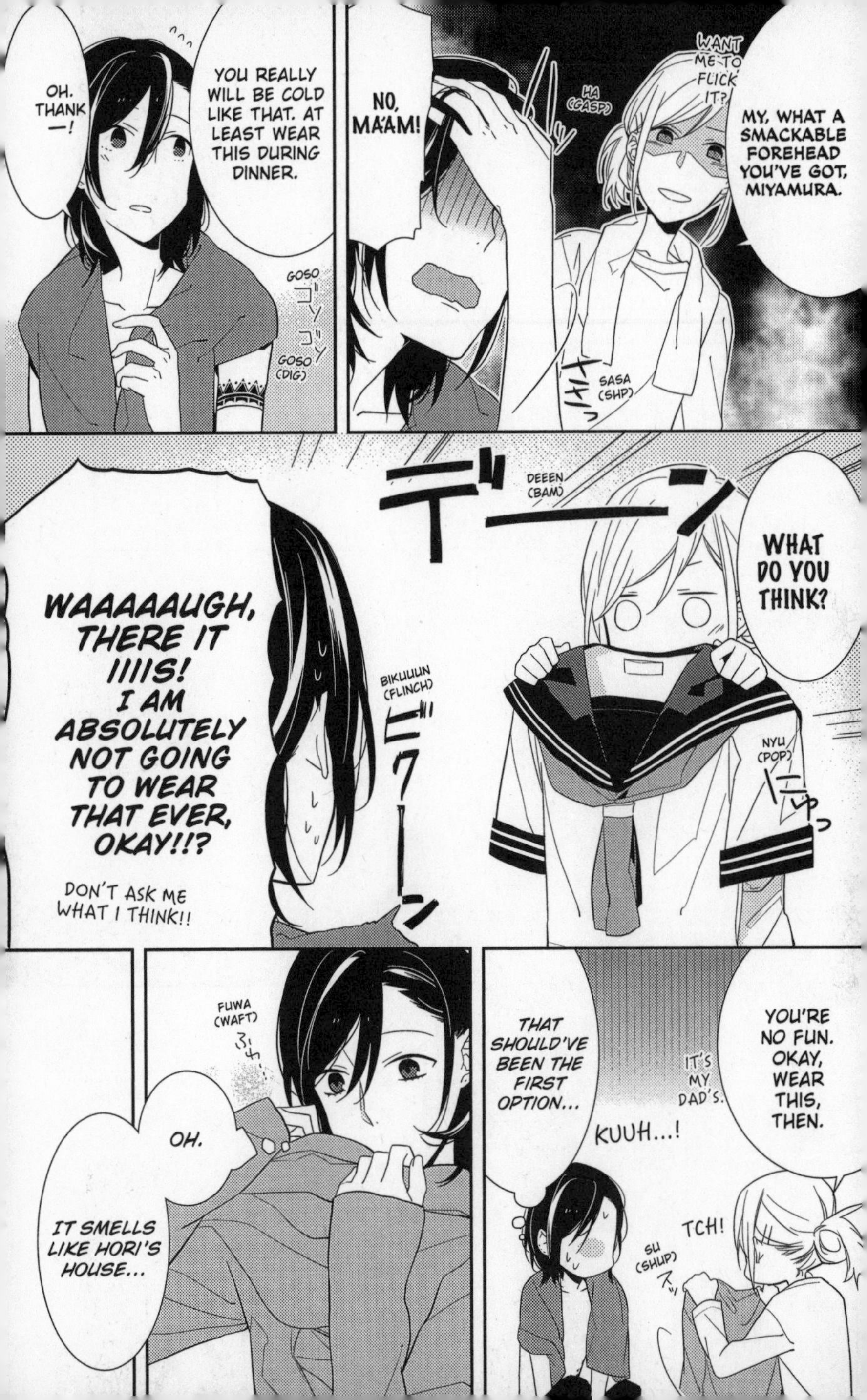
MY, WHAT A SMACKABLE FOREHEAD YOU'VE GOT, MIYAMURA.
WANT ME TO FLICK IT?
HA (GASP)
NO, MA'AM!
SASA (SHP)
YOU REALLY WILL BE COLD LIKE THAT. AT LEAST WEAR THIS DURING DINNER.
OH. THANK—!
GOSO GOSO (DIG)
WHAT DO YOU THINK?
DEEEN (BAM)
NYU (POP)
BIKUUUN (FLINCH)
WAAAAAUGH, THERE IT IIIIS! I AM ABSOLUTELY NOT GOING TO WEAR THAT EVER, OKAY!!?
DON'T ASK ME WHAT I THINK!!
YOU'RE NO FUN. OKAY, WEAR THIS, THEN.
IT'S MY DAD'S.
THAT SHOULD'VE BEEN THE FIRST OPTION...
KUUH...!
TCH!
SU (SHUP)
FUWA (WAFT)
OH.
IT SMELLS LIKE HORI'S HOUSE...

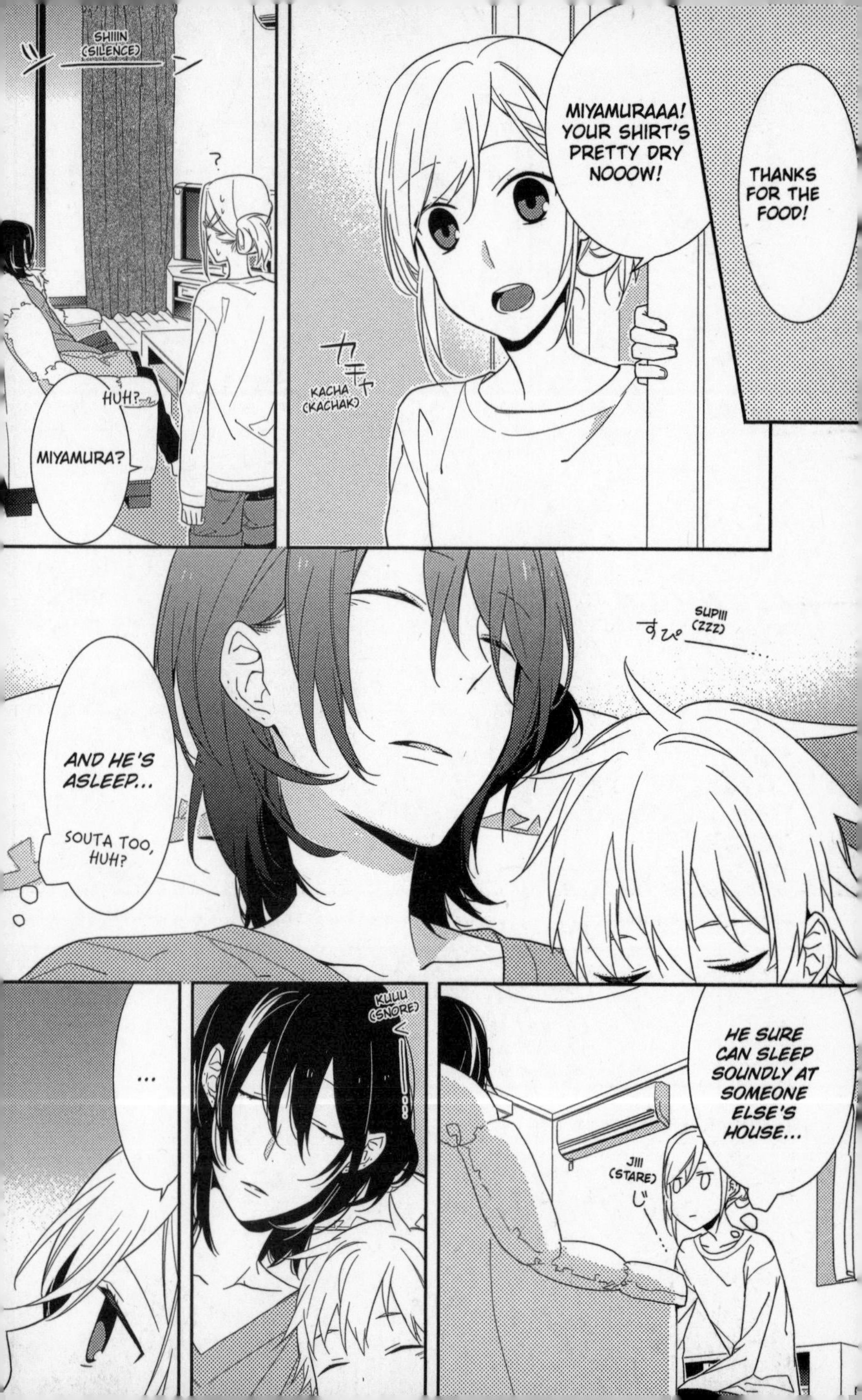
THANKS FOR THE FOOD!
MIYAMURAAA! YOUR SHIRT'S PRETTY DRY NOOOW!
カチャ
KACHA (KACHAK)
SHIIIN (SILENCE)
?
HUH?
MIYAMURA?
すぴ
SUPIII (ZZZ)
AND HE'S ASLEEP...
SOUTA TOO, HUH?
HE SURE CAN SLEEP SOUNDLY AT SOMEONE ELSE'S HOUSE...
じ
JIII (STARE)
KUUU (SNORE)
...

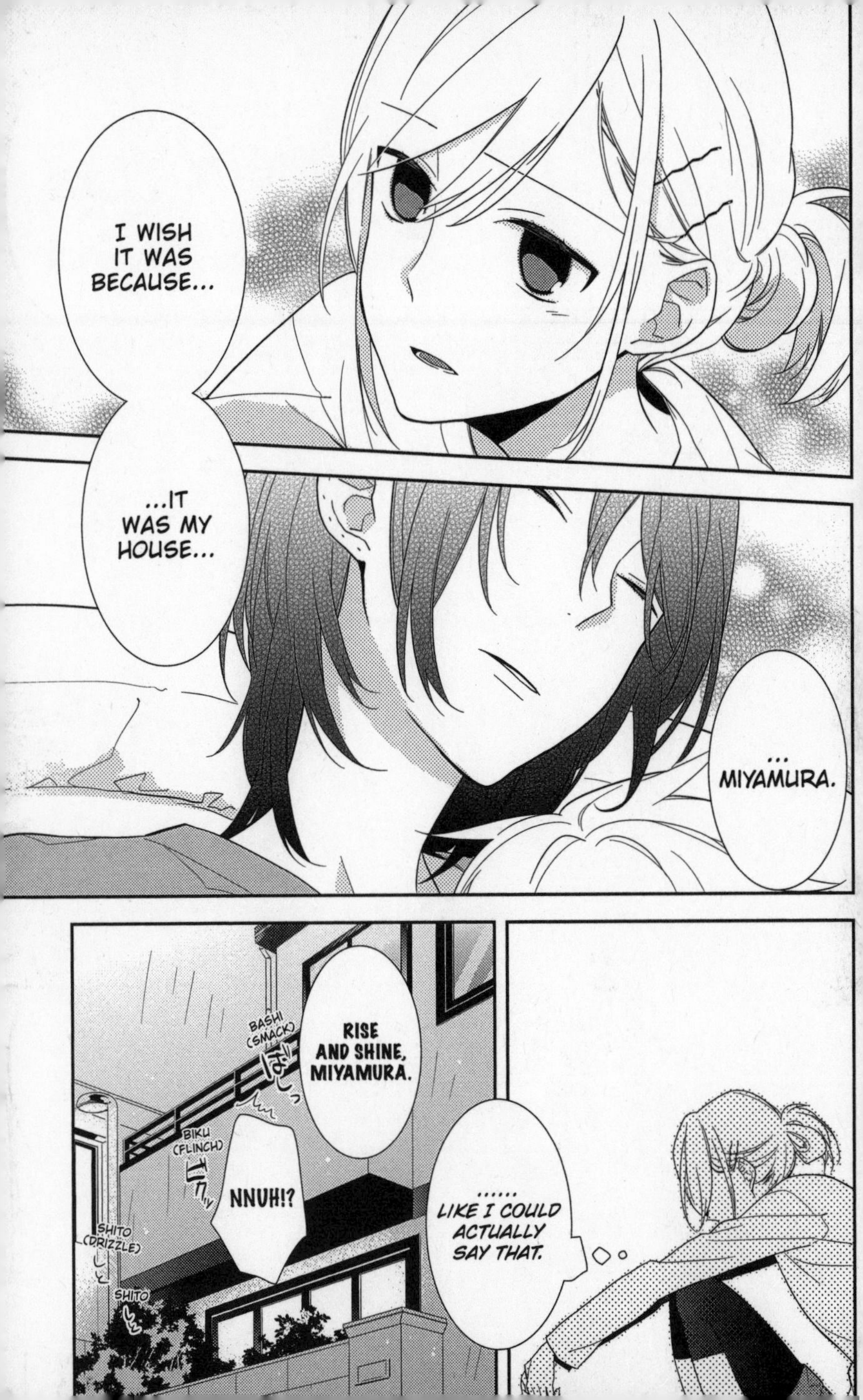
I WISH IT WAS BECAUSE...
...IT WAS MY HOUSE...
...MIYAMURA.
......LIKE I COULD ACTUALLY SAY THAT.
BASHI (SMACK)
RISE AND SHINE, MIYAMURA.
BIKU (FLINCH)
NNUH!?
SHITO (DRIZZLE)
SHITO

HORIMIYA

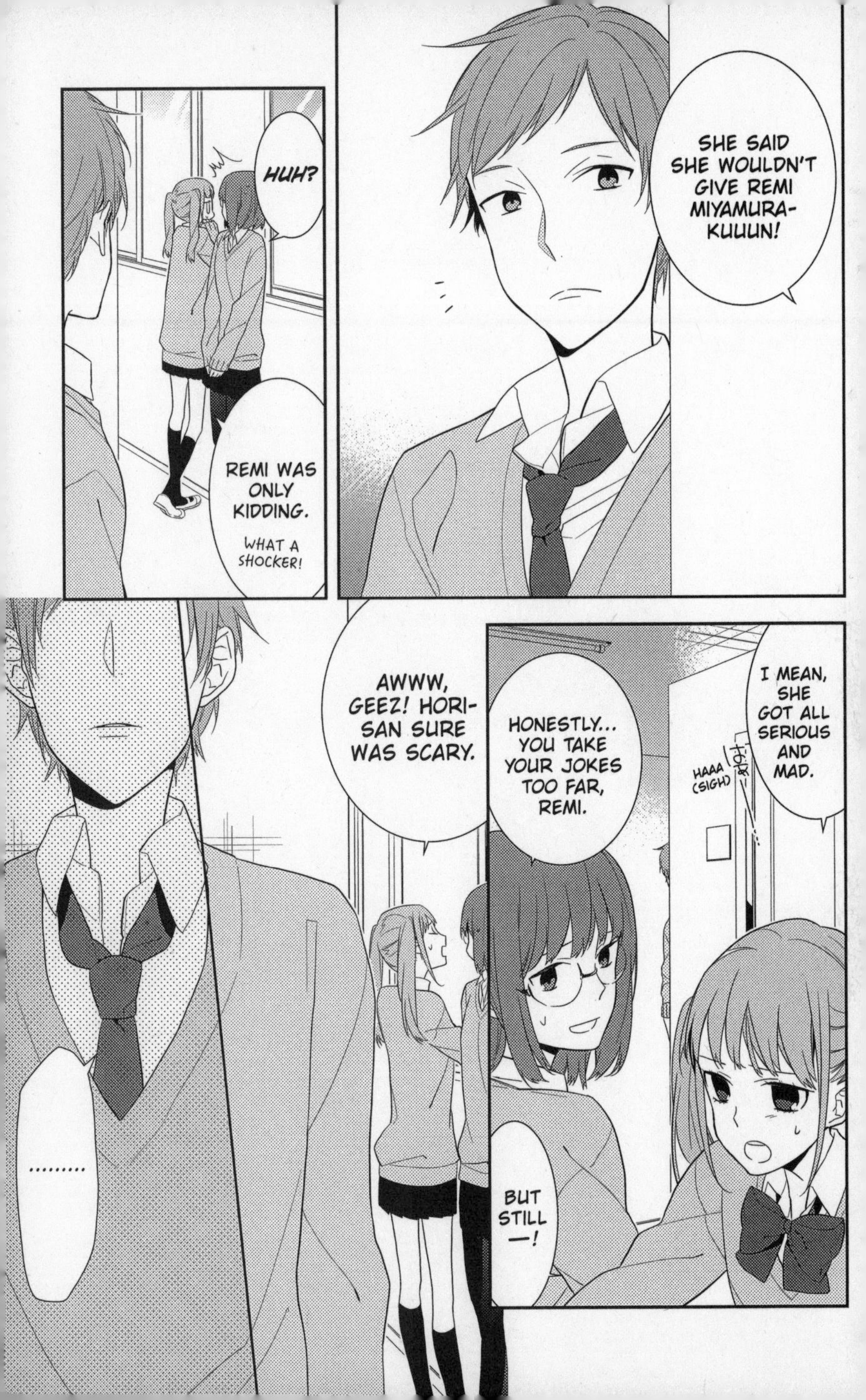
SHE SAID SHE WOULDN'T GIVE REMI MIYAMURA-KUUUN!
HUH?
REMI WAS ONLY KIDDING.
WHAT A SHOCKER!
I MEAN, SHE GOT ALL SERIOUS AND MAD.
HAAA (SIGH)
HONESTLY... YOU TAKE YOUR JOKES TOO FAR, REMI.
BUT STILL—!
AWWW, GEEZ! HORI-SAN SURE WAS SCARY.
....

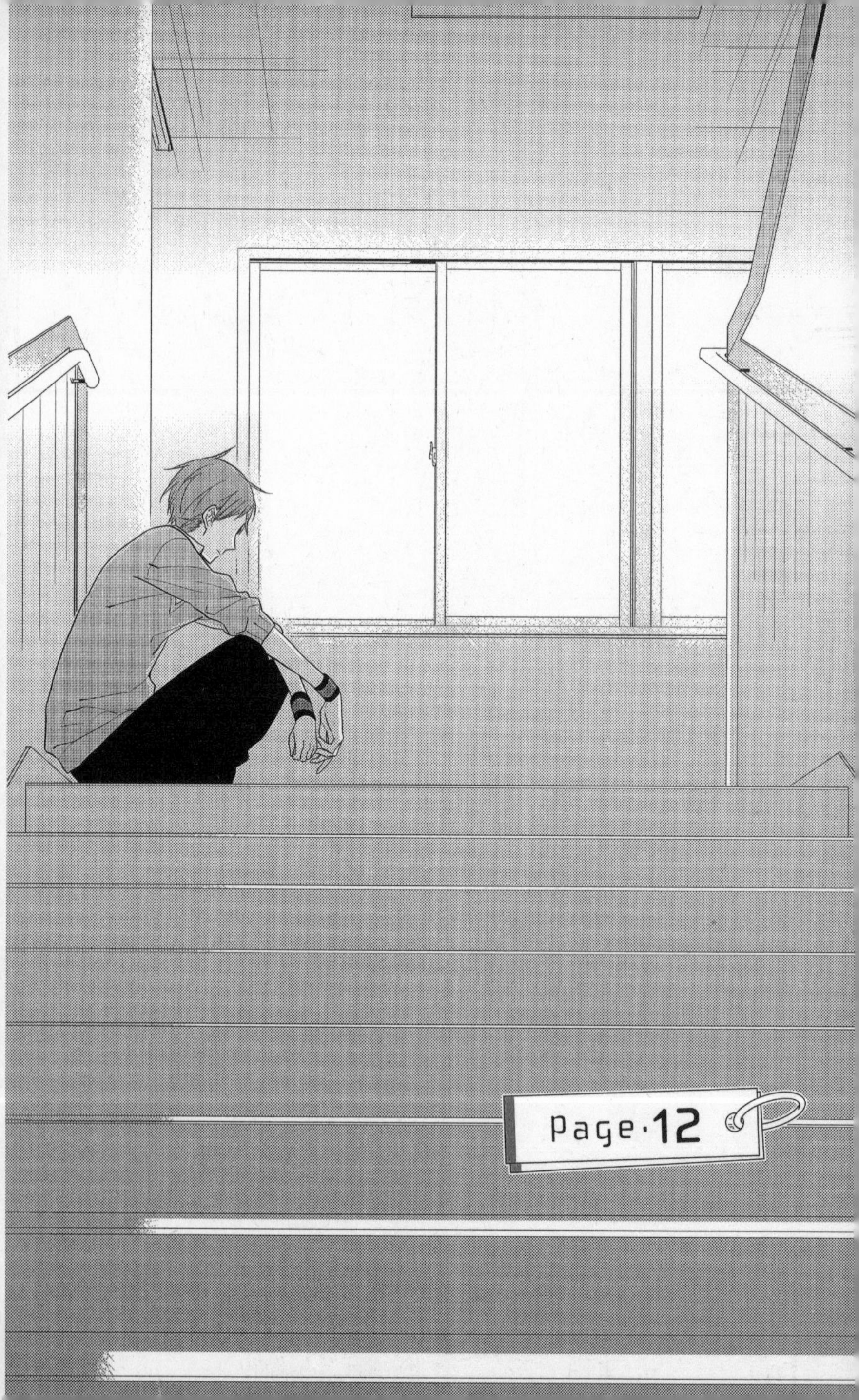
page·12

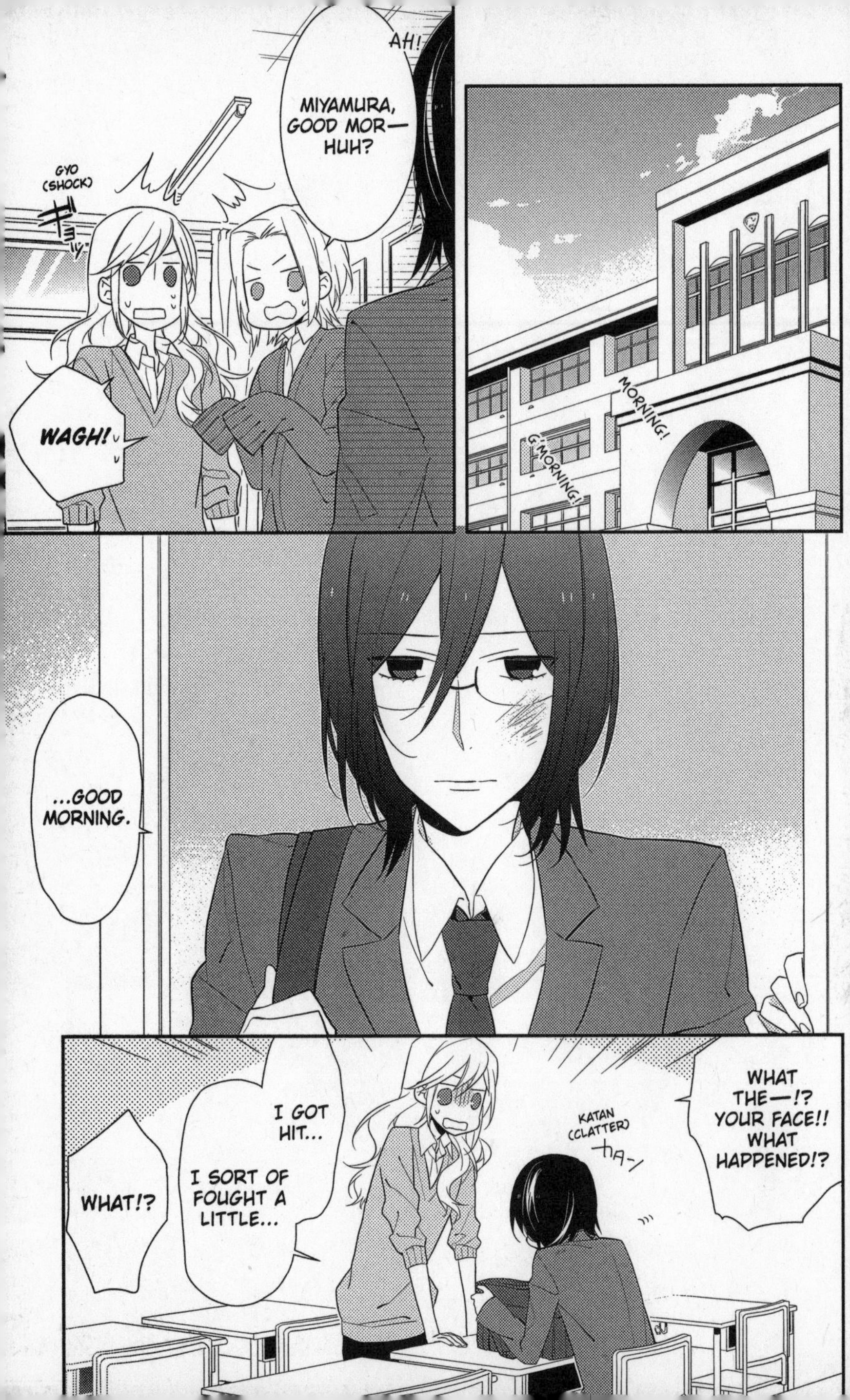
MORNING!
G'MORNING!
AH!
MIYAMURA, GOOD MOR— HUH?
GYO (SHOCK)
WAGH!
...GOOD MORNING.
WHAT THE—!? YOUR FACE!! WHAT HAPPENED!?
KATAN (CLATTER)
I GOT HIT...
I SORT OF FOUGHT A LITTLE...
WHAT!?

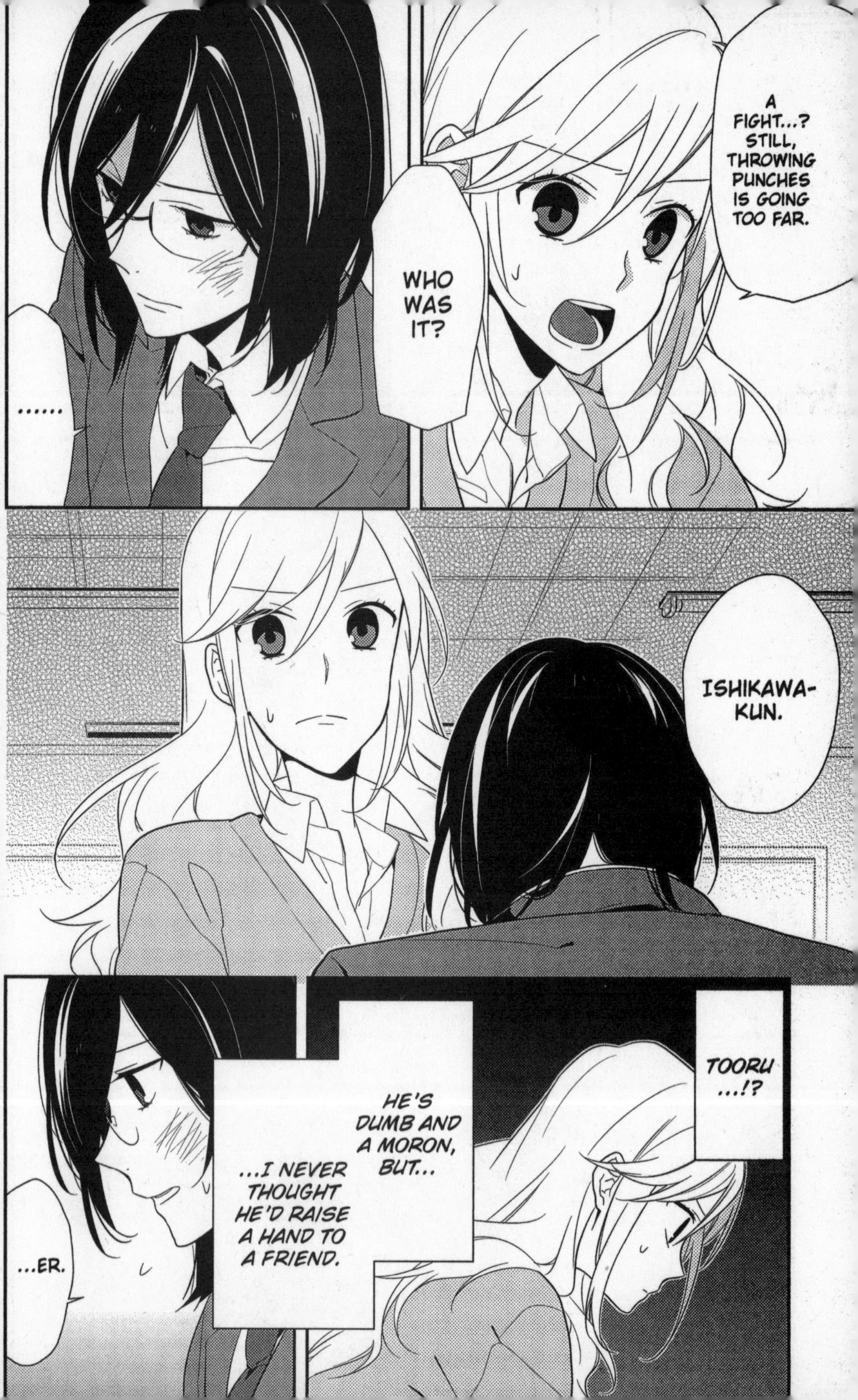
A FIGHT...? STILL, THROWING PUNCHES IS GOING TOO FAR.
WHO WAS IT?
......
ISHIKAWA-KUN.
TOORU ...!?
HE'S DUMB AND A MORON, BUT...
...I NEVER THOUGHT HE'D RAISE A HAND TO A FRIEND.
...ER.

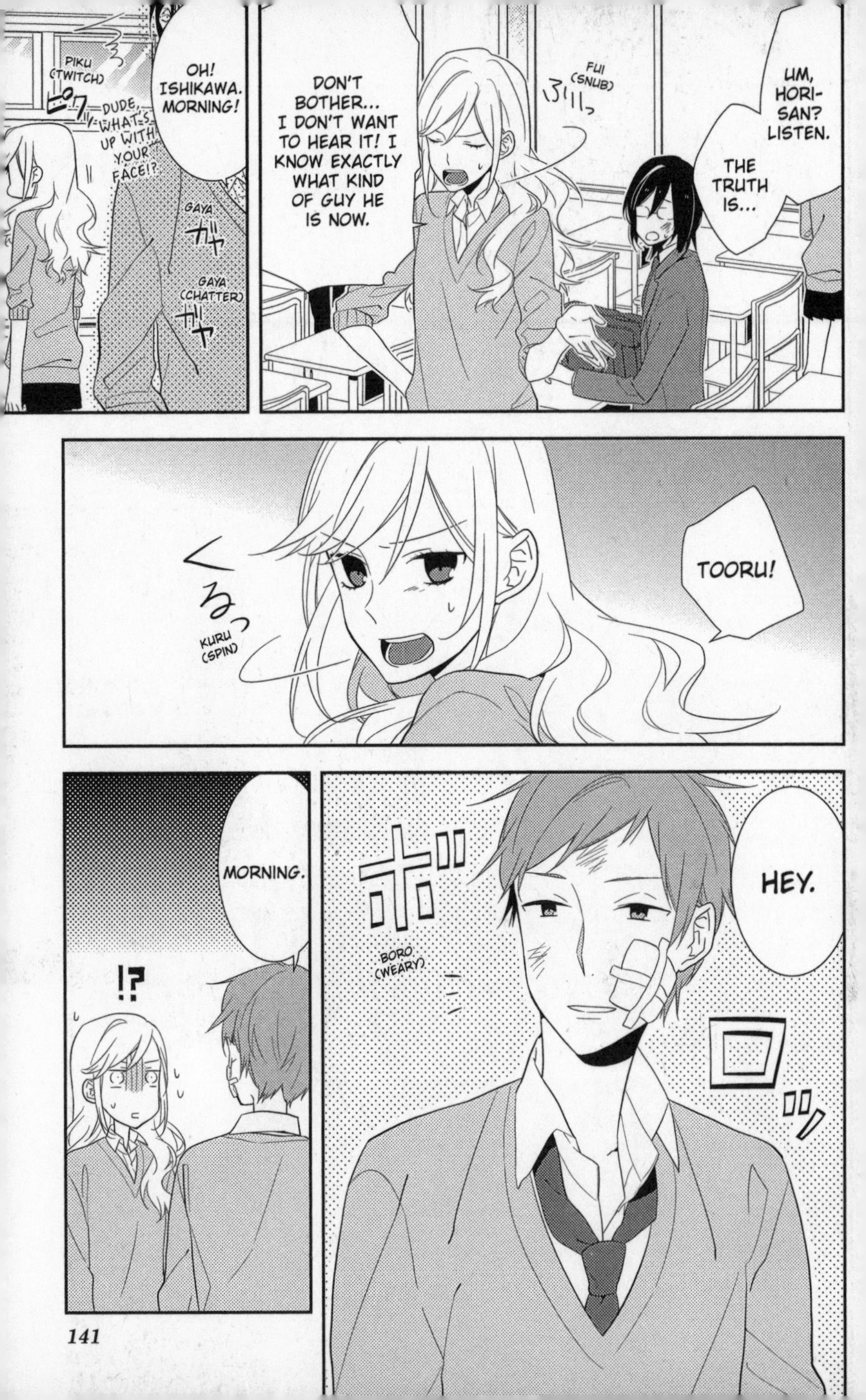
UM, HORI-SAN? LISTEN.
THE TRUTH IS...
FUI (SNUB)
DON'T BOTHER... I DON'T WANT TO HEAR IT! I KNOW EXACTLY WHAT KIND OF GUY HE IS NOW.
OH! ISHIKAWA. MORNING!
PIKU (TWITCH)
DUDE, WHAT'S UP WITH YOUR FACE!?
GAYA
GAYA (CHATTER)
TOORU!
KURU (SPIN)
HEY.
BORO (WEARY)
MORNING.
!?

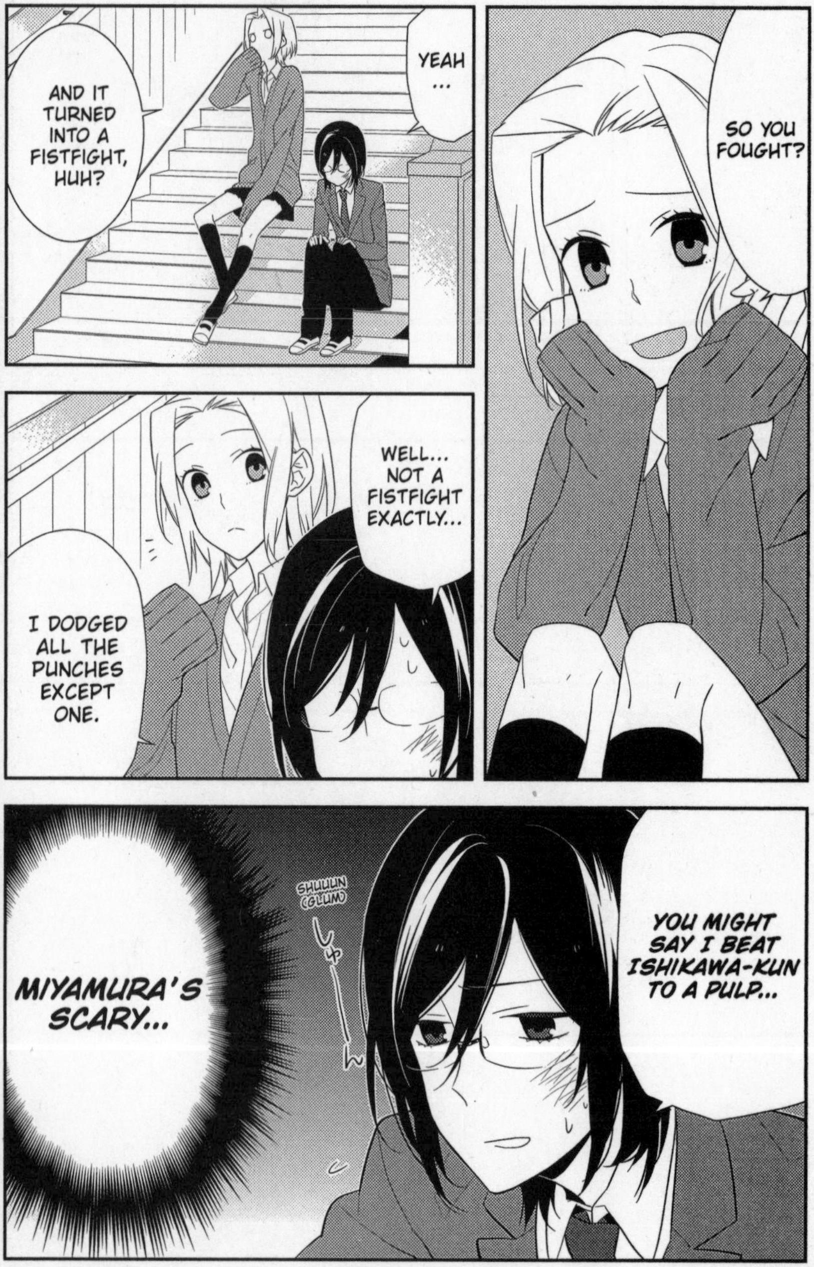
SO YOU FOUGHT?
YEAH ...
AND IT TURNED INTO A FISTFIGHT, HUH?
WELL... NOT A FISTFIGHT EXACTLY...
I DODGED ALL THE PUNCHES EXCEPT ONE.
YOU MIGHT SAY I BEAT ISHIKAWA-KUN TO A PULP...
SHUUUN (GLUM)
しゅーーん
MIYAMURA'S SCARY...

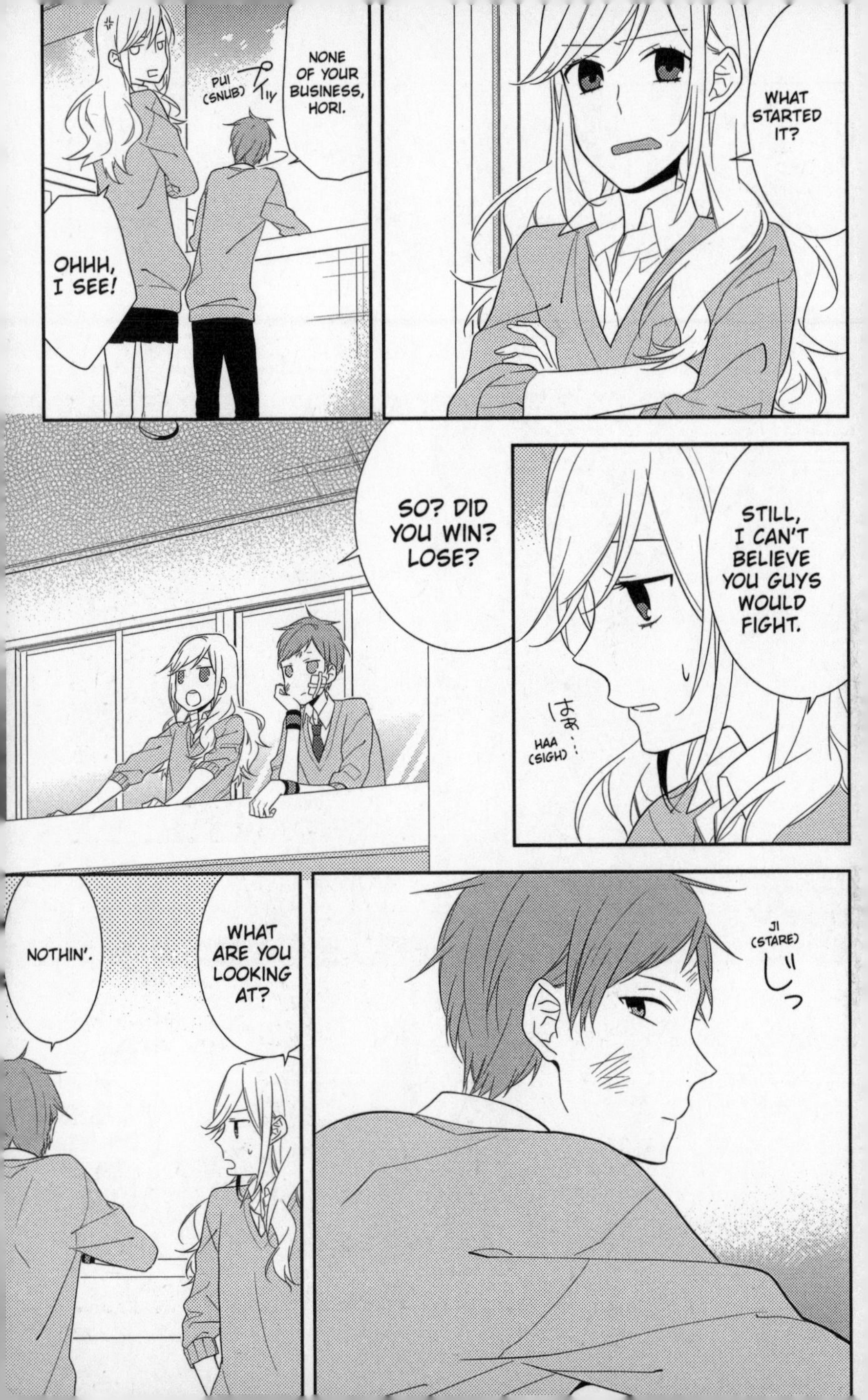
WHAT STARTED IT?
NONE OF YOUR BUSINESS, HORI.
PUI (SNUB)
OHHH, I SEE!
STILL, I CAN'T BELIEVE YOU GUYS WOULD FIGHT.
HAA (SIGH)
SO? DID YOU WIN? LOSE?
JI (STARE)
WHAT ARE YOU LOOKING AT?
NOTHIN'.

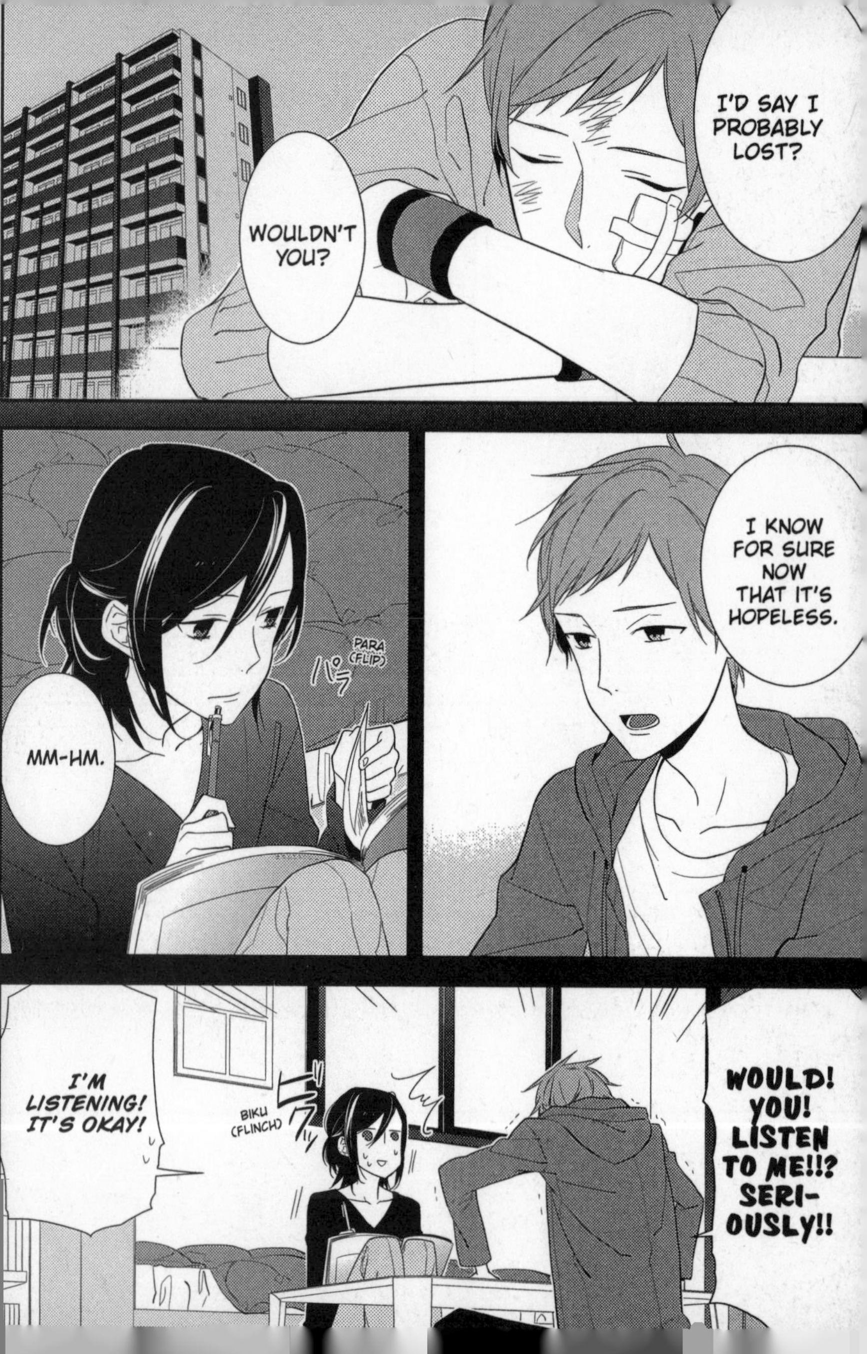
I'D SAY I PROBABLY LOST?
WOULDN'T YOU?
I KNOW FOR SURE NOW THAT IT'S HOPELESS.
パラ
PARA (FLIP)
MM-HM.
WOULD! YOU! LISTEN TO ME!!? SERI-OUSLY!!
BIKU (FLINCH)
I'M LISTENING! IT'S OKAY!

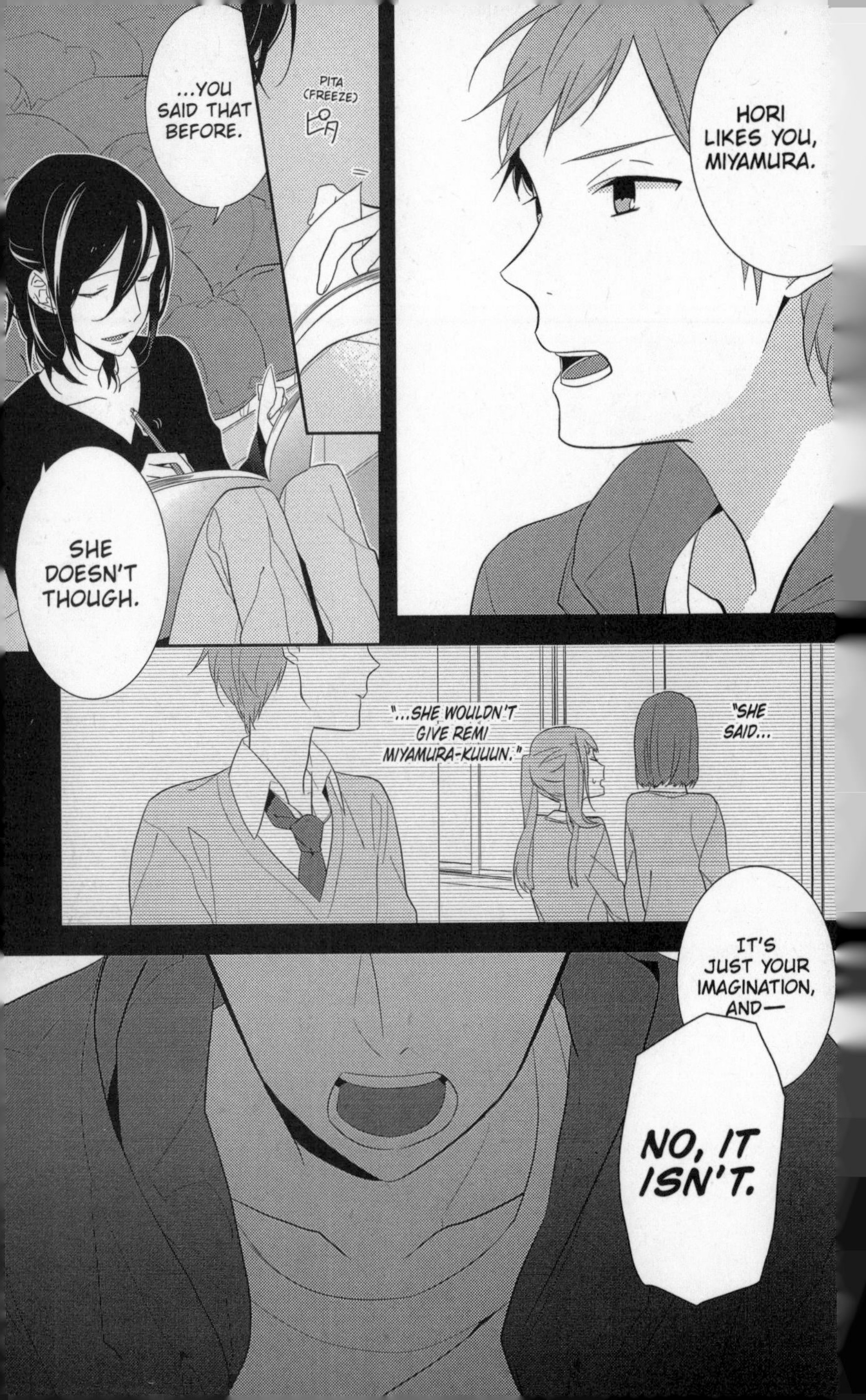
HORI LIKES YOU, MIYAMURA.
PITA (FREEZE)
...YOU SAID THAT BEFORE.
SHE DOESN'T THOUGH.
"SHE SAID...
"...SHE WOULDN'T GIVE REMI MIYAMURA-KUUUN."
IT'S JUST YOUR IMAGINATION, AND—
NO, IT ISN'T.

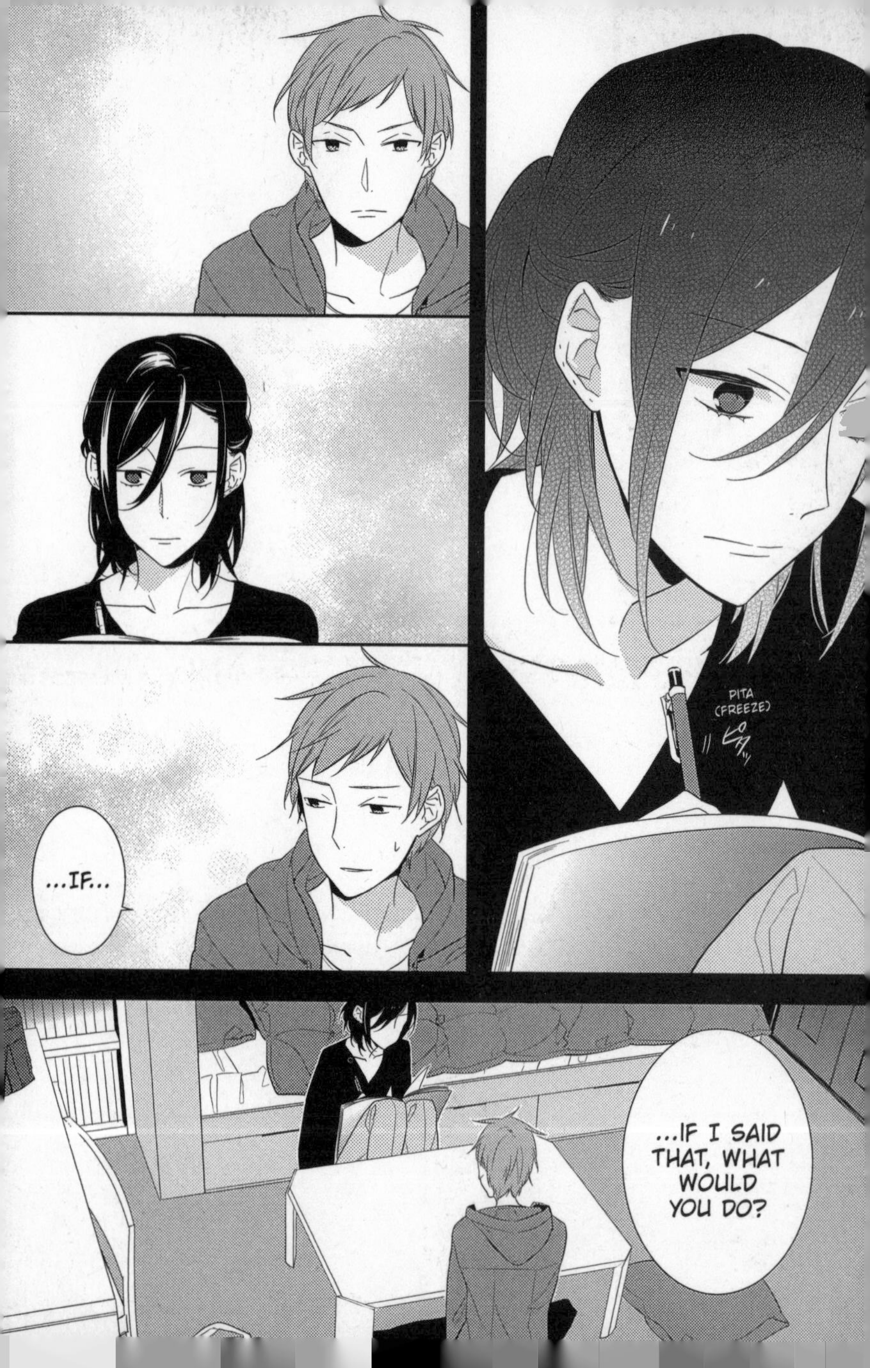
PITA
(FREEZE)
...IF...
...IF I SAID THAT, WHAT WOULD YOU DO?

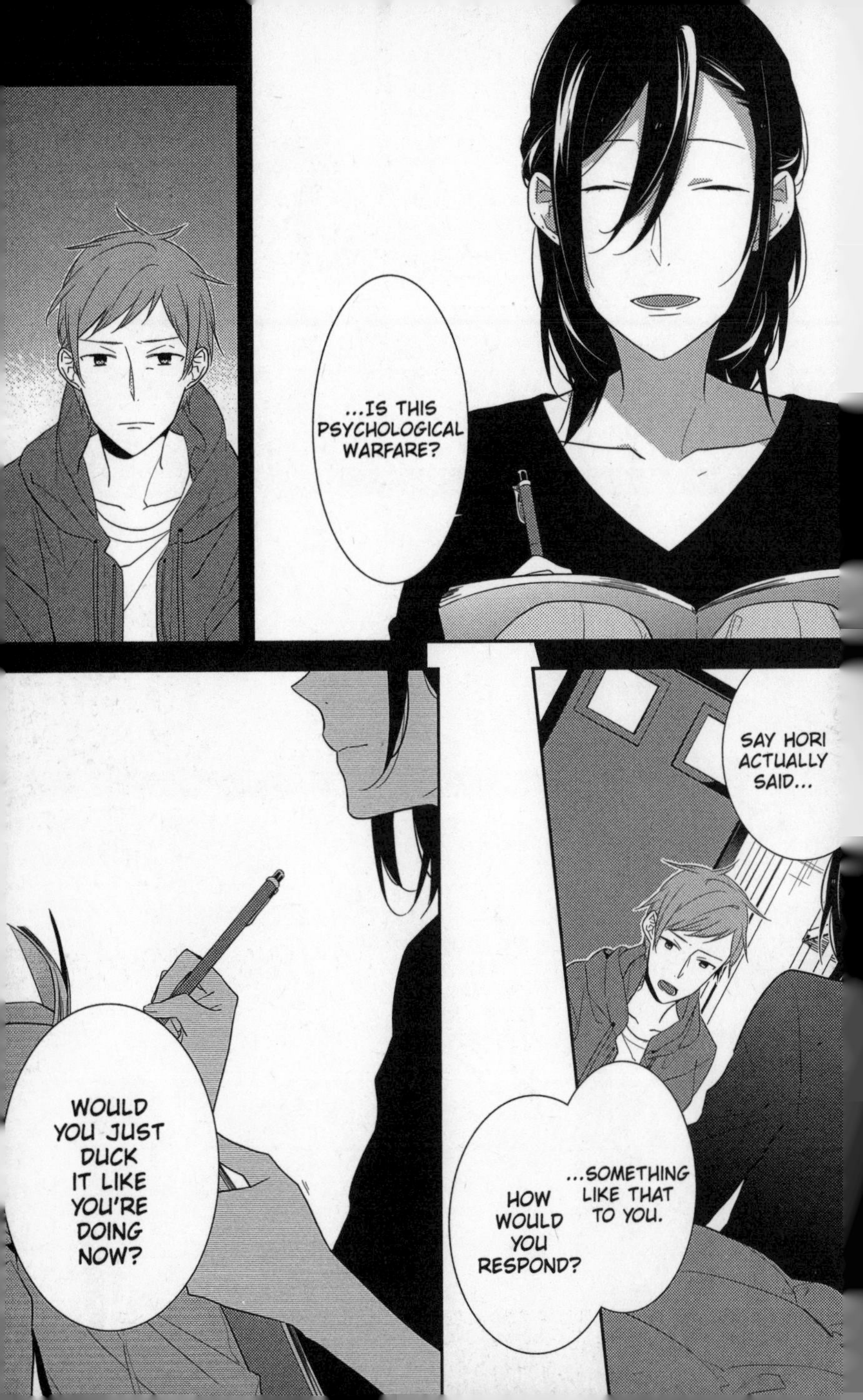
...IS THIS PSYCHOLOGICAL WARFARE?
SAY HORI ACTUALLY SAID...
...SOMETHING LIKE THAT TO YOU.
HOW WOULD YOU RESPOND?
WOULD YOU JUST DUCK IT LIKE YOU'RE DOING NOW?

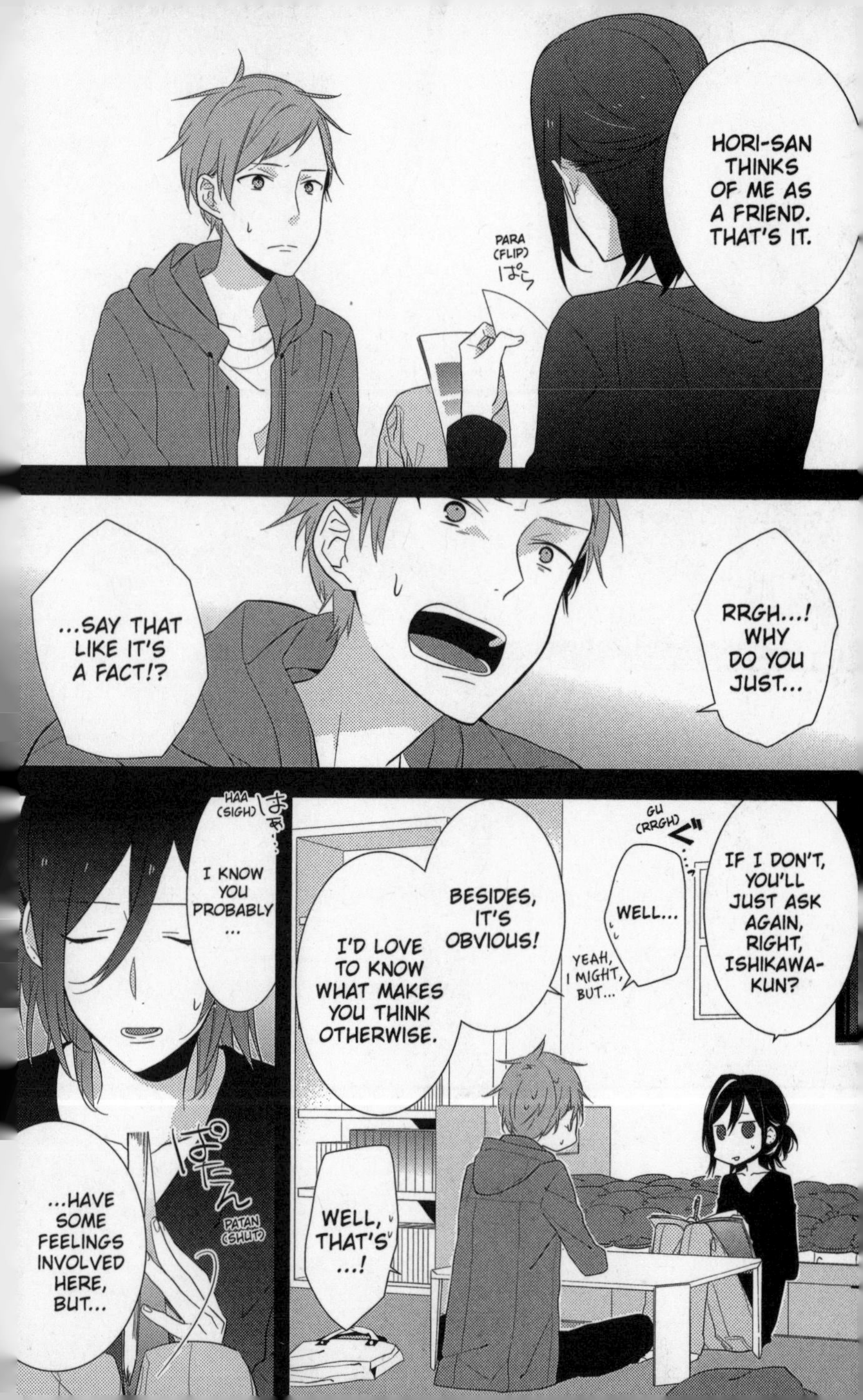
HORI-SAN THINKS OF ME AS A FRIEND. THAT'S IT.
PARA (FLIP) ぱら
RRGH...! WHY DO YOU JUST...
...SAY THAT LIKE IT'S A FACT!?
IF I DON'T, YOU'LL JUST ASK AGAIN, RIGHT, ISHIKAWA-KUN?
GU (RRGH) ぐ
WELL...
YEAH, I MIGHT, BUT...
BESIDES, IT'S OBVIOUS!
I'D LOVE TO KNOW WHAT MAKES YOU THINK OTHERWISE.
WELL, THAT'S ...!
HAA (SIGH) はあ…
I KNOW YOU PROBABLY ...
...HAVE SOME FEELINGS INVOLVED HERE, BUT...
PATAN (SHUT) ぱたん

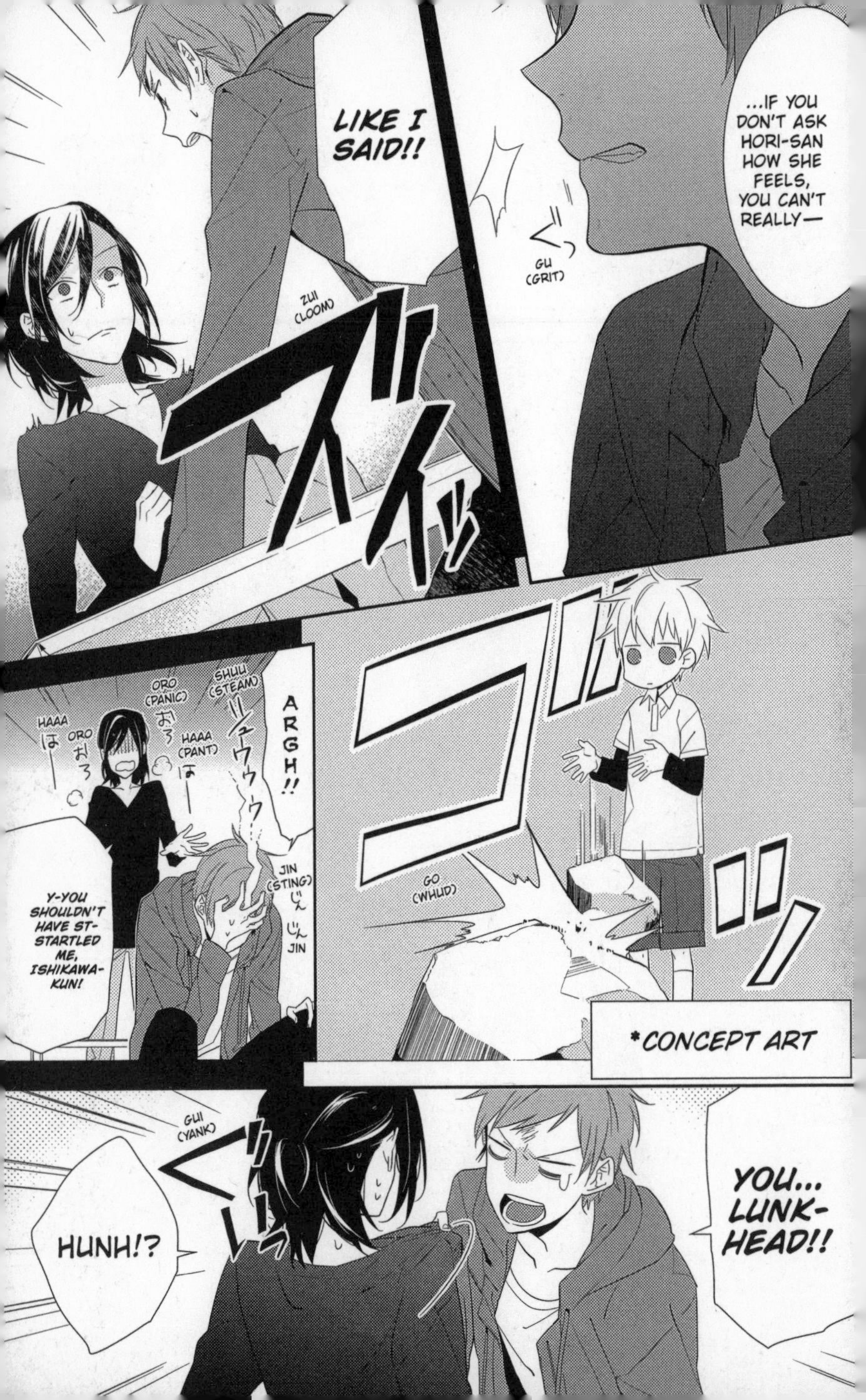

...IF YOU DON'T ASK HORI-SAN HOW SHE FEELS, YOU CAN'T REALLY—
ぐっ
GU (GRIT)
LIKE I SAID!!
ZUI (LOOM)
GO (WHUD)
*CONCEPT ART
ARGH!!
SHUU (STEAM)
シュウウウ
JIN (STING) じん
じん JIN
ORO (PANIC) おろ
ORO おろ
HAAA (PANT) は—
HAAA は—
Y-YOU SHOULDN'T HAVE ST-STARTLED ME, ISHIKAWA-KUN!
YOU... LUNK-HEAD!!
GUI (YANK)
HUNH!?

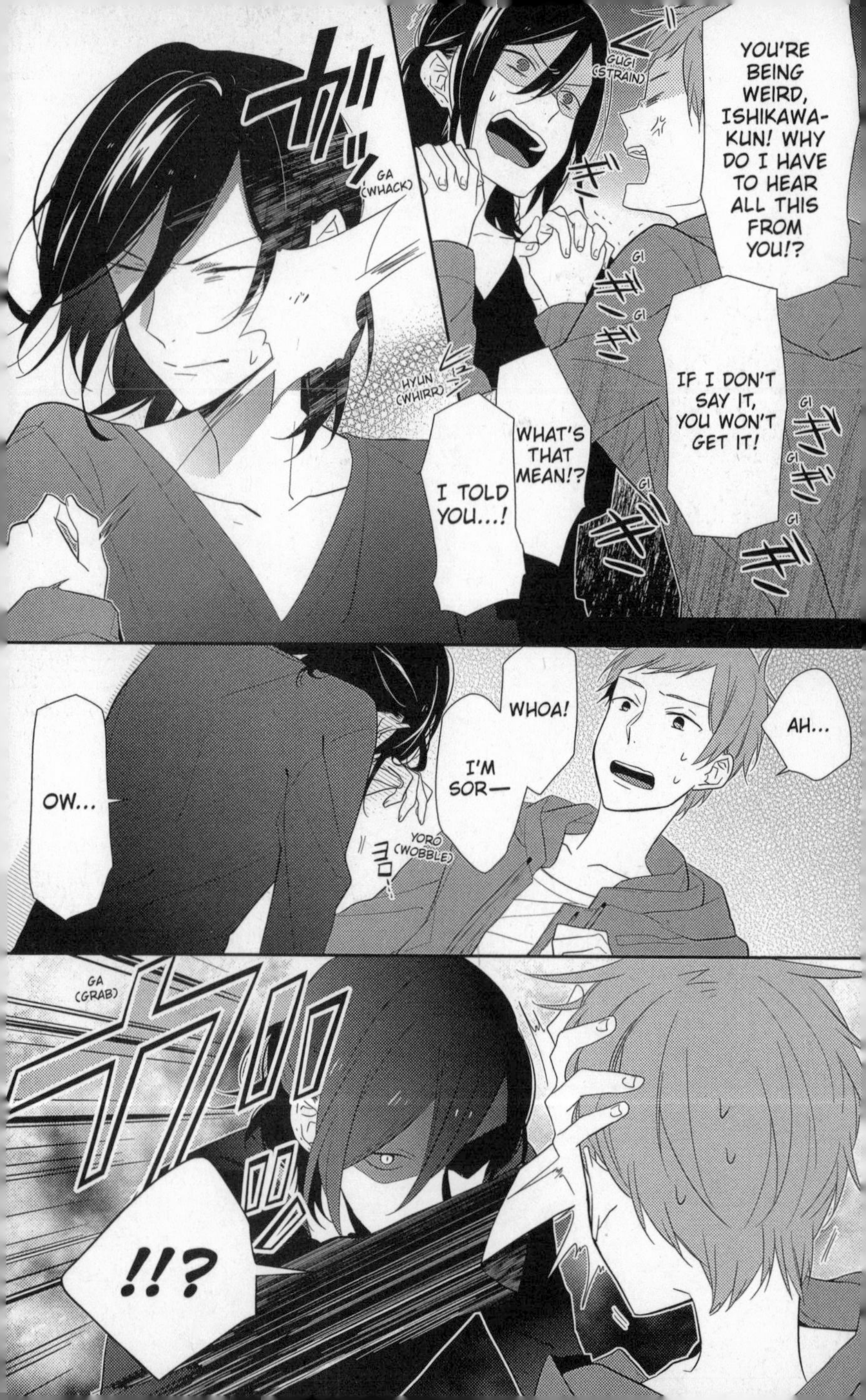
GUGI (STRAIN)
YOU'RE BEING WEIRD, ISHIKAWA-KUN! WHY DO I HAVE TO HEAR ALL THIS FROM YOU!?
GI
GI
IF I DON'T SAY IT, YOU WON'T GET IT!
GI
GI
GI
GI
WHAT'S THAT MEAN!?
I TOLD YOU...!
HYUN (WHIRR)
GA (WHACK)
AH...
WHOA!
I'M SOR—
YORO (WOBBLE)
OW...
GA (GRAB)
!!?

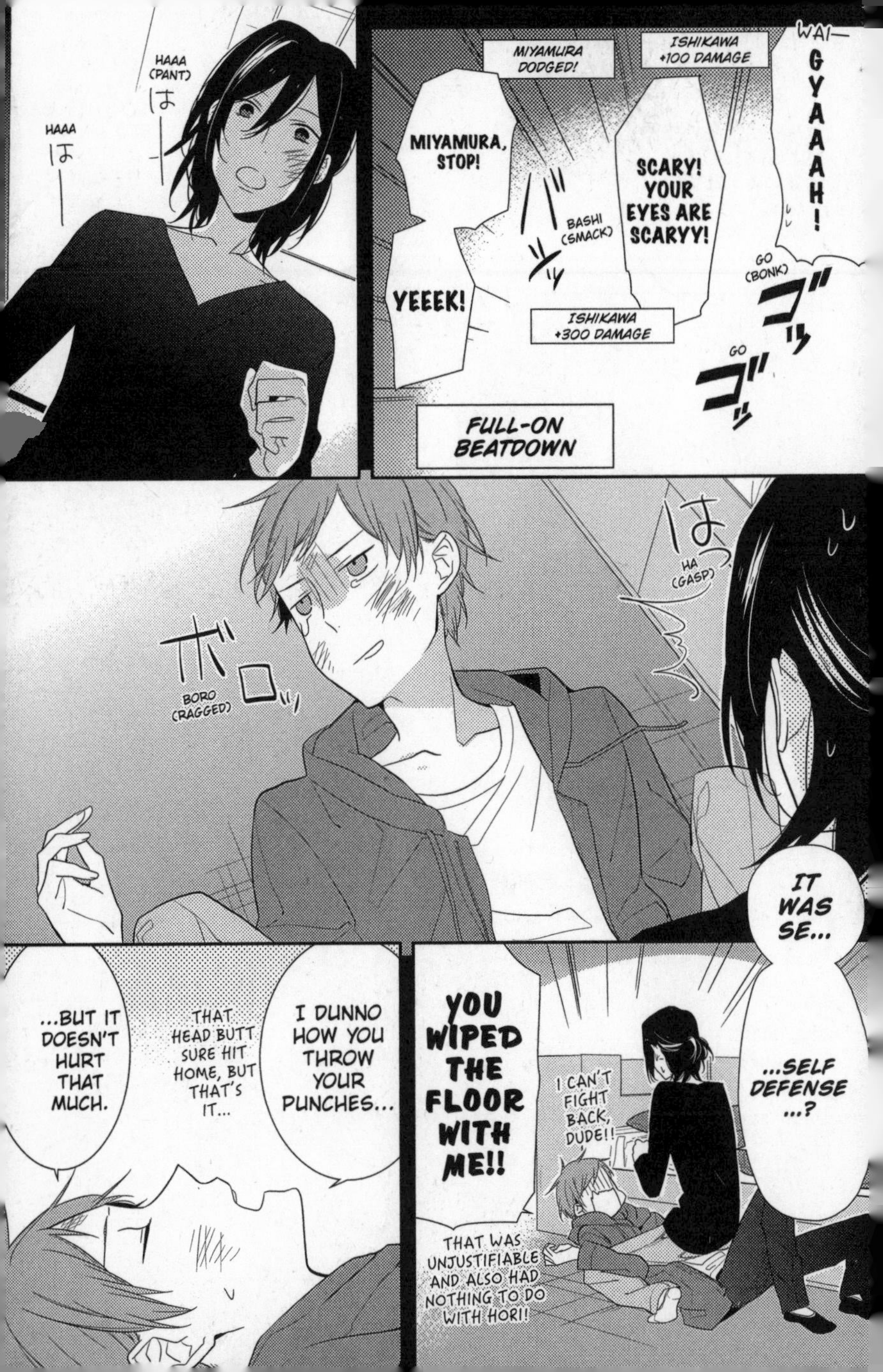
WAI— GYAAAH!
ISHIKAWA +100 DAMAGE
MIYAMURA DODGED!
SCARY! YOUR EYES ARE SCARYY!
MIYAMURA, STOP!
バシッ
BASHI (SMACK)
ゴッ
GO (BONK)
ゴッ
GO
ISHIKAWA +300 DAMAGE
YEEEK!
FULL-ON BEATDOWN
HAAA (PANT)
は—
HAAA
は—
はっ
HA (GASP)
IT WAS SE...
ボロッ
BORO (RAGGED)
...SELF DEFENSE ...?
I CAN'T FIGHT BACK, DUDE!!
YOU WIPED THE FLOOR WITH ME!!
THAT WAS UNJUSTIFIABLE AND ALSO HAD NOTHING TO DO WITH HORI!
I DUNNO HOW YOU THROW YOUR PUNCHES...
THAT HEAD BUTT SURE HIT HOME, BUT THAT'S IT...
...BUT IT DOESN'T HURT THAT MUCH.

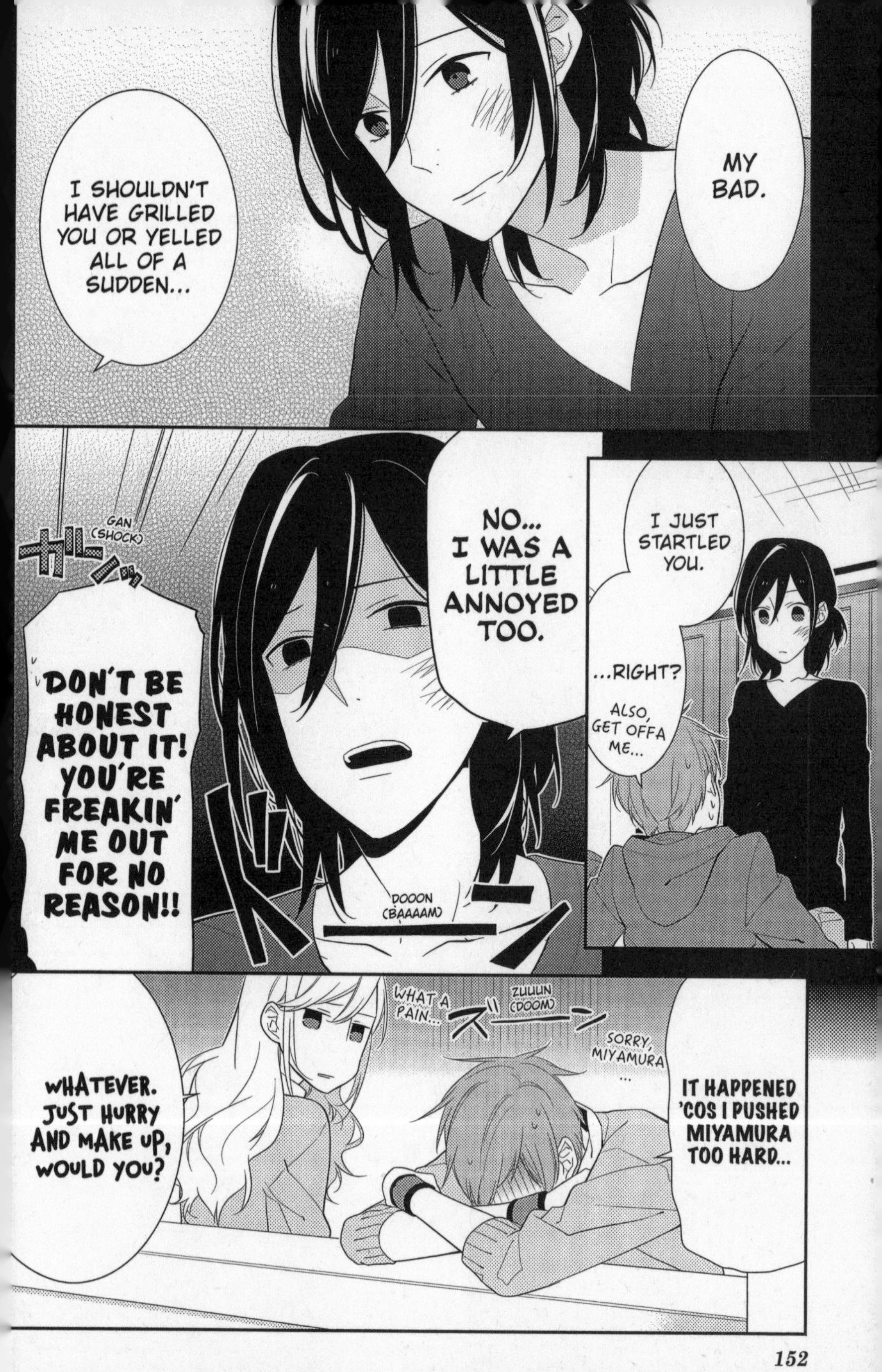
MY BAD.
I SHOULDN'T HAVE GRILLED YOU OR YELLED ALL OF A SUDDEN...
I JUST STARTLED YOU.
...RIGHT?
ALSO, GET OFFA ME...
NO... I WAS A LITTLE ANNOYED TOO.
GAN (SHOCK)
DON'T BE HONEST ABOUT IT! YOU'RE FREAKIN' ME OUT FOR NO REASON!!
DOOON (BAAAAM)
IT HAPPENED 'COS I PUSHED MIYAMURA TOO HARD...
SORRY, MIYAMURA...
ZUUUN (DOOM)
WHAT A PAIN...
WHATEVER. JUST HURRY AND MAKE UP, WOULD YOU?

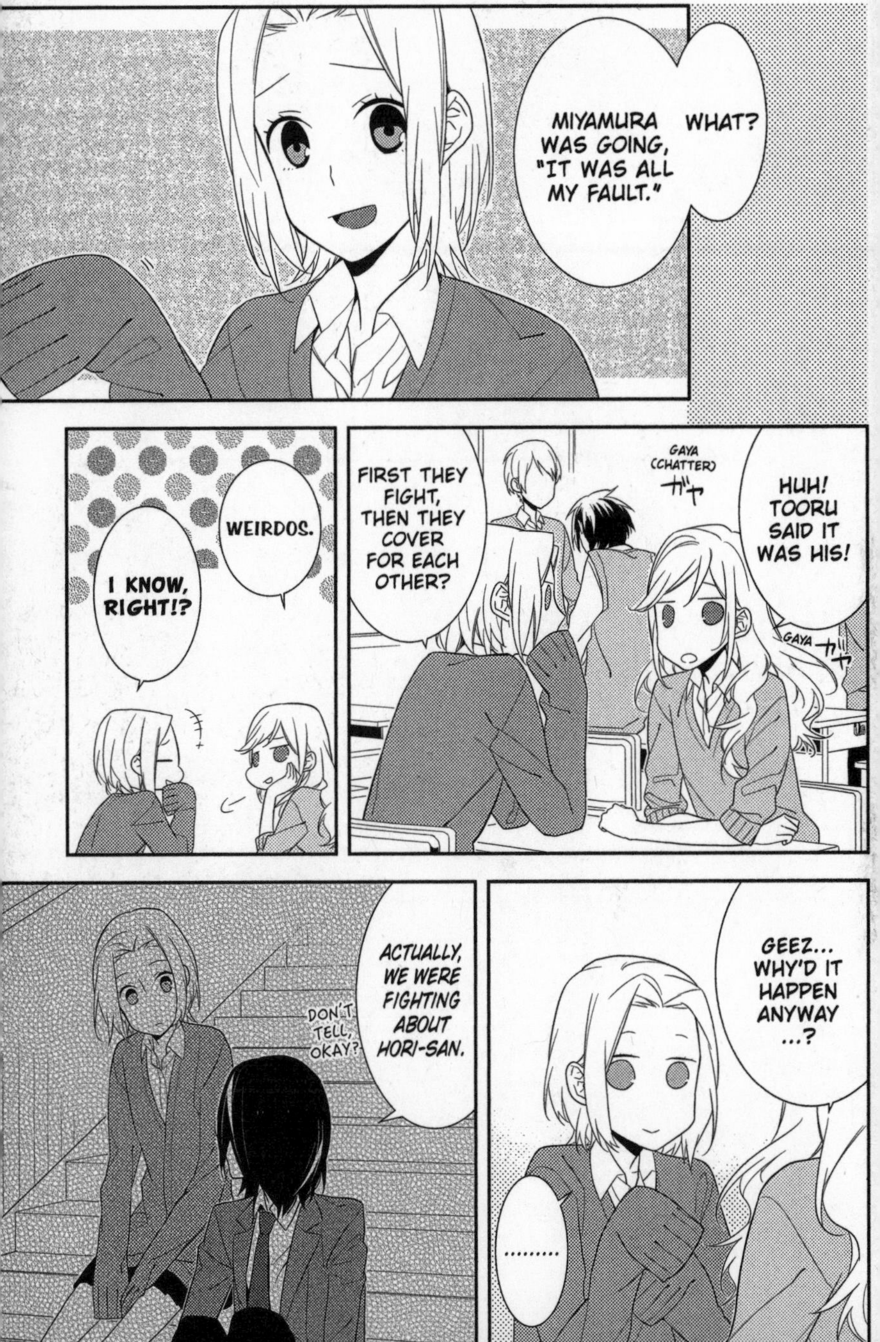
WHAT?
MIYAMURA WAS GOING, "IT WAS ALL MY FAULT."
GAYA (CHATTER) ガヤ
HUH! TOORU SAID IT WAS HIS!
GAYA ガヤ
FIRST THEY FIGHT, THEN THEY COVER FOR EACH OTHER?
WEIRDOS.
I KNOW, RIGHT!?
GEEZ... WHY'D IT HAPPEN ANYWAY ...?
....
ACTUALLY, WE WERE FIGHTING ABOUT HORI-SAN.
DON'T TELL, OKAY?

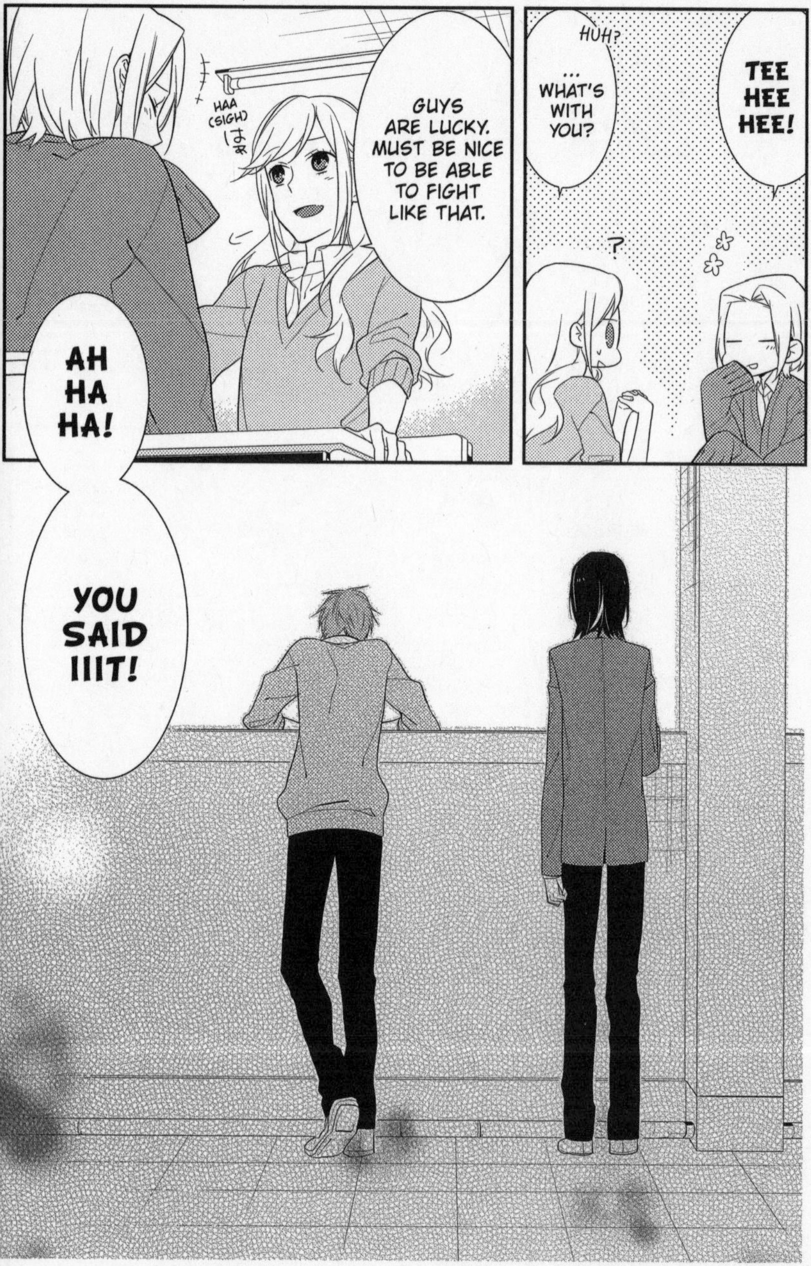
TEE HEE HEE!
HUH?
... WHAT'S WITH YOU?
?
GUYS ARE LUCKY. MUST BE NICE TO BE ABLE TO FIGHT LIKE THAT.
HAA (SIGH) はぁ
AH HA HA!
YOU SAID IIIT!

HORIMIYA

HORIMIYA

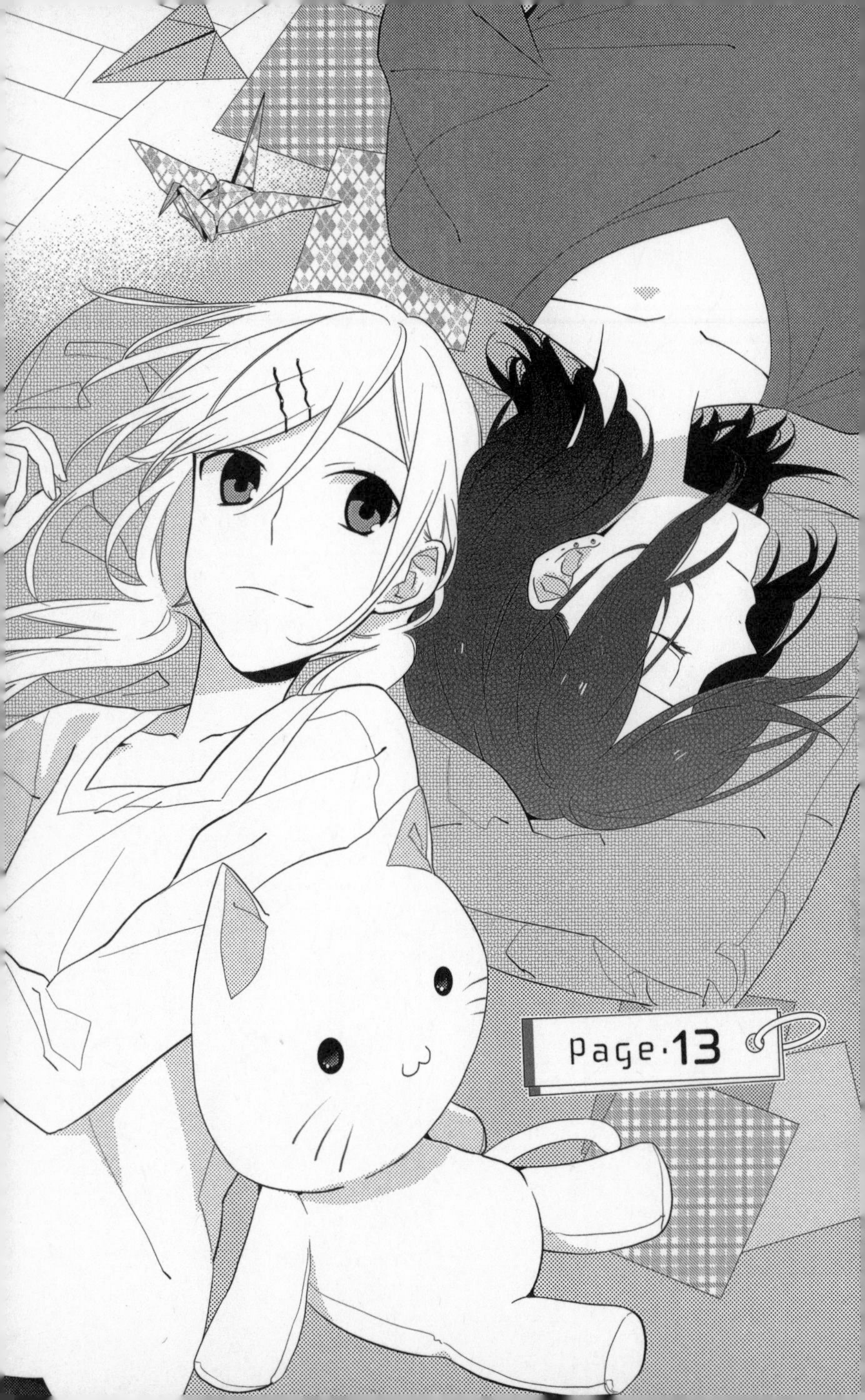
page·13

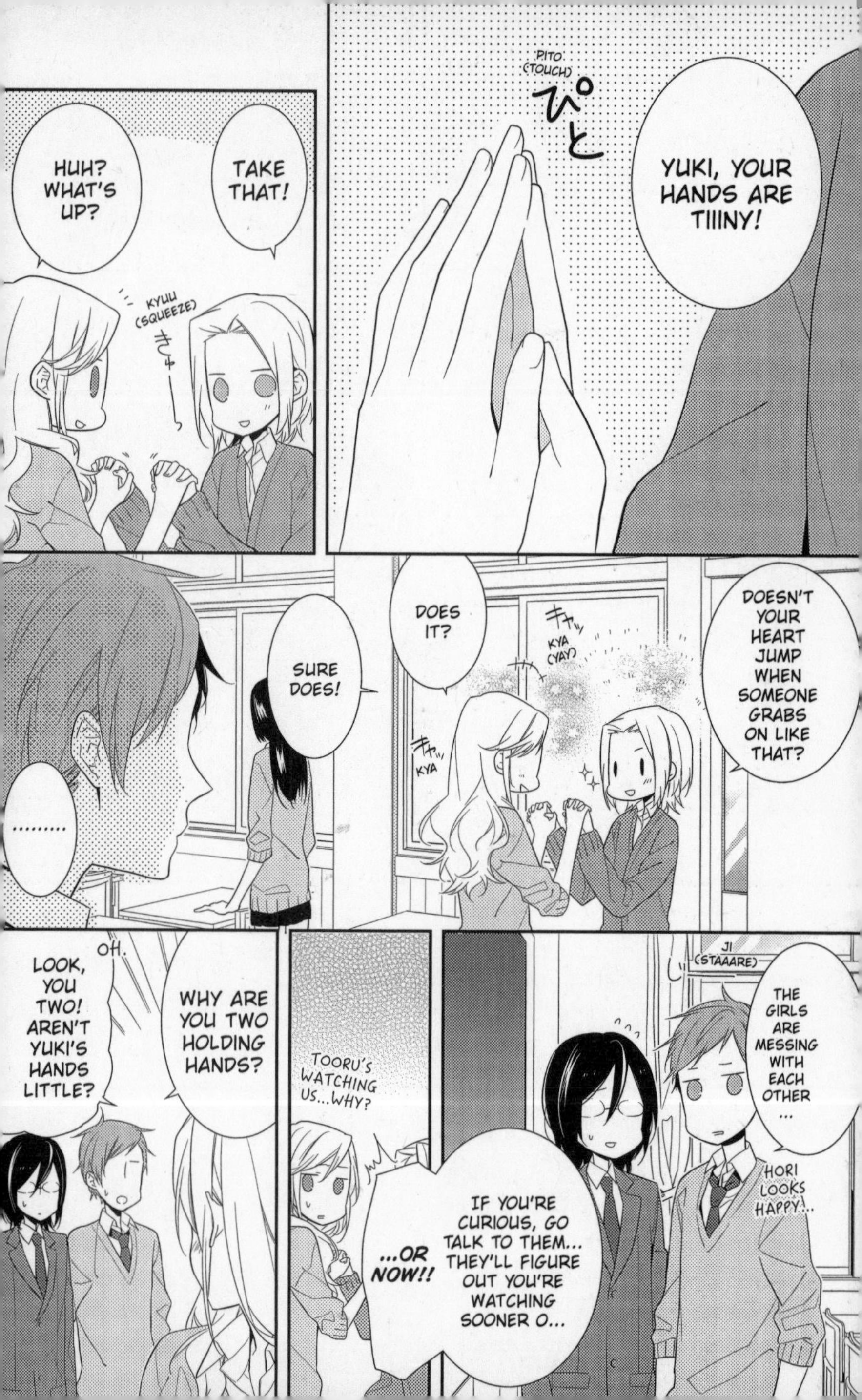
PITO (TOUCH)
ぴと
YUKI, YOUR HANDS ARE TIIINY!
TAKE THAT!
HUH? WHAT'S UP?
KYUU (SQUEEZE)
きゅー
DOESN'T YOUR HEART JUMP WHEN SOMEONE GRABS ON LIKE THAT?
DOES IT?
キャッ
KYA (YAY)
SURE DOES!
キャッ
KYA
....
JI (STAAARE)
THE GIRLS ARE MESSING WITH EACH OTHER...
HORI LOOKS HAPPY...
IF YOU'RE CURIOUS, GO TALK TO THEM... THEY'LL FIGURE OUT YOU'RE WATCHING SOONER O...
...OR NOW!!
TOORU'S WATCHING US...WHY?
WHY ARE YOU TWO HOLDING HANDS?
OH.
LOOK, YOU TWO! AREN'T YUKI'S HANDS LITTLE?

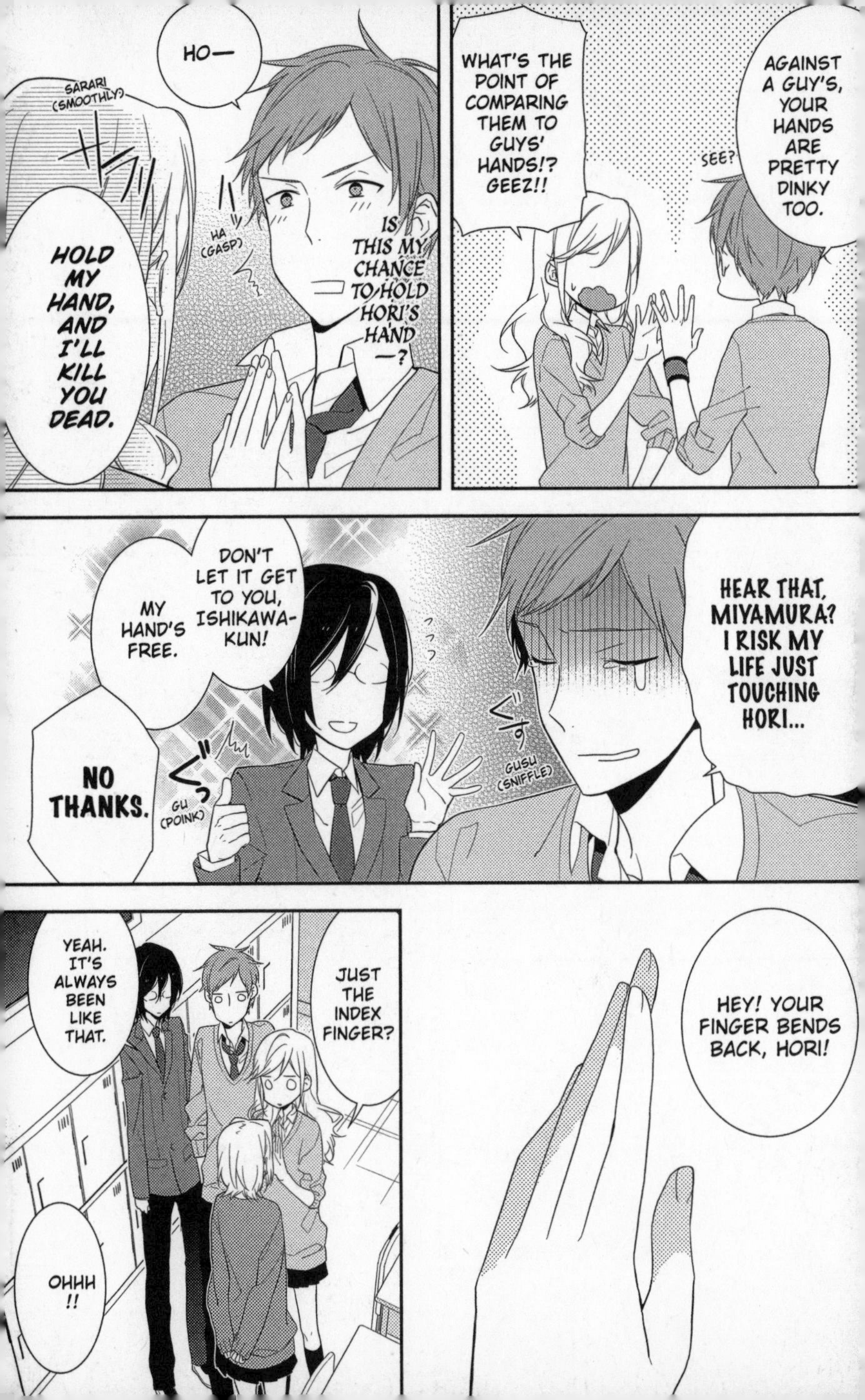
AGAINST A GUY'S, YOUR HANDS ARE PRETTY DINKY TOO.
SEE?
WHAT'S THE POINT OF COMPARING THEM TO GUYS' HANDS!? GEEZ!!
HO—
SARARI (SMOOTHLY)
IS THIS MY CHANCE TO HOLD HORI'S HAND—?
HA (GASP)
HOLD MY HAND, AND I'LL KILL YOU DEAD.
HEAR THAT, MIYAMURA? I RISK MY LIFE JUST TOUCHING HORI...
GUSU (SNIFFLE)
DON'T LET IT GET TO YOU, ISHIKAWA-KUN!
MY HAND'S FREE.
GU (POINK)
NO THANKS.
HEY! YOUR FINGER BENDS BACK, HORI!
JUST THE INDEX FINGER?
YEAH. IT'S ALWAYS BEEN LIKE THAT.
OHHH !!

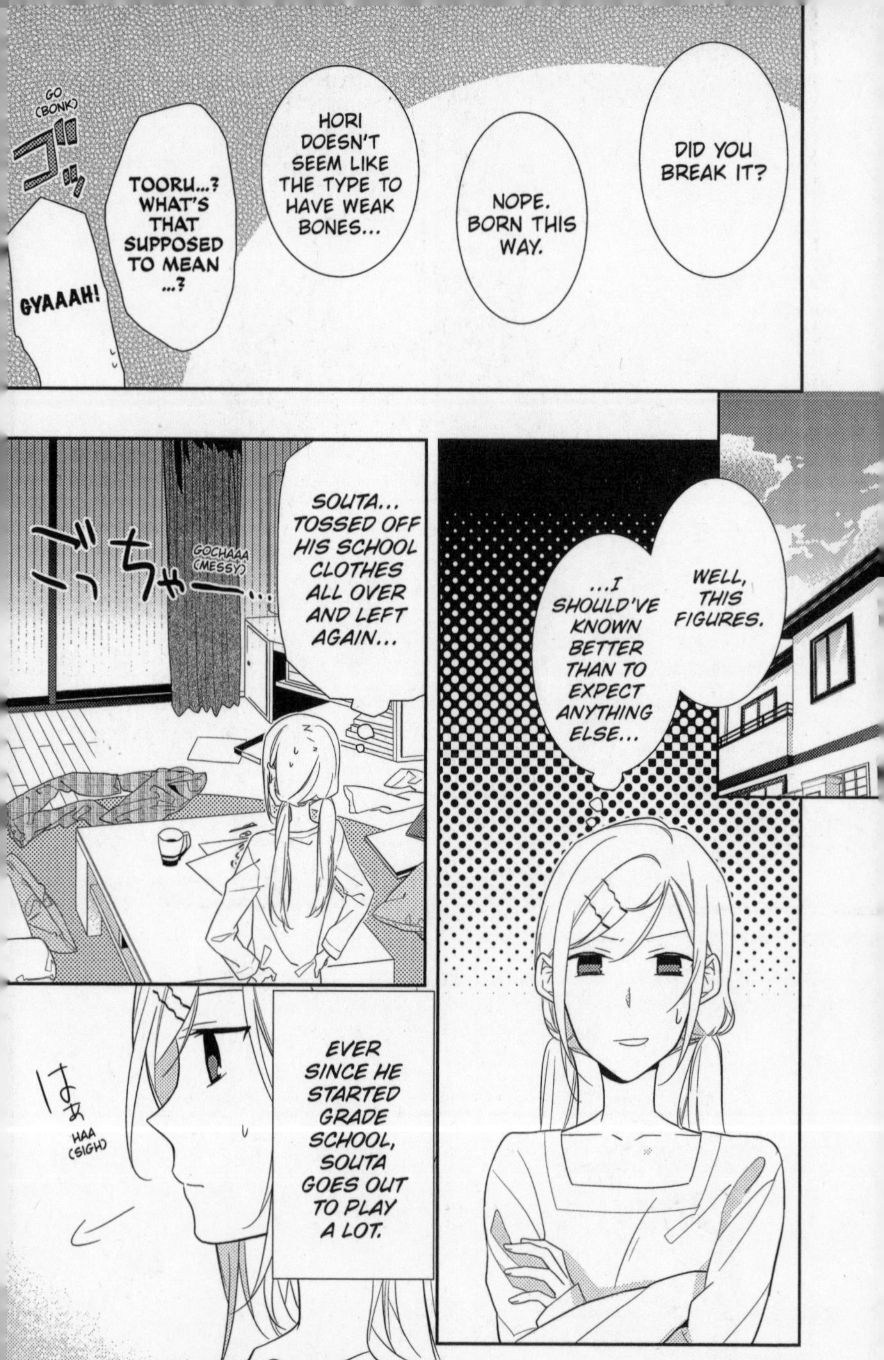
DID YOU BREAK IT?
NOPE. BORN THIS WAY.
HORI DOESN'T SEEM LIKE THE TYPE TO HAVE WEAK BONES...
TOORU...? WHAT'S THAT SUPPOSED TO MEAN ...?
GO (BONK)
GYAAAH!
WELL, THIS FIGURES.
...I SHOULD'VE KNOWN BETTER THAN TO EXPECT ANYTHING ELSE...
SOUTA... TOSSED OFF HIS SCHOOL CLOTHES ALL OVER AND LEFT AGAIN...
GOCHAAA (MESSY)
EVER SINCE HE STARTED GRADE SCHOOL, SOUTA GOES OUT TO PLAY A LOT.
HAA (SIGH)

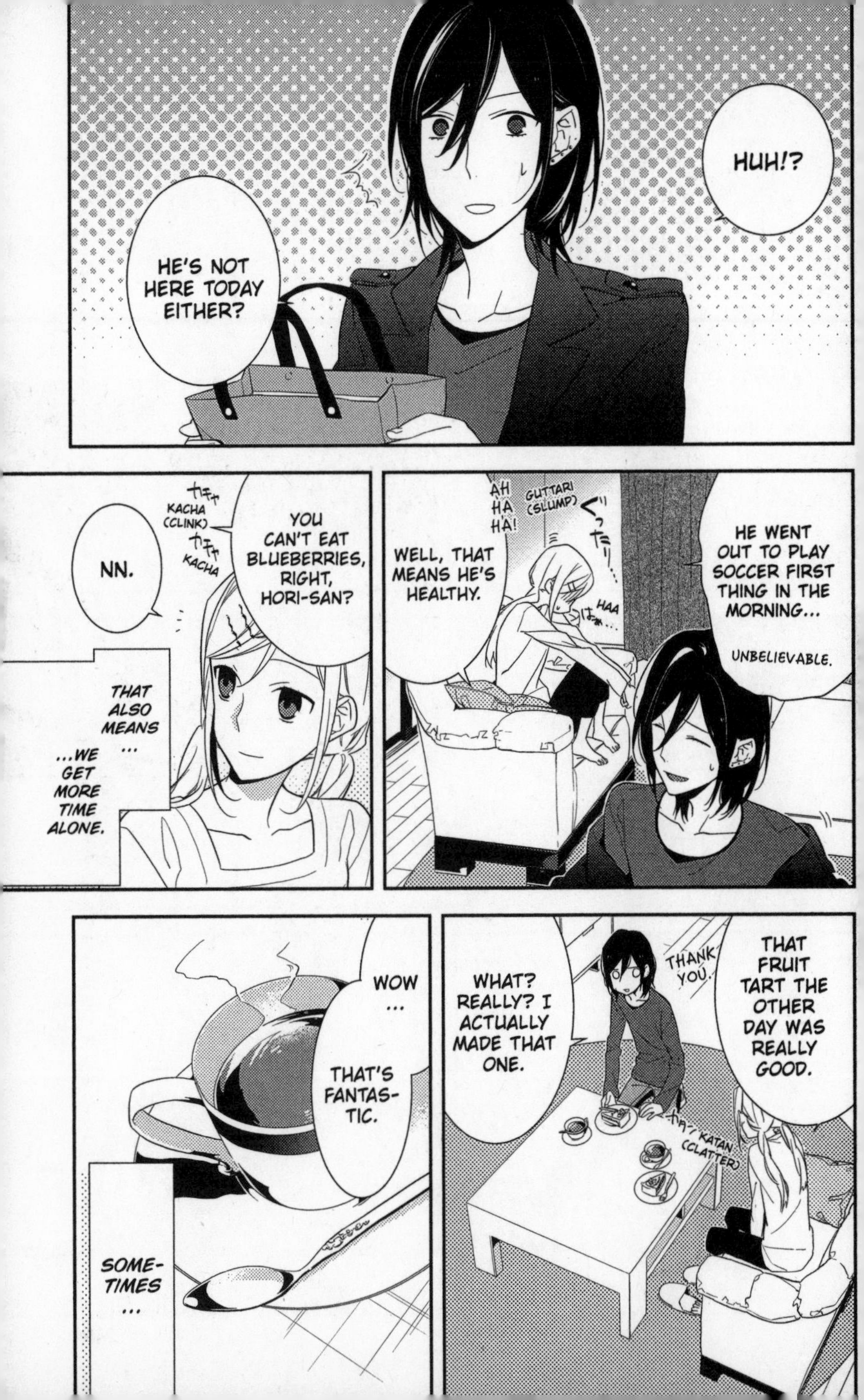
HUH!?
HE'S NOT HERE TODAY EITHER?
HE WENT OUT TO PLAY SOCCER FIRST THING IN THE MORNING...
UNBELIEVABLE.
GUTTARI (SLUMP)
AH HA HA!
HAA
WELL, THAT MEANS HE'S HEALTHY.
YOU CAN'T EAT BLUEBERRIES, RIGHT, HORI-SAN?
KACHA (CLINK) KACHA
NN.
THAT ALSO MEANS...
...WE GET MORE TIME ALONE.
THAT FRUIT TART THE OTHER DAY WAS REALLY GOOD.
THANK YOU.
WHAT? REALLY? I ACTUALLY MADE THAT ONE.
KATAN (CLATTER)
WOW... THAT'S FANTASTIC.
SOMETIMES...

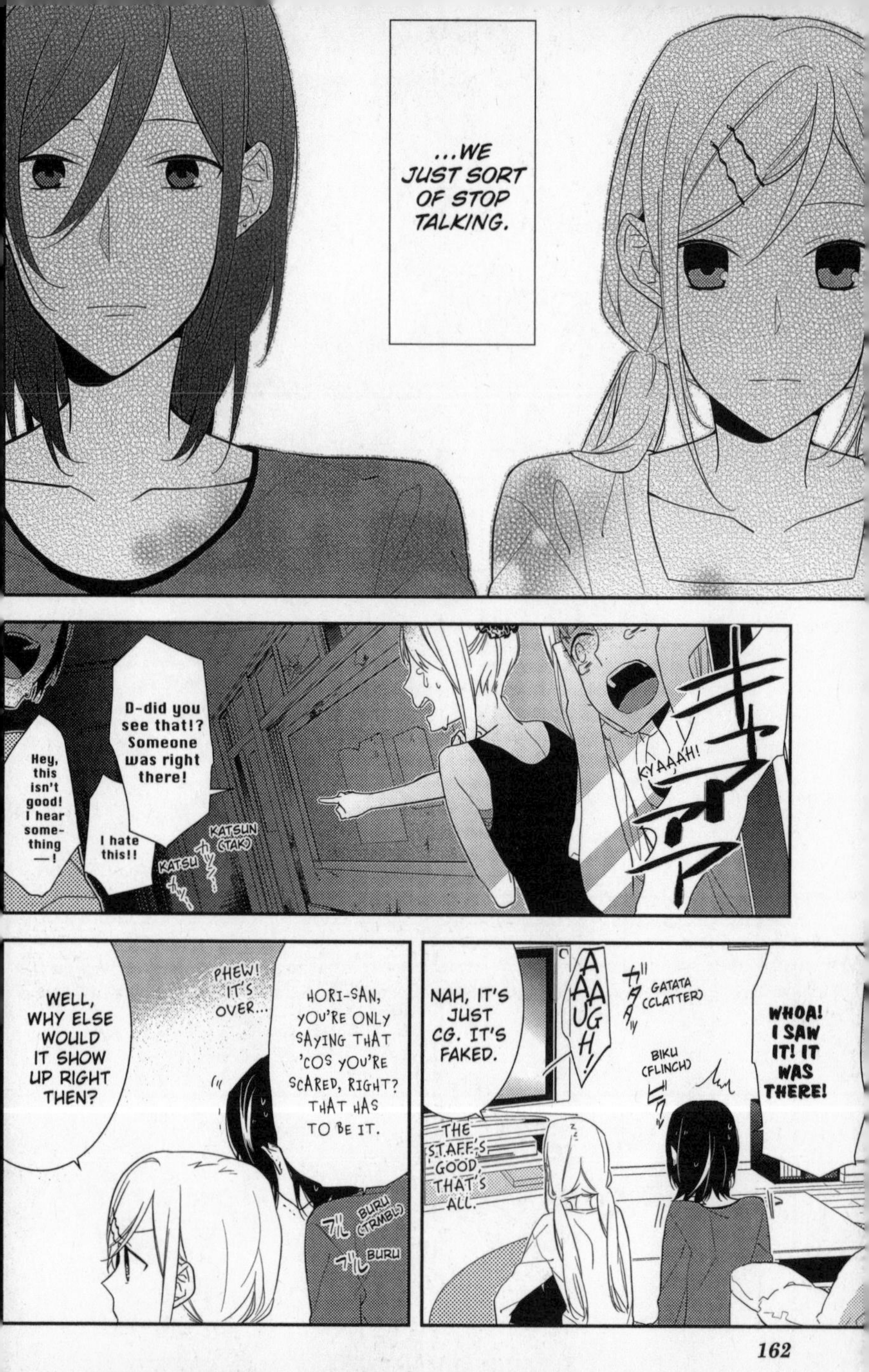
...WE JUST SORT OF STOP TALKING.
KYAAAH!
D-did you see that!? Someone was right there!
Hey, this isn't good! I hear some-thing—!
I hate this!!
KATSUN (TAK)
KATSU
WHOA! I SAW IT! IT WAS THERE!
GATATA (CLATTER)
AAAUGH!
BIKU (FLINCH)
NAH, IT'S JUST CG. IT'S FAKED.
THE STAFF'S GOOD, THAT'S ALL.
HORI-SAN, YOU'RE ONLY SAYING THAT 'COS YOU'RE SCARED, RIGHT? THAT HAS TO BE IT.
PHEW! IT'S OVER...
WELL, WHY ELSE WOULD IT SHOW UP RIGHT THEN?
BURU (TRMBL)
BURU

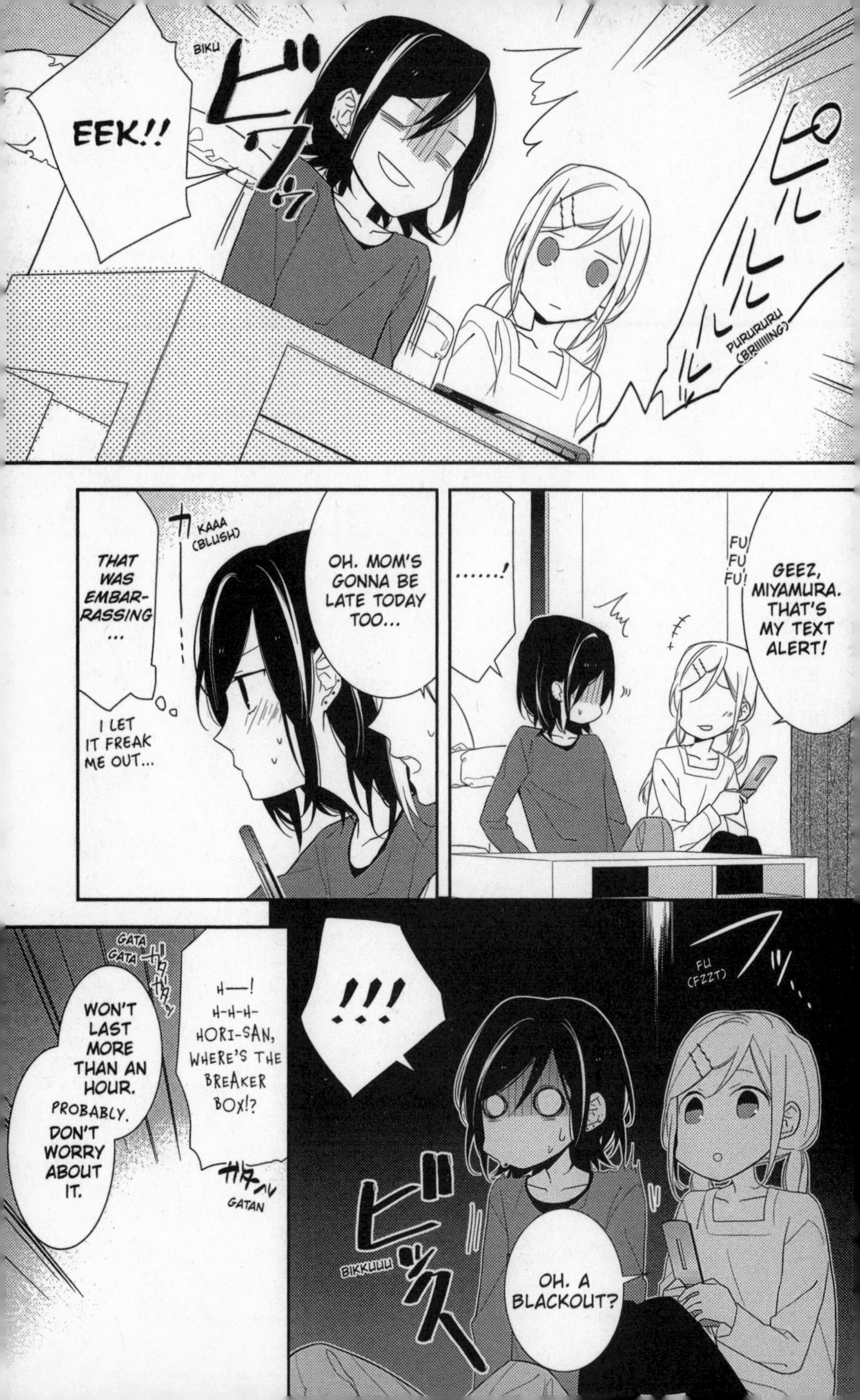
PURURURU (BRIIIIING)
BIKU
EEK!!
OH. MOM'S GONNA BE LATE TODAY TOO...
KAAA (BLUSH)
THAT WAS EMBARRASSING...
I LET IT FREAK ME OUT...
FU FU FU!
GEEZ, MIYAMURA. THAT'S MY TEXT ALERT!
......!
FU (FZZT)
!!!
BIKKUUU
OH. A BLACKOUT?
GATA GATA
H—! H-H-H-HORI-SAN, WHERE'S THE BREAKER BOX!?
GATAN
WON'T LAST MORE THAN AN HOUR. PROBABLY. DON'T WORRY ABOUT IT.

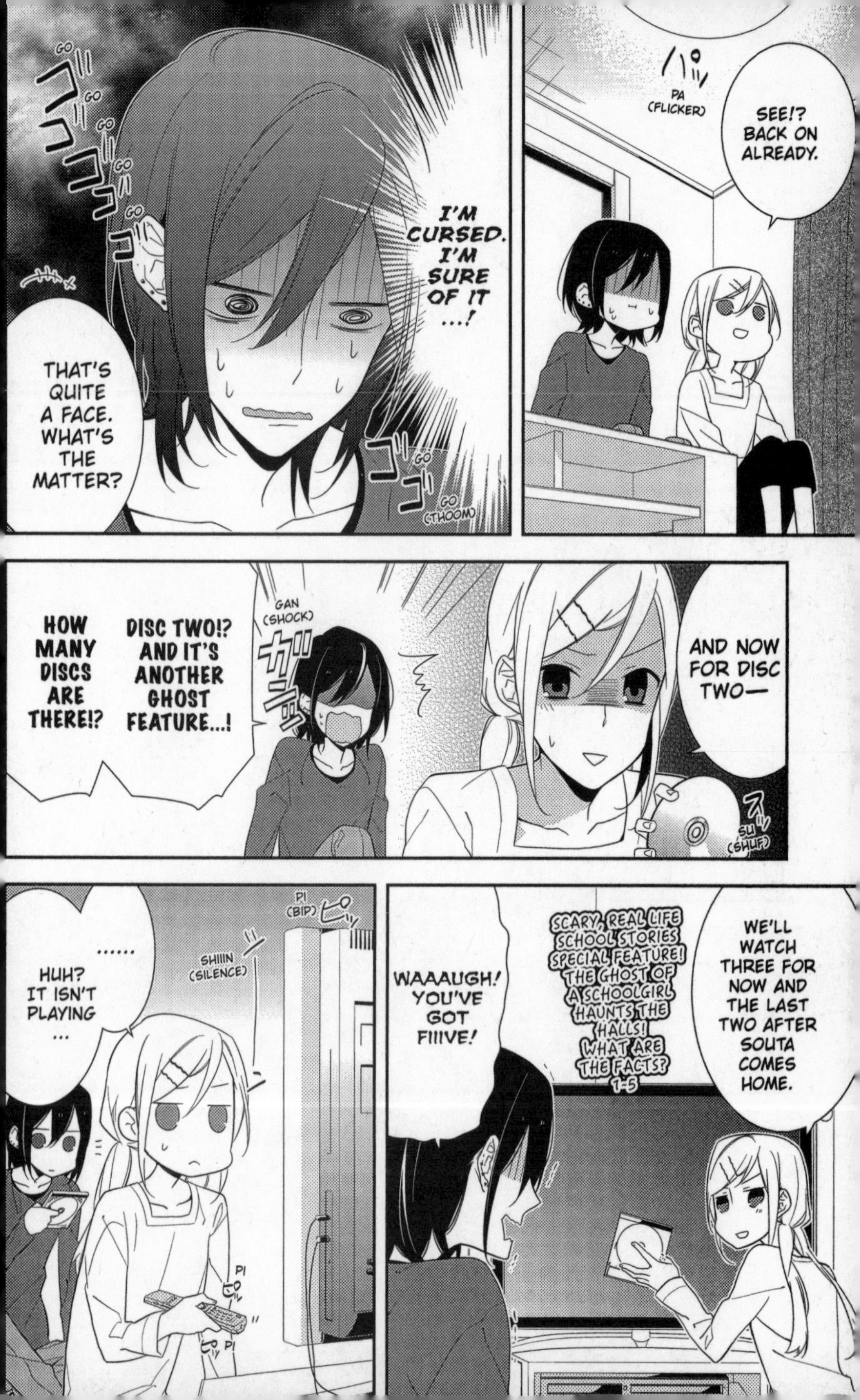
PA (FLICKER)
SEE!? BACK ON ALREADY.
GO GO GO GO GO
I'M CURSED. I'M SURE OF IT ...!
THAT'S QUITE A FACE. WHAT'S THE MATTER?
GO GO (THOOM)
AND NOW FOR DISC TWO—
SU (SHUF)
GAN (SHOCK)
DISC TWO!? AND IT'S ANOTHER GHOST FEATURE...!
HOW MANY DISCS ARE THERE!?
WE'LL WATCH THREE FOR NOW AND THE LAST TWO AFTER SOUTA COMES HOME.
SCARY, REAL LIFE SCHOOL STORIES SPECIAL FEATURE! THE GHOST OF A SCHOOLGIRL HAUNTS THE HALLS! WHAT ARE THE FACTS? 1-5
WAAAUGH! YOU'VE GOT FIIIVE!
PI (BIP)
SHIIN (SILENCE)
......
HUH? IT ISN'T PLAYING ...
PI
PI

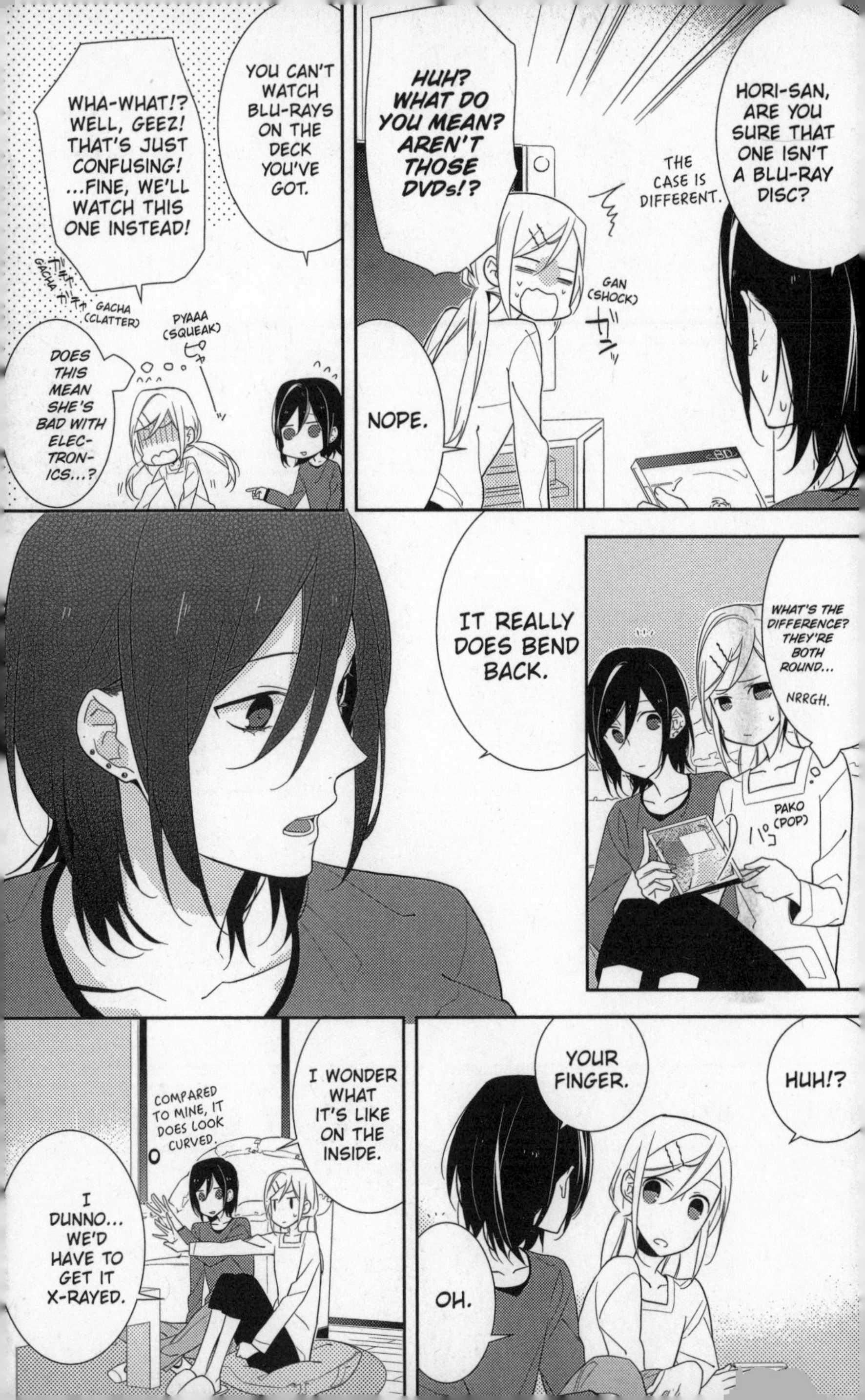
HORI-SAN, ARE YOU SURE THAT ONE ISN'T A BLU-RAY DISC?
THE CASE IS DIFFERENT.
HUH? WHAT DO YOU MEAN? AREN'T THOSE DVDs!?
GAN (SHOCK)
NOPE.
YOU CAN'T WATCH BLU-RAYS ON THE DECK YOU'VE GOT.
WHA-WHAT!? WELL, GEEZ! THAT'S JUST CONFUSING! ...FINE, WE'LL WATCH THIS ONE INSTEAD!
GACHA GACHA (CLATTER)
PYAAA (SQUEAK)
DOES THIS MEAN SHE'S BAD WITH ELEC-TRON-ICS...?
WHAT'S THE DIFFERENCE? THEY'RE BOTH ROUND...
NRRGH.
PAKO (POP)
IT REALLY DOES BEND BACK.
HUH!?
YOUR FINGER.
OH.
I WONDER WHAT IT'S LIKE ON THE INSIDE.
COMPARED TO MINE, IT DOES LOOK CURVED.
I DUNNO... WE'D HAVE TO GET IT X-RAYED.

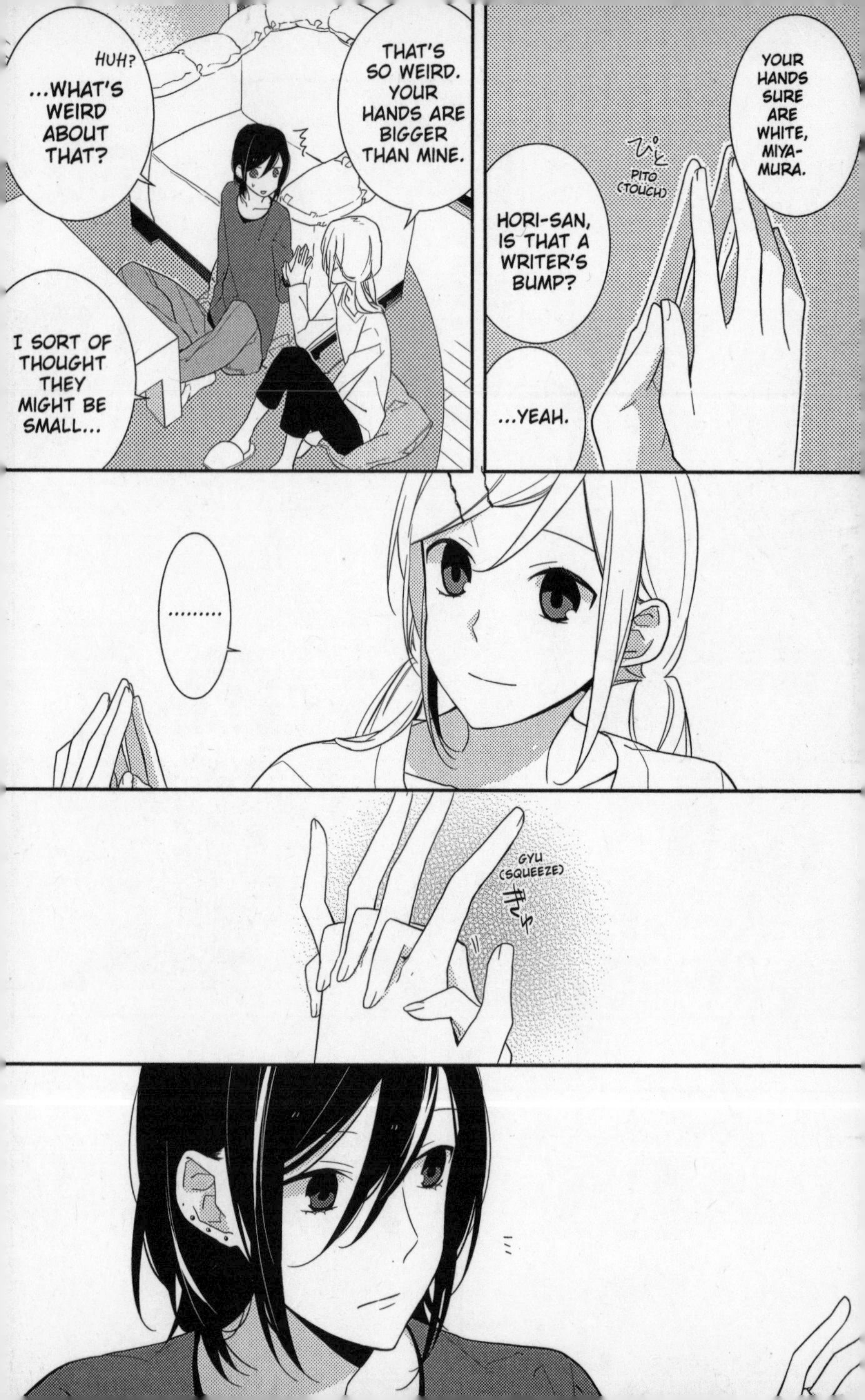
YOUR HANDS SURE ARE WHITE, MIYA-MURA.
PITO (TOUCH)
HORI-SAN, IS THAT A WRITER'S BUMP?
...YEAH.
THAT'S SO WEIRD. YOUR HANDS ARE BIGGER THAN MINE.
HUH?
...WHAT'S WEIRD ABOUT THAT?
I SORT OF THOUGHT THEY MIGHT BE SMALL...
....
GYU (SQUEEZE)

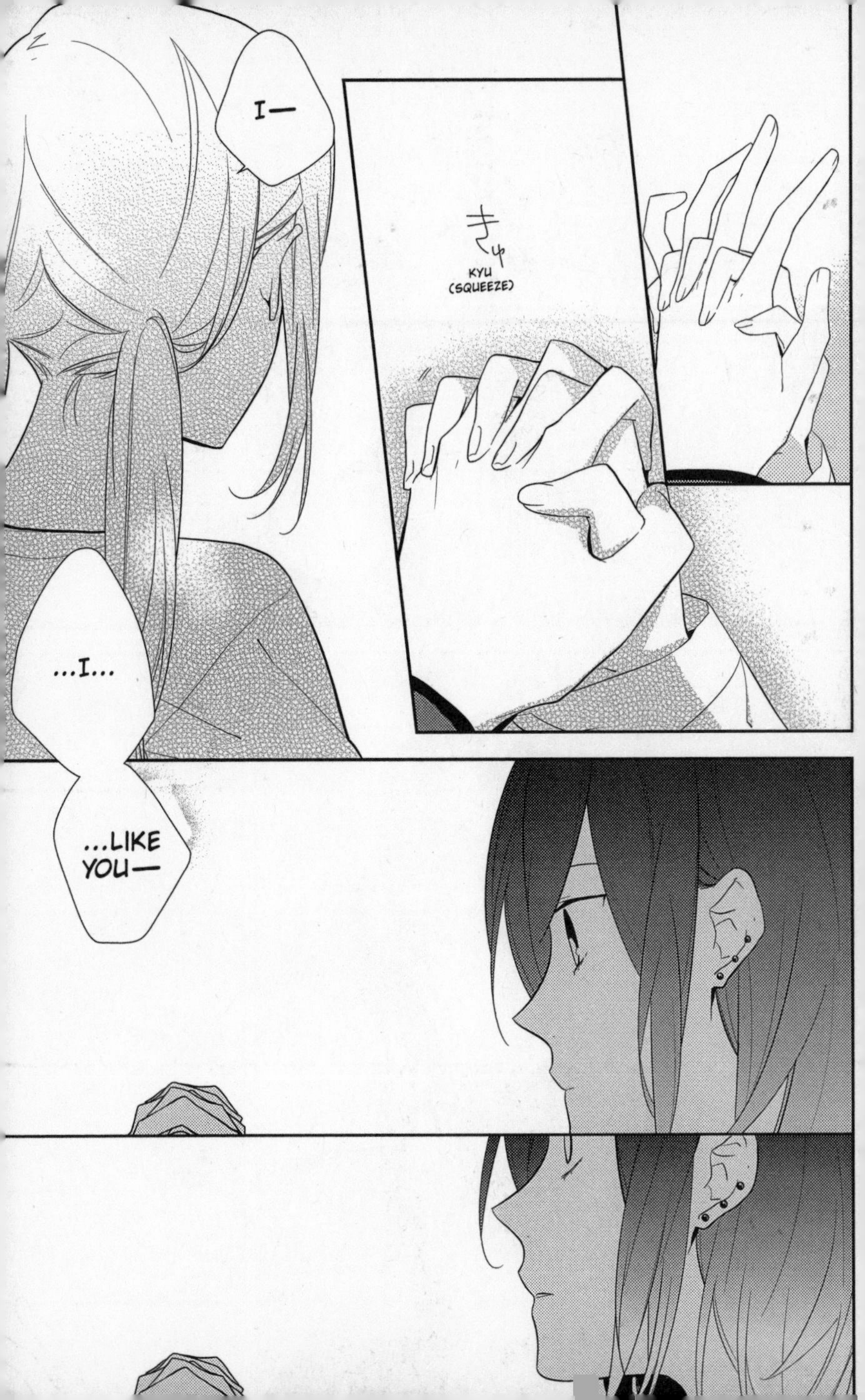
きゅ
KYU (SQUEEZE)
I—
...I...
...LIKE YOU—

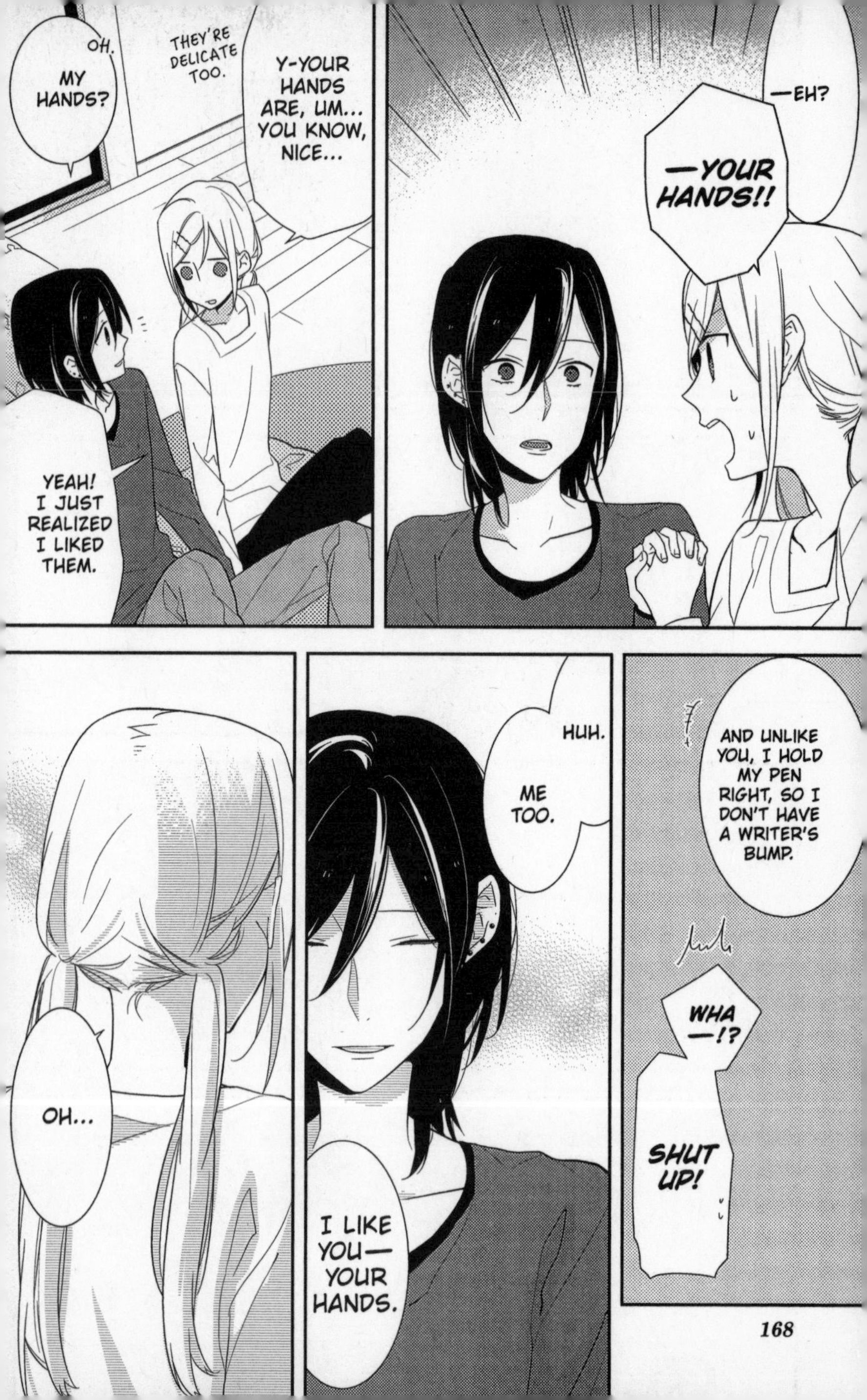
—EH?
—YOUR HANDS!!
Y-YOUR HANDS ARE, UM... YOU KNOW, NICE...
THEY'RE DELICATE TOO.
OH.
MY HANDS?
YEAH! I JUST REALIZED I LIKED THEM.
AND UNLIKE YOU, I HOLD MY PEN RIGHT, SO I DON'T HAVE A WRITER'S BUMP.
WHA—!?
SHUT UP!
HUH.
ME TOO.
I LIKE YOU— YOUR HANDS.
OH...

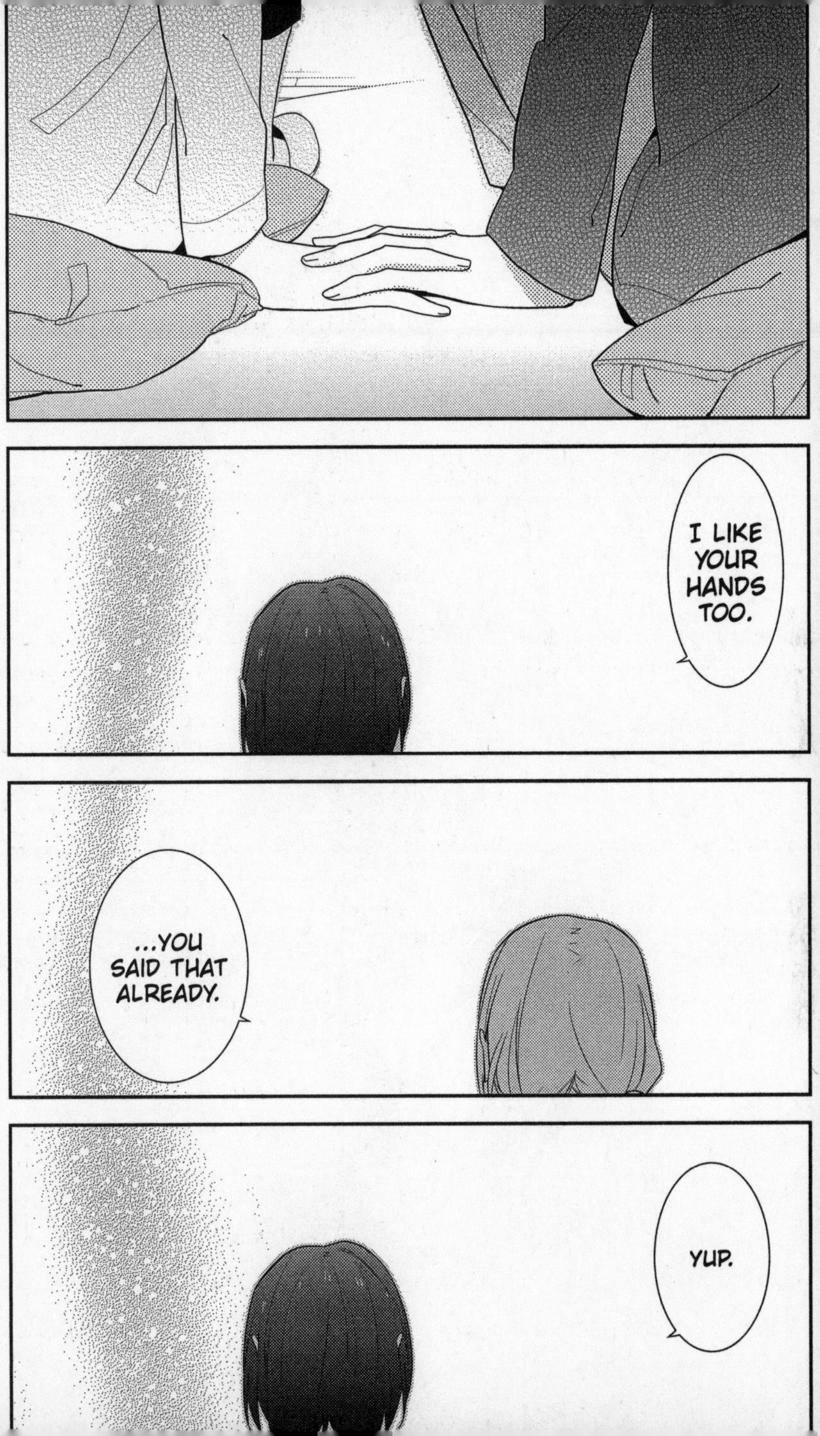
I LIKE YOUR HANDS TOO.
...YOU SAID THAT ALREADY.
YUP.

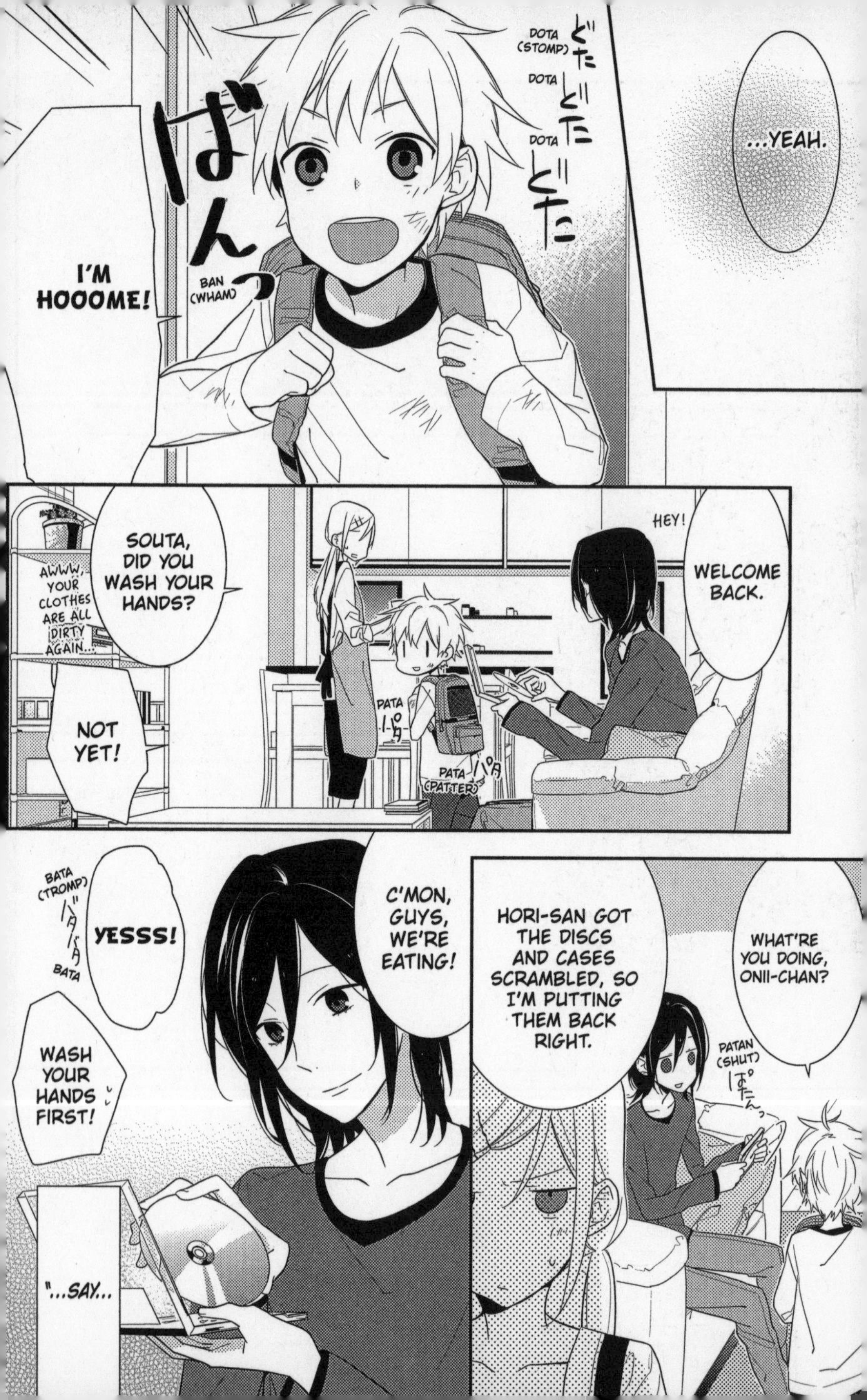
...YEAH.
DOTA (STOMP) どた
DOTA どた
DOTA どた
BAN (WHAM) ばんっ
I'M HOOOME!
HEY!
WELCOME BACK.
SOUTA, DID YOU WASH YOUR HANDS?
AWWW, YOUR CLOTHES ARE ALL DIRTY AGAIN...
PATA パタ
PATA (PATTER) パタ
NOT YET!
WHAT'RE YOU DOING, ONII-CHAN?
PATAN (SHUT) ぱたんっ
HORI-SAN GOT THE DISCS AND CASES SCRAMBLED, SO I'M PUTTING THEM BACK RIGHT.
C'MON, GUYS, WE'RE EATING!
YESSS!
BATA (TROMP) バタバタ BATA
WASH YOUR HANDS FIRST!
"...SAY...

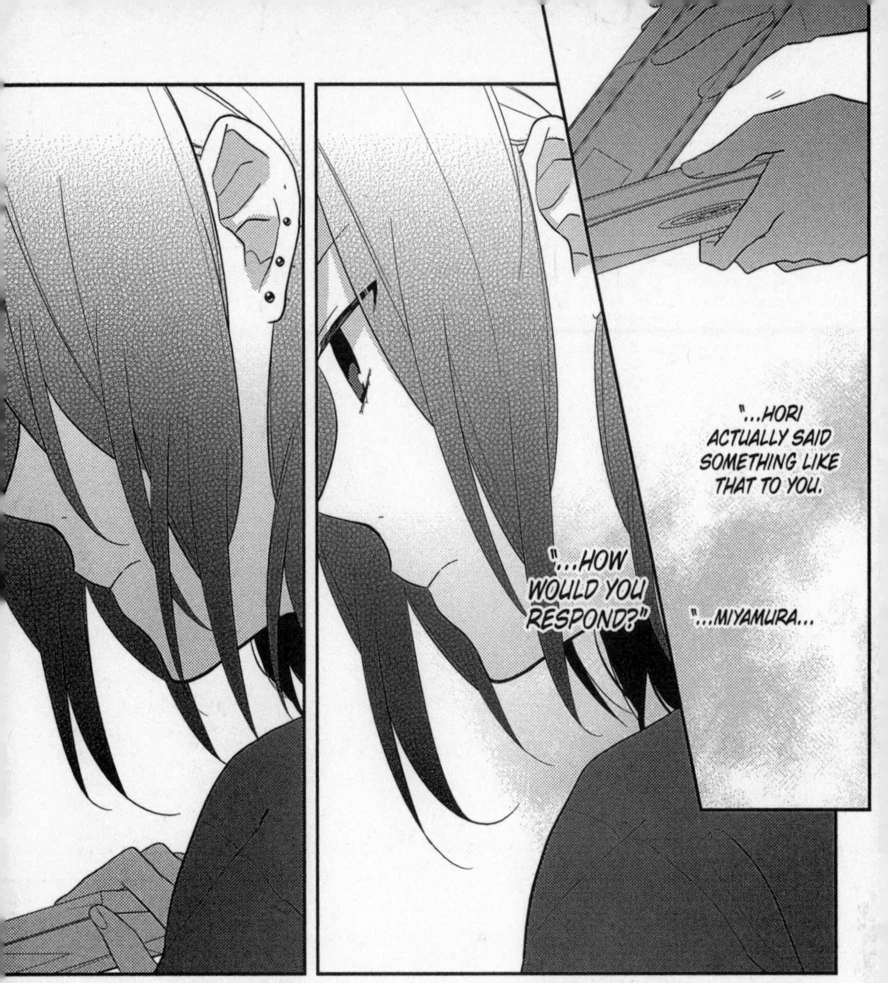
"...HORI ACTUALLY SAID SOMETHING LIKE THAT TO YOU.
"...MIYAMURA...
"...HOW WOULD YOU RESPOND?"
パタン
PATAN

HORIMIYA 2 END

To Be Continued...

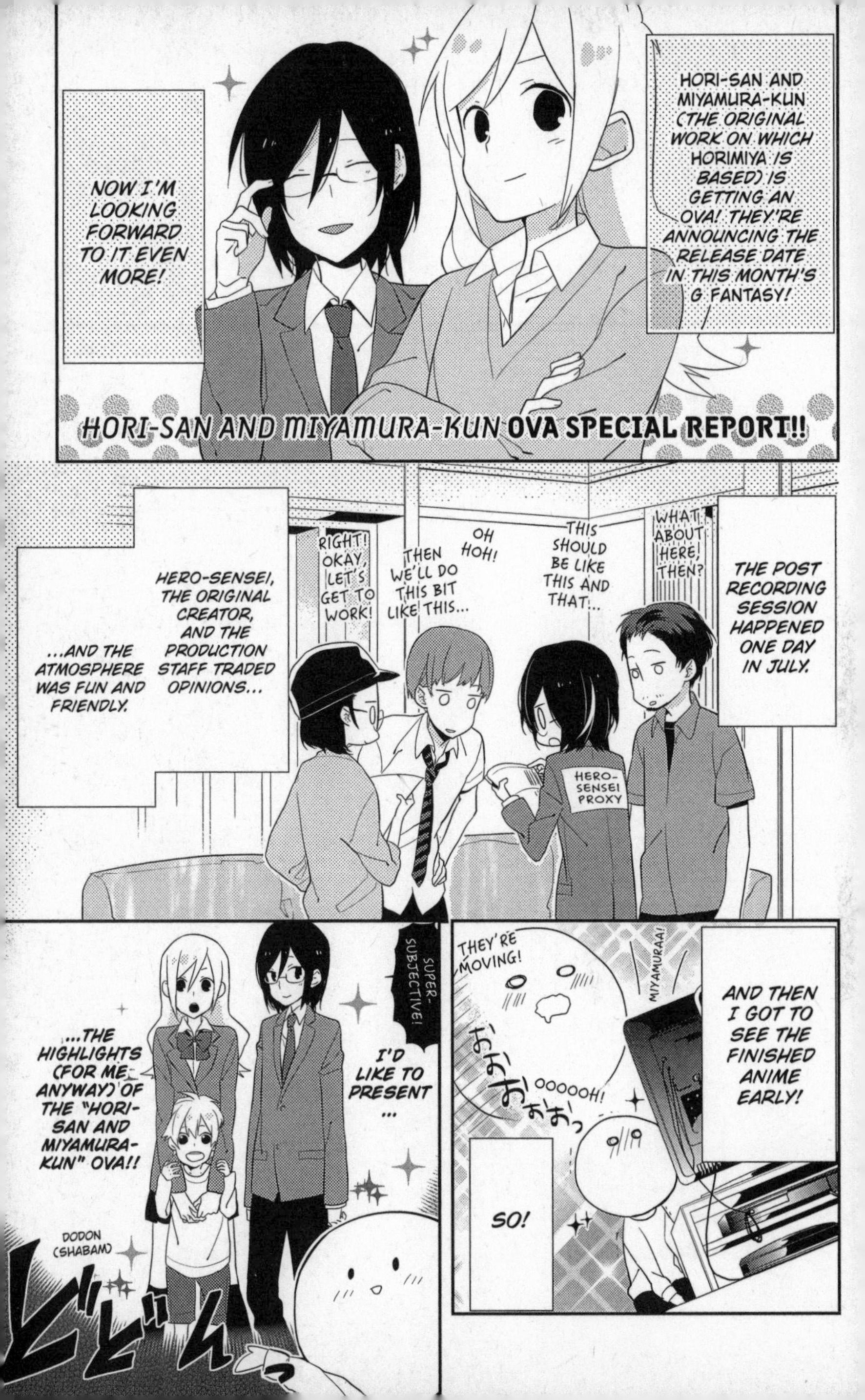
HORI-SAN AND MIYAMURA-KUN (THE ORIGINAL WORK ON WHICH HORIMIYA IS BASED) IS GETTING AN OVA! THEY'RE ANNOUNCING THE RELEASE DATE IN THIS MONTH'S G FANTASY!
NOW I'M LOOKING FORWARD TO IT EVEN MORE!
HORI-SAN AND MIYAMURA-KUN OVA SPECIAL REPORT!!
THE POST RECORDING SESSION HAPPENED ONE DAY IN JULY.
WHAT ABOUT HERE, THEN?
THIS SHOULD BE LIKE THIS AND THAT...
OH HOH!
THEN WE'LL DO THIS BIT LIKE THIS...
RIGHT! OKAY, LET'S GET TO WORK!
HERO-SENSEI PROXY
HERO-SENSEI, THE ORIGINAL CREATOR, AND THE PRODUCTION STAFF TRADED OPINIONS...
...AND THE ATMOSPHERE WAS FUN AND FRIENDLY.
AND THEN I GOT TO SEE THE FINISHED ANIME EARLY!
MIYAMURAA!
THEY'RE MOVING!
OOOOOOH!
SO!
SUPER-SUBJECTIVE!
I'D LIKE TO PRESENT ...
...THE HIGHLIGHTS (FOR ME ANYWAY) OF THE "HORI-SAN AND MIYAMURA-KUN" OVA!!
DODON (SHABAM)

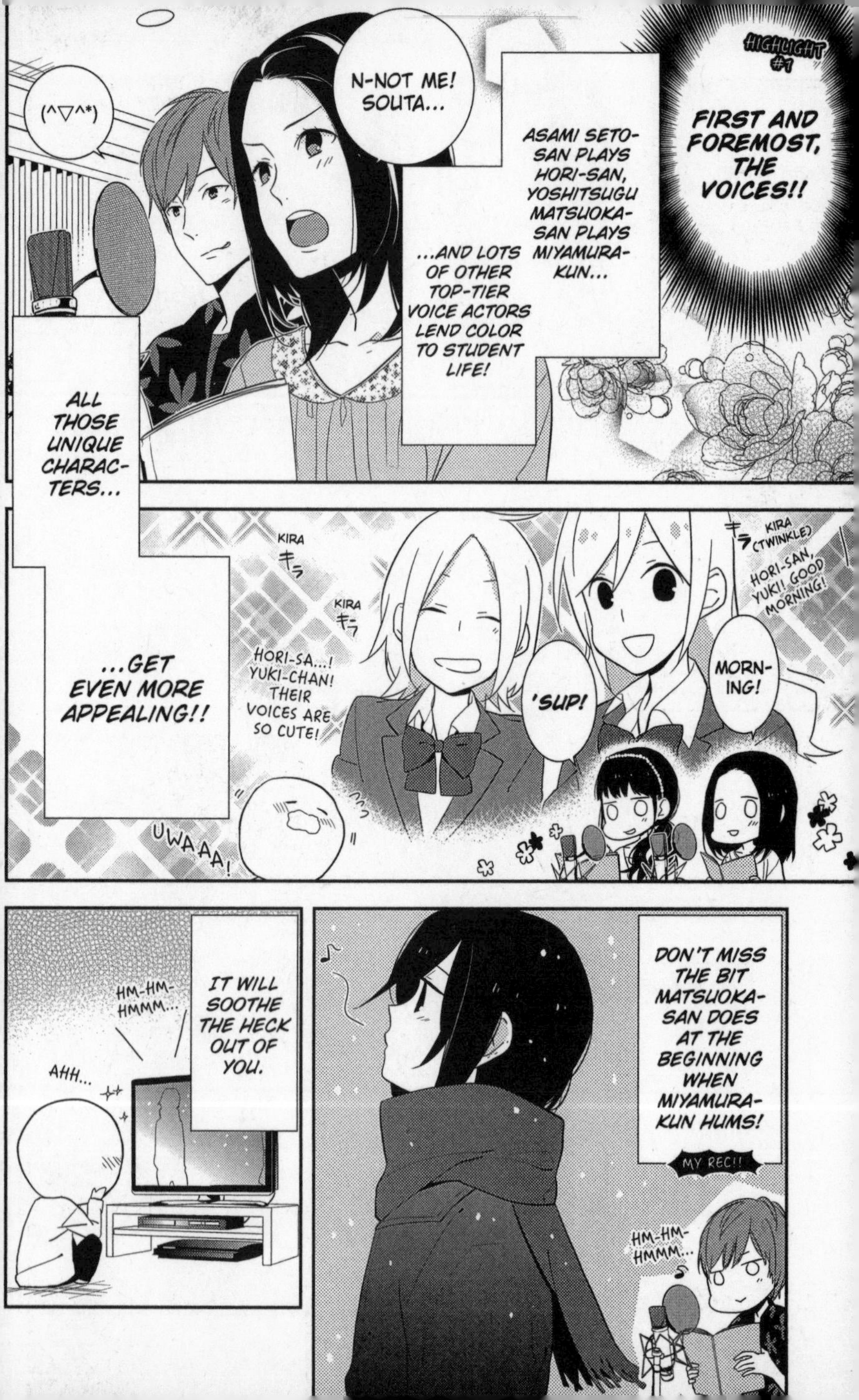
HIGHLIGHT #1
FIRST AND FOREMOST, THE VOICES!!
ASAMI SETO-SAN PLAYS HORI-SAN, YOSHITSUGU MATSUOKA-SAN PLAYS MIYAMURA-KUN...
...AND LOTS OF OTHER TOP-TIER VOICE ACTORS LEND COLOR TO STUDENT LIFE!
N-NOT ME! SOUTA...
(^▽^*)
ALL THOSE UNIQUE CHARACTERS...
キラ KIRA (TWINKLE)
HORI-SAN, YUKI! GOOD MORNING!
MORNING!
'SUP!
KIRA キラ
KIRA キラ
HORI-SA...! YUKI-CHAN! THEIR VOICES ARE SO CUTE!
UWAAAA!
...GET EVEN MORE APPEALING!!
DON'T MISS THE BIT MATSUOKA-SAN DOES AT THE BEGINNING WHEN MIYAMURA-KUN HUMS!
MY REC!!
HM-HM-HMMM...
IT WILL SOOTHE THE HECK OUT OF YOU.
HM-HM-HMMM...
AHH...

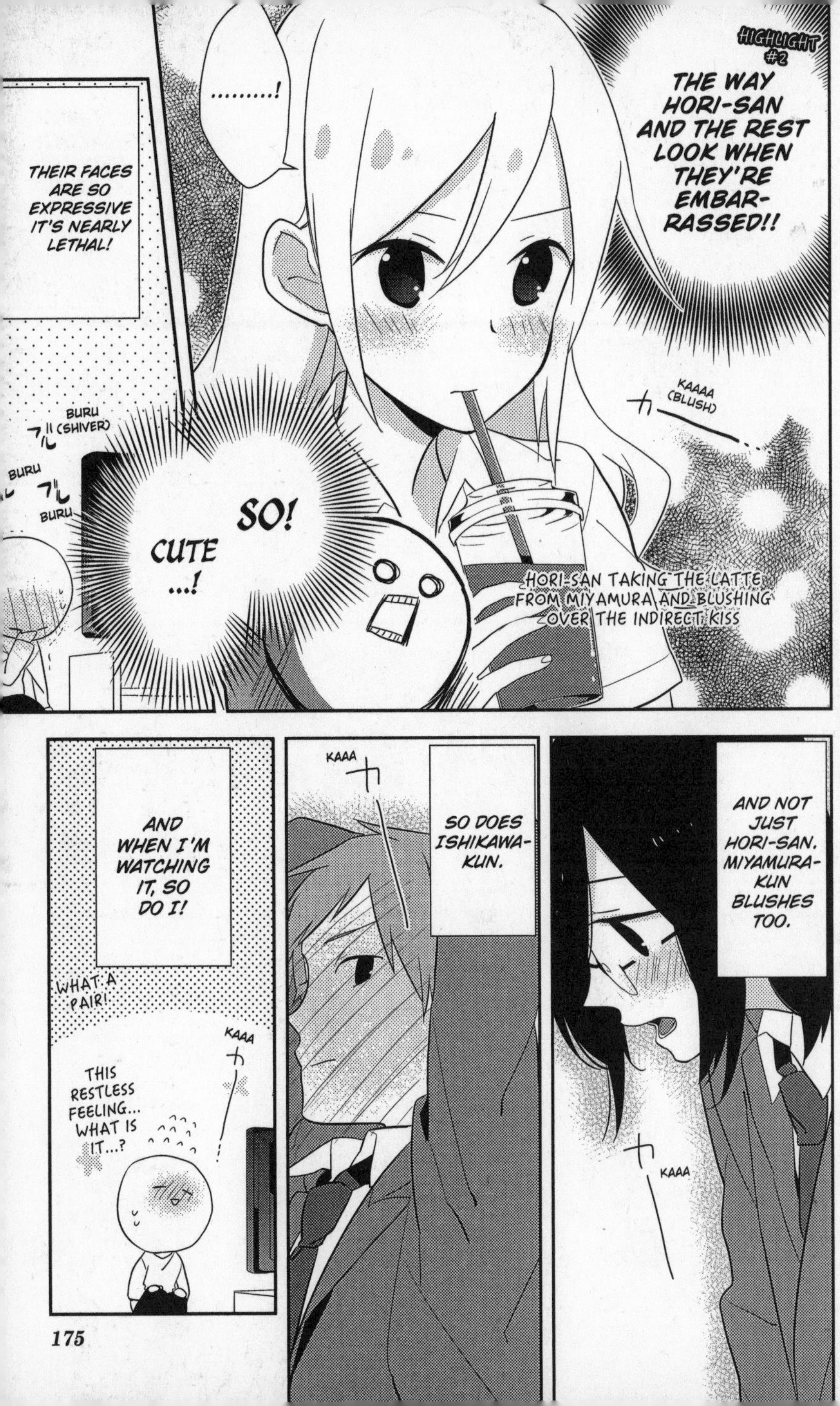
HIGHLIGHT #2
THE WAY HORI-SAN AND THE REST LOOK WHEN THEY'RE EMBAR-RASSED!!
.........!
THEIR FACES ARE SO EXPRESSIVE IT'S NEARLY LETHAL!
KAAAA (BLUSH)
HORI-SAN TAKING THE LATTE FROM MIYAMURA AND BLUSHING OVER THE INDIRECT KISS
SO! CUTE ...!
BURU (SHIVER)
BURU
BURU
AND NOT JUST HORI-SAN. MIYAMURA-KUN BLUSHES TOO.
KAAA
SO DOES ISHIKAWA-KUN.
KAAA
AND WHEN I'M WATCHING IT, SO DO I!
WHAT A PAIR!
KAAA
THIS RESTLESS FEELING... WHAT IS IT...?

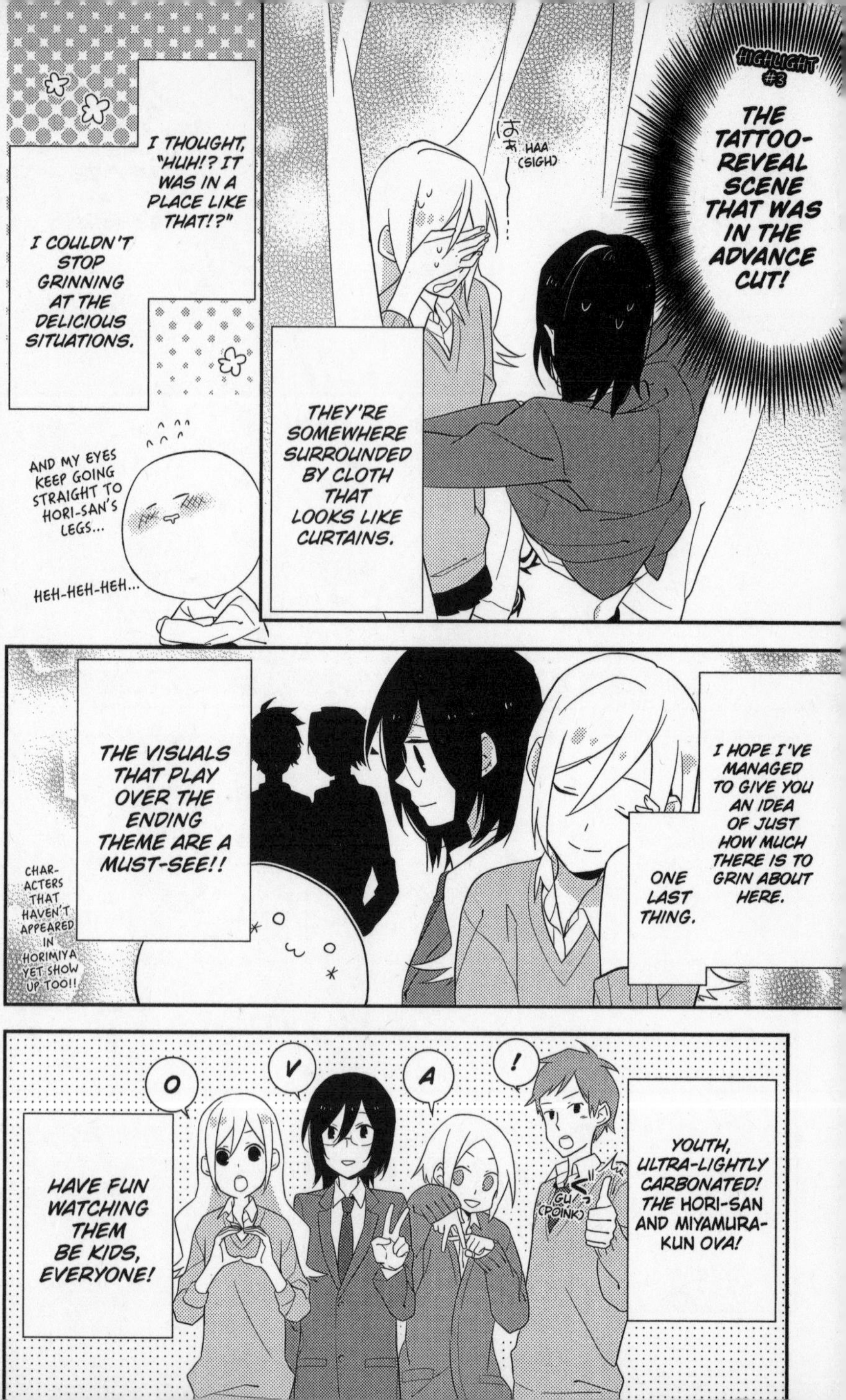
HIGHLIGHT #3
THE TATTOO-REVEAL SCENE THAT WAS IN THE ADVANCE CUT!
はぁ HAA (SIGH)
THEY'RE SOMEWHERE SURROUNDED BY CLOTH THAT LOOKS LIKE CURTAINS.
I THOUGHT, "HUH!? IT WAS IN A PLACE LIKE THAT!?"
I COULDN'T STOP GRINNING AT THE DELICIOUS SITUATIONS.
AND MY EYES KEEP GOING STRAIGHT TO HORI-SAN'S LEGS...
HEH-HEH-HEH...
I HOPE I'VE MANAGED TO GIVE YOU AN IDEA OF JUST HOW MUCH THERE IS TO GRIN ABOUT HERE.
ONE LAST THING.
THE VISUALS THAT PLAY OVER THE ENDING THEME ARE A MUST-SEE!!
CHARACTERS THAT HAVEN'T APPEARED IN HORIMIYA YET SHOW UP TOO!!
YOUTH, ULTRA-LIGHTLY CARBONATED! THE HORI-SAN AND MIYAMURA-KUN OVA!
GU (POINK)
O V A !
HAVE FUN WATCHING THEM BE KIDS, EVERYONE!

HORIMIYA

BONUS: PRESIDENT SENGOKU

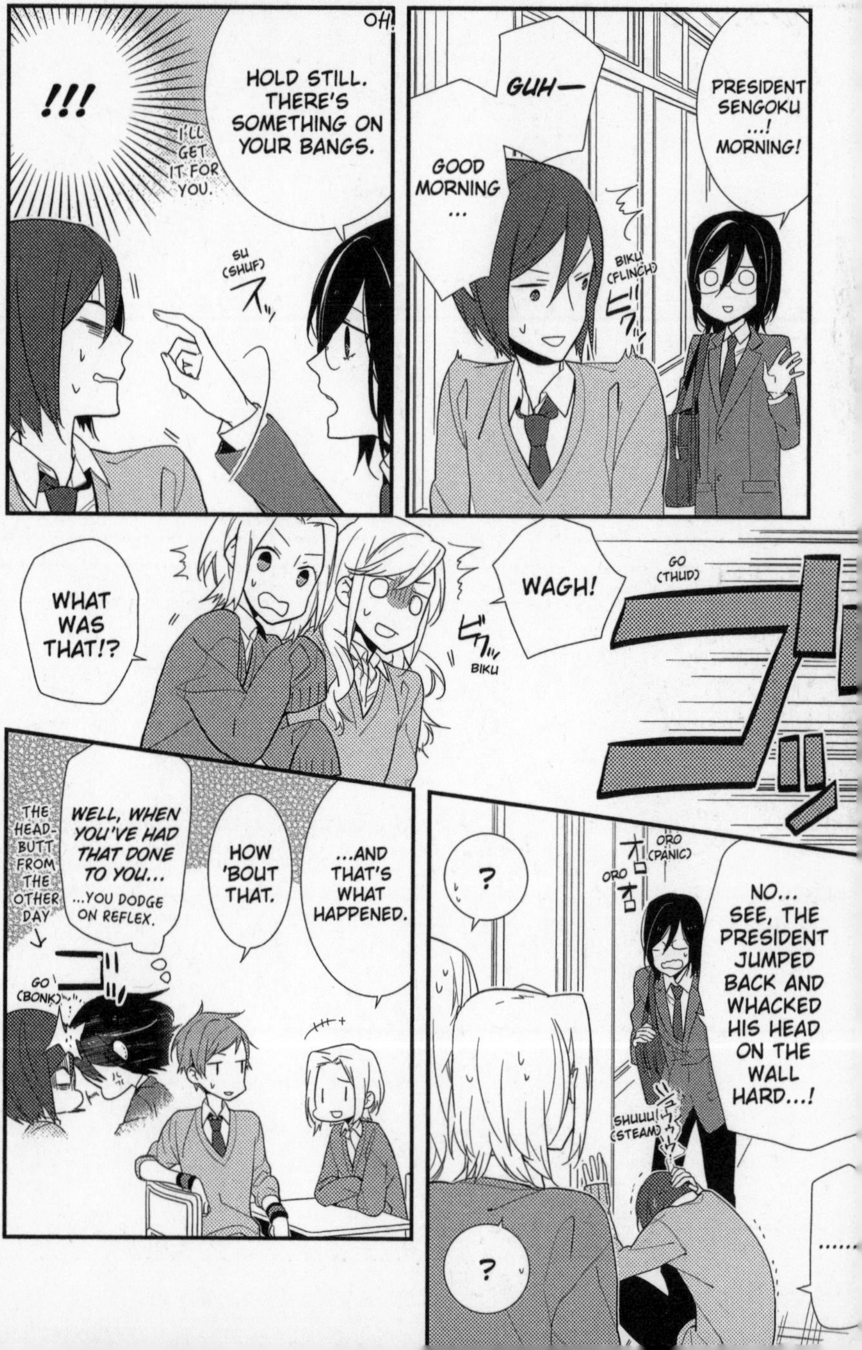
PRESIDENT SENGOKU ...! MORNING!
BIKU (FLINCH)
GOOD MORNING ...
GUH—
OH!
HOLD STILL. THERE'S SOMETHING ON YOUR BANGS.
I'LL GET IT FOR YOU.
SU (SHUF)
!!!
GO (THUD)
WAGH!
BIKU
WHAT WAS THAT!?
NO... SEE, THE PRESIDENT JUMPED BACK AND WHACKED HIS HEAD ON THE WALL HARD...!
ORO (PANIC)
ORO
?
SHUUU (STEAM)
?
......
...AND THAT'S WHAT HAPPENED.
HOW 'BOUT THAT.
WELL, WHEN YOU'VE HAD THAT DONE TO YOU...
...YOU DODGE ON REFLEX.
THE HEAD-BUTT FROM THE OTHER DAY
GO (BONK)

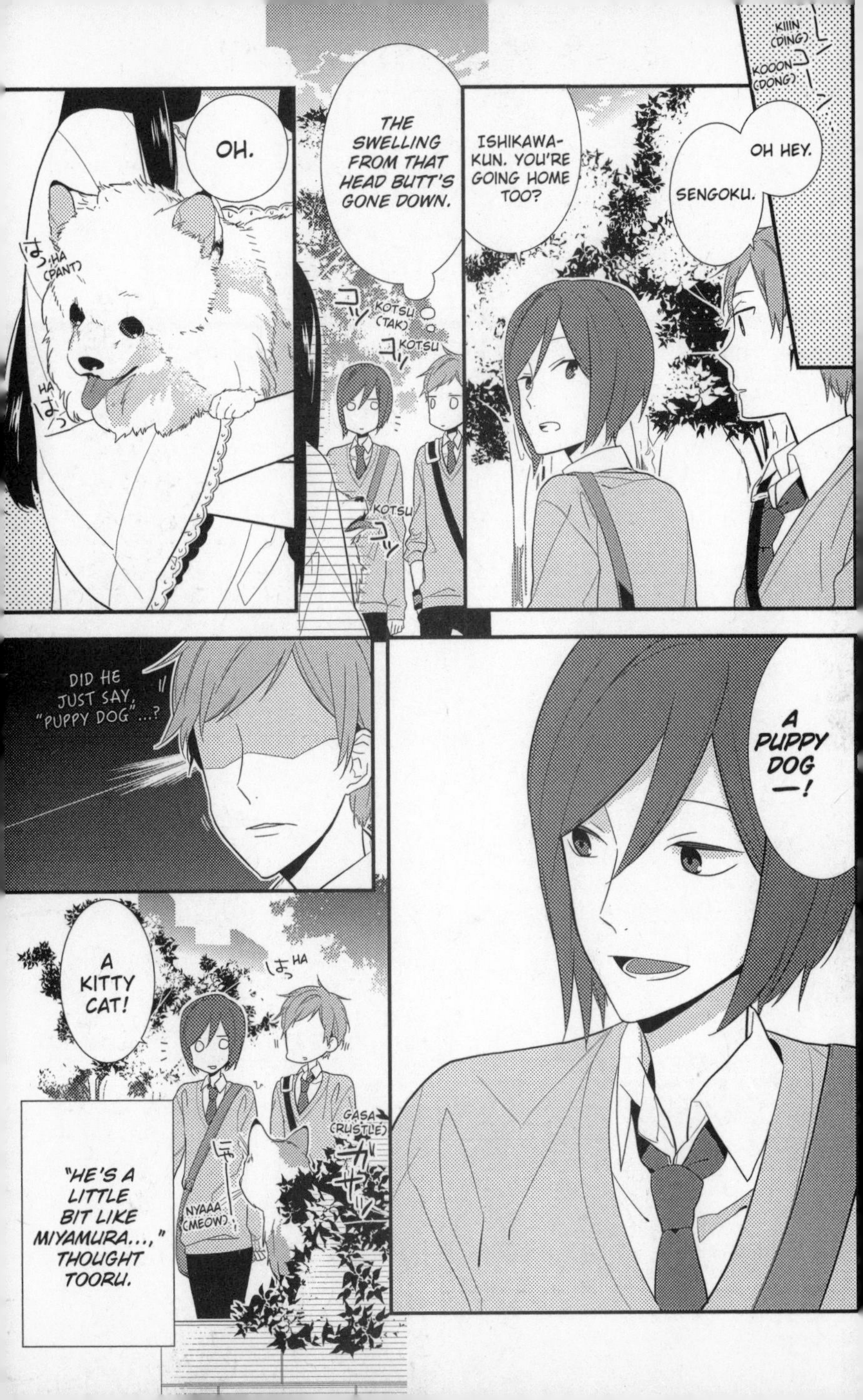
KIIIN (DING)
KOOON (DONG)
OH HEY.
SENGOKU.
ISHIKAWA-KUN. YOU'RE GOING HOME TOO?
THE SWELLING FROM THAT HEAD BUTT'S GONE DOWN.
KOTSU (TAK)
KOTSU
KOTSU
OH.
HA (PANT)
HA
A PUPPY DOG—!
DID HE JUST SAY, "PUPPY DOG"...?
A KITTY CAT!
HA
GASA (RUSTLE)
NYAAA (MEOW)
"HE'S A LITTLE BIT LIKE MIYAMURA...," THOUGHT TOORU.

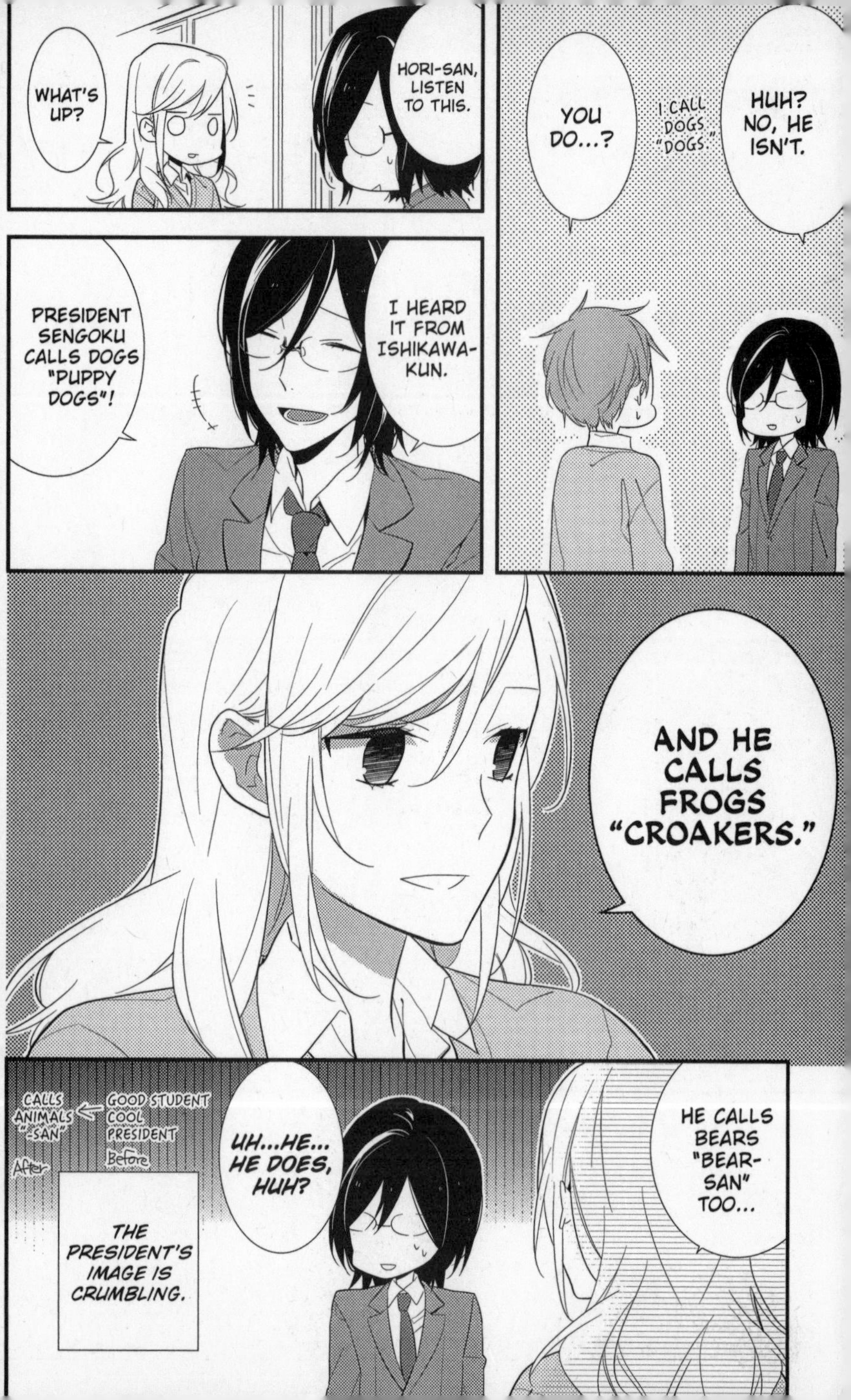
HUH? NO, HE ISN'T.
I CALL DOGS "DOGS."
YOU DO...?
HORI-SAN, LISTEN TO THIS.
WHAT'S UP?
I HEARD IT FROM ISHIKAWA-KUN.
PRESIDENT SENGOKU CALLS DOGS "PUPPY DOGS"!
AND HE CALLS FROGS "CROAKERS."
HE CALLS BEARS "BEAR-SAN" TOO...
UH...HE... HE DOES, HUH?
GOOD STUDENT COOL PRESIDENT
Before
CALLS ANIMALS "-SAN"
After
THE PRESIDENT'S IMAGE IS CRUMBLING.

Afterword

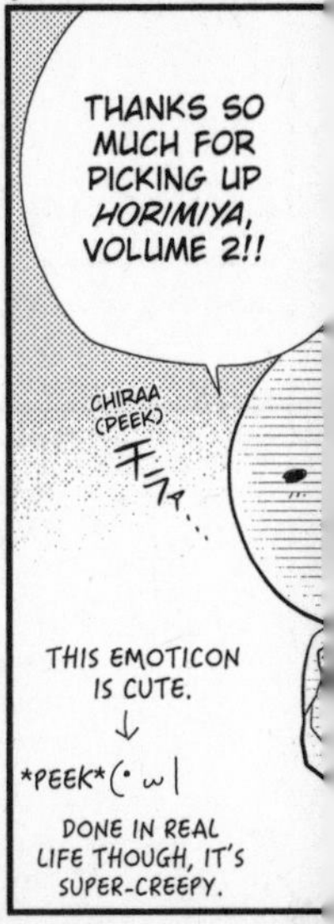
THANKS SO MUCH FOR PICKING UP *HORIMIYA*, VOLUME 2!!
CHIRAA (PEEK)
THIS EMOTICON IS CUTE.
↓
PEEK(・ω|
DONE IN REAL LIFE THOUGH, IT'S SUPER-CREEPY.

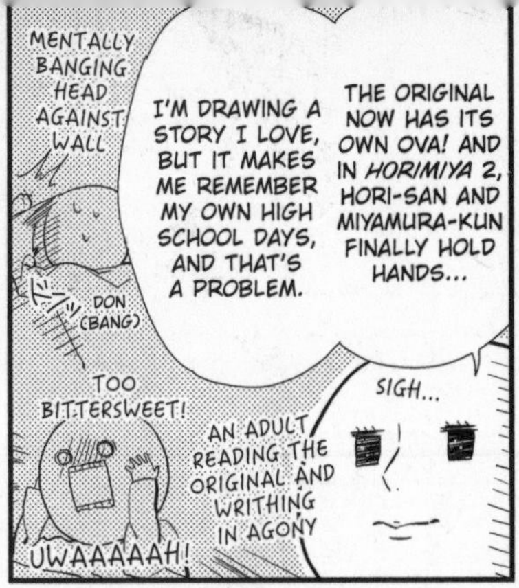
THE ORIGINAL NOW HAS ITS OWN OVA! AND IN *HORIMIYA* 2, HORI-SAN AND MIYAMURA-KUN FINALLY HOLD HANDS...
I'M DRAWING A STORY I LOVE, BUT IT MAKES ME REMEMBER MY OWN HIGH SCHOOL DAYS, AND THAT'S A PROBLEM.
MENTALLY BANGING HEAD AGAINST WALL
DON (BANG)
SIGH...
AN ADULT READING THE ORIGINAL AND WRITHING IN AGONY
TOO BITTERSWEET!
UWAAAAAH!

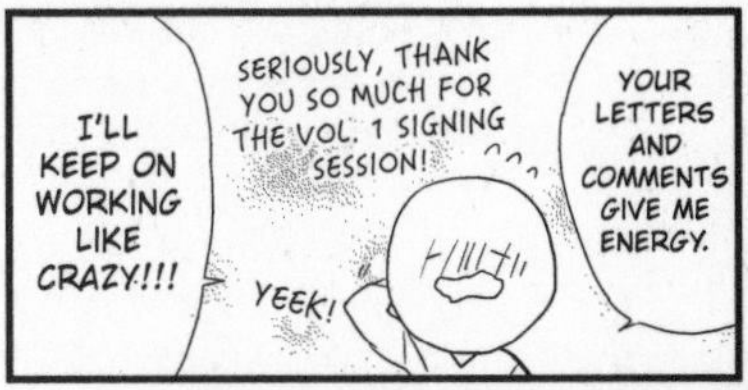
YOUR LETTERS AND COMMENTS GIVE ME ENERGY.
SERIOUSLY, THANK YOU SO MUCH FOR THE VOL. 1 SIGNING SESSION!
I'LL KEEP ON WORKING LIKE CRAZY!!!
YEEK!

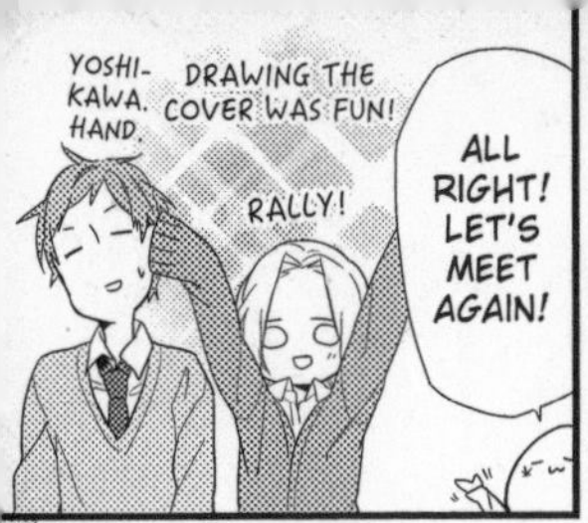
ALL RIGHT! LET'S MEET AGAIN!
RALLY!
DRAWING THE COVER WAS FUN!
YOSHIKAWA. HAND.

STAFF

Original story: HERO-sama

HORI-SAN AND MIYAMURA-KUN

Assistant: Yossan

Editor: Ishikawa-sama

Thank you for everything!

Special Thanks

My family, my friends, and everyone who picked up this book.

Thank you!!

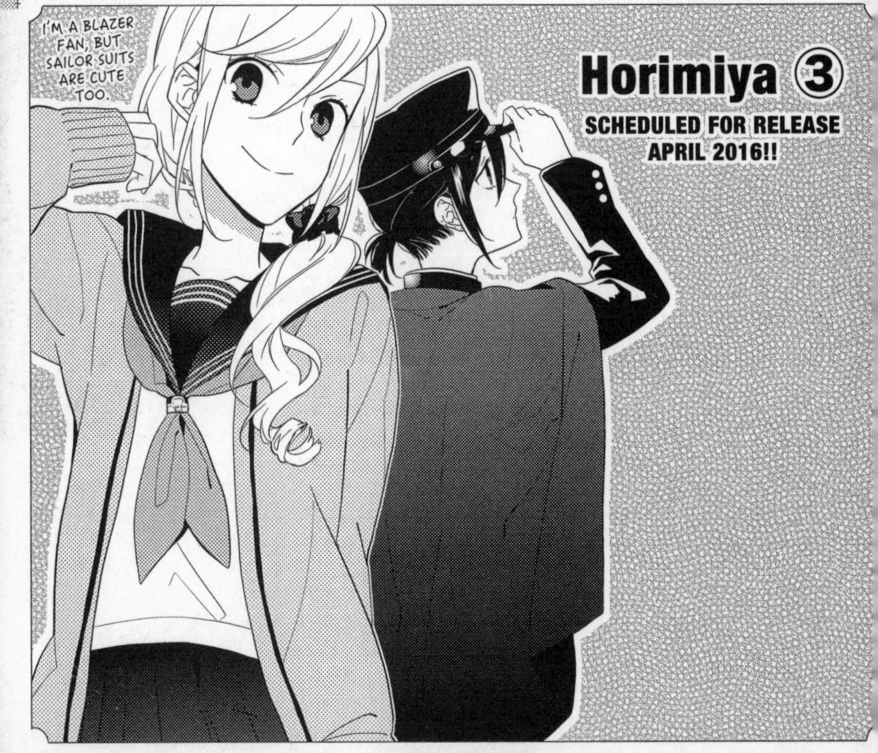
I'M A BLAZER FAN, BUT SAILOR SUITS ARE CUTE TOO.
Horimiya ③
SCHEDULED FOR RELEASE APRIL 2016!!

Translation Notes

Page 31 – Three-way meeting
A meeting between a student, one of their parents, and their teacher.

Page 46 – Scantron quiz
A scantron quiz is one with a multiple choice answer sheet that is machine readable and can be computer graded by running it through a special scanner.

Page 65 – Visual *kei*
Visual *kei* is a Japanese music subculture with a prominent visual component. The music can range from hard rock to playful pop, but the style is usually characterized by colorful, elaborate costumes and hair design, extensive makeup, and a generally androgynous look.

Page 71 – The porch of Kiyomizu
The main hall of the Buddhist temple of Kiyomizu in Kyoto has a wide veranda to accommodate the numerous pilgrims who visit. Hanging over a steep cliffside, this veranda, or porch, is approximately thirteen meters off of the ground. During the Edo period, there was a superstition that anyone who entrusted their life to the goddess Kannon and jumped off would not only survive, but also have their wish granted. About 85 percent of the 234 jumpers recorded during that period did in fact survive, possibly because there were thick trees below the veranda at the time. Jumping was made illegal in 1872, but Shuu is implying that Tooru should jump, since they're at the actual place. These days, to "jump off the porch at Kiyomizu" is a Japanese expression similar to "take the plunge."

Page 75 – Rings in school
Japanese school rules are quite strict, and personal items like jewelry and accessories are often forbidden.

HORIMIYA

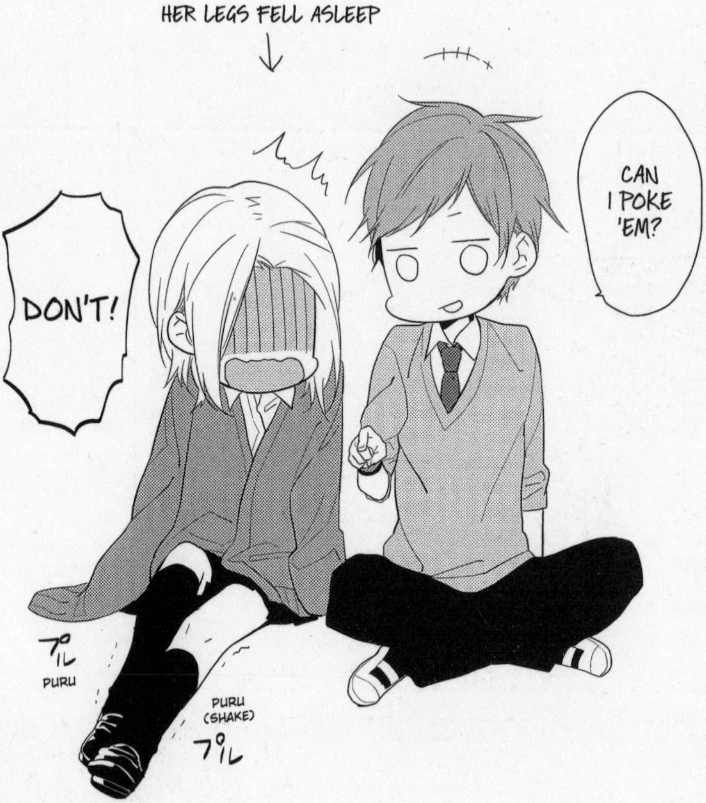
HER LEGS FELL ASLEEP
CAN I POKE 'EM?
DON'T!
プル
PURU (SHAKE)
プル
PURU

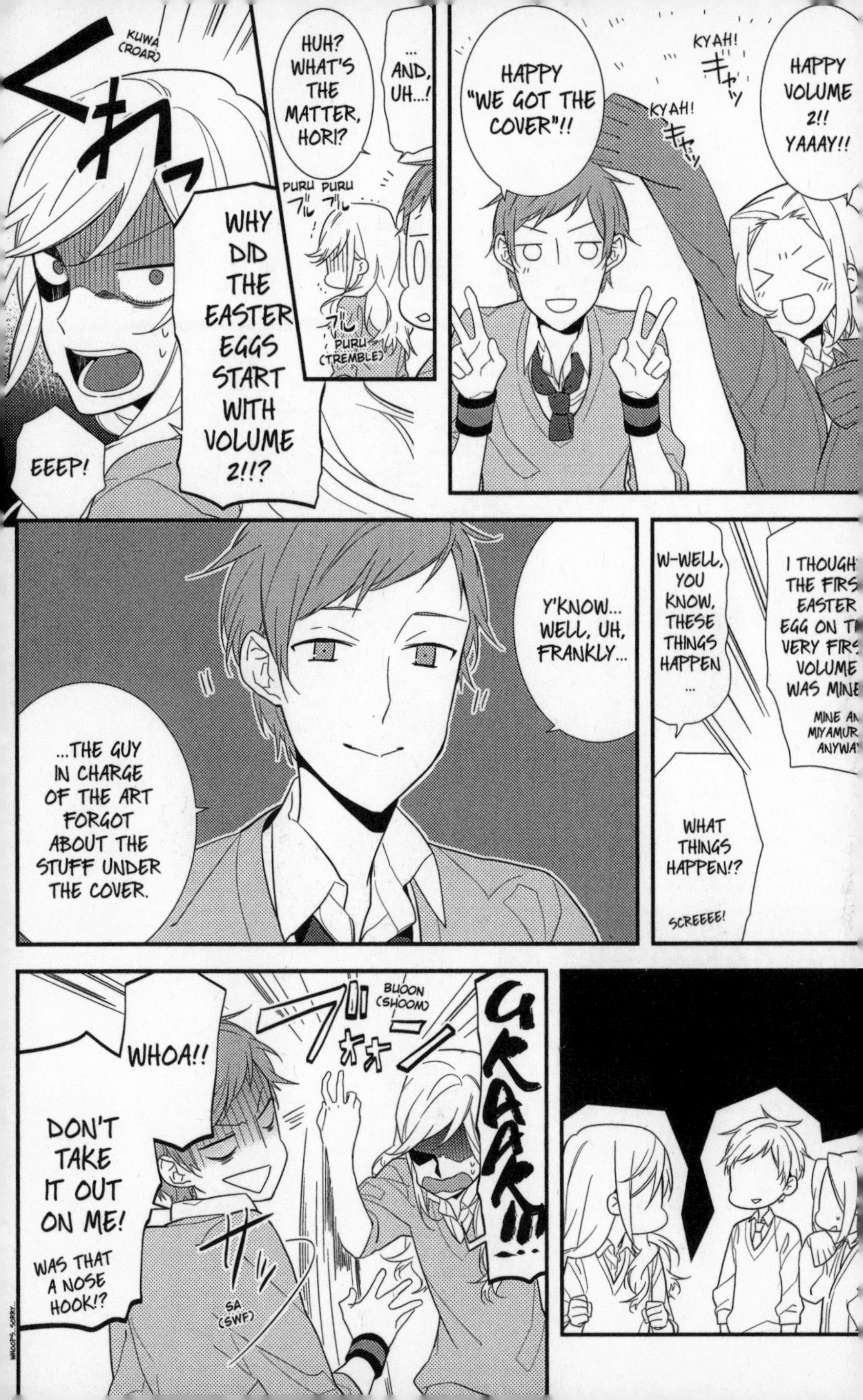

HAPPY VOLUME 2!! YAAAY!!
KYAH!
KYAH!
HAPPY "WE GOT THE COVER"!!
... AND, UH...!
HUH? WHAT'S THE MATTER, HORI?
PURU PURU
PURU (TREMBLE)
KUWA (ROAR)
WHY DID THE EASTER EGGS START WITH VOLUME 2!!?
EEEP!
I THOUGH THE FIRS EASTER EGG ON TH VERY FIRS VOLUME WAS MINE
MINE AN MIYAMUR ANYWAY
W-WELL, YOU KNOW, THESE THINGS HAPPEN ...
WHAT THINGS HAPPEN!?
SCREEEE!
Y'KNOW... WELL, UH, FRANKLY...
...THE GUY IN CHARGE OF THE ART FORGOT ABOUT THE STUFF UNDER THE COVER.
BUOON (SHOOM)
GUAAK!!
WHOA!!
DON'T TAKE IT OUT ON ME!
WAS THAT A NOSE HOOK!?
SA (SWF)
WHOOPS, SORRY...

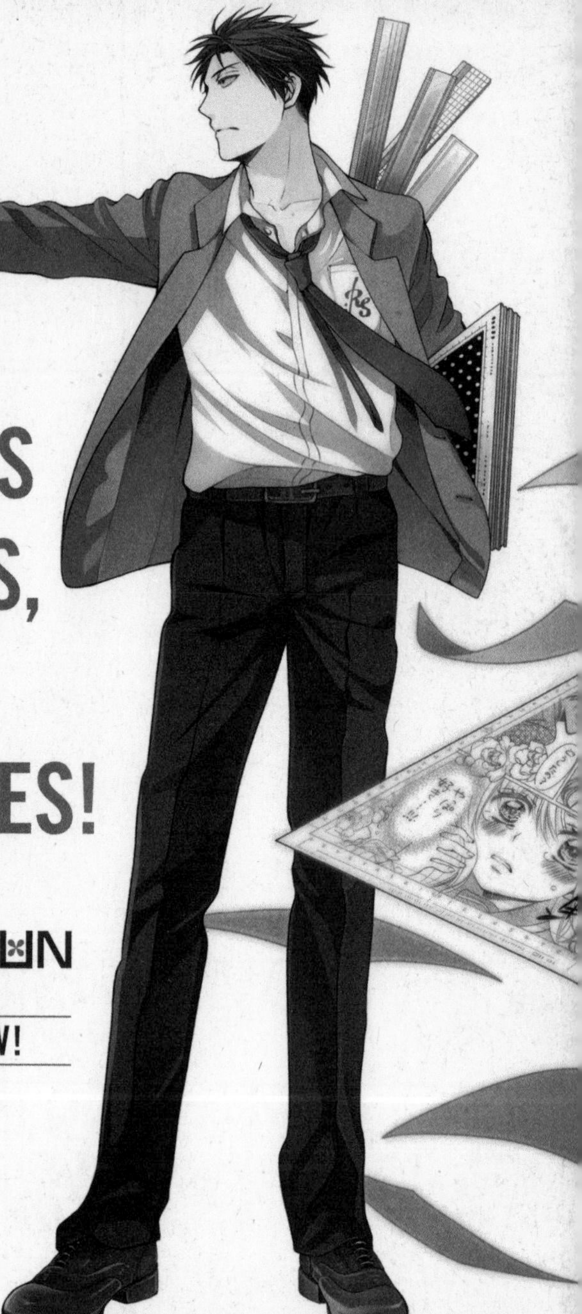

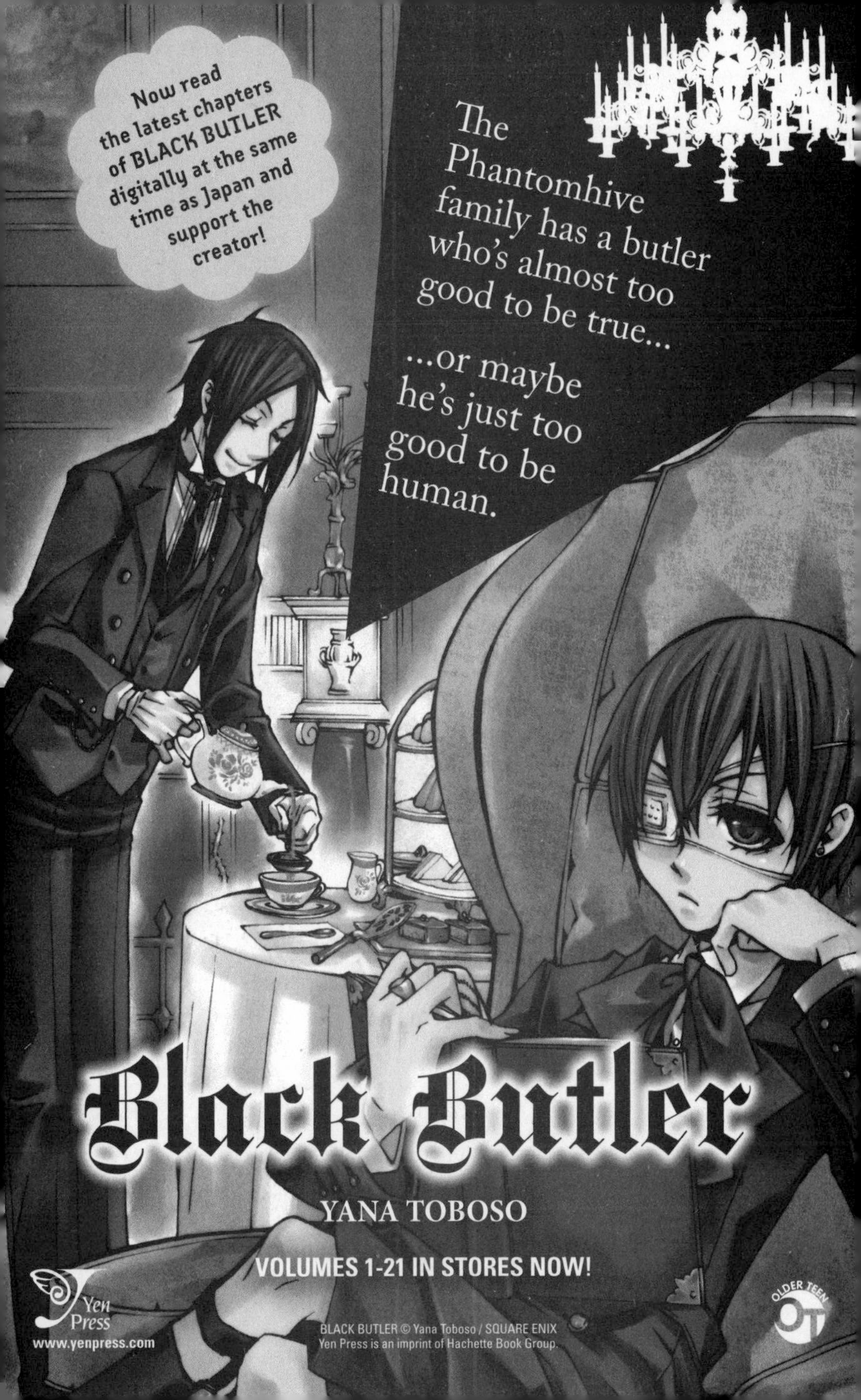

Now read the latest chapters of BLACK BUTLER digitally at the same time as Japan and support the creator!
The Phantomhive family has a butler who's almost too good to be true...
...or maybe he's just too good to be human.
Black Butler
YANA TOBOSO
VOLUMES 1-21 IN STORES NOW!
Yen Press
www.yenpress.com
BLACK BUTLER © Yana Toboso / SQUARE ENIX
Yen Press is an imprint of Hachette Book Group.
OLDER TEEN
OT

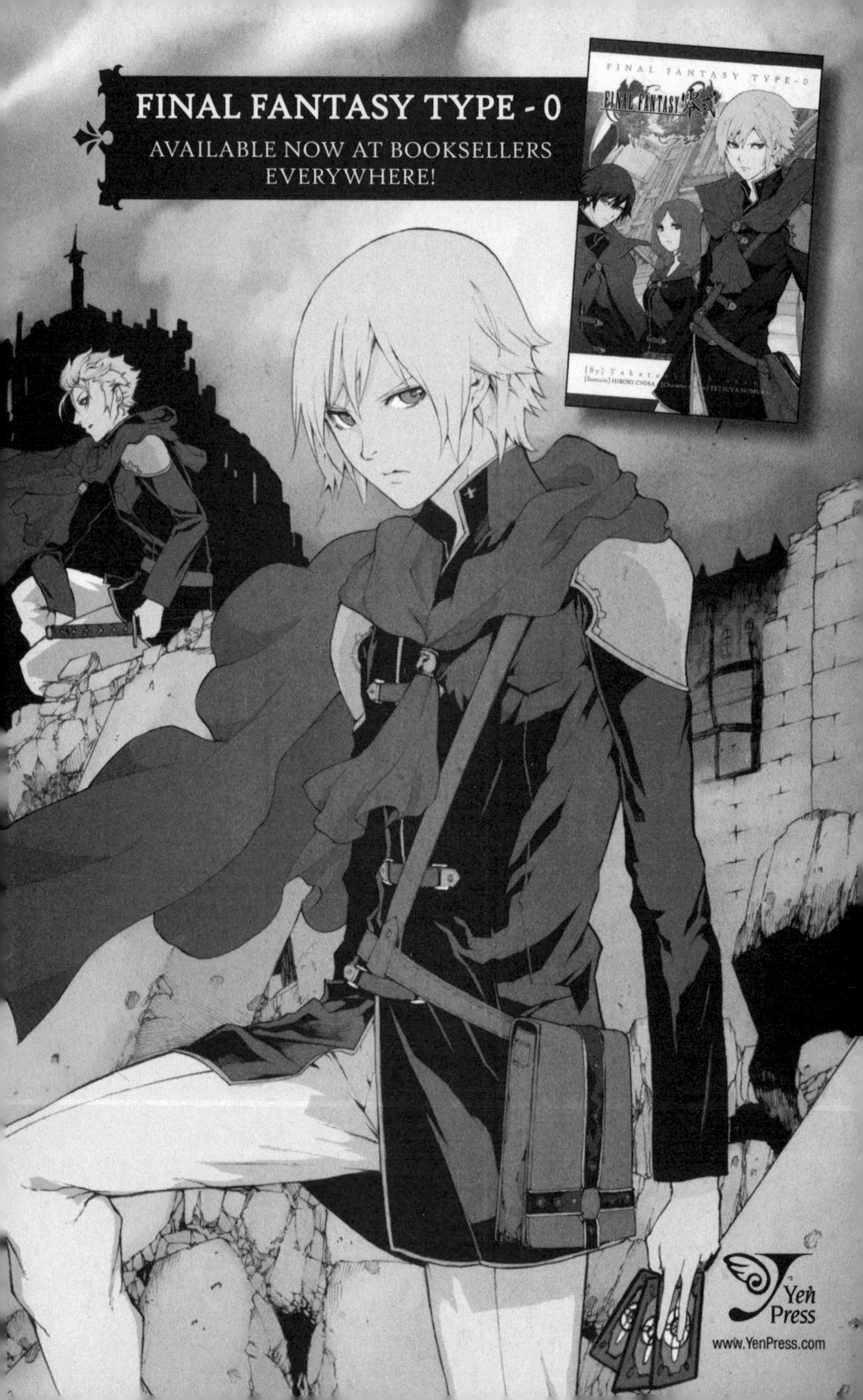
FINAL FANTASY TYPE - 0
AVAILABLE NOW AT BOOKSELLERS
EVERYWHERE!
FINAL FANTASY TYPE-0
Yen Press
www.YenPress.com

FINAL FANTASY 零式 TYPE-0

Art: TAKATOSHI SHIOZAWA
Character Design: TETSUYA NOMURA
Scenario: HIROKI CHIBA

The cadets of Akademeia's Class Zero are legends, with strength and magic unrivaled, and crimson capes symbolizing the great Vermilion Bird of the Dominion. But will their elite training be enough to keep them alive when a war breaks out and the Class Zero cadets find themselves at the front and center of a bloody political battlefield?!

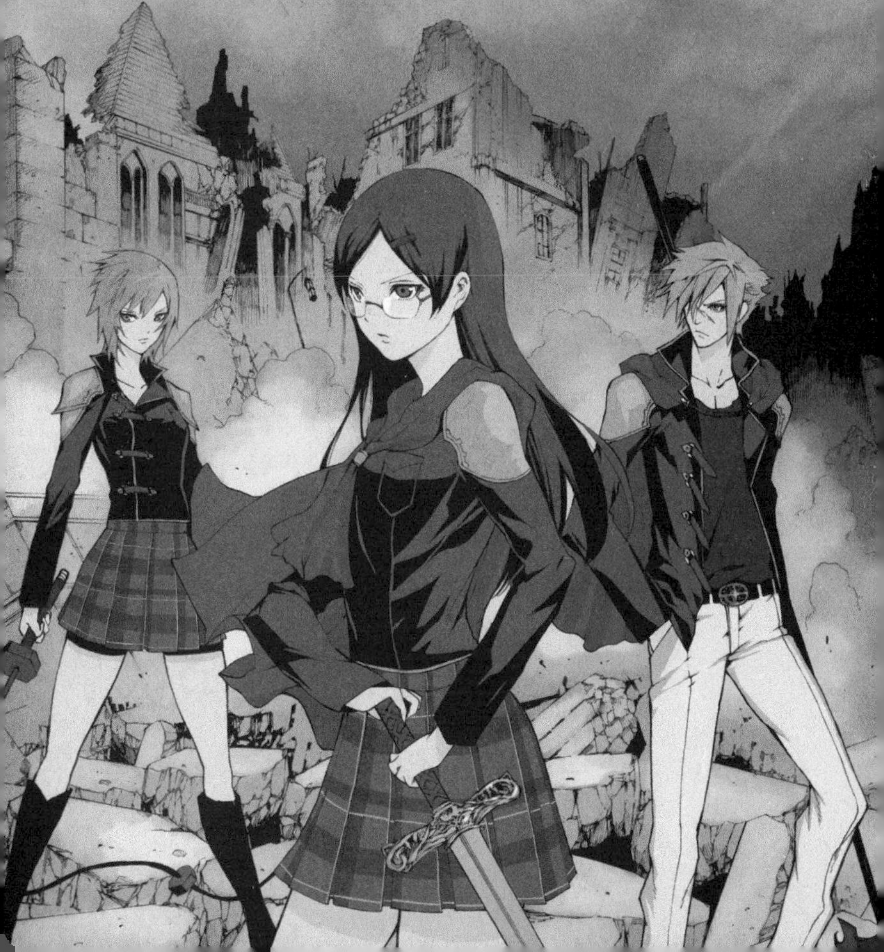

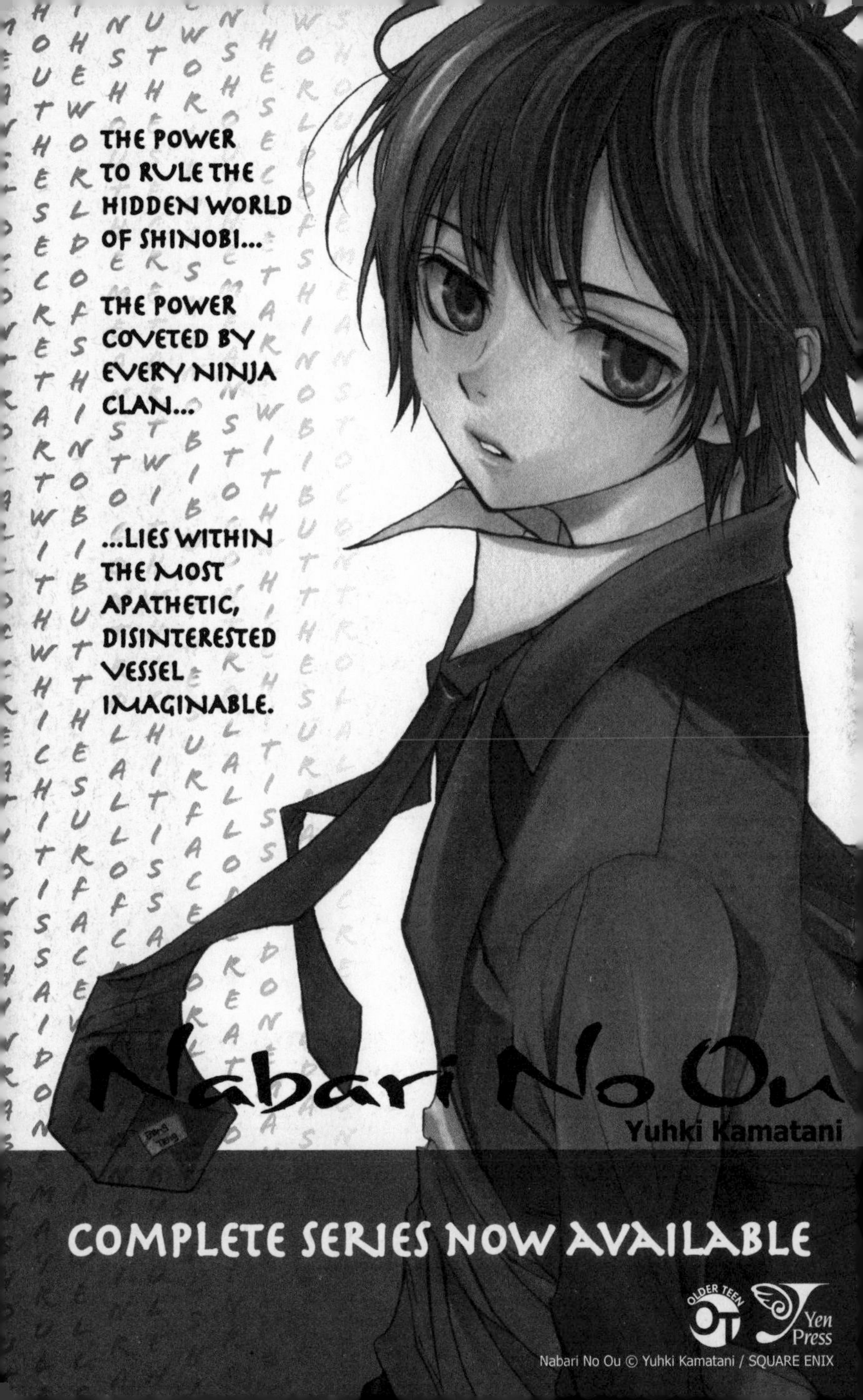
THE POWER TO RULE THE HIDDEN WORLD OF SHINOBI...
THE POWER COVETED BY EVERY NINJA CLAN...
...LIES WITHIN THE MOST APATHETIC, DISINTERESTED VESSEL IMAGINABLE.
Nabari No Ou
Yuhki Kamatani
COMPLETE SERIES NOW AVAILABLE
OLDER TEEN OT
Yen Press
Nabari No Ou © Yuhki Kamatani / SQUARE ENIX

To become the ultimate weapon, one boy must eat the souls of 99 humans...

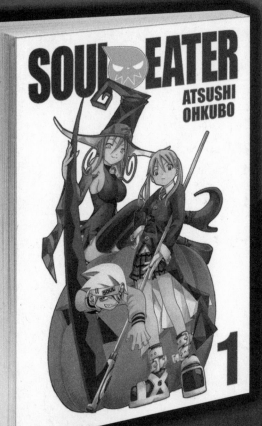

...and one witch.

Maka is a scythe meister, working to perfect her demon scythe until it is good enough to become Death's Weapon—the weapon used by Shinigami-sama, the spirit of Death himself. And if that isn't strange enough, her scythe also has the power to change form—into a human-looking boy!

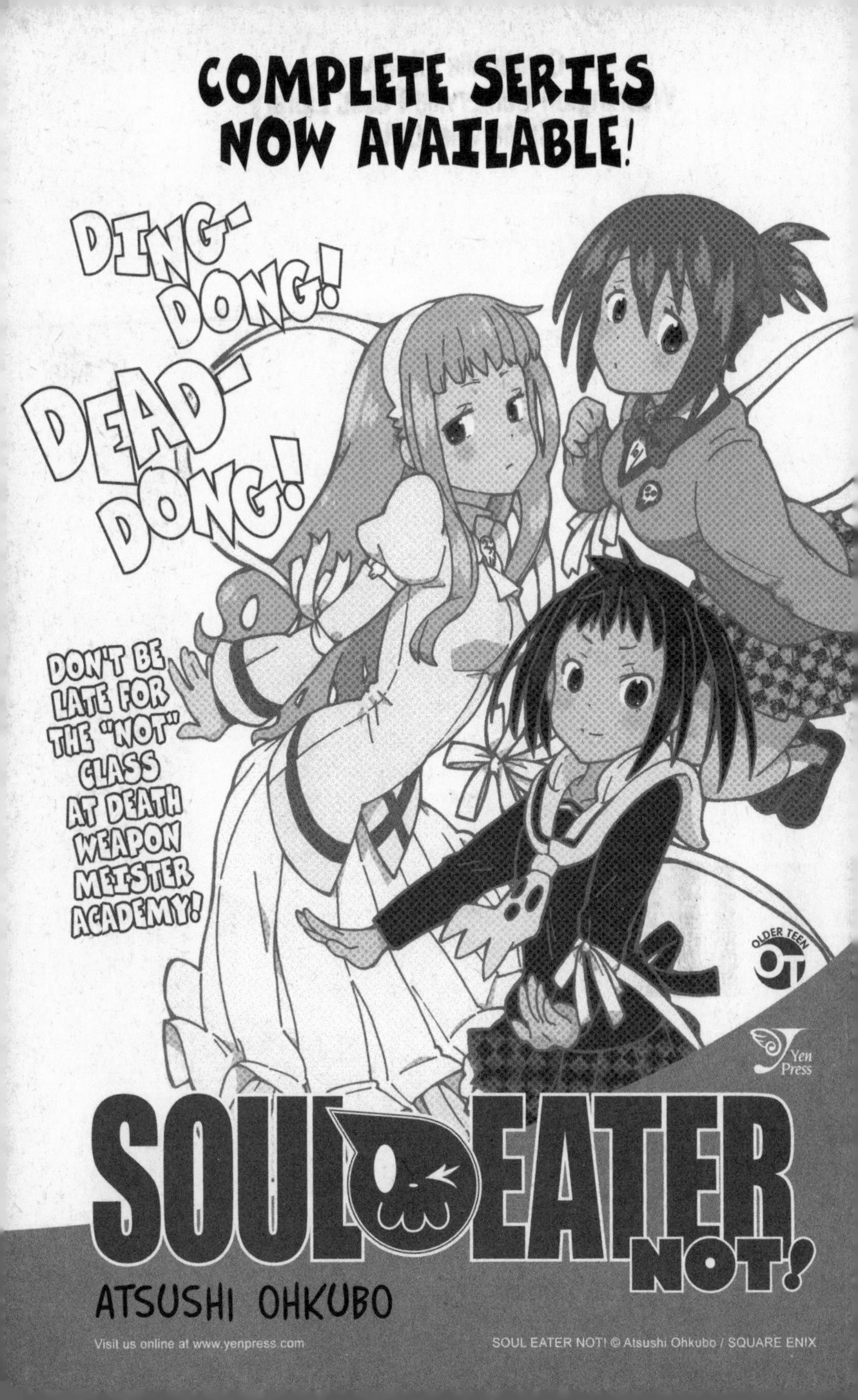
COMPLETE SERIES
NOW AVAILABLE!
DING-DONG!
DEAD-DONG!
DON'T BE LATE FOR THE "NOT" CLASS AT DEATH WEAPON MEISTER ACADEMY!
OLDER TEEN OT
Yen Press
SOUL EATER NOT!
ATSUSHI OHKUBO
Visit us online at www.yenpress.com
SOUL EATER NOT! © Atsushi Ohkubo / SQUARE ENIX

HERO × DAISUKE HAGIWARA

Translation: Taylor Engel
Lettering: Alexis Eckerman

HORIMIYA vol. 2
© HERO · OOZ
© 2012 Daisuke Hagiwara / SQUARE ENIX CO., LTD. First published in Japan in 2012 by SQUARE ENIX CO., LTD. English translation rights arranged with SQUARE ENIX CO., LTD. and Yen Press, LLC through Tuttle-Mori Agency, Inc.

English translation © 2016 by SQUARE ENIX CO., LTD.

Yen Press
1290 Avenue of the Americas
New York, NY 10104

Visit us at yenpress.com · facebook.com/yenpress ·
twitter.com/yenpress · yenpress.tumblr.com ·
instagram.com/yenpress

First Yen Press Edition: January 2016

Yen Press is an imprint of Yen Press, LLC.
The Yen Press name and logo are trademarks
of Yen Press, LLC.

The publisher is not responsible for websites
(or their content) that are not owned by the
publisher.

Library of Congress Control Number: 2015960115

ISBNs: 978-0-316-26869-1 (paperback)
978-0-316-35660-2 (ebook)
978-0-316-35661-9 (app)

10 9 8 7 6 5 4 3

BVG

Printed in the United States of America